Sentences, Paragraphs, and Beyond

Sentences, Paragraphs, and Beyond

A WORKTEXT WITH READINGS

Fourth Edition

Lee Brandon
Mt. San Antonio College

Kelly Brandon
Santa Ana College

HOUGHTON MIFFLIN COMPANY
Boston   New York

To Sharon

Publisher: Patricia A. Coryell
Development Editor: Kellie Cardone
Editorial Assistant: Peter Mooney
Associate Project Editor: Shelley Dickerson
Manufacturing Manager: Florence Cadran
Marketing Manager: Annamarie Rice

Cover image: © Annie Phillips/Illustration Works/Getty Images

Text credits and acknowledgments appear on page 496, which constitutes an extension of the copyright page.

Printed in the U.S.A.

Library of Congress Control Number: 2003110174

Student Text ISBN: 0-618-42676-0
Instructor's Annotated Edition ISBN: 0-618-42677-9

23456789 - DBH - 08 07 06 05

Contents

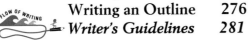

Part IV: Writing Paragraphs and Essays:
Instruction, with Reading Selections   **301**

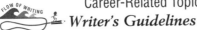

Terisita Castellanos, "Festival of the Dead"   434

Several days before the occasion, markets and bakeries are filled with special breads baked in human forms, sweets shaped into skulls. . . .

Sheila Ferguson, "Soul Food at a Black American Family Reunion"   435

A black American family reunion stands for a great deal more than just the sharing of a really fine meal. It is a testimonial both to the past and to what the future holds in store for the entire family.

Linda Hogan, "Thanksgiving"   438

During that ceremony, I also drank bitter tea, telling the herb in the cup, thank you, *telling the sun,* thank you, *and thanking the land.*

Patricia Hampl, "Grandmother's Sunday Dinner"   440

Something sweet and starry was in the kitchen and I lay down beside it, my stomach full, warm, so safe I'll live the rest of my life off the fat of that vast family security.

Grace Paley, "The Loudest Voice"   444

In a Christmas play performed by Jewish children, Celia lay in the straw with Cindy Lou, her favorite doll. . . . Little Eddie Braunstein wandered upstage and down with his shepherd's stick, looking for sheep.

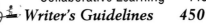

Preface

The phrase "flow of writing" has been prominent in the previous three editions of *Sentences, Paragraphs, and Beyond*. In this fourth edition, it takes shape as a unifying and reinforcing icon, demonstrating with coastal waves and a merry surf writer on a pencil that writing is cyclical, moving forward and backward and forward again. The surf writer will always be searching for the "perfect wave," meaning the best possible expression. That recursive movement, or revision, is the essence of good writing. Instruction in this book—comprehensive, flexible, relevant, and stimulating—is predicated on systematic, relentless revision.

Comprehensive Instruction

The text's four parts and the appendixes cover the full range of instruction for developmental writing.

- **Part One: Reading Leading to Writing** includes instruction in underlining, annotating, summarizing, paraphrasing, and critiquing. Because summary writing provides structure and content, this part offers a good opportunity for diagnosing problems in basic writing at the beginning of the semester. It is also a rich source of useful introductory assignments and ice-breaking discussions.
- **Part Two: Writing Sentences** covers matters such as sentence structure, phrases and clauses, kinds of sentences, sentence combining, omissions, sentence problems, verbs, pronouns, modifiers, punctuation, spelling, and wordiness. Chapters 2 through 11 feature Microthemes, which connect exercises with paragraph writing. A student answer key at the back of the book gives answers to selected exercises so that students can do some work independently.
- **Part Three: Using the Writing Process** contains instruction, examples, demonstrations, and exercises in freewriting, brainstorming, clustering, listing, topic sentence writing, outlining, revising, and editing.
- **Part Four: Writing Paragraphs and Essays: Instruction, with Reading Selections** provides guidance in writing with patterns. An abundance of readings is grouped dually by theme and form of discourse. Student writing is shown in stages through use of the Writing Process Worksheet.
- The **Appendixes** cover parts of speech, taking tests, writing a letter of application and a résumé, and a brief guide for ESL students. The student **Answer Key** gives answers to selected exercises so that students can do some work on fundamentals independently.

Adaptable Organization

Instructors can move easily between parts according to their course designs. Sentence skills can be taught separately or interspersed in response to student need. These are some of the basic course needs that *Sentences, Paragraphs, and Beyond* can serve:

- a course mixing paragraphs and essay writing with assignments of different patterns
- a course mixing paragraph and essay writing with assignments that vary from student to student, depending on students' abilities and student-instructor contract or other agreement
- a course dealing exclusively with paragraph writing
- a course beginning with paragraphs and ending with essays
- a course (a one-unit design) dealing almost exclusively with grammar and the sentence
- a course moving from sentences to paragraphs to essays

Relevant and Stimulating Readings

The readings are dually grouped by pattern and theme and serve as examples of good writing by student and professional authors. Selected to stimulate reader interest and lively discussion, they reflect a wide range of current and enduring concerns:

"Growing Pains and Pleasures"
"Prized and Despised Possessions"
"Living in the Age of Irritations"
"The Joy and Grief of Work"
"Heroes—Who, Where, and Why"
"Cultural Blends and Clashes"
"To Regulate or Not"
"Celebrations—More Same Than Different"

Functional Student Demonstrations

All writers—beginners and professionals—depend on examples for guidance. When confronted with new writing tasks, we are likely to say, "Show me what one looks like." Instruction in *Sentences, Paragraphs, and Beyond* fulfills that need. Examples in Chapters 16–22 in Part Four show how students just like those using this book have begun with assignments and ended with well-crafted compositions, presenting the pertinent stages of the writing process.

Time-Tested Techniques

Written especially for developmental writing courses, the fourth edition continues to feature highly accessible, easily remembered techniques that will enable students initially to survive and then to thrive. For example, the acronym **CLUESS** is a memory aid, with the letters representing key parts of rewriting: Coherence, Language, Unity, Emphasis, Support, and Sentences. Inexperienced writers can easily remember

CLUESS and use it as a checklist. Another acronym (**COPS**—Capitalization, Omissions, Punctuation, and Spelling) is used for editing. Those considerations of drafting paragraphs and essays are prominent in this book: fundamentals of grammar, usage, rhetoric, organization, and development.

New and Special Features in the Fourth Edition

- More than 60 percent new reading selections
- New content for exercises in sentence writing (Chapters 2–11)
- New feature to connect sentence-writing exercises with writing: the Microtheme
- New feature on cross-curricular writing topics
- New feature in sentence variety
- New feature in word omissions
- New feature in avoiding wordiness
- Additional career-related writing topics
- Additional emphasis on organization and revision
- Refined Writing Process Worksheet suitable for photocopying and designed to provide guidance for students and to save time and effort for instructors
- Streamlined Self-Evaluation Chart to help students track their needs and goals and to promote self-reliance

Support Material for Instructors

- The Instructor's Annotated Edition (IAE) contains immediate answers for exercises
- Instructor's Guide with all the following parts included in the IAE:
    Reproducible diagnostic tests and sentence-writing quizzes
    Reproducible quizzes for selected readings in Part Four
    Suggestions for effective and time-saving approaches to instruction
    Sample annotated syllabi to adopt or adapt for different course designs
- Software resources include
    Updated Expressways 5.0 CD-ROM: Interactive software that guides students as they write and revise paragraphs and essays
    Houghton Mifflin Grammar CD-ROM
    American Heritage Dictionary CD-ROM
- Online options include
    Dolphinville: An online writing center
    SMARTHINKING™: Live, online tutoring and academic support. Offer your students live, quality online tutoring from SMARTHINKING's trained e-structors.

Web Resources

Sentences, Paragraphs, and Beyond offers instructors and students more opportunities to explore writing through the student and instructor websites.

Instructor Website

- Tips for new instructors on how to approach the text
- Information on how to integrate ESL instruction into the classroom and how to work with basic writers
- PowerPoint slides that can be downloaded and used to enhance classroom instruction
- Dolphinville 2.0: an online writing community for any level writer
- Reproducible quizzes for selected readings in Part Four
- Reproducible diagnostic tests and sentence-writing quizzes
- Sample annotated syllabi to adopt or adapt for different course designs

Student Website

- Additional exercises and readings
- Dolphinville 2.0: an online writing community for any level writer
- Additional instruction in writing résumés

Acknowledgments

We are grateful to the following instructors who have reviewed this textbook: Kathryn Beckwith, Arizona State University; John Bell, New York City Technical College; Christena T. Biggs, DePauw University; Wendy Bishop, Florida State University; Marilyn Black, Middlesex Community College; Betty Bluman, Community College of Allegheny; Curtis Bobbitt, University of Great Falls; Marlene Bosanko, Tacoma Community College; Elizabeth Breen, Pierce College; Deborah Burson-Smith, Southern University-A&M; Janet Cutshall, Sussex County Community College; Dr. Scott Earle, Tacoma Community College; Eddye Gallagher, Tarrant County Junior College; Nicole Greene, University of Southwestern Louisiana; Roslyn J. Harper, Trident Technical College; Carolyn G. Hartnett, College of the Mainland; Bradley S. Hayden, Western Michigan University; Grady Hinton, Jr., St. Louis Community College at Forest Park; Wayne P. Hubert, Chaffey Community College; Anna Jo Johnson, Community College of Western Kentucky University; James C. McDonald, University of Southwestern Louisiana; Tracy A. Peyton, Pensacola Junior College; James Rice, Quinsigamond Community College; Athene Sallee, Forsyth Technical Community College; Susan Schiller, University of California-Davis; Ann Shackleford; Bacone College; and David White, Walters State Community College. Thanks also go to the faculty members at Mt. San Antonio College (with special appreciation to the Basic Courses Review Committee) and Santa Ana College for their suggestions.

We deeply appreciate the work of freelance editors Ann Marie Radaskiewicz, Mary Dalton-Hoffman, Nancy Benjamin of Books By Design, and Robin Hogan, as well as my colleagues at Houghton Mifflin: Pat Coryell, Kellie Cardone, Peter Mooney, Anna Rice, Laura Hemrika, and Shelley Dickerson.

We are grateful to our families for their cheerful, enduring support, especially Sharon, Erin, Michael, Shane, Lauren, Jarrett, and Matthew.

Lee Brandon
Kelly Brandon

Student Overview

As you work with writing skills, don't compare yourself with others. Compare yourself then with yourself now.

The Flow of Writing: Icon and Theme

You will see this icon frequently in *Sentences, Paragraphs, and Beyond*:

Follow the line from top left over the waves, then down and around to the pencil with the little surf writer getting ready to hang ten.

Like the surf writer, you follow that pattern in writing, the pattern of the tide near the shore. In flowing cycles, the tide advances and withdraws, then regroups and proceeds again. The tide doesn't merely rush forward at one time and be done with it. Writing also has a repetitive, rhythmic flow. You don't just write your message and walk away. Instead, you write—and, for revision and editing—back up, and rewrite, following that pattern until you're through. In writing, the back-and-forth movement is called *recursive*. It is the essence of the writing process.

In the coming pages, the icon will identify features that enable your own flow of writing and remind you of the importance of rewriting.

Sentences, Paragraphs, and Beyond shows how to proceed from fragmented ideas to effective expression by blending instruction, examples, and practice. Like the surf writer going back again and again in quest of that perfect wave, you as a writer will go back again and again looking for that perfect composition.

Writing efffectively is not as difficult as you may think. You can learn to be a good writer if you practice effective techniques. The operative words are the last three: "practice effective techniques." A good piece of written material includes clear organization, solid content, and good use of language skills. You should have something to say, present it in appropriate order, and write correctly. All of those points will be covered in the four main parts of this book: Reading Leading to Writing, Writing Sentences, Using the Writing Process, and Writing Paragraphs and Essays: Instruction, with Reading Selections.

Part One: Reading Leading to Writing

Much of your college writing will be related to what you read. Reading is a principal way of learning, and writing is a principal way of using learned information, especially in college. If you don't get the reading right, you won't get the writing right. If you can't read well, your learning will be restricted, and if you can't write well, you may not be able to show others what you really know and receive proper credit. This part links techniques of effective reading and effective writing. Expect to sharpen your skills in reading comprehension as you study how to underline, annotate, and outline. Then link that comprehension to written expression by composing outlines, summaries, evaluations, and reactions.

2

Part Two: Writing Sentences

The second part, Writing Sentences, concentrates on effectiveness. Beginning with the simplest aspects of sentences, namely subjects and verbs, the text moves to the larger word units of clauses and sentences, with their numerous patterns. It shows you the difference between complete sentences and incomplete sentences, between sound and unsound arrangements of words, and between correct and incorrect punctuation. While giving you the opportunity to experiment and develop your own style, it leads you through the problem areas of verbs, pronouns, and modifiers. If you are not sure when to use *lie* and when to use *lay,* when to use *who* and when to use *whom,* or when to use *good* and when to use *well,* this book can help you. If you're not sure whether the standard expression is *between you and I* or *between you and me,* or if you're not sure about the difference between a colon and a semi-colon, you will find the answers here. That line of *if* statements could be applied to almost every page in this book. Perhaps you are not sure of the correct answer to most of these questions. The good news is that by the end of the course, you will be sure—and if your "sure" is still a bit shaky, then you will know where to find the rules, examples, and discussion in this book.

The text in Part Two follows a pattern: rules, examples, exercises, and writing activity. Again, you learn by practicing sound principles. As you complete assignments, you can check your answers to selected exercises in the Answer Key in the back of the book so that you can monitor your understanding.

Part Three: Using the Writing Process

The third part, Using the Writing Process, presents writing as a process, not as something that is supposed to emerge complete on demand. Writing begins with a topic, either generated or provided, and moves through stages of exploration, organization, development, revision, and editing. If you have suffered, at least at times, from writer's block, this book is for you. If you have sometimes produced material that was organized poorly so that you did not receive full credit for what you knew, then this book is for you. If you have sometimes had ideas, but you did not fully develop them, so that your work was judged as "sketchy" or "lacking in content," then this book is for you.

Part Four: Writing Paragraphs and Essays: Instruction, with Reading Selections

The fourth part, Writing Paragraphs and Essays: Instruction, with Reading Selections, gives you models of good writing and lively ideas for discussion and writing. The selections are presented with observations and exercises to help you develop effective reading techniques. In working with these assignments, you may discover that you can learn a great deal from other writers—if you can read perceptively, understanding both what the writers say and how they say it.

Some reading selections are paragraphs and others are essays. They are rich in invention, style, and cultural perspective. Several are written by celebrated authors. Some are written by students, individuals like you who entered college, worked on language skills, and learned. Well-written and fresh in thought, these models are especially useful because they were done as college English assignments. Each of the students whose writing is included in this book learned writing skills in a developmental program before taking freshman composition. Several of them also studied in English as a Second Language (ESL) programs.

The selections are grouped in two ways: according to theme and according to form of writing. For example, the writings in "Prized and Despised Possessions" are all descriptions. Of course, no one selection is entirely in a single form, although one may predominate. Many forms are presented—narration, description, exemplification, process analysis, analysis by division, comparison and contrast, and argument—because you will need to use many of these forms in your college work. Topics such as "Explain how to (analyze a rock, perform the Heimlich procedure, or sell a product)" and "Compare and contrast (two theories, two leaders, two programs)" abound across the curriculum. Studying the principles for these forms and reading good examples of pieces that demonstrate the effective use of these forms will help you get full credit for what you know, in your college classes and elsewhere.

Appendixes

This book also has four appendixes, a collection of support materials that were too valuable to be omitted from a college book on writing: Parts of Speech, Taking Tests, Writing a Letter of Application and a Résumé, and Brief Guide for ESL Students.

Strategies for Self-Improvement

Here are some strategies you can follow to make the best use of this book and to jump-start the improvement in your writing skills.

1. *Be active and systematic in learning.* Take advantage of your instructor's expertise by being an active class member—one who takes notes, asks questions, and contributes to discussion. Become dedicated to systematic learning: Determine your needs, decide what to do, and do it. Make learning a part of your everyday thinking and behavior.

2. *Read widely.* Samuel Johnson, a great English scholar, once said he didn't want to read anything by people who had written more than they had read. William Faulkner, a Nobel Prize winner in literature, said, "Read, read, read. Read everything—trash, classics, good and bad, and see how writers do it." Read to learn technique, to acquire ideas, and to be stimulated to write. Especially read to satisfy your curiosity and to receive pleasure. If reading is a main component of your course, approach it as systematically as you do writing.

3. *Keep a journal.* Keep a journal, even though it may not be required in your particular class. It is a good practice to jot down your observations in a notebook. Here are some topics for daily, or almost daily, journal writing:

   - Summarize, evaluate, or react to reading assignments.

   - Summarize, evaluate, or react to what you see on television and in movies and what you read in newspapers and in magazines.

   - Describe and narrate situations or events you experience.

   - Write about career-related matters you encounter in other courses or on the job.

Your journal entries may read like an intellectual diary, a record of what you are thinking about at certain times. Keeping a journal will help you to understand reading material better, to develop more language skills, and to think more clearly—as well as to become more confident and to write more easily so that writing becomes a comfortable, everyday activity. Your entries may also provide subject material for longer, more carefully crafted pieces. The most important thing is to get into the habit of writing something each day.

4. *Evaluate your writing skills.* Use the Self-Evaluation Chart inside the front cover of this book to assess your writing skills by listing problem areas you need to work on. You may be adding to these lists throughout the entire term. Drawing on your instructor's comments, make notes on matters such as organization, development, content, spelling, vocabulary, diction, grammar, sentence structure, punctuation, and capitalization. Use this chart for self-motivated study assignments and as a checklist in all stages of writing. As you master each problem area, you can erase it or cross it out. Most of the elements you record in your Self-Evaluation Chart probably are covered in *Sentences, Paragraphs, and Beyond*. The table of contents, the index, and the Correction Chart on the inside back cover of the book will direct you to the additional instruction you decide you need.

- *Organization/Development/Content:* List aspects of your writing, including the techniques of all stages of the writing process, such as freewriting, brainstorming, and clustering; the phrasing of a good topic sentence or thesis; and the design, growth, and refinement of your ideas.

- *Spelling/Vocabulary/Diction:* List common spelling words marked as incorrect on your college assignments. Here, *common* means words that you use often. If you are misspelling these words now, you may have been doing so for years. Look at your list. Is there a pattern to your misspellings? Consult Chapter 11 for a set of useful rules. Whatever it takes, master the words on your list. Continue to add troublesome words as you accumulate assignments. If your vocabulary is imprecise or your diction is inappropriate (if you use slang, trite expressions, or words that are too informal), note those problems as well.

- *Grammar/Sentence Structure:* List recurring problems in your grammar or sentence structure. Use the symbols and page references listed on the Correction Chart (inside back cover of this book) or look up the problem in the index.

- *Punctuation/Capitalization:* Treat these problems the same way you treat grammar problems. Note that the punctuation and capitalization section in Chapter 10 numbers some rules; therefore, you can often give exact locations of the remedies for your problems.

Here is an example of how your chart might be used.

Self-Evaluation Chart

Organization/ Development/ Content	Spelling/ Vocabulary/ Diction	Grammar/ Sentence Structure	Punctuation/ Capitalization
needs more specific support such as examples, 337	avoid slang, 284	fragments, 88	difference between semicolons and commas, 219
	avoid clichés such as "be there for me," 284	subject-verb agreement, 130	
refine outline, 276		comma splice, 101	comma after long introductory modifier, 211, #2
use clear topic sentence, 273	it's, its, 251		
	you're, your, 252	vary sentence patterns, 79	comma in compound sentence, 211, #1
	rec<u>e</u>ive, rule on, 248		

5. *Use the Writing Process Worksheet.* Record details about each of your assignments, such as the due date, topic, length, and form. The worksheet will also remind you of the stages of the writing process: explore, organize, and write. A blank Writing Process Worksheet for you to photocopy for assignments appears on page 7. Discussed in Chapter 2, it illustrates student work in almost every chapter. Your instructor may ask you to complete the form and submit it with your assignments.

6. *Take full advantage of technology.* Although using a computer will not by itself make you a better writer, it will enable you to write and revise more swiftly as you move, alter, and delete material with a few keystrokes. Devices such as the thesaurus, spell checker, grammar checker, and style checker will help you revise and edit. Many colleges have writing labs with good instruction and facilities for networking and researching complicated topics. The Internet, used wisely, can provide resource material for compositions.

7. *Be positive.* To improve your English skills, write with freedom, but revise and edit with rigor. Work with your instructor to set attainable goals, and proceed at a reasonable pace. Soon, seeing what you have mastered and checked off your list will give you a sense of accomplishment.

   Finally, don't compare yourself with others. Compare yourself then with yourself now and, as you improve, consider yourself what you are—a student on the path toward effective writing, a student on the path toward success.

Writing Process Worksheet

Title _____

Name _____ **Due Date** _____

ASSIGNMENT In the space below, write whatever you need to know about your assignment, including information about the topic, audience, pattern of writing, length, whether to include a rough draft or revised drafts, and whether your paper must be typed.

STAGE ONE **Explore** Freewrite, brainstorm (list), cluster, or take notes as directed by your instructor. Use the back of this page or separate paper, if you need more space.

STAGE TWO **Organize** Write a topic sentence or thesis; label the subject and treatment parts.

Write an outline or an outline alternative.

STAGE THREE **Write** On separate paper, write and then revise your paragraph or essay as many times as necessary for **c**oherence, **l**anguage (usage, tone, and diction), **u**nity, **e**mphasis, **s**upport, and **s**entences (**CLUESS**). Read your work aloud to hear and correct any grammatical errors or awkward-sounding sentences.

Edit any problems in fundamentals, such as **c**apitalization, **o**missions, **p**unctuation, and **s**pelling (**COPS**).

Reading Leading to Writing

Reading and writing are joined without seam. Reading activates your memory and provides you with substance for writing. Writing helps you examine your ideas and clarify what you have read. In all areas—personal, cross-curricular, and career-related—what you learn in reading strengthens your writing, and what you learn in writing makes you a better reader.

Chapter

1

From Reading to Writing

Reading and writing are like the chicken and egg sequence—each needs the other, and each is a product of the other.

FLOW OF WRITING

Learning Objectives

Working with this chapter, I will learn to

~ underline and annotate.

~ outline and summarize.

~ write a reaction paper.

~ write a two-part response.

Reading to Write

Much of your college and career writing will require you to evalute and to reflect on what you read, rather than write from a purely personal perspective. In college, you will write in response to reading material in textbooks and in collateral assignments. Research papers will be firmly based on reading material. At the workplace, you will read and respond to in-house reports, research studies, and proposals. Executive summaries, in which employees present a digested version of lengthy documents, are common.

Whether on campus or at the workplace, your skill in identifying main ideas and their support through reading and then commenting on them in writing will serve you well. The writings you will do in this textbook is commonly called *reading-related writing*. It includes

- reading effectively (which may include underlining, annotating, and outlining).
- writing a *summary* (main ideas in your own words).
- writing a *reaction* (usually a statement of how the reading relates specifically to you, your experiences, and your attitudes but also often a critique, involving the worth and logic of a piece).
- writing a *two-part response* (both a summary and a reaction, although they are separate).

These kinds of writing have certain points in common; they all

- originate as a response to something you have read.
- indicate, to some degree, content from that piece.
- demonstrate a knowledge of the piece of writing.

Working with the outline, summary, and reaction will give you practice in reading analytically and in recording the main ideas and their support in a clear, direct manner. In Part Four, you will be able to put these skills to good use in your work with assignments of paragraphs and essays. In other courses and finally at the workplace, you will have many other opportunites to work with the principles introduced here.

Reading Techniques

Good reading begins with desire; and concentration, or focus, is the first product of desire. *Focus is no problem if you have a strong purpose in reading.* If you go to a cookbook to find a recipe for enchiladas, you will find the recipe, read it, and refer back to it periodically while you prepare the dish. It is unlikely that you will put the book aside and say, "I wanted to read about making enchiladas, but I just couldn't concentrate." If you can capture that sense of concentration and apply it to all of your reading experiences, you will become a stronger reader.

Of course, a desire that naturally emerges from a situation is different from a need that occurs because, let's say, a teacher has assigned three chapters in a history book. In the latter case, you may be motivated or you may not be. If not, you will want to manufacture that concentration somehow.

Underlining

One way to build concentration is to develop a relationship with the reading material. Imagine you are reading a chapter of several pages, and you decide to underline and write in the margins. Immediately, the underlining takes you out of the passive, television-watching frame of mind. You are involved. You are participating. It is now necessary for you to discriminate, to distinguish more important from less important ideas. Perhaps you have thought of underlining as a method designed only to help you with reviewing. That is, when you study the material the next time, you won't have to read all of the material; instead, you can review only the most important, underlined parts. However, even while you are underlining, you are benefiting from an imposed concentration, because this procedure forces you to think, to focus. Consider the following guidelines for underlining:

1. Underline the main ideas in paragraphs. The most important statement, the topic sentence, is likely to be at the beginning of the paragraph.

2. Underline the support for those main ideas.

3. Underline answers to questions that you bring to the reading assignment. These questions may have come from the end of the chapter, from subheadings that you turn into questions, or from your independent concern about the topic.

4. Underline only the key words. You would seldom underline all the words in a sentence and almost never a whole paragraph.

Does that fit your approach to underlining? Possibly not. Most students, in their enthusiasm to do a good job, overdo underlining.

Maybe you have had this experience: You start reading about something you have not encountered before. The idea seems important. You highlight it. The next idea is equally fresh and significant. You highlight it. A minute or two later, you have changed the color of the page from white to orange, but you haven't accomplished anything.

The trick is how to figure out what to underline. You would seldom underline more than about 30 percent of a passage, although the amount would depend on your purpose and the nature of the material. Following the preceding four rules will be useful. Learning more about the principles of sentence, paragraph, and essay organization will also be helpful. These principles are presented in Chapters 2 through 15.

Consider this passage with effective underlining.

Youth and the Counterculture

Main idea   <u>Rock music helped tie</u> this <u>international subculture together</u>. Rock <u>grew out of</u> the <u>black music culture</u> of <u>rhythm and blues</u>, which was <u>flavored with country and western</u> to make it <u>more accessible</u> to <u>white</u>

Support   <u>teenagers</u>. The <u>mid-1950s signaled</u> a <u>breakthrough</u> as <u>Billy Hailey</u> called

Support   on record buyers to <u>"Rock Around the Clock"</u> and <u>Elvis Presley</u> warned

Support   them to keep off his <u>"Blue Suede Shoes."</u> In the <u>1960s</u>, the <u>Beatles</u> thrilled millions of young people, often to their parents' dismay. Like Elvis, the Beatles <u>suggested personal and sexual freedom</u> that many older people found disturbing.

Main idea

It was <u>Bob Dylan</u>, a young folksinger turned rock poet with an acoustic guitar, who <u>best expressed the radical political</u> as well as <u>cultural aspirations</u> of the <u>"younger generation."</u> In a song that became a rallying cry, <u>Dylan sang</u> that <u>"the times they are a'changing."</u> The song captured the spirit of <u>growing alienation between the generation</u> whose defining experiences had been the <u>Great Depression and World War II</u> and the <u>generation ready to reject</u> the <u>complacency</u> of the <u>1950s</u>. <u>Increasing discontent with middle-class conformity and the injustices of racism and imperialism fueled</u> the young leaders of <u>social protest</u> and <u>reflected</u> a <u>growing spirit of rebellion</u>.

Support

Support

Closing statement

John P. McKay et al., *A History of Western Society*

EXERCISE 1

Underlining

Using the four rules of underlining on page 13, mark the following paragraphs. (See Answer Key for possible answers. It is unlikely that any two readers will underline precisely the same words.)

The Leadership of Martin Luther King Jr.

1   On December 1, 1955, in Montgomery, Alabama, a black woman named Rosa Parks was arrested for refusing to give up her bus seat to a white man. In protest, Montgomery blacks organized a year-long bus boycott. The boycott forced white city leaders to recognize the blacks' determination and economic power.

2   One of the organizers of the bus boycott was a Baptist minister, the Reverend Martin Luther King Jr. King soon became a national leader in the growing civil rights movement. With stirring speeches and personal courage, he urged blacks to demand their rights. At the same time, he was completely committed to nonviolence. Like Gandhi, . . . he believed that justice could triumph through moral force.

3   In April 1963, King began a drive to end segregation in Birmingham, Alabama. He and his followers boycotted segregated businesses and held peaceful marches and demonstrations. Against them, the Birmingham police used electric cattle prods, attack dogs, clubs, and fire hoses to break up marches.

4   Television cameras brought those scenes into the living rooms of millions of Americans, who were shocked by what they saw. On May 10, Birmingham's city leaders gave in. A committee of blacks and whites oversaw the gradual desegregation of the city and tried to open more jobs for blacks. The victory was later marred by grief, however, when a bomb exploded at a Birmingham church, killing four black children.

Steven L. Jantzen, *World History: Perspectives on the Past*

Annotating

Annotating, a practice related to underlining, is writing in the margins. You can do it independently, although it usually appears in conjunction with underlining to mark the understanding and to extend the involvement.

Writing in the margins represents intense involvement because it makes the reader a writer. If you read material and write something in the margin as a reaction to it, then in a way you have had a conversation with the author. The author has made a statement and you have responded. In fact, you may have added something to the text; therefore, for your purposes you have become a co-author or collaborator. The comments you make in the margin are of your own choosing according to your interests and the purpose you bring to the reading assignment. Your response in the margin may merely echo the author's ideas, it may question them critically, it may relate them to something else, or it may add to them.

In the following example, you can see how the reader has reinforced the underlining by commenting in the margin.

Women and Witchcraft

Mary Beth Norton

<table>
<tr>
<td>Salem witchcraft—
broad interest</td>
<td>1</td>
<td>The <u>Salem withcraft crisis</u> of 1692 to 1693, in which a small number of adolescent girls and young women accused hundreds of older women (and a few men) of having bewitched them, <u>has fascinated Americans ever since</u>. It has provided material for innumerable books, plays, movies, and television productions. To twentieth-century Americans, the belief in witchcraft in the seventeenth-century colonies is difficult to explain or understand; perhaps that is why the Salem episode has attracted so much attention. For those interested in studying women's experiences, of course, witchcraft incidents are particulary intriguing. The vast majority of <u>suspected witches</u> were <u>female</u>, and <u>so, too</u>, were many of their <u>accusers</u>. Although colonial women rarely played a role on the public stage, in witchcraft cases they were the primary actors. <u>What accounts for their prominence under these peculiar circumstance</u>?</td>
</tr>
<tr>
<td>Why mostly women?</td>
</tr>
<tr>
<td>Historical/cultural background</td>
<td>2</td>
<td>To answer that question, the <u>Salem crises</u> must be placed into its <u>proper historical and cultural context</u>. People in the early modern world <u>believed</u> in <u>witchcraft because</u> it <u>offered</u> a <u>rationale</u> for <u>events</u> that <u>otherwise seemed random</u> and <u>unfathomable</u>. In the <u>absence</u> of <u>modern scientific knowledge about</u> such <u>natural phenomena</u> as <u>storms</u> and <u>diseases</u>, and <u>clear explanations</u> for <u>accidents</u> of various sorts, the <u>evil actions of a witch</u> could provide a <u>ready answer</u> to a person or community inquiring about the causes of a disaster.</td>
</tr>
<tr>
<td>Without modern science</td>
</tr>
<tr>
<td>Witch hunts in Europe—
the extent</td>
<td>3</td>
<td>Therefore, <u>witchcraft accusations</u>—and some large-scale "witch hunts"—were <u>not uncommon</u> in <u>Europe between</u> the early <u>fourteenth</u> and the late <u>seventeenth centuries</u> (1300 to 1700). In short, the <u>immigrants</u> to the <u>colonies came from a culture</u> in which <u>belief</u> in <u>witchcraft</u> was <u>widespread</u> and in which <u>accusations</u> could <u>result</u> in formal <u>prosecutions</u> and <u>executions</u>. Recent research has demonstrated that the Salem incident, although the largest and most important witch hunt in New England, was just one of a number of such episodes in the American colonies.</td>
</tr>
<tr>
<td>Question—repeated</td>
<td>4</td>
<td><u>But why were witches women</u>? Admittedly, historians have not yet answered that question entirely satisfactorily. Certain observations can be made: <u>women gave birth</u> to <u>new life</u> and <u>seemed to have</u> the <u>potential</u> to <u>take life away</u>. In <u>Western culture</u>, <u>women were seen</u> as <u>less rational than men, more linked</u> to the "<u>natural" world</u>, in which <u>magic</u> held sway. <u>Men</u>, who <u>dominated European society, defined</u> the characteristics</td>
</tr>
<tr>
<td>Answers: 1
2
3</td>
</tr>
</table>

Women seen as
"out of their place"

Mary Beth Norton, *Major Problems
in American Women's History*

of a "<u>proper woman</u>," who was <u>submissive</u> and <u>accepted a subordinate
position</u>. The <u>stereotypical witch</u>, usually described as an <u>aggressive</u>
and <u>threatening older woman</u>, represented the <u>antithesis</u> of that <u>image</u>.
These broad categories need further refinement, and historians are currently looking closely at the women who were accused of practicing
witchcraft to identify the crucial characteristics that set them apart from
their contemporaries and made them a target for accusations.

EXERCISE 2

Underlining and Annotating

**Mark the following paragraphs with underlining and annotation. Compare your marks
with those of your classmates.**

Buddha Taught Nonviolence

1   Buddha gave his first sermon to the five wisdom seekers who had been his com-
panions. That sermon was a landmark in the history of world religions. Buddha
taught the four main ideas that had come to him in his enlightenment, calling them
the Four Noble Truths.

2   *First Noble Truth:* Everything in life is suffering and sorrow.

3   *Second Noble Truth:* The cause of all this pain is people's self-centered cravings
and desires. People seek pleasure that cannot last and leads only to rebirth and more
suffering.

4   *Third Noble Truth:* The way to end all pain is to end all desires.

5   *Fourth Noble Truth:* People can overcome their desires and attain enlightenment
by following the Eightfold Path.

6   The Eightfold Path was like a staircase. According to Buddha, those who sought
enlightenment had to master one step at a time. The steps of the Eightfold Path were
right knowledge, right purpose, right speech, right action, right living, right effort,
right mindfulness, and right meditation. By following the Eightfold Path, anyone
could attain *nirvana* (nur-VAHN-uh), Buddha's word for release from pain and self-
ishness.

7   Buddha taught his followers to treat all living things (humans, animals, and even
insects) with loving kindness. A devout Buddhist was not even supposed to swat a
mosquito.

8   Buddhist and Hindus both sought to escape from the woes of this world, but their
paths of escape were very different. Unlike traditional Hinduism, Buddhism did not
require complex rituals. Moreover, Buddha taught in everyday language, not in the
ancient Sanskrit language of the Vedas and the Upanishads, which most Indians in
500 B.C. could no longer understand. Buddha's religion was also unique in its concern for all human beings—women as well as men, lowborn as well as highborn.

Written Responses to Reading

Among the forms of writing that will be suggested as assignments in this book are outlines, summaries, and reading-related compositions. In some instances, you will be asked to use all three forms after reading a passage. The three forms are also tied to reading and critical thinking, in that they contribute to reading comprehension and use systematic and analytical thought.

To show how a reading selecion can be dealt with by more than one form, the next two writing examples will be based on the following brief passage.

The Roman Toga

1   Practicality has never been a requirement of fashion. The Roman toga was an uncomfortable garment. It was hot in summer, cold in winter, and clumsy for just about any activity but standing still. The toga was, however, practical in one way: It was easy to to make, since it involved no sewing. Not even a buttonhole was needed. An adult's toga was basically a large wool blanket measuring about 18 by 7 feet. It was draped around the body in a variety of ways without the use of buttons or pins.

2   In the early days of the Roman republic, both women and men wore togas. Women eventually wore more dresslike garments, called *stolas,* with separate shawls. For men, however, the toga remained in fashion with very little change.

3   Soon after the republic was formed, the toga became a symbol of Roman citizenship. Different styles of togas indicated a male citizen's place in society. For example, a young boy would wear a white toga with a narrow purple band along the border. When his family decided he was ready for adult responsibilities, he would don a pure white toga. On that day, usually when he was about 16, his family would take him to the Forum, where he would register as a full citizen. For the rest of his life, he would wear a toga at the theater, in court, for religious ceremonies, and on any formal occasion. At his funeral his body would be wrapped in a toga to mark him, even in death, as a Roman citizen.

Steven L. Jantzen, *World History: Perspectives on the Past*

Outlining

Following is a topic outline by student Leon Batista. Note the parallel structure.

    I. Practicality
      A. Not practical
        1. Hot in summer
        2. Cold in winter
        3. Clumsy
      B. Practical
        1. Easy to make
        2. Easy to put on and take off
   II. Fashion in Roman republic
      A. Worn by men and women
        1. Changes little with men
        2. Alternates with stolas and shawls for women

B. Symbol of citizenship

    1. One style for young male

    2. Another style for adult male

       a. Presented at point of adulthood

       b. Worn on all occasions

EXERCISE 3

Organizing an Outline

Use the outline form to organize these sentences about college English into an outline.

1. It can help you express yourself more effectively in speaking and writing.

2. It can help you with your reading.

3. It will present the difference between fact and opinion.

4. It can help you to recognize and avoid logical fallacies.

5. It will offer complex courses in the interpretation of literature.

6. It will teach that a fact is something that can be verified.

7. It will offer courses in reading skills.

8. It will teach that an opinion is a subjective view.

9. It will offer courses in composition.

10. It will offer instruction in inductive and deductive thinking.

11. It will offer courses that involve discussion.

12. It can help you think critically.

13. College English can benefit you in many ways.

14. It will help you understand causes and effects.

Main idea: _____

    I. _____

       A. _____

       B. _____

    II. _____

       A. _____

       B. _____

    III. _____

       A. _____

1. _____

2. _____

B. _____

C. _____

D. _____

Summarizing

A **summary** is a rewritten, shortened version of a piece of writing in which you use your own wording to express the main ideas. Learning to summarize effectively will help you in many ways. Summary writing reinforces comprehension skills in reading. It requires you to discriminate among the ideas in the target reading passage. Summaries are usually written in the form of a well-designed paragraph. Frequently, they are used in collecting material for research papers and in writing conclusions to essays.

The following rules will guide you in writing effective summaries.

1. Cite both the author and title of the text.

2. Reduce the length of the original by about two-thirds, although the exact reduction will vary depending on the content of the original.

3. Concentrate on the main ideas and include details only infrequently.

4. Change the wording without changing the idea.

5. Do not evaluate the content or give an opinion in any way (even if you see an error in logic or fact).

6. Do not add ideas (even if you have an abundance of related information).

7. Do not include any personal comments (that is, do not use "I," referring to self).

8. Seldom use quotations. (If you do use quotations, however, enclose them in quotation marks.)

9. Use author tags ("says York," "according to York," or "the author explains") to remind the reader that you are summarizing the material of another writer.

10. Begin with the main idea (as you usually do in middle paragraphs) and cover the main points in an organized fashion while using complete sentences.

The following is a summary of "The Roman Toga," written by the same student who prepared the sample outline. The writing process used by Batista was direct and systematic. When first reading the material, he had underlined key parts and written comments and echo phrases in the margin. Then he wrote his outline. Finally, referring to both the marked passage and the outline, he wrote this summary. Had he not been assigned to write the outline, he would have done so anyway, as preparation for writing his summary.

Summary of "The Roman Toga" by Steven L. Jantzen

According to Steven Jantzen in *World History: Perspectives on the Past*, the toga was the main form of dress for citizens of the Roman republic, despite its being "hot in summer, cold in winter, and clumsy" to wear. Perhaps the Romans appreciated the simplicity of wearing a piece of woolen cloth about eighteen by seven feet "without the use of buttons or pins." Jantzen explains that the women also wore another garment similar to a dress called the *stola*, but Roman male citizens were likely to wear only the toga—white with a purple edge for the young and solid white for the adult. This apparel was worn from childhood to death.

EXERCISE 4

Evaluating a Summary

Compare this summary with the original passage and with the student summary you just read. Then mark the instances of poor summary writing by underlining and by using rule numbers from the preceding list.

Summary About One of My Favorite Garments

For citizens of the Roman republic, the toga was the main form of dress, despite its being hot in summer, cold in winter, and clumsy to wear. Frankly, I don't see why a bright bunch of people like the Romans couldn't have come up with a better design. Perhaps the Romans appreciated the simplicity of wearing a piece of woolen cloth about eighteen by seven feet without buttons or pins; but I've read elsewhere that the togas were sometimes stolen at the public baths. The women also wore another garment similar to a dress called the *stola*, but the Roman male citizen was likely to wear only the toga—white with a purple edge for the young and solid white for the adult. For the rest of his life, he would wear a toga at the theater, in court, for religious ceremonies, and on any formal occasion. At his funeral, his body would be wrapped in a toga to mark him, even in death, as a Roman citizen.

Other Reading-Related Writing Forms:
The Reaction and the Two-Part Response

The following three paragraphs are further examples of reading-related writing: the reaction and the two-part response.

The Reaction

The reaction is usually concerned with how a reading relates specifically to you, your experiences, and your attitudes, but also is often a critique, involving the worth and logic of a piece.

In this reading-related writing, student Shanelle Watson takes a basic idea from the original on pages 15–16 and finds parallels. She could have written about one parallel situation or condition—personal or historical.

Sticks and Stones
Shanelle Watson

Reading "Women and Witchcraft" by Mary Beth Norton reminded me of a long line of indignities against women. If something goes wrong, and women can be blamed, they are. For centuries if a woman didn't have babies, it was said *she* couldn't, although the man was just as likely as the woman to be the cause of her childlessness. If, heaven forbid, the woman kept having female babies, that woman, it was said, couldn't produce a male. Yet we know now that it is the male who determines the sex of the child. If the child was not bright, as recently as a hundred years ago some doctors said it was because the woman was reading during pregnancy and took away the brain power from the fetus. As a result, many women were not allowed to open a book during pregnancy. Of course, because it was believed that women were so weak, husbands were allowed to beat their wives, but, according to English law, the stick could be no thicker than the man's thumb, hence "the rule of thumb." Even voting was argued against by some who said that the typical woman, controlled by emotions, would allow her husband to tell her how to vote, and each married man would then have two votes. It's no wonder that three hundred years ago men looked around and, finding many misfortunes, decided that women were the culprits and should be punished. Sticks were not enough. It was time for stones.

The Two-Part Response

As you have seen, the reaction includes an idea or ideas from a reading or is written with the assumption that readers have read the original piece. However, your instructor may prefer that you separate the forms and present a clear, concise summary followed by another type of reading-related writing. This format is especially useful for critical reactions or problem-solving assignments because it requires you to understand and repeat another's views or experiences before responding. The two-part response also helps you avoid the common problem of writing only a summary of the text when your instructor wants you to both summarize and evaluate or to otherwise react. In writing a summary and an evaluation, it is a good idea to ask your instructor if you should separate your summary from your response.

This reading-related writing first summarizes in a separate paragraph and then analyzes, evaluates, and interprets the original passage on pages 15–16. Thus the second paragraph is a form of the reaction.

"Women and Witchcraft" by Mary Beth Norton: A Summary and a Reaction

Jeanne Garcia

Part 1: Summary

Americans have long been fascinated by the Salem witchcraft plight in 1692 to 1693. One perplexing factor is that most of the people accused and many who blamed them were women. In "Women and Witchcraft," Mary Beth Norton says the whole issue should be placed in a historical context. In those times, much was unknown about the causes of disasters and illnesses, and the people came to believe that these things could be attributed to evil supernatural forces. Consequently, from about 1300 to 1700 "witchhunts" occurred, and Salem was just one of the locations. Historians are not certain about why women were often victims and accusers. They may have been involved because they had the power to produce life and, therefore, maybe had "the potential to take life away." Women were thought to be more emotional than rational and even connected to nature, as in magic. Moreover, the stereotypical witch was characterized as a mature, assertive woman, unlike the "proper woman" of the time "who was submissive and accepted a subordinate position." Norton says that historians now seek to discover the precise causes that made assertive women the victims of persecution as witches.

Part 2: Reaction

The "witchcraft crisis of 1692 to 1693," which Mary Beth Norton discusses in "Women and Witchcraft," is not so surprising to some of us who look back after three hundred years at the way some men treat some women. One doesn't have to read between Norton's lines. She makes it clear that "usually" the people were "aggressive and threatening older women." The charges came mainly from adolescent girls and young women, but the power structure was adult men. Out of ignorance, the men, often with female accomplices, were looking around to find reasons for the misfortunes—bad weather, diseases, and accidents—that their society faced. It is a fact that if people are foolish and desperate enough to look for witches, they are foolish and desperate enough to find them. And they did: They found mainly a few old women who didn't know their place, individuals of a gender associated with the emotions. If these women had been meek and mild, if they had been properly submissive to the menfolk, and if they had still been young and sexy, they would not have been vulnerable. But they were what they were—mature and relatively independent women, who seemed to be different—and that made them witches to those who were said not to be emotionally based—the men.

EXERCISE 5

Writing a Response to a Reading

Read, underline, and annotate the following text and then complete one of the assignments below. Some of the annotation and underlining have been done for you. One possible response is for you to pose as a psychologist, counselor, or thoughtful friend and offer advice to McGraw. Is she thinking clearly? What should she do?

- **Write a summary.**

- **Write an outline.**

- **Write a reaction. Include enough summary to establish clear and logical connections between the text and your own ideas.**

- **Write a two-part response composed of a summary separated from a reaction.**

Everyone Pays the Price

HADLEY MCGRAW

Sitting in a college classroom, Hadley McGraw doesn't remind one of the stereotypical gang member. Apparently tattoo- and puncture-free, she is fair-skinned, well-groomed, and soft-spoken. She does her homework, contributes to class discussion, and writes well. So much for stereotypes!

1   It is ten o'clock and time for me to start my day. I put an X on my calendar to signify that another twenty-four hours has passed. I now have one hundred and nine days until Martin, my boyfriend, comes home. He has been in jail for the last year. I guess you could say I was not surprised by his sentence. This is not the first time, and I'm afraid it will not be the last. Eighteen months of our three-and-a-half-year relationship, he has spent in correctional institutions. Martin is a gang

Thesis   member. He has been a gang member for nine years now. Gang membership of a loved one affects everyone around that person. Three-and-a-half years later I live each day in fear and grief.

Topic sentence 2   I guess what attracted me to Martin at first was his bad-boy image and his carefree way of life. He was good looking and well known. He was tough and exciting. I, however, was good and obedient. I had been told often that I was pretty. I made good grades and came from a good home. My parents, still married and drug-free,

Causes   lived comfortably in a middle-class neighborhood. Martin, on the contrary, came from a broken home. His parents hated each other. His father was a cold, heartless man, and his mother was a "flakey" drug addict. His uncles and cousins were all members of a very large gang that "controlled" an area where he lived. Soon he too was a gang member.

3   Martin quit school when he was a freshman and spent his days on a street corner drinking Olde English forty-ouncers. Soon I was joining him. I began ditching school to hang out. In no time, I was a gang member myself, and as I look back, I

Effects   see what an awful person I became. We used drugs all day and all night. I didn't care about anything and neither did he. I left home and devastated my family and lost my friends. I didn't care because I had a new family and new friends. Martin spent his nights committing crimes and dealing drugs. I was by his side, carrying his gun. The drugs made him irritable and violent, and small disagreements turned into huge battles between us. Jail sentences made him angrier and closer to his gang. Each day Martin became farther from me. Life was a nonstop party with his homeboys, and I was his woman. It was exciting and risky. It was self-destructive.

Topic sentence   4   <u>My breaking point was one year ago</u>. Martin and I were at a party. Everyone was drinking and joking. Oldies were playing and a noisy, wild game of poker was taking place. Suddenly a car was approaching us rapidly. Martin told me to run and hide, so I did. The homeboys began reaching for their guns. I heard five gunshots before the car drove away. I ran to the front of the house where Martin's cousin lay bleeding. I tried to wake him, speak to him. He wasn't responding. I screamed for an ambulance. Finally Martin appeared from behind a car and ran inside to call 911. When the ambulance arrived, I was hysterical and covered in blood. They took Martin's cousin to the hospital where he was pronounced dead. Because of the gunshot wounds, the funeral was a closed casket affair and very hard on everyone. It made Martin stronger, meaner, and colder, and it made me wiser. Martin was out committing crimes again, and two months later would be jailed again.

5   It is hard for me to imagine what I did to myself, knowing that any day I could have died senselessly. It is even harder for me to accept the fact that my boyfriend would die for a dirty, trashy street gang, but not for me.

Topic sentence   6   <u>This last year I have been moving back to the right track. I have gotten sober,</u>
Effects   <u>started college, and returned home. I have nightmares</u> about things I have seen and things I have done. I struggle every day to stay sober, to do the right thing. I'm doing a lot of thinking. I live each day in fear for Martin's safety as well as my own. I fear for our future in a society that doesn't understand us. I count down the days until Martin can see the sunlight. I pray every day that this time will be the last time he goes to jail. I pray Martin will trade his gun for me, even get an education. I cry every night and try to live every day.

EXERCISE 6   # Discussion and Critical Thinking

1. Why did McGraw become associated with Martin and finally become a gang member?

2. Were there deeper reasons for her dropping out of mainstream, middle-class society and joining a gang?

3. What were the effects on her life and those who were close to her?

4. What happened before the killing to set the stage for her change?

5. To what extent has she changed?

6. Why doesn't she leave Martin?

7. What is your reaction to the statement "I fear for our future in a society that doesn't understand us"?

EXERCISE 7

Writing a Response to a Reading

Read, underline, and annotate the following text and then complete one of the assignments below.

- Write a summary.

- Write a reaction. Include enough summary to establish clear and logical connections between the text and your own ideas.

- Write a two-part response composed of a summary separated from a reaction.

American Space, Chinese Place

YI-FU TUAN

What can you learn about people by studying the design of their homes?
According to Yi-Fu Tuan, you can learn a great deal.

1   Americans have a sense of space, not of place. Go to an American home in exurbia, and almost the first thing you do is drift toward the picture window. How curious that the first compliment you pay your host inside his house is to say how lovely it is outside his house! He is pleased that you should admire his vistas. The distant horizon is not merely a line separating earth from sky, it is a symbol of the future. The American is not rooted in his place, however lovely: His eyes are drawn by the expanding space to a point on the horizon, which is his future.

2   By contrast, consider the traditional Chinese home. Blank walls enclose it. Step behind the spirit wall and you are in a courtyard with perhaps a miniature garden around the corner. Once inside the private compound you are wrapped in an ambiance of calm beauty, an ordered world of buildings, pavement, rock, and decorative vegetation. But you have no distant view: Nowhere does space open out before you. Raw nature in such a home is experienced only as weather, and the only open space is the sky above. The Chinese is rooted in his place. When he has to leave, it is not for the promised land on the terrestrial horizon, but for another world altogether along the vertical, religious axis of his imagination.

3   The Chinese tie to place is deeply felt. Wanderlust is an alien sentiment. The Taoist classic *Tao Te Ching* captures the idea of rootedness in place with these words: "Though there may be another country in the neighborhood so close that they are within sight of each other and the crowing of cocks and barking of dogs in one place can be heard in the other, yet there is no traffic between them; and

throughout their lives the two peoples have nothing to do with each other." In theory if not in practice, farmers have ranked high in Chinese society. The reason is not only that they are engaged in the "root" industry of producing food but that, unlike pecuniary merchants, they are tied to the land and do not abandon their country when it is in danger.

4   Nostalgia is a recurrent theme in Chinese poetry. An American reader of translated Chinese poems may well be taken aback—even put off—by the frequency as well as the sentimentality of the lament for home. To understand the strength of this sentiment, we need to know that the Chinese desire for stability and rootedness in place is prompted by the constant threat of war, exile, and the natural disasters of flood and drought. Forcible removal makes the Chinese keenly aware of their loss. By contrast, Americans move, for the most part, voluntarily. Their nostalgia for home town is really longing for childhood to which they cannot return: In the meantime the future beckons and the future is "out there," in open space. When we criticize American rootlessness we tend to forget that it is a result of ideals we admire, namely, social mobility and optimism about the future. When we admire Chinese rootedness, we forget the word "place" means both location in space and position in society: To be tied to place is also to be bound to one's station in life, with little hope of betterment. Space symbolizes hope; place, achievement and stability.

EXERCISE 8 — Discussion and Critical Thinking

1. According to the author, if you visit a traditional American home, what will your host invite you to enjoy? Why?

2. On the contrary, if you visit a Chinese home, what will your host invite you to enjoy? Why?

3. Why do the Chinese admire their farmers?

4. In the same vein, what station in life do Americans, in contrast with Chinese, admire?

5. What are the different views, good and bad, held by Chinese and Americans on moving?

6. What is positive and negative in both the American and Chinese views?

Writer's Guidelines

1. Underlining will help you to prepare for review and to concentrate when reading.
   a. Underline the main idea in each paragraph.
   b. Underline the support for those main ideas.
   c. Underline answers to questions.
   d. Underline only key words; almost never underline entire sentences.

2. Annotating along with underlining will make you an engaged, active reader.

3. Outlining reading selections will show main and supporting ideas.

4. Summarizing will help you concentrate on main ideas; this is helpful in both reading and writing. (See page 19 for specific rules.)

5. Reading-related writing can take two forms in addition to the summary:
   a. The reaction is usually a statement of how the reading relates specifically to you, your experiences, and your attitudes, but it is also often a critique, involving the worth and logic of a piece.
   b. A two-part response includes both a summary and a reaction but separates them.

Writing Sentences

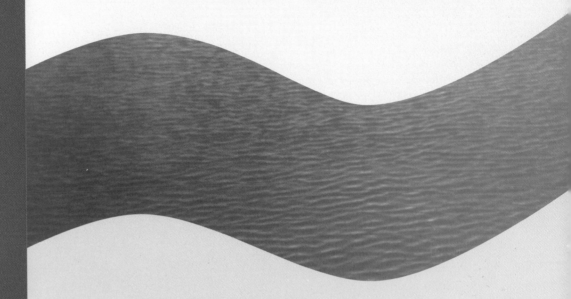

Almost all of your most important writing will be in sentences. Good sentences, those you write correctly and effectively, will convey what you intend to say and perhaps even enhance the message. Incorrect and awkward sentences will detract from your message. Even an original, insightful idea may be discredited if it is carried by weak phrasing, faulty mechanics, or poor word choice. Chapters 2 through 11 will help you get full credit for communicating your ideas.

Chapter 2

Subjects and Verbs

Look carefully and you will see that each sentence has a skeleton and that the skeleton's two indispensable bones are the subject and the verb.

FLOW OF WRITING

Learning Objectives

Working with this chapter, I will learn to

~ identify subjects and verbs.
~ respect subjects and verbs as key elements in sentence structure.
~ not confuse subjects with objects of prepositions.
~ not confuse verbs with verbals and adverbs.

MICROTHEME

EXERCISE A

Writing Activity in Miniature
Two Purposes

Writing Diagnostic: Before you work on this chapter, the Microtheme will give you an opportunity to write briefly on an engaging topic without pressure.

Chapter Learning Application: After you have studied this chapter, return to your Microtheme to check your work and practice what you have just learned.

Form and Procedure

Like an executive summary (written for a busy boss), the Microtheme conveys ideas concisely (using no more than the space on a 5- by 8-inch card) in a specified form. Indent only once, and write small enough to leave room for marking later. Directions for practicing your chapter writing skills appear in Exercise B.

Suggested Microtheme Topic

Write a Microtheme of 80 to 100 words about an event that took place in no more than five minutes. Perhaps it had a special meaning as a discovery, a reason for change, or a transformation. The event could be outstanding because of the pain, pleasure, or insight it gave you.

_____

_____

_____

_____

_____

_____

_____

_____

_____

_____

_____

_____

_____

EXERCISE B

Connecting Your Learning Objectives with Your Microtheme

Complete this exercise after you have studied this chapter.

1. Underline the subjects and circle the verbs in your first two sentences.

2. Check to make certain you have not confused objects of prepositions with subjects.

3. Check to make certain you have not confused verbs with verbals or adverbs.

FLOW OF WRITING

The two most important parts of any sentence are the subject and the verb. The **subject** is who or what causes the action or expresses a state of being. The **verb** indicates what the subject is doing or is being. Many times, the subject and verb taken together carry the meaning of the sentence. Consider this example:

The <u>woman</u> <u>left</u> for work.
         subject   verb

The subject *woman* and the verb *left* indicate the basic content of the sentence while providing structure.

Subjects

The **simple subject** of a sentence is usually a single noun or pronoun.

The judge's <u>reputation</u> for order in the courtroom is well known.
              simple subject

The **complete subject** is the simple subject with all its modifiers—that is, with all the words that describe or qualify it.

<u>The judge's reputation for order in the courtroom</u> is well known.
                   complete subject

To more easily understand and identify simple subjects of sentences, you may want to review the following information about nouns and pronouns. See Appendix A, pages 452–457, for more information about all eight parts of speech.

Nouns

Nouns are naming words. Nouns may name persons, animals, plants, places, things, substances, qualities, or ideas—for example, *Bart, armadillo, Mayberry, tree, rock, cloud, love, ghost, music, virtue.*

Pronouns

A **pronoun** is a word that is used in place of a noun.

- Pronouns that can be used as subjects of sentences may represent specific persons or things and are called **personal pronouns:**

I	*we*
you	*you*
he, she, it	*they*

    Example: <u>They</u> recommended my sister for the coaching position.
           subject

- **Indefinite pronouns** refer to nouns (persons, places, things) in a general way:

    each   everyone   nobody   somebody

    Example: <u>Everyone</u> wants a copy of that photograph.
           subject

- Other pronouns point out particular things:

  Singular: *this, that*   **Plural:** *these, those*

  This is my treasure.   *These* are my jewels.
  That is your junk.   *Those* are your trinkets.

- Still other pronouns introduce questions:

  Which is the best CD player?
  What are the main ingredients in a Twinkie?
  Who understands this computer command?

Note: To be the subject of a sentence, a pronoun must stand alone.

> *This* is a treasure. [Subject is *this*; pronoun stands alone.]
> This *treasure* is mine. [Subject is *treasure. This* is an **adjective**—a word that describes a noun; *this* describes *treasure*.]

Compound Subjects

A subject may be **compound.** That is, it may consist of two or more subjects, usually joined by *and* or *or*, that function together.

> The *prosecutor* and the *attorney* for the defense made opening statements.
> *He* and his *friends* listened carefully.
> *Steven, Juan,* and *Alicia* attended the seminar. [Note the placement of commas for three or more subjects.]

Implied Subjects

A subject may be **implied,** or understood. An **imperative sentence**—a sentence that gives a command—has *you* as the implied subject.

> (You) Sit in that chair, please.
> (You) Now take the oath.
> (You) Please read the notes carefully.

Trouble Spot: Prepositional Phrases

A **prepositional phrase** is made up of a preposition (a word such as *at, in, of, to, with*) and one or more nouns or pronouns with their modifiers: *at the time, by the jury, in the courtroom, to the judge and the media, with controlled anger.* Be careful not to confuse the subject of a sentence with the noun or pronoun (known as the object of the preposition) in a prepositional phrase. The object of a preposition cannot be the subject of a sentence.

> The <u>car</u> <u>with the dents</u> is mine.
>   subject   prepositional
>   phrase

The subject of the sentence is *car.* The word *dents* is the object of the preposition *with* and cannot be the subject of the sentence.

> <u>Most</u> <u>of the pie</u> has been eaten.
> subject   prepositional
>   phrase

> The <u>person</u> <u>in the middle</u> <u>of the crowd</u> has disappeared.
>   subject   prepositional   prepositional
>   phrase   phrase

Trouble Spot: The Words *Here* and *There*

The words *here* and *there* are adverbs (used as filler words) and cannot be subjects.

There is no <u>problem</u>.
subject

Here is the <u>issue</u>.
subject

EXERCISE 1

Finding Subjects

Circle the subjects in the following sentences. You will have to supply the subject of one sentence. (See Answer Key for answers.)

1. Mahatma Gandhi gave his life for India and for peace.

2. Through a practice of nonviolent resistance, he led his people to freedom from the British.

3. Ponder his preference for behavior rather than accomplishment.

4. There was only good in his behavior and in his accomplishments.

5. His fasts, writings, and speeches inspired the people of India.

6. He taught his people self-sufficiency in weaving cloth and making salt for themselves against British law.

7. Gandhi urged the tolerance of all religions.

8. Finally, the British granted freedom to India.

9. Some leaders in India and a few foreign agitators questioned the freedom of religion.

10. Gandhi, the Indian prince of peace, was killed by an intolerant religious leader.

EXERCISE 2

Finding Subjects

Circle the subjects in the following sentences. You will have to supply the subject of one sentence.

1. More than two hundred years ago, some tractors were powered by steam.

2. They could travel at about three miles per hour for about ten minutes.

3. Consider that information in relation to the following material.

4. There was a great future ahead for these self-powered vehicles.

5. About a hundred years later, in 1897, Freelan O. Stanley and his associates produced the Stanley steamer, the best-known steam automobile.

6. Around the same time, William Morrison built an electric car.

7. Without polluting the atmosphere, it could go twenty miles an hour.

8. After traveling for about fifty miles, its batteries had to be recharged.

9. Meanwhile in Germany, Gottlieb Daimler, Karl Benz, and their engineers were developing the internal-combustion engine.

10. In the 1890s, the first successful gasoline-powered automobiles took to the roads.

Verbs

Verbs show action or express being in relation to the subject of a sentence.

Types of Verbs

Action verbs indicate movement or accomplishment in idea or deed. Someone can "consider the statement" or "hit the ball." Here are other examples:

She *sees* the arena.

He *bought* the book.

They *adopted* the child.

He *understood* her main theories.

Being verbs indicate existence. Few in number, they include *is, was, were, am,* and *are.*

The movie *is* sad.

The book *was* comprehensive.

They *were* responsible.

I *am* concerned.

We *are* organized.

Verb Phrases

Verbs may occur as single words or as phrases. A **verb phrase** is made up of a main verb and one or more helping verbs such as the following:

is	*was*	*can*	*have*	*do*	*may*	*shall*
are	*were*	*could*	*had*	*does*	*might*	*should*
am		*will*	*has*	*did*	*must*	
		would				

Here are some sentences that contain verb phrases:

The judge *has presided* over many capital cases.

His rulings seldom *are overturned* on appeal.

Trouble Spot: Words Such as *Never, Not,* and *Hardly*

Never, not, hardly, seldom, and so on, are modifiers, not verbs.

The attorney could *not* win the case without key witnesses.
[*Not* is an adverb. The verb phrase is *could win.*]

The jury could *hardly* hear the witness. [*Hardly* is an adverb; *could hear* is
the verb phrase.]

Compound Verbs

Verbs that are joined by a word such as *and* or *or* are called **compound verbs.**

As a district attorney, Barbara *had presented* and *had won* famous cases.

She *prepared* carefully and *presented* her ideas with clarity.

We *will go* out for dinner or *skip* it entirely.

Trouble Spot: Verbals

Do not confuse verbs with verbals. **Verbals** are verblike words in certain respects,
but they do not function as verbs. They function as other parts of speech. There are
three kinds of verbals.

An **infinitive** is made up of the word *to* and a verb. An infinitive provides information, but, unlike the true verb, it is not tied to the subject of the sentence. It acts
as a modifier or a noun.

His drive *to succeed* would serve him well.

He wanted *to get* a bachelor's degree.

His main objective was *to get* a bachelor's degree.

In the first example, *to succeed* is an infinitive acting as a modifier. In the second and
third examples *to get* is an infinitive acting as a noun.

A **gerund** is a verblike word ending in *-ing* that acts as a noun.

Retrieving her e-mail was her main objective.

She thought about *retrieving* her e-mail.

Retrieving in each sentence acts as a noun.

A **participle** is a verblike word that usually has an *-ing* or an *-ed* ending.

Walking to town in the dark, he lost his way.

Wanted by the FBI, she was on the run.

The *starved* dog barked for food.

In the first example, the word *walking* answers the question *when.* In the second example, the word *wanted* answers the question *which one.* In the third example,
starved describes the dog. *Walking, wanted,* and *starved* are describing words; they
are not the true verbs in the sentences.

EXERCISE 3

Finding Verbs

Underline the verb(s) in each sentence. (See Answer Key for answers.)

1. Chimpanzees live and travel in social groups.

2. The composition of these groups varies in age and gender.

3. The habitat of the chimpanzees is mainly forests.

4. They spend more time in the trees than on the ground.

5. Each night they make a nest of branches and leaves in trees.

6. Sometimes a proud male will beat on his chest.

7. Chimpanzees are violent at times but usually live peacefully.

8. After finding food, a chimp hoots and shakes branches.

9. Other chimps hear the commotion and go to the food source.

10. Chimp tools, such as leaf sponges and sticks, are primitive.

EXERCISE 4

Finding Verbs

Underline the verb(s) in each sentence.

1. Chimpanzees share many features with human beings.

2. More than 90 percent of basic genetic make-up is shared.

3. Both human beings and chimps can use reason.

4. Chimps have a remarkable talent for communication.

5. Chimps do not have the capacity for human speech.

6. However, chimps can use other symbols.

7. In one experiment, chimps learned American Sign Language.

8. Chimps can learn a complex system of language.

9. Chimp scholar Washoe has learned more than 160 signs and can ask questions.

10. Another chimp, Lana, uses a computer.

Location of Subjects and Verbs

Although the subject usually appears before the verb, it may follow the verb instead:

Into the court <u>stumbled</u> the <u>defendant</u>.
　　　　　　　verb　　　　　subject

From tiny acorns <u>grow</u> mighty <u>oaks</u>.
　　　　　　　　verb　　　　　subject

There <u>was</u> little <u>support</u> for him in the audience.
　　　　verb　　　　subject

Here <u>are</u> your <u>books</u> and your <u>papers</u>.
　　　verb　　　subject　　　　　subject

Verb phrases are often broken up in a question. Do not overlook a part of the verb that is separated from another in a question such as "Where had the defendant gone on that fateful night?" If you have trouble finding the verb phrase, recast the question, making it into a statement: "The defendant *had gone* where on that fateful night?" The result will not necessarily be a smooth or complete statement, but you will be able to see the basic elements more easily.

Can the defense lawyer *control* the direction of the trial?

Change the question to a statement to find the verb phrase:

The defense lawyer *can control* the direction of the trial.

As you will see in Chapter 3, a sentence may have more than one set of subjects and verbs. In the following passsage, the subjects are circled; the verbs are underlined.

(We) <u>should be</u> careful to get out of an experience only the wisdom (that) <u>is</u>

in it—and <u>stop</u> there; lest (we) <u>be</u> like the cat (that) <u>sits</u> down on a hot stove

lid. (She) <u>will</u> never <u>sit</u> down on a hot stove lid again—and (that) <u>is</u> well; but

also (she) <u>will</u> never <u>sit</u> down on a cold one any more.

Mark Twain, *Epitaph for His Daughter*

EXERCISE 5 | ## Finding Subjects and Verbs

Circle the subject(s) and underline the verb(s) in the following sentences. You will have to supply the subject for one sentence. (See Answer Key for answers.)

1. Read this exercise and learn about the Aztec empire in Mexico.

2. Aztec cities were as large as those in Europe at that time.

3. Government and religion were important concerns.

4. There was little difference between the two institutions.

5. They built huge temples to their gods and sacrificed human beings.

6. The religious ceremonies related mainly to their concerns about plentiful harvests.

7. Aztec society had nobles, commoners, serfs, and slaves.

8. The family included a husband, a wife, children, and some relatives of the husband.

9. At the age of ten, boys went to school, and girls either went to school or learned domestic skills at home.

10. The Aztecs wore loose-fitting garments, they lived in adobe houses, and they ate tortillas.

11. Scholars in this culture developed a calendar of 365 days.

12. Huge Aztec calendars of stone are now in museums.

13. The Aztec language was similar to that of the Comanche and Pima Indians.

14. The Aztec written language was pictographic and represented ideas and sounds.

15. Both religion and government required young men to pursue warfare.

16. By pursuing warfare, the soldiers could capture others for slaves and sacrifice, and enlarge the Aztec empire.

17. In 1519, Hernando Cortez landed in Mexico.

18. He was joined by Indians other than Aztecs.

19. After first welcoming Cortez and his army, the Aztecs then rebelled.

20. The Spaniards killed Emperor Montezuma II, and then they defeated the Aztecs.

EXERCISE 6

Finding Subjects and Verbs

Circle the subject(s) and underline the verb(s) in the following sentences.

1. Who are the Eskimos?

2. Where did they come from?

3. How do they live?

4. How has their way of life changed in the last century?

5. These questions are all important.

6. There may be different views on some of the answers.

7. They live in the Arctic from Russia east to Greenland.

8. Their ancestors came from Siberia in Northern Asia.

9. They have learned to live in a land of perpetual snow.

10. The word *Eskimo* means *eaters of raw meat* in a Native American language.

11. Their own name for themselves is *Inuit* or *Yuit,* meaning *people.*

12. For hundreds of years, their homes during hunting and fishing excursions were made of blocks of ice or packed snow and called *igloos.*

13. They ate the raw flesh of caribou, seals, whales, and fish.

14. During the 1800s, the whalers enlisted the Eskimos as helpers.

15. Later the traders came and bought furs from the Eskimos.

16. The traders and whalers brought guns, tools, technology, and disease to the Eskimos.

17. The Eskimos used their new harpoons and guns, and killed more game.

18. Their simple, traditional way of life changed.

19. Now most Eskimos live in settlements.

20. Despite the many changes, Eskimos still treasure their ancient ways.

CHAPTER REVIEW   SUBJECTS AND VERBS

The **subject** carries out the action or expresses the state of being in a sentence. The **verb** indicates what the subject is doing or is being.

Subjects

You can recognize the **simple subject** by asking who or what causes the action or expresses the state of being found in the verb.

1. The **simple subject** can be single or compound.

    My *friend* and *I* have much in common. [compound subject]

    My *friend* brought a present. [single subject]

2. The command, or **imperative,** sentence has a "you" as the implied subject and no stated subject.

    (*You*) Read the notes.

3. Although the subject usually appears before the verb, it may follow the verb.

    There was *justice* in the verdict.

4. The object of a preposition cannot be a subject.

    The *chairperson* [subject] of the department [object of the preposition] directs the discussion.

Verbs

Verbs show action or express being in relation to the subject.

1. Action verbs suggest movement or accomplishment in idea or deed.

He *dropped* the book. [movement]

He *read* the book. [accomplishment]

2. Being verbs indicate existence.

They *were* concerned.

3. Verbs may occur as single words or phrases.

He *led* the charge. [single word]

She *is leading* the charge. [phrase]

4. A **verb phrase** may be separated in a question.

Where *had* the defendant *gone* on that fateful night?

5. Compound verbs are joined by a word such as *and* or *or*.

She *worked* for twenty-five years and *retired*.

6. Words such as *never, not,* and *hardly* are not verbs; they modify verbs.

7. Verbals are not verbs; **verbals** are verblike words that function as other parts of speech.

Singing [gerund acting as a noun subject] is fun.

I want *to sing*. [infinitive acting as a noun object]

Singing [participle acting as a modifier], he walked in the rain.

CHAPTER REVIEW EXERCISES

REVIEW 1

Finding Subjects and Verbs

Circle the subject(s) and underline the verb(s) in the following sentences. You will have to supply the subject for one sentence. (See Answer Key for answers.)

1. Read this exercise carefully.

2. What causes earthquakes?

3. How much damage can they do?

4. Earthquakes shake the earth.

5. There is no simple answer to the question of cause.

6. The earth is covered by rock plates.

7. Instead of merely covering, they are in constant motion.

8. These plates bump into each other and then pass over each other.

9. The rocks are squeezed and stretched.

10. They pull apart or pile up and cause breaks in the earth's surface.

11. These breaks are called *faults*.

12. The formation of a fault is an earthquake.

13. During the breaking or shifting, a seismic wave travels across the earth's surface.

14. These quaking vibrations are especially destructive near the point of the breaking or shifting.

15. Their force is equal to as much as ten thousand times that of an atomic bomb.

16. For many years, scientists have tried to predict earthquakes.

17. There has been little success in their endeavors.

18. Earthquakes are identified only after the fact.

19. Some states, such as California, experience many earthquakes.

20. Somewhere in the earth, a quake of some magnitude is almost certainly occurring now.

REVIEW 2

Finding Subjects and Verbs

Circle the subject(s) and underline the verb(s) in the following sentences. You will have to supply the subject for one sentence.

1. Consider this information about Puerto Rico.

2. Just where is Puerto Rico?

3. What do the words *Puerto Rico* mean?

4. Are Puerto Ricans citizens?

5. How is Puerto Rico different from our states?

6. Will it ever become a state?

7. The Commonwealth of Puerto Rico is located southeast of Florida.

8. *Puerto Rico* means "rich port."

9. Puerto Rico became a U.S. territory in 1898 after the Spanish-American War.

10. It became a commonwealth with its own constitution in 1952.

11. Puerto Ricans are citizens of the United States.

12. They cannot vote in presidential elections and do not pay federal income taxes.

13. On several occasions, they have voted not to become a state.

14. However, there are many in favor of statehood.

15. The majority of the citizens speak Spanish.

16. Their economy is based on manufacturing, fishing, and agriculture.

17. The Caribbean National Forest is treasured by Puerto Ricans and visitors.

18. In this tropical rain forest parrots and orchids can be seen.

19. Tourists by the thousands visit the Phosphorescent Bay at La Parguera.

20. On moonless nights, the phosphorescent plankton light the water.

REVIEW 3

Writing Sentences with Subjects and Verbs

Using the topic of *work*, write five sentences. For variety, include one sentence with a compound subject, one with a compound verb, one with the verb before the subject, and one with the subject followed by a prepositional phrase. Circle the subjects and underline the verbs.

1. _____

   _____

2. _____

   _____

3. _____

   _____

4. _____

   _____

5. _____

   _____

MICROTHEME

To practice your skills acquired in this chapter, return to the Microtheme on page 32 and complete Exercise B.

Chapter 3

Kinds of Sentences

Is it not curious that though the English language has about two million words, we writers have only four ways of arranging them in basic sentence patterns?

FLOW OF WRITING

Learning Objectives

Working with this chapter, I will learn to

~ identify independent, dependent, and relative clauses.

~ distinguish phrases from clauses.

~ identify and write simple, compound, complex, and compound-complex sentences.

MICROTHEME

EXERCISE A

Writing Activity in Miniature
Two Purposes

Writing Diagnostic: Before you work on this chapter, the Microtheme will give you an opportunity to write briefly on an engaging topic without pressure.

Chapter Learning Application: After you have studied this chapter, return to your Microtheme to check your work and practice what you have just learned.

Form and Procedure

Like an executive summary (written for a busy boss), the Microtheme conveys ideas concisely (using no more than the space on a 5- by 8-inch card) in a specified form. Indent only once, and write small enough to leave room for marking later. Directions for practicing your chapter writing skills appear in Exercise B.

Suggested Microtheme Topic

Write a Microtheme of 80 to 100 words about the best or the worst decision you made during the past three years.

_____

_____

_____

_____

_____

_____

_____

_____

_____

_____

_____

_____

_____

_____

_____

_____

_____

EXERCISE B

Connecting Your Learning Objectives with Your Microtheme

Complete this exercise after you have studied this chapter.

1. Examine your Microtheme to make sure you have used a variety of sentence structures.

2. Label one simple sentence, one compound sentence, and one complex sentence. Revise sentences for variety if necessary.

FLOW OF WRITING

There are four kinds of basic sentences in English: simple, compound, complex, and compound-complex. The terms may be new to you, but if you can recognize subjects and verbs, with a little instruction and practice you should be able to identify and write any of the four kinds of sentences. The only new idea to master is the concept of the *clause*.

Clauses

A **clause** is a group of words with a subject and a verb that functions as a part or all of a complete sentence. There are two kinds of clauses: independent (main) and dependent (subordinate).

Independent Clause: I have the money.

Dependent Clause: When I have the money

Independent Clauses

An **independent (main) clause** is a group of words with a subject and a verb that can stand alone and make sense. An independent clause expresses a complete thought by itself and can be written as a separate sentence.

Sabrina plays the bass guitar.

The manager is not at fault.

Dependent Clauses

A **dependent clause** is a group of words with a subject and a verb that depends on the main clause to give it meaning.

since Carlotta came home [no meaning alone]

<u>Since Carlotta came home</u>, <u>her mother has been happy</u>. [has meaning]
       dependent clause   independent clause

because she was needed [no meaning alone]

<u>Kachina stayed in the game</u> <u>because she was needed</u>. [has meaning]
     independent clause   dependent clause

Relative Clauses

One type of dependent clause is called a **relative clause.** A relative clause begins with a relative pronoun, a pronoun such as *that, which,* or *who*. Relative pronouns *relate* the clause to another word in the sentence.

that fell last night [no meaning alone]

The snow <u>that fell last night</u> is nearly gone. [has meaning]
        dependent clause

independent clause

In the sentence above, the relative pronoun *that* relates the dependent clause to the subject of the sentence, *snow.*

who stayed in the game [no meaning alone]

Kachina was the only one who stayed in the game.
<small>independent clause</small>   <small>dependent clause</small>

In the sentence above, the relative pronoun *who* relates the dependent clause to the word *one*.

Trouble Spot: Phrases

A **phrase** is a group of words that go together. It differs from a clause in that a phrase does not have a subject and a verb. In Chapter 2, we discussed prepositional phrases (*in the house, beyond the horizon*) and saw some verbal phrases (infinitive phrase: *to go home*; participial phrase: *disconnected from the printer*; and gerund phrase: *running the computer*).

EXERCISE 1

Identifying Clauses and Phrases

Identify the following groups of words as an independent, or main, clause (has a subject and verb and can stand alone); a dependent clause (has a subject and verb but cannot stand alone); or a phrase (a group of words that go together but do not have a subject and verb). Use these abbreviations: IC (independent clause), DC (dependent clause), or P (phrase).

_____   1. Under the table

_____   2. After I scanned the document

_____   3. I scanned the document.

_____   4. To find a fossil

_____   5. Mr. Darwin found a fossil.

_____   6. Over the bridge and through the woods

_____   7. We chased the wind over the bridge and through the woods.

_____   8. Which is on the floor

_____   9. Find your new socks.

_____   10. Because of the new guidelines

_____   11. Standing on the corner

_____   12. Why are we standing on the corner?

Writing Sentences

This section covers sentence types according to this principle: On the basis of the number and kinds of clauses it contains, a sentence may be classified as simple, compound, complex, or compound-complex. In the examples in the following table, the dependent clauses are italicized, and the independent clauses are underlined.

Type	Definition	Example
Simple	One independent clause	She did the work well.
Compound	Two or more independent clauses	She did the work well, and she was paid well.
Complex	One independent clause and one or more dependent clauses	*Because she did the work well,* she was paid well.
Compound-Complex	Two or more independent clauses and one or more dependent clauses	*Because she did the work well,* she was paid well, and she was satisfied.

Simple Sentences

A **simple sentence** consists of one independent clause and no dependent clauses. It may contain phrases and have more than one subject or verb.

The *lake looks* beautiful in the moonlight. [one subject and one verb]

The *Army, Navy,* and *Marines sent* troops to the disaster area. [three subjects and one verb]

We sang the old songs and *danced* happily at their wedding. [one subject and two verbs]

My *father, mother,* and *sister came* to the school play, *applauded* the performers, and *attended* the party afterwards. [three subjects and three verbs]

EXERCISE 2

Writing Simple Sentences

Write six simple sentences. The first five have been started for you.

1. This school _____

_____

2. My desk _____

_____

3. My friend _____

_____

4. In the evening, I _____

_____

5. Last night the _____

_____

6. _____

_____

Compound Sentences

A **compound sentence** consists of two or more independent clauses with no dependent clauses. Take, for example, the following two independent clauses:

He opened the drawer. He found his missing disk.

Here are two ways to join the independent clauses to form a compound sentence.

1. The two independent clauses can be connected by a connecting word called a *coordinating conjunction*. The coordinating conjunctions are *for, and, nor, but, or, yet, so.* (An easy way to remember them is to think of the acronym FANBOYS, which is made up of the first letter of each conjunction.) Use a comma before the coordinating conjunction (FANBOYS) between two independent clauses (unless the clauses are extremely short).

He opened the drawer, *and* he found his missing disk.

He opened the drawer, *so* he found his missing disk.

2. Another way to join independent clauses to form a compound sentence is to put a semicolon between the clauses.

He opened the drawer; he found his missing disk.

EXERCISE 3   ## Writing Compound Sentences

Write five compound sentences using coordinating conjunctions. The sentences have been started for you. Then write the same five compound sentences without the coordinating conjunctions. Use a semicolon to join the independent clauses.

1. He played well in the first quarter, but he _____

_____

_____

2. She was happy for a while, and then _____

_____

_____

3. The dog is our best friend, for _____

_____

_____

4. She is not the best player, nor is _____

_____

_____

5. I will try to help, but _____

_____

_____

6. _____

_____

_____

7. _____

_____

_____

8. _____

_____

_____

9. _____

_____

_____

10. _____

_____

_____

Complex Sentences

A **complex sentence** consists of one independent clause and one or more dependent clauses. In the following sentences, the dependent clauses are italicized.

> *When lilacs are in bloom,* we love to visit friends in the country. [one dependent clause and one independent clause]

> *Although it rained last night,* we decided to take the path *that led through the woods.* [one independent clause and two dependent clauses]

Punctuation tip: Use a comma after a dependent clause that appears before the main clause.

> *When the bus arrived,* we quickly boarded.

A relative clause (see page 47) can be the dependent clause in a complex sentence.

I knew the actress *who played that part in the 1980s.*

EXERCISE 4

Writing Complex Sentences

Write six complex sentences. The first five have been started for you.

1. Although he did the work quickly, _____

   _____

2. _____

   because we got caught in a storm. _____

3. After you go to the party, _____

   _____

4. Because you are smart, _____

   _____

5. _____

   _____ when he turned to leave.

6. _____

   _____

Compound-Complex Sentences

A **compound-complex sentence** consists of two or more independent clauses and one or more dependent clauses.

Compound-Complex Sentence:	Albert enlisted in the Army, and Robert, who was his older brother, joined him a day later.
Independent Clauses:	Albert enlisted in the Army Robert joined him a day later
Dependent Clause:	who was his older brother
Compound-Complex Sentence:	Because Mr. Yamamoto was a talented teacher, he was voted teacher of the year, and his students prospered.
Independent Clauses:	he was voted teacher of the year his students prospered
Dependent Clause:	Because Mr. Yamamoto was a talented teacher

EXERCISE 5

Writing Compound-Complex Sentences

Write six compound-complex sentences. The first five have been started for you.

1. Because he was my friend, I had to defend him, and I _____

   _____

2. Although he started late, he finished rapidly, and he _____

   _____

3. She had not eaten since the clock struck twelve, and she _____

   _____

4. The man who was sick tried to rise, but _____

   _____

5. If you want to leave, _____

   _____

6. _____

   _____

Procedure for Sentence Analysis

Here is a systematic approach some students find helpful.

1. Underline all the verbs and circle all the subjects in the sentence.

2. Draw a box around each clause.

3. Label each box as either IC (independent clause) or DC (dependent clause).

4. Add up the number of each kind of clause and apply the following formula. (See the chart on page 49 for a more detailed explanation and examples.)

   One IC = Simple
   Two or more ICs = Compound
   One IC and one or more DCs = Complex
   Two or more ICs and one or more DCs = Compound-Complex

   Example:

   DC
   | Although (he) played well all season, |

   IC
   | his (team) lost ten games and finished in last place. |

   1 DC + 1 IC = Complex

Identifying Types of Sentences

Indicate the kind of sentence by writing the appropriate letter(s) in the blank.

S   simple

CP   compound

CX   complex

CC   compound-complex

Underline the verbs and circle the subjects. Consider using labeled boxes as shown above. (See Answer Key for answers.)

_____   1. The most popular sport in the world is soccer.

_____   2. People in ancient China and Japan had a form of soccer, and even Rome had a game that resembled soccer.

_____   3. The game as it is played today got its start in England.

_____   4. In the Middle Ages, whole towns played soccer on Shrove Tuesday.

_____   5. Goals were built at opposite ends of town, and hundreds of people who lived in those towns would play on each side.

_____   6. Such games resembled full-scale brawls.

_____   7. The first side to score a goal won and was declared village champion.

_____   8. Then both sides tended to the wounded, and they didn't play again for a whole year.

_____   9. The rules of the game were written in the late 1800s at British boarding schools.

_____ 10. Now nearly every European country has a national soccer team, and the teams participate in international tournaments.

EXERCISE 7

Identifying Types of Sentences

Indicate the kind of sentence by writing the appropriate letter(s) in the blank.

S	simple
CP	compound
CX	complex
CC	compound-complex

Underline the verbs and circle the subjects. Consider using labeled boxes as shown on page 53.

_____ 1. Leonardo da Vinci was one of the greatest painters of the Italian Renaissance

_____ 2. His portrait *Mona Lisa* and his religious scene *The Last Supper* rank among the most famous pictures ever painted.

_____ 3. Da Vinci was trained to be a painter, but he was also one of the most versatile geniuses in all of history.

_____ 4. His interests and achievements spread into an astonishing variety of fields that are usually considered scientific specialties.

_____ 5. Da Vinci studied anatomy, astronomy, botany, and geology, and he designed machines and drew plans for hundreds of inventions.

_____ 6. He recorded his scientific observations and his ideas for inventions in notebooks.

_____ 7. About 4,200 pages still exist; they are filled with brilliant drawings that reveal da Vinci's powers of observation and skill as a draftsman.

_____ 8. Many of the ideas and designs preserved in these notebooks were ahead of their time; for example, he drew plans for a flying machine, and he came up with the parachute, too.

_____ 9. These drawings rank among da Vinci's greatest masterpieces.

_____ 10. Although scientists of his day believed in an Earth-centered universe, da Vinci's notebooks reveal his understanding of the Earth's movement around the Sun.

EXERCISE 8

Identifying Types of Sentences

Indicate the kind of sentence by writing the appropriate letter(s) in the blank.

S   simple

CP   compound

CX   complex

CC   compound-complex

Underline the verbs and circle the subjects. Consider using labeled boxes as shown on page 53. (See Answer Key for answers.)

_____ 1. The American Society of Civil Engineers (ASCE) compiled a list of the seven wonders of the modern world.

_____ 2. These engineering experts based their decisions upon several factors; for example, they evaluated the pioneering quality of structures' design or construction, the structures' contributions to humanity, and the engineering challenges that were overcome to build the structures.

_____ 3. One structure on the list is the 31-mile Channel Tunnel, or Chunnel, which connects England and France through a system of tunnels under the English Channel.

_____ 4. Another marvel is the Panama Canal; it took 42,000 workers ten years to dig a canal across Panama to connect the Atlantic and Pacific oceans.

_____ 5. Although it was completed back in 1937, San Francisco's Golden Gate Bridge remains the world's tallest suspension bridge.

_____ 6. The bridge's construction involved many difficulties, for workers faced strong tides, frequent storms and fog, and the problem of blasting rock under deep water for earthquake-resistant foundations.

_____ 7. Two of the structures on the ASCE's list of wonders are buildings.

_____ 8. One of them is New York's Empire State Building, and the other is the CN Tower in Toronto, Canada.

_____ 9. Even though it is no longer the tallest building in the world, the well-engineered Empire State Building held that record for forty years, and its construction revolutionized the skyscraper construction industry.

_____ 10. The Itaipu Dam at the Brazil/Paraguay border and the dams, floodgates, and storm surge barriers of the Netherlands' North Sea Protection Works illustrate humanity's ability to master the forces of nature, so they are the sixth and seventh items on the list.

EXERCISE 9

Identifying Types of Sentences

Indicate the kind of sentence by writing the appropriate letter(s) in the blank.

S   simple
CP   compound
CX   complex
CC   compound-complex

Underline the verbs and circle the subjects. Consider using labeled boxes as shown on page 53.

_____ 1. Around 500 B.C.E., the Mayans began to create their civilization in the southern Gulf Coast region and present-day Guatemala.

_____ 2. The result was remarkable for its brilliant achievements.

_____ 3. Although they had no wheeled vehicles and no beasts of burden such as horses or oxen, they moved great pieces of stone to build their temples.

_____ 4. They had no iron tools; however, because they shaped their stone blocks so skillfully, their pyramids still stand.

_____ 5. The pyramids were the center of Mayan religious ceremonies.

_____ 6. The Mayans built many city-states, and the ruins of at least eighty have been found.

_____ 7. The tallest pyramid was as high as a twenty-story building.

_____ 8. A small temple was constructed at the top, where priests conducted ceremonies.

_____ 9. These pyramids were surrounded by plazas and avenues.

_____ 10. The Mayans were able to build complex structures and to invent an accurate calendar because they knew mathematics well.

CHAPTER REVIEW   KINDS OF SENTENCES

On the basis of number and kinds of clauses, sentences may be classified as simple, compound, complex, and compound-complex.

Clauses

1. A **clause** is a group of words with a subject and a verb that functions as a part or all of a complete sentence. There are two kinds of clauses: independent (main) and dependent (subordinate).

2. An **independent (main) clause** is a group of words with a subject and a verb that can stand alone and make sense. An independent clause expresses a complete thought by itself and can be written as a separate sentence.

> I have the money.

3. A **dependent clause** is a group of words with a subject and a verb that depends on a main clause to give it meaning.

> When you are ready

Types of Sentences

Type	Definition	Example
Simple	One independent clause	Susan was having trouble with her spelling.
Compound	Two or more independent clauses	Susan was having trouble with her spelling, and she purchased a computer with a spell checker.
Complex	One independent clause and one or more dependent clauses	Because Susan was having trouble with her spelling, she purchased a computer with a spell checker.
Compound-Complex	Two or more independent clauses and one or more dependent clauses	Because Susan was having trouble with her spelling, she purchased a computer with a spell checker, and the results made her expenditure worthwhile.

Punctuation

1. Use a comma before a coordinating conjunction (FANBOYS) between two independent clauses.

> The movie was good, but the tickets were expensive.

2. Use a comma after a dependent clause that appears before the main clause.

> When the bus arrived, we quickly boarded.

3. Use a semicolon between two independent clauses in one sentence if there is no coordinating conjunction.

> The bus arrived; we quickly boarded.

CHAPTER REVIEW EXERCISES

Identifying Types of Sentences

Indicate the kind of sentence by writing the appropriate letter(s) in the blank.

S   simple

CP   compound

CX   complex

CC   compound-complex

Underline the verbs and circle the subjects. Consider using labeled boxes as shown on page 53. (See Answer Key for answers.)

_____ 1. For more than forty years, dolphins have served in the U.S. Navy.

_____ 2. Dolphins use *echolocation,* which involves transmitting sound waves at objects and then reading the "echoes" from those objects.

_____ 3. They can distinguish a BB pellet from a kernel of corn from fifty feet away.

_____ 4. They can also tell the difference between natural and man-made objects, so the navy has trained dolphins to detect explosive anti-ship mines.

_____ 5. After unmanned undersea vehicles use sonar to identify suspicious objects, a dolphin and his team of humans go into watery combat zones to evaluate those objects.

_____ 6. When a dolphin positively identifies a mine, the location is marked, and divers arrive later to remove the mine.

_____ 7. During the 2003 war with Iraq, dolphins helped to disarm 100 mines and underwater booby traps planted in the water near the port city of Umm Qasr.

_____ 8. The dolphins are not in jeopardy because they are trained to stay a safe distance from the mines.

_____ 9. Dolphins also protected warships during the Vietnam War; in 1970, for example, the presence of five navy dolphins prevented enemy divers from destroying an army pier.

_____ 10. Many people do not realize that dolphins have used their extraordinary abilities to protect American lives during wartime, so the navy considers them to be very valuable assets.

Identifying Types of Sentences

Indicate the kind of sentence by writing the appropriate letter(s) in the blank.

S   simple

CP   compound

CX   complex

CC   compound-complex

Underline the verbs and circle the subjects. Consider using labeled boxes as shown on page 53.

_____ 1. Most hummingbirds weigh less than a nickel.

_____ 2. Because they're so tiny, people think of them as cute, sweet little birds.

_____ 3. However, hummingbirds are very mean, and they have been dubbed the "junkyard dogs" of the bird world.

_____ 4. A male hummingbird will fiercely guard a nectar feeder or a patch of flowers, and if any other hummingbirds come near, he will attack them.

_____ 5. The bird will threaten intruders, chase them, ram them in mid-air, and try to stab them with its beak.

_____ 6. Hummingbirds can even intimidate birds like hawks, which are a hundred times their size.

_____ 7. These territorial birds can be vicious, but they do have a good reason.

_____ 8. They expend a lot of energy; as a matter of fact, their hearts beat 1,200 times a minute, and their wings beat at over 2,000 revolutions per minute.

_____ 9. To survive, a hummingbird must consume 7 to 12 calories per day; in human terms, that would be 204,300 calories per day, which is the amount in 171 pounds of hamburger.

_____ 10. If you had to round up that much grub every day, you, too, might get very protective of your food source.

REVIEW 3   Writing Types of Sentences

Write a paragraph or two (a total of about ten sentences) on the topic of food (eating or preparing). Then examine your sentences and mark at least one example of each kind: simple (S), compound (CP), complex (CX), and compound-complex (CC). If any kinds are not represented, do some simple sentence revision.

MICROTHEME

To practice your skills acquired in this chapter, return to the Microtheme on page 46 and complete Exercise B.

Chapter

4

Combining Sentences

A piece of writing made up of a long series of choppy sentences probably suffers from a bad case of the monotony blues. The remedy may be found in a judicious dose of sentence combining.

FLOW OF WRITING

Learning Objectives

Working with this chapter, I will learn to

~ **combine sentences for effective expression.**

~ **punctuate sentences.**

~ **write sentences with variety.**

MICROTHEME

EXERCISE A

Writing Activity in Miniature
Two Purposes

Writing Diagnostic: Before you work on this chapter, the Microtheme will give you an opportunity to write briefly on an engaging topic without pressure.

Chapter Learning Application: After you have studied this chapter, return to your Microtheme to check your work and practice what you have just learned.

Form and Procedure

Like an executive summary (written for a busy boss), the Microtheme conveys ideas concisely (using no more than the space on a 5- by 8-inch card) in a specified form. Indent only once, and write small enough to leave room for marking later. Directions for practicing your chapter writing skills appear in Exercise B.

Suggested Microtheme Topic

Write a Microtheme of 80 to 100 words about the breakup of a relationship. It could be a friendship, romance, or work situation. Concentrate on causes or effects.

_____

_____

_____

_____

_____

_____

_____

_____

_____

_____

_____

_____

_____

EXERCISE B

Connecting Your Learning Objectives with Your Microtheme

Complete this exercise after you have studied this chapter.

1. Check to make sure that you have combined the sentences that could be combined. Revise as necessary.

2. Check to make sure that you have properly used commas and semicolons in compound, complex, and compound-complex sentences.

The simple sentence, the most basic sentence in the English language, can be exceptionally useful and powerful. Some of the greatest statements in literature have been presented in the simple sentence. Its strength is in its singleness of purpose. However, a piece of writing made up of a long series of short simple sentences is likely to be monotonous. Moreover, the form may suggest a separateness of ideas that does not serve your purpose well. If your ideas are closely associated and some are equal in importance and some not, you may be able to combine sentences to show a clearer relationship among those ideas.

Coordination: The Compound Sentence

If you intend to communicate two equally important and closely related ideas, you certainly will want to place them close together, probably in a **compound sentence**.

Suppose we take two simple sentences that we want to combine:

> I am very tired. I worked very hard today.

We have already looked at coordinating conjunctions as a way of joining independent clauses to create compound sentences. Depending on which coordinating conjunction you use, you can show different kinds of relationships. (The following list is arranged according to the FANBOYS acronym discussed in Chapter 3. Only the first conjunction joins the original two sentences.)

For shows a reason:

> I am very tired, *for* I worked very hard today.

And shows equal ideas:

> I am very tired, *and* I want to rest for a few minutes.

Nor indicates a negative choice or alternative:

> I am not tired, *nor* am I hungry right now.

But shows contrast:

> I am very tired, *but* I have no time to rest now.

Or indicates a choice or an alternative:

> I will take a nap, *or* I will go out jogging.

Yet indicates contrast:

> I am tired, *yet* I am unable to relax.

So points to a result:

> I am tired, *so* I will take a nap.

Punctuation with Coordinating Conjunctions

When you combine two sentences by using a coordinating conjunction, drop the first period, change the capital letter that begins the second sentence to a small letter, and insert a comma before the coordinating conjunction.

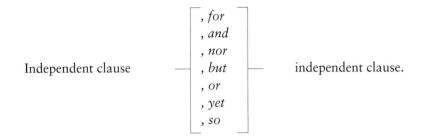

Independent clause

, for
, and
, nor
, but
, or
, yet
, so

independent clause.

| EXERCISE 1 | **Combining Sentences: Compound** |

Combine the following pairs of sentences by deleting the first period, changing the capital letter that begins the second sentence to a small letter, and inserting a comma and an appropriate coordinating conjunction from the FANBOYS list. Feel free to reword the sentences as necessary. (See Answer Key for answers.)

1. James Francis "Jim" Thorpe, a Sac and Fox Indian, was born in 1888 near Prague, Oklahoma. At the age of sixteen, he left home to enroll in the Carlisle Indian School in Pennsylvania.

2. He had had little experience playing football. He led his small college to victories against championship teams.

3. He had scarcely heard of other sports. He golfed in the 70s, bowled above 200, and played varsity basketball and lacrosse.

4. In the 1912 Olympic Games for amateur athletes at Stockholm, Jim Thorpe entered the two most rigorous events, the decathlon and the pentathlon. He won both.

5. King Gustav V of Sweden told him, "You, Sir, are the greatest athlete in the world." Jim Thorpe said, "Thanks, King."

6. Later it was said he had once been paid fifteen dollars a week to play baseball, making him a professional athlete. The Olympic medals were taken from him.

7. Soon a Major League baseball scout did offer Thorpe a respectable contract. He played in the National League for six seasons.

8. Not content to play only one sport, he also earned a good salary for that time in professional football. After competing for fifteen years, he said he had never played for the money.

9. Many regard Jim Thorpe as the greatest athlete of the twentieth century. He excelled in many sports at the highest levels of athletic competition.

10. Off the playing fields, he was known by his friends as a modest, quiet man. On the fields, he was a person of joyful combat.

Combining Sentences: Compound

Combine the following pairs of sentences by deleting the first period, changing the capital letter that begins the second sentence to a small letter, and inserting a comma and an appropriate coordinating conjunction from the FANBOYS list. Feel free to reword the sentences as necessary.

1. Sailing on its maiden voyage, the *Titanic* was considered unsinkable. On April 14, 1912, it struck an iceberg.

2. The ship sank 1,600 miles northeast of New York City. About 1,500 lives were lost.

3. The *Titanic* had been designed with great care. Its structure included sixteen watertight compartments.

4. Four of the compartments could be flooded without the ship's sinking. On that night five of the compartments flooded.

5. There were not enough lifeboats for the passengers. Lifeboats were considered unnecessary.

6. The management of the *Titanic* was supremely confident about the safety of the passengers. No lifeboat drills were required.

7. The killer iceberg was spotted just before the crash. It was too late.

8. At the time of the collision, another ship, the *Californian,* was only twenty miles away. The radio operator aboard the *Californian* was not on duty.

9. Some people behaved heroically. Others thought only of saving themselves.

10. Most of the survivors were women and children. The victims included the

rich and famous.

Semicolons and Conjunctive Adverbs

In Chapter 3 we saw that a semicolon can join independent clauses to make a compound sentence. Here are two more simple sentences to combine:

We were late. We missed the first act.

We can make one compound sentence out of them by joining the two clauses with a semicolon:

We were late; we missed the first act.

We can also use words called **conjunctive adverbs** after semicolons to make the relationship between the two clauses clearer. Look at how the conjunctive adverb *therefore* adds the idea of "as a result."

We were late; *therefore*, we missed the first act.

Conjunctive adverbs include the following words and phrases: *also, consequently, furthermore, hence, however, in fact, moreover, nevertheless, now, on the other hand, otherwise, soon, therefore, similarly, then, thus.*
    Consider the meaning you want when you use a conjunctive adverb to coordinate ideas.

As a result of: *therefore, consequently, hence, thus, then*

To the contrary or with reservation: *however, nevertheless, otherwise, on the other hand*

In addition to: *moreover, also*

To emphasize or specify: *in fact, for example*

To compare: *similarly*

Punctuation with Semicolons and Conjunctive Adverbs

When you combine two sentences by using a semicolon, replace the first period with a semicolon and change the capital letter that begins the second sentence to a small letter. If you wish to use a conjunctive adverb, insert it after the semicolon and put a comma after it. (However, no comma follows *then, now, thus,* and *soon*.) The first letters of ten common conjunctive adverbs make up the acronym HOTSHOT CAT.

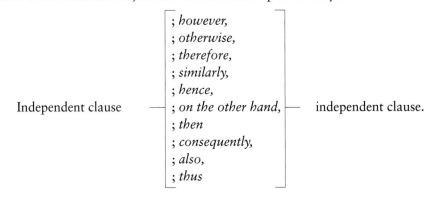

Independent clause
; *however,*
; *otherwise,*
; *therefore,*
; *similarly,*
; *hence,*
; *on the other hand,*
; *then*
; *consequently,*
; *also,*
; *thus*
independent clause.

Combining Sentences: Compound

Combine the following pairs of sentences by replacing the first period with a semi-colon, changing the capital letter that begins the second sentence to a small letter, and inserting a conjunctive adverb if appropriate. Consider the list of conjunctive adverbs (HOTSHOT CAT and others). Do not use a conjunctive adverb in every sentence. (See Answer Key for answers.)

1. The legendary island of Atlantis has fascinated people for centuries. It probably never existed.

2. According to the Greek writer Plato, the people of Atlantis were very ambitious and warlike. They planned to conquer all of the Mediterranean.

3. Initially, they were successful in subduing areas to the west. They became wealthy.

4. Then the people of Atlantis became proud. They became corrupt and wicked.

5. They were confident and attacked Athens. Athens and its allies defeated the invaders.

6. The story of Atlantis is probably just a tale. Many people have believed it.

7. Some writers have tried to link the legend with such real places as America and the Canary Islands. No link has been found.

8. The Minoan civilization on Crete was destroyed by tidal waves. A similar fate may have befallen Atlantis.

9. Some people speculate about a volcanic explosion on Atlantis. A volcanic eruption did destroy part of the island Thera in the Eastern Mediterranean in 1500 B.C.E.

10. Some writers have conjectured that American Indians migrated to the New World by way of Atlantis. Archaeologists dispute that idea.

EXERCISE 4   ## Combining Sentences: Compound

Combine the following pairs of sentences by replacing the first period with a semi-colon, changing the capital letter that begins the second sentence to a small letter, and inserting a conjunctive adverb if appropriate. Consider the list of conjunctive adverbs (HOTSHOT CAT and others). Do not use a conjunctive adverb in every sentence.

1. Camels can cover much distance in heat with little or no water. They are well adapted to the desert.

2. They can walk easily on soft sand and carry heavy loads. They are useful pack animals for human beings traveling in the desert.

3. The typical desert offers little vegetation. That circumstance does not affect the camel.

4. A camel stores food in one or two humps of fat on its back. When food is scarce, the camel uses that fat for energy.

5. The Arabian camel has one hump. The Bactrian has two.

6. Camels are known for their bad temper. Most people are not surprised when camels bite, kick, and spit.

7. Camels grunt and groan when mounted. Once under way, they carry their loads patiently.

8. Camels have mouth linings as tough as leather. They can eat a thorny cactus without injuring themselves.

9. In the 1850s the U.S. Army imported camels for desert transportation. The development of the railroads made camels unnecessary.

10. Working camels in Africa live for as long as fifty years. In circuses and zoos they die by the age of thirty.

Subordination: The Complex Sentence

Whereas a compound sentence contains independent clauses that are equally important and closely related, a **complex sentence** combines ideas of unequal value. The following two sentences can be combined as either a compound sentence or a complex sentence, depending on whether the writer thinks the ideas are of equal value.

My neighbors are considerate. They never play loud music.

Combined as a compound sentence, suggesting that the ideas are of equal value, the new sentence looks like this:

<u>My neighbors are considerate</u>, and <u>they never play loud music</u>.
       independent clause   independent clause
         (main idea)   (main idea)

Here are the same two ideas combined as a complex sentence, suggesting that the ideas are of unequal value:

<u>Because my neighbors are considerate</u>, <u>they never play loud music</u>.
      dependent clause   independent clause
     (less important idea)   (main idea)

Although both the compound and complex forms are correct, the complex form conveys the ideas more precisely because one idea does seem to be more important—one idea depends on the other.

Thus if you have two sentences with closely related ideas and one is clearly more important than the other, consider combining them in a complex sentence. Compare these two paragraphs:

- Version 1 contains six simple sentences, implying that the ideas are of equal value:

    (1) I was very upset. (2) The Fourth of July fireworks were especially loud. (3) My dog ran away. (4) The animal control officer made his morning rounds. (5) He found my dog in another part of town. (6) I was relieved.

- Version 2 consists of two simple sentences and two complex sentences, showing that some ideas are more important than others:

    (1) I was very upset. (2) Because the Fourth of July fireworks were especially loud, my dog ran away. (3) When the animal control officer made his morning rounds, he found my dog in another part of town. (4) I was relieved.

You will probably consider Version 2 superior to Version 1. Sentences 2 and 3 are closely related, but 3 is more important. Sentences 4 and 5 are closely related, but 5 is more important. In Version 2, the revision made each pair into a complex sentence.

Although you could combine sentences 1 and 2, the result would be illogical because the wrong idea would be conveyed:

Illogical Combination: I was very upset because the Fourth of July fireworks were especially loud.

The person was very upset because the dog ran away, not because the fireworks were especially loud.

Subordinating Conjunctions

As you learned in Chapter 3, a complex sentence is composed of one independent clause and one or more dependent clauses. In combining two independent clauses to write a complex sentence, your first step is to decide on a word that will best show the relationship between the clauses. Words that show the relationship of a dependent clause to an independent one are called **subordinating conjunctions.** The italicized words in the following sentences are subordinating conjunctions. Consider the meaning as well as the placement of each one.

Because the storm hit, the game was canceled.

After the storm passed, the dogs began to bark.

When Colette told her joke, the class was moved to fits of hysterics.

Vernon did not volunteer to work on the holiday, *although* the pay was good.

No one has visited Patty *since* she moved into town.

They decided to wait *until* the cows came home.

They refused to work *unless* they were allowed to wear chef's hats.

Before the session ended, all the "hep cats" blew some sweet sounds.

Other subordinating conjunctions include the following:

as	*provided that*	*whereas*
as if	*rather than*	*wherever*
even if	*so that*	*whether*
even though	*than*	*while*
if	*whenever*	
in order that	*where*	

Punctuation with Subordinating Conjunctions

If the dependent clause comes *before* the main clause, set it off with a comma.

Before Mike wrote his final draft, he looked over his outline.

If the dependent clause comes *after* or *within* the main clause, set it off only if the clause is not necessary to the meaning of the main clause or if the dependent clause begins with the word *although, though,* or *even though.*

We went home *after* the concert had ended.

Vincent continued painting, *although* he had repainted the cabinet twice.

Punctuation with Relative Pronouns

As you learned in Chapter 3, a relative clause begins with a relative pronoun, a pronoun such as *that, which,* or *who.*

The decision <u>that I made</u> is final.
relative clause

A student <u>who uses a computer</u> can save time in revising.
relative clause

Set off the dependent (relative) clause with commas when it is not necessary to the sentence. Do not set off the clause if it is necessary for the meaning of the sentence.

Everyone *who tries* will pass this class. [The dependent clause is necessary because one would not say, "Everyone will pass this class."]

Juan, *who tries,* will pass this class. [The dependent clause is not necessary because one can say, "Juan will pass this class."]

The relative pronoun *which* usually refers to things. The word *which* almost always indicates that a clause is not necessary for the meaning of the sentence. Therefore, a clause beginning with *which* is almost always set off by commas.

> My car, *which* is ten years old, has a flat tire.

The relative pronoun *that* also usually refers to things. However, the word *that* almost always indicates that the clause *is* necessary for the meaning of the sentence. Therefore, a clause beginning with *that* usually is *not* set off by commas.

> The car *that* has a flat tire is ten years old.

The relative pronouns *who* and *whom*, as well as *whoever* and *whomever*, usually refer to people. Clauses that begin with those relative pronouns are not set off by commas if they are necessary for the meaning of the sentence; if they are not necessary, they are set off.

> A person *who* has a way with words is often quoted. [necessary for the meaning of the sentence]

> Uncle Colby, *whom* I quote often, has a way with words. [not necessary for the meaning of the sentence]

EXERCISE 5

Combining Sentences: Complex

Combine the following pairs of sentences into one complex sentence. Insert an appropriate subordinating conjunction or relative pronoun, add or fix punctuation, and make other minor changes as needed. Sentences that should be combined by using a relative pronoun are indicated. (See Answer Key for answers.)

1. (relative pronoun) The freeway congestion was under study. The problem occurred every Friday at noon.

2. The vacationers had a good time. The bears destroyed a few tents and ate people's food.

3. The teenagers loved their senior prom. The band played badly.

4. Farmers gathered for miles around. Jeff had grown a fifty-pound cucumber.

5. Back-seat drivers make unwanted suggestions in the nag-proof model. They can be ejected from the vehicle.

6. (relative pronoun) The marriage counselor gave bad advice. He charged only half price.

7. (relative pronoun) The robots would not do their work. They needed fresh batteries.

8. The hurricane was expected to hit during the night. The residents checked their flashlights.

9. The ice sculptor displayed his work in the dining hall. The customers applauded.

10. Someone stole the artwork of ice. No evidence was found.

EXERCISE 6

Combining Sentences: Complex

Combine the following pairs of sentences into one complex sentence. Insert an appropriate subordinating conjunction or relative pronoun, add or fix punctuation, and make other minor changes as needed. Sentences that should be combined by using a relative pronoun are indicated.

1. (relative pronoun) Mary Hayes was one of the first female soldiers in American warfare. She is better known as Molly Pitcher.

2. (relative pronoun) At the outbreak of the War of Independence, Mary was the wife of John Hayes. He soon joined the army.

3. Following established practice, Mary Hayes also went to war. She was the wife of a soldier.

4. He performed military duties. She washed and mended clothes and cooked meals.

5. John Hayes's regiment fought at the Battle of Monmouth. The day was hot.

6. Mary Hayes brought the soldiers water in pitchers. Some men started calling her Molly Pitcher, "Molly" for "Mary" and "Pitcher" for what she carried.

7. She was immediately proud of the name. Others started using it.

8. John Hayes suffered a heat stroke. Mary Hayes took over his job, firing his cannon.

9. A cannonball sailed between her knees and tore her dress. She refused to stop fighting.

10. Following the war, Mary Hayes received a pension for soldiers. She was truly a patriotic veteran.

Coordination and Subordination: The Compound-Complex Sentence

At times you may want to show the relationship of three or more ideas within one sentence. If that relationship involves two or more main ideas and one or more supporting ideas, the combination can be stated in a **compound-complex sentence** (two or more independent clauses and one or more dependent clauses).

<u>Before Kafka learned how to operate a word processor,</u>
dependent clause

<u>he had trouble with his typewritten assignments,</u>
independent clause

but now <u>he produces clean, attractive pages.</u>
independent clause

In our previous discussion of the complex sentence, we presented this group of six sentences:

I was very upset. The Fourth of July fireworks were especially loud. My dog ran away. The animal control officer made his morning rounds. He found my dog in another part of town. I was relieved.

We then converted the group of six sentences to four.

I was very upset. Because the Fourth of July fireworks were especially loud, my dog ran away. When the animal control officer made his morning rounds, he found my dog in another part of town. I was relieved.

But what if we wanted to show an even closer relationship of ideas? One solution would be to combine the two complex sentences in this way (the italicized sentence is compound-complex):

I was very upset. *Because the Fourth of July fireworks were especially loud, my dog ran away; but when the animal control officer made his morning rounds, he found my dog in another part of town.* I was relieved.

Punctuation of Complicated Compound or Compound-Complex Sentences

If a compound or compound-complex sentence has one or more commas in the first clause, you may want to use a semicolon before the coordinating conjunction between the two clauses. Its purpose is to show the reader very clearly the division between the two independent clauses. The preceding example illustrates this use of the semicolon.

EXERCISE 7

Combining Sentences: Compound-Complex

Combine each group of sentences into one compound-complex sentence. Use the rules of sentence combining and punctuation discussed in this chapter. (See Answer Key for answers.)

1. A grumpy bear had stalked the grounds. Summer camp had been a great experience for the campers. They vowed to return.

2. The stuffed cabbage ran out. The party ended. The guests went home.

3. It was a costume party. All the guests dressed as movie legends. Ten were Elvis impersonators.

4. A new Elvis theme park opened in our town. I attended. I think I saw the King.

5. My father encouraged me to take up a hobby. I began collecting stamps. Now my hobby has become a business.

6. They were in a wilderness camp. They were not allowed to bring pets. They were allowed to bring toys.

7. He had no leather shoes to wear. Young Stu could not go to the prom. He hoped there would be a prom next year.

8. People were hungry. They ate massive quantities of hot dogs at the game. They knew the dogs were made of mystery meat.

9. The ambulance drivers were taking a break. A man had a choking fit. The drivers came to his rescue.

10. The film was filled with scenes of violence. It included a charming love story. The public liked it.

Combining Sentences: Compound-Complex

Combine each group of sentences into one compound-complex sentence. Use the rules of sentence combining and punctuation discussed in this chapter.

1. Helen Keller suffered a serious childhood illness. She became blind and deaf. At first her parents did not know what to do.

2. Her parents would not give up despite discouraging advice. They advertised for a teacher. A tutor named Anne Sullivan agreed to help.

3. Young Helen began to discover the world through her sense of touch. She learned the alphabet. She started connecting words with objects.

4. Her physical condition was irreversible. Her progress was rapid. In three years she could read Braille.

5. She could not talk. She used sign language for speech. She used a special typewriter to write.

6. She reached the age of ten. She took speech lessons from a teacher of the deaf. In six years she could speak well enough to be understood.

7. She attended college. She still needed help. Anne Sullivan continued as her tutor and interpreter.

8. She graduated from college with honors. She became involved in programs to help the deaf and blind communicate. She wrote books and articles about problems of the disabled.

9. The effects of World War II presented special problems. Helen Keller helped disabled people in other countries. She helped soldiers blinded in the war.

10. Helen Keller died in 1968. She had an international reputation as a humanitarian. Her books had been translated into more than fifty languages.

Other Ways to Combine Ideas

In this chapter you have learned how to combine simple sentences into compound, complex, and compound-complex sentences that show the coordination and subordination of ideas. There are other methods of combining ideas, too. Here are four you may want to use in your own writing.

1. Use an appositive, which is a noun or noun phrase that immediately follows a noun or pronoun and renames it.

   > Kyoko is the leading scorer on the team. Kyoko is a quick and strong player.

   > Kyoko, *a quick and strong player,* is the leading scorer on the team.

2. Use a prepositional phrase, a preposition followed by a noun or pronoun object.

   > Dolly Parton wrote a song about a coat. The coat had many colors.

   > Dolly Parton wrote a song about a coat *of many colors.*

3. Drop the subject in the sentence that follows and combine the sentences.

   > Some items are too damaged for recycling. They must be discarded.

   > Some items are too damaged for recycling *and* must be discarded.

4. Use a participial phrase, a group of words that includes a participle, which is a verbal that usually ends in -*ing* or -*ed*.

   > Jamal rowed smoothly. He reached the shore.

   > *Rowing smoothly,* Jamal reached the shore.

| EXERCISE 9 | **Combining Sentences** |

Combine each group of sentences into a single sentence in the ways indicated. (See Answer Key for answers to the odd-numbered sentence sets.)

Use an appositive.

1. Ernest Hemingway won the Nobel Prize for literature in 1954. He was mainly an American writer of fiction.

2. Ernest spent his childhood summers in Michigan. He was the second of six children of Clarence and Grace Hemingway.

Use a prepositional phrase.

3. After high school he became a reporter. He worked for the Kansas City *Star*.

4. During World War I he volunteered to serve as a Red Cross ambulance driver. The Red Cross unit was stationed in Italy.

Drop the subject of the second sentence.

5. In 1920 he returned to journalism with the Toronto *Star*. He met his future first wife, Hadley Richardson.

6. Hemingway and his wife moved to France. They lived in a walk-up flat in the Latin Quarter of Paris.

Use a participial phrase.

7. Hemingway worked conscientiously on his writing. He soon became a leader of the so-called Lost Generation.

8. He always sought adventure. He hunted, fished, loved, drank, fought, and wrote his way through the next three decades.

Use any of the above ways.

9. During World War II Hemingway armed his fishing boat and hunted for German submarines. He patrolled the waters of the Caribbean.

10. He died as a life-weary, broken man in 1961 at his home in Ketchum, Idaho. He was suffering from both physical and psychological problems.

Omissions: When Parts Are Missing

Do not omit words that are needed to make your sentences clear and logical. Of the many types of undesirable construction in which necessary words are omitted, the following are the most common.

1. **Subjects.** Do not omit a necessary subject in a sentence with two verbs.

    Illogical: The cost of the car was $12,000 but would easily last me through college. (subject of *last*)

    Logical: The cost of the car was $12,000, but the car would easily last me through college.

2. **Verbs.** Do not omit verbs that are needed because of a change in the number of the subject or a change of tense.

    Illogical: The bushes were trimmed and the grass mowed.

    Logical: The bushes were trimmed and the grass was mowed.

    Illogical: True honesty always has and always will be admired by most people. (tense)

    Logical: True honesty always has been and always will be admired by most people.

3. *That* **as a conjunction.** The conjunction *that* should not be omitted from a dependent clause if there is danger of misreading the sentence.

    Misleading: We believed Eric, if not stopped, would hurt himself.

    Clear: We believed that Eric, if not stopped, would hurt himself.

4. **Prepositions.** Do not omit prepositions in idiomatic phrases, in expressions of time, and in parallel phrases.

    Illogical: Weekends the campus is deserted. (time)

    Logical: During weekends the campus is deserted.

    Illogical: I have neither love nor patience with untrained dogs. (parallel phrases)

    Logical: I have neither love for nor patience with untrained dogs.

    Illogical: Glenda's illness was something we heard only after her recovery.

    Logical: Glenda's illness was something we heard about only after her recovery.

| EXERCISE 10 | Omissions |

Identify the kinds of omissions by writing one of the following words in the blanks to the right: preposition, verb, subject, that. Insert the necessary words in the sentences.

1. Charles had neither love nor patience with small pets.   _____

2. Because he was careless, a branch caught on the trigger of his gun, and went off.   _____

3. In the newspaper, the radio, and TV, the story was the same.   _____

4. We saw the car, if not stopped, would hit the tree.   _____

5. Since Jim had not worked that summer, money was scarce in the fall and expenses burdensome.   _____

6. Harry's ignorance was one of the things that we learned on the trip.   _____

7. We believed the lie, if not revealed, would harm people.   _____

8. The truck was creeping up the hill, and had no thought at all of the traffic behind.   _____

9. I do not believe and never have that a person's life is not his or her own responsibility.   _____

10. When Joe got his second wind, his breathing slowed, and was able to go on running without fatigue.   _____

Variety in Sentences: Types, Order, Length, Beginnings

Sentences can be written in a variety of ways to achieve freshness and clarity. Much of this polishing takes place during revision. Here are a few techniques for the main variations.

Types

You have learned that all four types of sentences are sound. Your task as a writer is to decide which one to use for a particular thought. That decision may not be made until you revise your composition. Then you can choose on the basis of the relationship of ideas:

Simple: a single idea
Compound: two closely related ideas
Complex: one idea more important than the other
Compound-complex: a combination of the two parts

These types were all covered in the previous chapter. This chapter provides further practice, as you combine sentences.

Order

You will choose the order of parts and information according to what you want to emphasize. Typically the most emphatic location is at the end of any unit.

Length

Uncluttered and direct, short sentences commonly draw attention. But that focus occurs only when they stand out from longer sentences. Therefore, you would usually avoid a series of short sentences.

Beginnings

A long series of sentences with each beginning containing a subject followed by a verb may become monotonous. Consider beginning sentences in different ways:

With a prepositional phrase: *In the distance* a dog barked.

**With a transitional connective (conjunctive adverb) such as *then, however,* or *therefore:* Then the game was over.

**With a coordinating conjunction such as *and* or *but:* But* no one moved for three minutes.

With a dependent clause: *Although he wanted a new Corvette*, he settled for a used Ford Taurus.

With an adverb: *Carefully* he removed the thorn from the lion's paw.

EXERCISE 11

Providing Sentence Variety

Revise the following passage to achieve better sentence variety through changes in types of sentences, order of information, length of sentences, and beginnings of sentences. Also, combine sentences for improved expression. Compare your revisions with those of others in your class. There is no single correct way of making these changes.

Power Rangers to the Rescue

Leewan Yeomans

I do promotions on the weekends for TV's "Power Rangers." I'm Trini. She's supposed to be Chinese. I'm Chinese-American, the kids think I'm the real Ranger when I take off my mask. I've never felt very much like a Ranger except for one occasion. It was a weekend promotion, held at a park. We were doing our routine. I looked around and saw a little boy collapse. I guess he had been in distress for a while. Wearing the mask, I could hardly see anything. Anyway, this little boy was lying there, thrashing around and trying to throw up. No one was doing anything. The

Pink Ranger started running around trying to find the child's parents. No one answered. I ran over when no one touched the boy, took off my mask, and put my finger in his mouth to clear his throat. There I found the problem. He had been chewing on, or maybe blowing, a long balloon He had swallowed it. I pulled it out of his throat. It was almost a foot long. The whole spectacle must have looked like a magic trick. The child still wasn't breathing well. The paramedics were called. They quickly helped him back to good health. His parents, who lived across the street, came to carry him home. We Rangers put our masks back on. The audience cheered us as if we had planned the whole scene. We resumed our routine. It was just another day of work for the Power Rangers.

CHAPTER REVIEW COMBINING SENTENCES

Coordination

If you want to communicate two equally important and closely related ideas, place them close together, probably in a **compound sentence** (two or more independent clauses).

1. When you combine two sentences by using a coordinating conjunction (FANBOYS), drop the first period, change the capital letter of the second sentence to a small letter, and insert a comma before the coordinating conjunction.

   I like your home. I can visit for only three months.

   I like your home, *but* I can visit for only three months.

2. When you combine two sentences by using a semicolon, replace the first period with a semicolon and change the capital letter that begins the second sentence to a small letter. If you wish to use a conjunctive adverb, insert it after the semicolon and usually follow it with a comma.

   I like your home. I can visit for only three months.

   I like your home; I can visit for only three months.

   I like your home; *however,* I can visit for only three months.

Subordination

If you have two ideas that are closely related, but one is secondary or dependent on the other, you may want to use a **complex sentence**.

   My neighbors are considerate. They never play loud music.

   Because my neighbors are considerate, they never play loud music.

1. If the dependent clause comes first, set it off with a comma.

   Because my dog has no hands or words, he licks me to show affection.

2. If the dependent clause comes after the main clause, set it off with a comma only if you use some form of the word *though* or if the words are not necessary to convey the basic meaning in the sentence.

   Edmund Hillary was knighted by Queen Elizabeth II because he was one of the first two men to climb Mt. Everest.

   Other mountain climbers soon duplicated his feat, *though* they received less recognition.

3. One type of dependent clause is called a **relative clause.** A relative clause begins with a relative pronoun, a pronoun such as *that, which,* or *who.* Relative pronouns *relate* the clause to another word in the sentence.

   Orlando purchased a used computer. It had hardly been touched.

   Orlando purchased a used computer *that* had hardly been touched.

4. A relative clause should be set off with commas when it is not necessary to the sentence. Do not set the clause off if it is necessary for the meaning of the sentence.

   Necessary: No one who fails the eye test will get a driver's license.

   Unnecessary: Mr. McGoo, who failed his eye test, did not get a driver's license.

Coordination and Subordination

At times you may want to show the relationship of three or more ideas within one sentence. If that relationship involves two or more main ideas and one or more supporting ideas, the combination can be stated in a **compound-complex sentence** (two or more independent clauses and one or more dependent clauses).

   Kafka produced illegible handwritten papers. At that time he had not learned how to operate a word processor. Now he hands in clean, attractive pages.

   Before Kafka learned how to operate a word processor, he produced illegible handwritten papers, but now he hands in clean, attractive pages.

Use punctuation consistent with that of the compound and complex sentences.

Other Ways to Combine Ideas

1. Use an **appositive phrase,** a group of words that immediately follows a noun or pronoun and renames it.

   Garth Brooks claims Yukon, Oklahoma, as his hometown. He is a famous singer.

   Garth Brooks, a famous singer, claims Yukon, Oklahoma, as his hometown.

2. Use a **prepositional phrase,** a preposition followed by a noun or pronoun object.

   John Elway led the Denver Broncos to two Super Bowl victories. Both triumphs occurred in the 1990s.

John Elway led the Denver Broncos to two Super Bowl victories *in the 1990s.*

3. Drop the subject in the sentence that follows and combine the sentences.

Emily Dickinson's poetry went mostly unpublished during her lifetime. It was finally discovered and celebrated more than a half century later.

Emily Dickinson's poetry went mostly unpublished during her lifetime *but was finally discovered and celebrated more than a half century later.*

4. Use a **participial phrase,** a group of words that includes a participle, which is a verbal that usually ends in *-ing* or *-ed.*

The turtle plodded without rest stops. It won the race against the rabbit.

Plodding without rest stops, the turtle won the race against the rabbit.

CHAPTER REVIEW EXERCISES

REVIEW 1   ## Combining Sentences

Combine two or more sentences from each group by using any pattern. (See Answer Key for possible answers.)

1. The Mercury Comet was judged the winner. It had imitation zebra-skin seat covers. It had an eight-ball shift knob.

2. Koko had a great plan to make some money. She had financial problems. She could not develop her plan.

3. The mixture could not be discussed openly. Competitors were curious. Corporate spies were everywhere.

4. Babette's bowling ball is special. It is red and green. It is decorated with her phone number in metal-flake.

5. The young bagpiper liked Scottish food. He enjoyed doing Scottish dances. Wearing a kilt in winter left him cold.

6. Ruby missed the alligator farm. She fondly remembered the hissing and snapping of the beasts as they scrambled for raw meat. Her neighbors were indifferent to the loss.

7. Many people are pleased to purchase items with food preservatives. Others are fearful. They think these chemicals may also preserve consumers.

8. Leewan loves her new in-line roller skates. They look and perform much like ice skates. They are not as safe as her conventional roller skates.

9. Fish sold at Discount Fish Market were not of the highest quality. Some of them had been dead for days without refrigeration. They were suitable only for bait.

10. Cliff wanted to impress his date. He splashed on six ounces of He-Man cologne. He put on his motorcycle leathers and a flying scarf.

REVIEW 2

Combining Sentences

Use appropriate methods to combine sentences as needed. Add and delete words sparingly.

Muhammad Ali was arguably the greatest heavyweight boxing champion. He won the title on four occasions. He loved to perform for the press. He made up sayings and poems about himself and his opponents. He said he would "float like a butterfly and sting like a bee." Ali announced that he would win each fight. He even named the round. He became a Black Muslim. He refused induction into the armed services. He was convicted of a crime for having done so. As a result he lost his championship. Later the decision was reversed by the U.S. Supreme Court. He won back the championship by defeating George Foreman in 1974. In 1978 he lost it to Leon Spinks. He won it back one more time the next year. He retired in 1980. Then fought once more for the title. He quit for good.

REVIEW 3

Combining Sentences

Use appropriate methods to combine sentences as needed. Add and delete words sparingly.

Reba McEntire: No Secrets to Her Success

Good singers can be found anywhere, even in a local lounge or pizza parlor. Great singers are rare. They have the "something special" qualities. The qualities just seem to work together. Country singer Reba McEntire is definitely one of the greats. The reasons are obvious: voice, songs, and style. Her voice is like no other. Her Oklahoma "twangy" accent is known by everyone in country music. She is able to jump from note to note. She can cover two octaves with ease. Her voice is rich and sensitive, yet powerful. Reba sings. She takes up all the oxygen in the room. The songs she sings are another reason for her greatness. Her lyrics deal with the issues. Those issues really touch the heart. They inspire the mind. They make even the men cry. Her song "Is There Life Out There?" encourages women and men everywhere to follow their dreams, no matter what those dreams may be. That song came out. Reba got thousands of letters from people. The people thanked her for writing such a positive song during difficult times. The final reason for her greatness is her style. It is all its own, from her spunky attitude right down to her steel-toed boots. This fiery redhead really knows how to get the crowd going. She has been performing for about thirty years. She has produced more than twenty albums. With all those qualities, Reba McEntire will be around for a long, long time.

MICROTHEME

To practice your skills acquired in this chapter, return to the Microtheme on page 63 and complete Exercise B.

Correcting Fragments, Comma Splices, and Run-Ons

*Using principles you now understand, this
chapter will protect you against the most
dreaded diseases in student writing: the
scarlet frag's, CS's, and RO's.*

FLOW OF WRITING

Learning Objectives

Working with this chapter, I will learn to

~ identify and correct fragments.
~ identify comma splices and run-ons.
~ use four methods for correcting
   comma splices and run-ons.

MICROTHEME

EXERCISE A

Writing Activity in Miniature
Two Purposes

Writing Diagnostic: Before you work on this chapter, the Microtheme will give you an opportunity to write briefly on an engaging topic without pressure.

Chapter Learning Application: After you have studied this chapter, return to your Microtheme to check your work and practice what you have just learned.

Form and Procedure

Like an executive summary (written for a busy boss), the Microtheme conveys ideas concisely (using no more than the space on a 5- by 8-inch card) in a specified form. Indent only once, and write small enough to leave room for marking later. Directions for practicing your chapter writing skills appear in Exercise B.

Suggested Microtheme Topic

Write a Microtheme of 80 to 100 words about a problem on campus, such as registration, class schedules, counseling, student activities, or parking. Use at least one specific example of the problem and suggest a solution.

EXERCISE B

Connecting Your Learning Objectives with Your Microtheme

Complete this exercise after you have studied this chapter.

1. Check to make sure that you have used no fragments. If you have, correct them. If in doubt, underline subjects and verbs.

2. Check to make sure that you have used no comma splices. If you have, correct them. If in doubt, try placing a period in the questionable spot and see if you have two sentences.

FLOW OF WRITING

In Chapter 2, you learned about subjects and verbs. In Chapters 3 and 4, you identified and wrote different kinds of sentences. With the information you now have, you will be able to spot and correct three problems in sentence structure that sometimes creep into and insidiously destroy what is otherwise good writing. Those problems are sentence fragments, comma splices, and run-on sentences.

Fragments

A correct sentence signals completeness. The structure and punctuation provide those signals. For example, if I say to you, "She left in a hurry," you do not necessarily expect me to say anything else, but if I say, "In a hurry," you do. If I say, "Tomorrow I will give you a quiz on the reading assignment," and I leave the room, you will merely take note of my words. But if I say, "Tomorrow when I give you a quiz on the reading assignment," and I leave the room, you will probably be annoyed, and you may even chase after me and ask me to finish my sentence. Those examples illustrate the difference between completeness and incompleteness.

A **fragment** is a word or group of words without a subject ("Is going to town.") or without a verb ("He going to town.") or without both ("Going to town."). A fragment can also be a group of words with a subject and verb that cannot stand alone ("When he goes to town."). Although the punctuation signals a sentence (a capital letter at the beginning and a period at the end), the structure of a fragment signals incompleteness. If you said it or wrote it to someone, that person would expect you to go on and finish the idea.

Other specific examples of common unacceptable fragments are these:

- *Dependent clause only:* When she came.
- *Phrase(s) only:* Waiting there for some help.
- *No subject in main clause:* Went to the library.
- *No verb in main clause:* She being the only person there.

Acceptable Fragments

Sometimes, fragments are used intentionally. When we speak, we often use the following fragments:

- *Interjections:* Great! Hooray! Whoa!
- *Exclamations:* What a day! How terrible! What a bother!
- *Greetings:* Hello. Good morning. Good night. Good evening.
- *Questions:* What for? Why not? Where to?
- *Informal conversation:* (What time is it?) Eight o'clock. Really.

In novels, plays, and short stories, fragments are often used in conversation among characters. However, unless you are writing fiction, you need to be able to identify fragments in your college assignments and turn those fragments into complete sentences.

Dependent Clauses as Fragments:
Clauses with Subordinating Conjunctions

In Chapter 4, you learned that words such as *because, after, although, since,* and *before* (see page 71 for a more complete list) are subordinating conjunctions, words that show the relationship of a dependent clause to an independent one. A dependent clause punctuated like a sentence (capital letter at the beginning; period at the end) is a sentence fragment.

>*While the ship was sinking.*

You can choose one of many ways to fix that kind of fragment.

Incorrect: They continued to dance. *While the ship was sinking.*

Correct: They continued to dance *while the ship was sinking.*

Correct: *While the ship was sinking,* they continued to dance.

Correct: The ship was sinking. They continued to dance.

Correct: The ship was sinking; they continued to dance.

In the first two correct sentences above, the dependent clause *while the ship was sinking* has been attached to an independent clause. Note that a comma is used when the dependent clause appears at the beginning of the sentence. In the next two sentences, the subordinating conjunction *while* has been omitted. The two independent clauses can then stand alone as sentences or as parts of a sentence, joined by a semicolon.

Dependent Clauses as Fragments: Clauses with Relative Pronouns

You learned in Chapter 3 that words such as *that, which,* and *who* can function as relative pronouns, words that relate a clause back to a noun or pronoun in the sentence. Relative clauses are dependent. If they are punctuated as sentences (begin with a capital letter; end with a period), they are incorrect. They are really sentence fragments.

>*Which is lying on the floor.*

The best way to fix such a fragment is to attach it as closely as possible to the noun to which it refers.

Incorrect: That new red sweater is mine. *Which is lying on the floor.*

Correct: The new red sweater, *which is lying on the floor,* is mine.

Reminder: Some relative clauses are restrictive (necessary to the meaning of the sentence) and should not be set off with commas. Some are nonrestrictive (not necessary to the meaning of the sentence), as in the example above, and are set off by commas.

EXERCISE 1   ## Correcting Fragments

Underline and correct each fragment. Some items may be correct as is. (See Answer Key for answers.)

1. When Leroy Robert Paige was seven years old. He was carrying luggage at a railroad station in Mobile, Alabama.

2. He was a clever young fellow. Who invented a contraption for carrying four satchels (small suitcases) at one time.

3. After he did that. He was always known as Satchel Paige.

4. His fame rests on his being arguably the best baseball pitcher. Who ever played the game.

5. Because of the so-called Jim Crow laws. He, as an African American, was not allowed to play in the Major Leagues. Until 1948 after the Major League color barrier was broken.

6. By that time he was already forty-two. Although he was in excellent condition.

7. He had pitched. Wherever he could, mainly touring around the country.

8. When he faced Major Leaguers in exhibition games. He almost always won.

9. Because people liked to see him pitch. He pitched almost every day. While he was on tour.

10. One year he won 104 games. During his career he pitched 55 no-hitters and won more than 2,000 games.

11. He pitched his last game in the majors at the age of fifty-nine.

12. In 1971 he was the first African-American player. Who was voted into the Baseball Hall of Fame in a special category for those. Who played in the old Negro Leagues.

EXERCISE 2

Correcting Fragments

Underline and correct each fragment.

1. When the Beatles began releasing hit records in the early 1960s. No one realized how profound an influence they would have on rock music and world culture.

2. Paul McCartney, John Lennon, George Harrison, and Ringo Starr formed a band. That would finally make rock music into an accepted art form.

3. Experimenting with new techniques, instruments, and musical effects. The group made highly innovative music.

4. For example, incorporating the sitar into songs like "Norwegian Wood" and creating the swirling, swishing sound now known as "flanging."

5. Because their songs are so interesting. Radio stations keep playing them for new generations of fans.

6. The Beatles have also inspired and influenced other musical artists. For over four decades.

7. In addition, the band's films anticipated the music video. Which is the essential promotional tool of today's musicians.

8. Their influence extended beyond their music. To hair and fashion, for example.

9. After "Beatlemania" hit the United States in 1964. Long hair became standard for rock-and-roll stars by the 1970s.

10. Besides Eastern instruments like the sitar. The Beatles introduced elements of Eastern philosophy, too, into Western culture.

Phrases as Fragments

Although a phrase may carry an idea, a phrase is a fragment because it is incomplete in structure. It lacks both a subject and a verb. See Chapter 2 for verbal phrases and prepositional phrases, and see Chapter 4 for appositive phrases.

Verbal Phrase

Incorrect: *Having studied hard all evening.* John decided to retire.

Correct: *Having studied hard all evening,* John decided to retire.

The italicized part of the incorrect example is a **verbal phrase.** As you learned in Chapter 2, a verbal is verblike without being a verb in sentence structure. Verbals include verb parts of speech ending in *-ed* and *-ing*. To correct a verbal phrase fragment, attach it to a complete sentence (independent clause). When the phrase begins the sentence, it is usually set off by a comma.

Prepositional Phrase

Incorrect: *For the past ten hours.* I have been designing my home page.

Correct: *For the past ten hours,* I have been designing my home page.

In this example, the fragment is a **prepositional phrase**—a group of words beginning with a preposition, such as *in, on, of, at,* and *with,* that connects a noun or pronoun object to the rest of the sentence. To correct a prepositional phrase fragment, attach it to a complete sentence (independent clause). If the prepositional phrase is long and begins the sentence, it is usually set off by a comma.

Appositive Phrase

Incorrect: He lived in the small town of Whitman. *A busy industrial center near Boston.*

Correct: He lived in the small town of Whitman, *a busy industrial center near Boston.*

Incorrect: Many readers admire the work of the nineteenth-century American poet. *Emily Dickinson.*

Correct: Many readers admire the work of the nineteenth-century American poet *Emily Dickinson.*

In these examples, the fragment is an **appositive phrase**—a group of words following a noun or pronoun and renaming it. To correct an appositive phrase fragment, connect it to a complete sentence (an independent clause). An appositive phrase fragment is set off by a comma or by commas only if it is not essential to the meaning of the sentence.

EXERCISE 3 | **Correcting Fragments**

Underline and correct each fragment. (See Answer Key for answers.)

1. As a subject of historical record. Dancing seems to be a natural human act.

2. Even prehistoric cave paintings depict dancing figures. Scrawled outlines of people in motion.

3. Dancing takes many forms, but mainly it is a matter of moving rhythmically. In time to music.

4. Most children jump up and down when they are excited. They sway back and forth when they are contented.

5. Having studied the behavior of many ethnic groups. Anthropologists confirm that dancing reveals much. About a group's culture.

6. People dance for various reasons. Such as to entertain others, to relax, to inspire others, and to celebrate life.

7. One stylized form of dancing is the ballet. A story told with graceful, rhythmic movement and music.

8. Folk dances relate stories. Of the dancers' culture.

9. Young people can get to know each other at social dances. While enjoying themselves.

10. Each generation of social dancers seems to have its own style. Sometimes a modified revival, such as swing.

EXERCISE 4   ## Correcting Fragments

Underline and correct each fragment.

1. Reflecting religious concerns. Ceremonial dances are still conducted in some cultures to promote good crops or successful warfare.

2. In the 1800s, an American Christian group called the Shakers performed a whirling, shaking dance. A ceremony to shake out the devil.

3. In the 1900s. Whirling Dervishes and Ghost Dancers believed that their dancing protected them in battle.

4. In Australia and North America. Aborigines had dances that imitated the movement of animals to be hunted.

5. Some of those dances are still performed. With few significant changes of style.

6. In Africa and the South Pacific. Groups have dances that signify the achievement of maturity.

7. In the United States and in many other countries. Young people gain popularity. By learning and demonstrating popular dance steps and movements.

8. It is hard to imagine human beings without dance. An activity transcending all time and cultures.

9. With the birth of rock 'n' roll music. Dancing styles became freer.

10. During the past hundred years. Dozens of dances, such as the lindy, twist, hustle, Charleston, big apple, frug, and mashed potato, have had their times of popularity.

Correcting Fragments

Correct the following phrase fragments by adding subjects and verbs and, perhaps, by changing or adding words. The story line is simple. Driving his Ford truck, Harry took Jane to the opening-day baseball game at Dodger Stadium. They arrived with high hopes, settled into their seats, had expectations, saw the game begin, and spotted some rain clouds. The questions in the boxes will help you follow the plot. (See Answer Key for possible answers.)

Example: A special date with Jane.

> Who had a special date with Jane?

Harry had a special date with Jane.

1. A Ford Ranger truck with fine Corinthian leather seats.

> What did he polish?

_____

_____

2. To pick up Jane for their date.

> What did he do then?

_____

_____

3. To go to the opening-day baseball game at Dodger Stadium.

> Where did Jane want to go on the date?

_____

_____

4. A never-to-be-forgotten experience.

> What satisfaction did she hope for?

_____

_____

5. Being seen on big-screen Diamond Vision in the stadium.

> What special experience did Jane dream of?

_____

_____

6. With the first sound of the bat on ball.

> When did they arrive?

_____

_____

7. Buying peanuts and Crackerjacks.

> Who bought peanuts and Crackerjacks and for whom?

_____

_____

8. A baseball glove to catch a well-hit ball.

> What did Jane bring so that she might catch a well-hit ball?

_____

_____

9. To hear and see heroes up close.

> What portable electronic device did Jane bring so she could follow the action on the field?

_____

_____

10. Seeing the rain clouds.

> Noticing the change in weather, what did they fear?

_____

_____

EXERCISE 6

Correcting Fragments

Correct the following phrase fragments by adding subjects and verbs and, perhaps, by changing or adding words. Continuing from Exercise 5 is the story of Harry and Jane at a baseball game where they got caught in a rainstorm. They ran for cover, contemplated leaving, waited, saw the game continue, watched the players slide in the mud, celebrated the Dodgers' victory, headed for the parking lot, and finally found Harry's truck. The questions in the boxes will help you follow the plot.

Example: In the last of the fourth inning.

> What began to fall from the clouds?

In the last of the fourth inning, *rain began to fall.*

1. Running for shelter.

> What happened to them as they ran through the rain?

_____

_____

2. Shivering and waiting for sunshine.

> Where did they wish they were?

_____

_____

3. To delay the game.

> What did the umpires decide to do?

_____

_____

4. To leave or not to leave.

> What question did Harry and Jane consider?

_____

_____

5. In less than an hour.

> What happened to the rain?

_____

_____

6. With the players back on the field.

> Following the change of weather, what happened to the game?

_____

_____

7. Sliding into bases on the wet field.

> What became easy for the players?

_____

_____

8. Winning the game at the end of the eleventh inning.

> How did the Dodgers delight their fans?

_____

_____

9. Finding Harry's truck in the parking lot.

> What problem did Harry and Jane have in finding Harry's truck?

_____

_____

10. By the light of the moon.

> How did they find Harry's truck?

_____

_____

Fragments as Word Groups Without Subjects or Without Verbs

Incorrect: Ayana studied many long hours. And received the highest grade in the class. [without subject]

Correct: Ayana studied many long hours and received the highest grade in the class.

Incorrect: Few children living in that section of the country. [without verb]

Correct: Few children live in that section of the country.

Each sentence must have an independent clause, a group of words that contains a subject and a verb and that can stand alone. As you may recall from the discussion of subjects in Chapter 2, a command or direction sentence, such as "Think," has an understood subject of _you_.

Correcting Fragments

The fragments in the following passage need either a subject or a verb. Underline the fragments and correct them. (See Answer Key for possible answers.)

(1) Two ice hotels the ultimate place for "chilling out." (2) One of these hotels in Quebec, Canada. (3) The other being in Sweden. (4) These structures built of 4,500 tons of snow and 250 tons of ice, like giant igloos. (5) The hotels' rooms even including furniture made of ice. (6) Room temperatures do not rise above 27 degrees Fahrenheit. (7) But outside temperatures well below freezing. (8) The hotels' ice walls actually trapping and holding some of the heat inside. (9) Guests sleep in thick sleeping bags piled with animal skins for warmth. (10) In the hotels' bars, even the glasses are made of ice. (11) Drinks served "in the rocks" instead of "on the rocks."

(12) Construction in December of every year. (13) In January, the hotels open for business. (14) Stay open until late March. (15) Then begin to melt. (16) These are two hotels having to be totally rebuilt every year.

Correcting Fragments

The fragments in the following passage need either a subject or a verb. Underline the fragments and correct them.

(1) Susan B. Anthony among the leaders in the early days of the women's rights movement. (2) Her parents being Quakers, who believed in the equality of the sexes. (3) As a young woman, wanted to argue against alcohol abuse. (4) Was not allowed to speak at rallies because she was a woman. (5) Susan B. Anthony not to be silenced. (6) She joined other women in fighting for women's rights in education, voting, and property ownership. (7) Also fought for the abolition of slavery. (8) When black men were given the right to vote in 1869, she was pleased. (9) However, was disappointed that women did not receive the same consideration. (10) For about sixty years, she was active in the National Woman Suffrage Movement. (11) Died fourteen years before the 19th Amendment gave women the right to vote. (12) In

1979, she was recognized for her civic contributions. (13) Placed her picture on a one-dollar coin.

Correcting Fragments

The following fragments need either a subject or a verb. Correct them. (See Answer Key for possible answers.)

1. One of the two main industries in Florida which is tourism.

2. People going to Florida to visit Disney World.

3. Others who go to watch sporting events such as the Orange Bowl.

4. Tourists regarding the Everglades National Park as a national wonder.

5. St. Augustine having the oldest house in the United States.

6. Many Major League baseball teams to Florida for spring training.

7. Can see a living coral reef formation at a state park.

8. Tours, demonstrations, and displays at the John F. Kennedy Space Center.

9. Some people who visit Florida for the pleasant weather and good beaches.

10. Circus World which offers opportunities for amateurs.

Correcting Fragments

The following fragments need either a subject or a verb. Correct them.

1. Australia as the "down under" country because it is south of the equator.

2. It being colonized by the English.

3. The first English residents being convicts.

4. The aborigines moving away from their traditional lands.

5. Had lived there for many thousands of years.

6. The population of Australia now well beyond twenty million.

7. More than two hundred thousand aborigines.

8. Many people living in the southeastern part of the country.

9. The inner region as the outback.

10. Australia being known for its unusual animals.

Correcting Fragments

Identify each of the following as a fragment (FRAG) or a complete sentence (OK). Correct the fragments. (They may be any of the kinds you have studied in this chapter: dependent clause, phrase, or word group without a subject or without a verb.) You can correct some fragments by adding them to a complete sentence.

_____ 1. Asia which developed much earlier than the West.

_____ 2. More than five thousand years ago, Asia had an advanced civilization.

_____ 3. People there who invented writing and created literature.

_____ 4. Involved in the development of science, agriculture, and religion.

_____ 5. The birthplace of the major religions of the world.

_____ 6. The most common religion in Asia being Hinduism.

_____ 7. The second most common religion is Islam.

_____ 8. Asia is the most populous continent.

_____ 9. With almost four billion people.

_____ 10. Hong Kong and Bangladesh which are among the most densely populated places in the world.

_____ 11. Asia having many ethnic groups.

_____ 12. Including the Chinese, the Indians, the Arabs, the Turks, and the Jews.

_____ 13. The Chinese have different groups.

_____

_____ 14. Speaking many dialects.

_____

_____ 15. Although they have different dialects.

_____

_____ 16. There is a national language.

_____

_____ 17. A language called Mandarin.

_____

_____ 18. Cultural differences exist in Taiwan.

_____

_____ 19. The main difference being between the Chinese from the mainland
and the Taiwanese.

_____

_____ 20. Despite the difference, all Chinese have much culture in common.

_____

Comma Splices and Run-Ons

The comma splice and the run-on are two other kinds of faulty "sentences" that give false signals to the reader. In each instance, the punctuation suggests that there is only one sentence, but, in fact, there is material for two.

The **comma splice** consists of two independent clauses with only a comma between them:

> The weather was disappointing, we canceled the picnic. [A comma by itself cannot join two independent clauses.]

The **run-on** differs from the comma splice in only one respect: It has no comma between the independent clauses. Therefore, the run-on is two independent clauses with _nothing_ between them:

> The weather was disappointing we canceled the picnic. [Independent clauses must be properly connected.]

Because an independent clause can stand by itself as a sentence and because two independent clauses must be properly linked, you can use a simple technique to identify the comma splice and the run-on. If you see a sentence that you think may contain one of these two errors, ask yourself this question: "Can I insert a period at some place in the word group and still have a sentence on either side?" If the answer is yes and there is no word such as *and* or *but* following the inserted period, then you have a comma splice or a run-on to correct. In our previous examples of the comma splice and the run-on, we could insert a period after the word *disappointing* in each case, and we would still have an independent clause—therefore, a sentence—on either side.

Four Ways to Correct Comma Splices and Run-Ons

Once you identify a comma splice or a run-on in your writing, you need to correct it. There are four different ways to fix these common sentence problems: Use a comma and a coordinating conjunction, use a subordinating conjunction, use a semicolon, or make each clause a separate sentence.

1. Use a comma and a coordinating conjunction.

>   Incorrect: We canceled the picnic the weather was disappointing. [run-on]

>   Correct: We canceled the picnic, *for* the weather was disappointing. [Here we inserted a comma and the coordinating conjunction *for*.]

Knowing the seven coordinating conjunctions will help you in writing sentences and correcting sentence problems. Remember the acronym FANBOYS: *for, and, nor, but, or, yet, so.*

EXERCISE 12

Correcting Comma Splices and Run-Ons

Identify each word group as a comma splice (CS), a run-on (RO), or a complete sentence (OK), and make needed corrections using commas and coordinating conjunctions. (See Answer Key for possible answers.)

>   Example: ___CS___ He did the assignment, ^*and*^ his boss gave him a bonus.

_____   1. In 1846 a group of eighty-two settlers headed for California with much optimism, a hard road lay ahead.

_____   2. They had expected to cross the mountains before winter they were in good spirits.

_____   3. They would not arrive in California before winter, nor would some of them get there at all.

_____   4. When they encountered a heavy snowstorm, they stopped to spend the winter they still thought they would be safe.

_____ 5. They made crude shelters of logs and branches, some also used moss and earth.

_____ 6. They had trouble managing they had not encountered such problems before.

_____ 7. They ran out of regular food, they ate roots, mice, shoe leather, and their horses.

_____ 8. Thirty-five members of the Donner Party died that winter, the survivors were so hungry that they ate the dead bodies.

_____ 9. They were weak, sick, and depressed they did not give up.

_____ 10. Fifteen people set out to get help seven survived and returned to rescue friends and relatives.

EXERCISE 13

Correcting Comma Splices and Run-Ons

Identify each word group as a comma splice (CS), a run-on (RO), or a complete sentence (OK), and make needed corrections using commas and coordinating conjunctions.

_____ 1. Comedian Woody Allen once observed that no one gets out of this world alive, we all know that no human is immortal.

_____ 2. But several famous dead people have managed to continue to _look_ alive they (or their admirers) had their bodies preserved and put on display.

_____ 3. Philosopher Jeremy Bentham wanted his body preserved, his wishes were carried out when he died in 1832.

_____ 4. Bentham left a lot of money to London's University College, the college couldn't have the money unless it agreed to let Bentham's body attend its annual board of directors meetings.

_____ 5. Bentham's dressed-up body was posed sitting in an armchair in his hand was his favorite walking stick.

_____ 6. Every year for ninety-two years, the college complied with Bentham's instructions the board's minutes for those years record Bentham as "present but not voting."

_____ 7. Bentham's body is still at University College, it's on display now in a permanent exhibit.

_____ 8. Soviet Union leader V. I. Lenin has been dead and on display since 1924 Russians and tourists can still visit his lifelike body enclosed in a glass coffin in Moscow.

_____ 9. The corpse of People's Republic of China founder Mao Tse-Tung was preserved for posterity, too, in his mausoleum, an elevator raises his glass coffin from underground to a public viewing area every morning.

_____ 10. Other famous people turned into modern mummies were national leaders Joseph Stalin, Eva Perón, and Ho Chi Minh, and opera singer Enrico Caruso.

2. Use a subordinating conjunction.

Incorrect: The weather was disappointing, we canceled the picnic.

Correct: *Because* the weather was disappointing, we canceled the picnic.

By inserting the subordinating conjunction *because,* you can transform the first independent clause into a dependent clause and correct the comma splice. Knowing the most common subordinating conjunctions will help you in writing sentences and correcting sentence problems. Here is a list of the subordinating conjunctions you saw in Chapter 4.

after	if	until
although	in order that	when
as	provided that	whenever
as if	rather than	where
because	since	whereas
before	so that	wherever
even if	than	whether
even though	unless	while

EXERCISE 14

Correcting Comma Splices and Run-Ons

Identify each word group as a comma splice (CS), a run-on (RO), or a complete sentence (OK), and correct the errors by making a dependent clause. (See Answer Key for possible answers.)

_____ 1. Chris Evert was one of the most successful tennis players of the 1970s and 1980s, she was not physically powerful.

_____ 2. She was intelligent and well coordinated, she became a top player.

_____ 3. She was still in her teens she won major championships.

_____ 4. She attracted much attention in 1974 she won fifty-five consecutive matches.

_____ 5. She reached the top, she had much competition there.

_____ 6. Evonne Goolagong was Evert's main competition at first Martina Navratilova soon assumed that role.

_____ 7. Financially Chris Evert's career was notable she made more than six million dollars.

_____ 8. Chris Evert helped to make women's tennis what it is today, she will not be forgotten.

_____ 9. She was called the "ice princess" she did not show her emotions.

_____ 10. She is regarded as one of the greatest athletes of the past forty years.

EXERCISE 15

Correcting Comma Splices and Run-Ons

Identify each word group as a comma splice (CS), a run-on (RO), or a complete sentence (OK), and correct the errors by making a dependent clause.

_____ 1. Jesse Owens won four gold medals in the 1936 Olympics he became a famous person.

_____ 2. The 1936 Olympics were held in Nazi Germany Owens was placed at a disadvantage.

_____ 3. Hitler believed in the superiority of the Aryans, he thought Owens would lose.

_____ 4. Jesse Owens won Hitler showed his disappointment openly.

_____ 5. Owens broke a record for the 200-meter race that had stood for thirty-six years.

_____ 6. Owens then jumped a foot farther than others in the long jump Hitler left the stadium.

_____ 7. Before the day was at last over, Owens had also won gold medals in the 100-meter dash and the 400-meter relay.

_____ 8. Hitler's early departure was a snub at Owens, but he did not care.

_____ 9. Owens returned to the United States, he engaged in numerous exhibitions, including racing against a horse.

_____ 10. In his later years Owens became an official for the U.S. Olympic Committee, he never received the recognition that many contemporary athletes do.

3. Use a semicolon.

Incorrect:	The weather was disappointing, we canceled the picnic.
Correct:	The weather was disappointing; we canceled the picnic.
Correct:	The weather was disappointing; *therefore,* we canceled the picnic.

This comma splice was corrected by a semicolon. The first correct example shows the semicolon alone. The second correct example shows a semicolon followed by the conjunctive adverb *therefore.* The conjunctive adverb is optional, but, as we have already seen, conjunctive adverbs can make the relationship between independent clauses stronger. Here is the list of conjunctive adverbs you saw in Chapter 4.

however	on the other hand
otherwise	then
therefore	consequently
similarly	also
hence	thus

Do you remember the acronym HOTSHOT CAT, made up of the first letter of each of these common conjunctive adverbs? The acronym will help you remember them. Other conjunctive adverbs include *in fact, for example, moreover, nevertheless, furthermore, now,* and *soon.*

EXERCISE 16

Correcting Comma Splices and Run-Ons

Identify each word group as a comma splice (CS), a run-on (RO), or a complete sentence (OK). Make corrections with a semicolon, and add a conjunctive adverb if appropriate. (See Answer Key for possible answers.)

_____ 1. Madonna Louise Veronica Ciccone became one of the biggest pop stars in the 1980s, she is known to most people as Madonna.

_____ 2. Madonna was talented in dance she even won a dance scholarship to the University of Michigan in the mid-1970s.

_____ 3. She was not interested in staying in school, with a mere thirty-five dollars in her possession, she moved to New York City.

_____ 4. After working in several small bands, she finally made her first album in 1983.

_____ 5. When her first album became number one on the *Billboard* list in 1984, she immediately had new opportunities.

_____ 6. Madonna continues to be a very popular singer, she can act.

_____ 7. She performed well in the comedy movie *Desperately Seeking Susan* she also starred in *Dick Tracy, A League of Their Own,* and *Evita.*

_____ 8. Madonna is an expert at manipulating the media, she increases her popularity each time she changes her image.

_____ 9. Her show business career has prospered, she has had problems in her private life.

_____ 10. She continues to promote herself other people do too.

EXERCISE 17

Correcting Comma Splices and Run-Ons

Identify each word group as a comma splice (CS), a run-on (RO), or a complete sentence (OK). Make corrections with a semicolon, and add a conjunctive adverb if appropriate.

_____ 1. Ants are highly social insects they live in colonies.

_____ 2. They work for the benefit of the group, cooperation is important.

_____   3. Ants have different roles they will, in some species, have different

sizes and shapes.

_____   4. An ant will be a queen, a worker, or a male, there is not an identity

problem among ants.

_____   5. A worker may be a soldier whose job is to defend the nest that ant

has large mandibles, or teeth.

_____   6. The worker that is a janitor will have the job of cleaning the nest

her head is big for pushing waste material through the tunnel.

_____   7. The queen is very large because she must lay many eggs.

_____   8. The workers are all female, their job is to do all of the work.

_____   9. The males have only one function, and that function is to mate with

the queen.

_____ 10. In some species, the workers may change roles in their work, the

males only mate and die young.

4. Make each clause a separate sentence.

Incorrect: The weather was disappointing, we canceled the picnic.

Correct: The weather was disappointing. We canceled the picnic.

This method is at once the simplest and most common method of correcting comma splices and run-ons. To correct the comma splice, replace the comma with a period, and begin the second sentence (the second independent clause) with a capital letter. For a run-on, insert a period between the two independent clauses and begin the second sentence with a capital letter.

EXERCISE 18   ## Correcting Comma Splices and Run-Ons

Identify each word group as a comma splice (CS), a run-on (RO), or a complete sentence (OK), and make corrections with a period and a capital letter. (See Answer Key for answers.)

_____   1. About a hundred and fifty years ago, British soldiers wore a bright

red coat, they also wore a black hat and white trousers.

_____   2. The soldiers looked good in parades the queen was very proud.

_____ 3. On the battlefield, the situation was different, and the uniform was regarded differently.

_____ 4. The coat could be seen at a great distance enemies aimed at the red coats.

_____ 5. This had long been a problem, even in the days of the American Revolution.

_____ 6. No one in high position was willing to change the colors of the uniform the soldiers decided to take action.

_____ 7. A solution was at hand, the soldiers would wear the red coats but change the colors.

_____ 8. At the time of their experiment, they were serving in India, they would use natural elements to solve their problem.

_____ 9. In the dry season, they would rub yellow-brown dust on their uniforms, and in the wet season they would use mud.

_____ 10. They liked the camouflage color so much that they finally changed the color of their uniforms to the drab color they called it _khaki_, the Indian word for _dust_.

EXERCISE 19

Correcting Comma Splices and Run-Ons

Identify each word group as a comma splice (CS), a run-on (RO), or a complete sentence (OK), and make corrections with a period and a capital letter.

_____ 1. The world's fastest steel-track roller coaster is the Top Thrill Dragster, it's at the Cedar Point Amusement Park in Ohio.

_____ 2. Riders rocket out of a starting gate they reach a speed of 120 miles per hour in four seconds.

_____ 3. The second-fastest roller coaster is in Japan, it goes a mere 106.8 miles per hour.

_____ 4. Wooden roller coasters are downright pokey in comparison the fastest reaches speeds of only 78.3 miles per hour.

_____ 5. If you're looking for the biggest drop, the Top Thrill Dragster has that distinction, too.

_____ 6. The largest drop on the Top Thrill Dragster is 400 feet, compare that to the largest drop on a wooden coaster, which is only 214 feet.

_____ 7. The longest roller coaster ride of them all is the Steel Dragon 2000 in Japan, that coaster is 8,133 feet long.

_____ 8. You want the steepest angle of descent, you can choose from several steel-track coasters that allow you to plummet downward at a 90-degree angle.

_____ 9. The steepest wooden coasters average about 55 degrees as a matter of fact, the steepest of all is only 61 degrees.

_____ 10. Most of the world's record-setting roller coasters were opened between 2000 and 2003 thrill-seekers hope they'll continue to get faster and steeper.

Techniques for Spotting Problem Sentences

1. For the fragment, ask yourself: "If someone were to say or write this to me, would I expect the person to add to the statement or rephrase it?"

2. In checking for the comma splice or run-on, ask yourself, "Is there a point in this word group at which I can insert a period and create a sentence on either side?" The question is not necessary if there is a coordinating conjunction (FANBOYS) at that point.

3. If you have trouble with comma splices and run-ons, check these constructions as you revise:

   a. A comma preceded by a noun or pronoun followed by a noun or pronoun

   b. A sentence beginning with a subordinating conjunction

4. If you have trouble with fragments, look for these clues:

   a. A word group with a single verb ending in *-ing*

   b. A word group without both a subject and a verb

5. Use the grammar checker on your word processor to alert you to possible problem sentences. Then use instruction from this book to make the necessary corrections.

CHAPTER REVIEW   ## CORRECTING FRAGMENTS, COMMA SPLICES, AND RUN-ONS

Fragments

1. A correct sentence signals completeness; a **fragment** signals incompleteness—it doesn't make sense. You expect the speaker or writer of a fragment to say or write more or to rephrase it.

2. A **dependent clause** cannot stand by itself because it begins with a subordinating word.

   Because he left.

   When she worked.

   Although they slept.

3. A **verbal phrase**, a **prepositional phrase**, and an **appositive phrase** may carry ideas, but each is incomplete because it lacks a subject and a verb.

Verbal Phrase:	*having completed his initial research*
Sentence:	Having completed his initial research, he refined his outline.
Prepositional Phrase:	*in the store*
Sentence:	She worked in the store.
Appositive Phrase:	*a successful business*
Sentence:	Marks Brothers, a successful business, sells clothing.

4. Each complete sentence must have an **independent clause,** a group of words that contains a subject and a verb, and can stand alone.

   He enrolled for the fall semester.

Comma Splices and Run-Ons

1. The **comma splice** consists of two independent clauses with only a comma between them.

   Maria exceeded her sales quota, she received a bonus. [A comma by itself cannot join two independent clauses.]

2. The **run-on** differs from the comma splice in only one respect: It has no comma between the independent clauses.

> Maria exceeded her sales quota she received a bonus. [Independent clauses must be properly connected.]

Correcting Comma Splices and Run-Ons

1. Use a comma and a **coordinating conjunction** (*for, and, nor, but, or, yet, so*) to correct the comma splice or run-on.

> Maria exceeded her sales quota, *and* she received a bonus.

2. Use a **subordinating conjunction** (such as *because, after, that, when, although, since, how, till, unless, before*) to make one clause dependent and correct the comma splice or run-on.

> *Because* Maria exceeded her sales quota, she received a bonus.

3. Use a **semicolon** (with or without a conjunctive adverb such as *however, otherwise, therefore, similarly, hence, on the other hand, then, consequently, also, thus*) to correct the comma splice or run-on.

> Maria exceeded her sales quota; *therefore,* she received a bonus.

> Maria exceeded her sales quota; she received a bonus.

4. Use a period to replace a comma and add a capital letter (to correct a comma splice), or use a period between two independent clauses and add a capital letter (to correct a run-on).

> Maria exceeded her sales quota. She received a bonus.

CHAPTER REVIEW EXERCISES

REVIEW 1   # Correcting Fragments, Comma Splices, and Run-Ons

Correct each fragment, comma splice, and run-on by using one of the methods you learned. Select the method you think is most effective for smoothness of expression and emphasis. You may find it helpful to read the material aloud as you work. (See Answer Key for possible answers.)

Dinosaurs were giant lizardlike animals, they lived more than a hundred million years ago. Some had legs like lizards and turtles, some had legs more like birds. The ones with legs like birds. Could walk easily with raised bodies. They varied in size, many were huge. The largest, the diplodocus, about ninety feet long, equal to the distance between the bases in baseball. Weighing more than ten elephants. The smallest weighed no more than two pounds and was no bigger than a chicken. Some dinosaurs ate meat, almost certainly some dinosaurs ate other dinosaurs. Used their strong claws and fierce teeth to tear at their victims. Dinosaurs were different. In design as well as size. They had horns, spikes, bills, armorlike plates, clublike tails, bony crests, and teeth in many sizes and shapes their heads were proportionately tiny or absurdly large. Their mouths varied. Depending on their eating habits.

REVIEW 2

Correcting Fragments, Comma Splices, and Run-Ons

Correct each fragment, comma splice, and run-on by using one of the methods you learned. Select the method you think is most effective for smoothness of expression and emphasis.

Deserts are often referred to as wastelands. It is true that not as many plants grow there as in a temperate zone, it is also true that animals do not live there in great numbers. However, many plants and animals live and do quite well in the desert. Because of their adaptations.

Not all deserts have the same appearance, many people think of the desert as a hot, sandy area. Actually, sand covers only about 20 percent of the desert. Some deserts have mountains some others have snow.

Because deserts are dry for most of the year. Plants must conserve and store water. Several kinds of cacti can shrink during a dry season and swell during a rainy season. Some shrubs simply drop their leaves and use their green bark to manufacture chlorophyll. Seeds sometimes lying in the desert for several years before sprouting to take advantage of a rainfall.

Animals have quite effectively adjusted to the desert, some animals obtain moisture from the food they eat and require no water. One animal of the desert, the camel, produces fat. Which it stores in its hump. The fat allows the camel to reserve more body heat it needs little water. Still other animals feed only at night or are inactive for weeks or even months.

About 15 percent of the land of the earth is covered by deserts. That area increasing every year. Because of overgrazing by livestock. Also because of the destruction of forests. Areas that were once green and fertile will now support little life and only

a small population of human beings.

MICROTHEME

To practice your skills acquired in this chapter, return to the Microtheme on page 87 and complete Exercise B.

Chapter

6

Verbs

Verbs are to strong sentences as gas is to fine cars. Choose the right kind and don't skimp on the octane.

FLOW OF WRITING

Learning Objectives

Working with this chapter, I will learn to

~ use verb tenses to show time.
~ make subjects and verbs agree.
~ make verbs consistent in tense.
~ use active and passive verbs appropriately.
~ use strong verbs.
~ use the subjunctive mood appropriately.

MICROTHEME

EXERCISE A

Writing Activity in Miniature

Two Purposes

Writing Diagnostic: Before you work on this chapter, the Microtheme will give you an opportunity to write briefly on an engaging topic without pressure.

Chapter Learning Application: After you have studied this chapter, return to your Microtheme to check your work and practice what you have just learned.

Form and Procedure

Like an executive summary (written for a busy boss), the Microtheme conveys ideas concisely (using no more than the space on a 5- by 8-inch card) in a specified form. Indent only once, and write small enough to leave room for marking later. Directions for practicing your chapter writing skills appear in Exercise B.

Suggested Microtheme Topic

Write a Microtheme of 80 to 100 words about people's driving habits that bother you. Give at least one real-life example.

_____

_____

_____

_____

_____

_____

_____

_____

_____

_____

_____

_____

_____

_____

_____

_____

EXERCISE B

Connecting Your Learning Objectives with Your Microtheme

Complete this exercise after you have studied this chapter.

1. Check to make sure your verbs are correct in form and consistent in tense.

2. Check to make sure your subjects and verbs agree.

3. Check to make sure you have used strong verbs in the appropriate voice and mood.

FLOW OF WRITING

This chapter covers the use of standard verbs. To some, the word *standard* implies "correct." A more precise meaning is "that which is conventional among educated people." Therefore, a standard verb is the right choice in most school assignments, most published writing, and most important public-speaking situations. We all change our language when we move from these formal occasions to informal ones: We don't talk to our families in the same way we would speak at a large gathering in public; we don't write letters to friends the same way we write a history report. Even with informal language, we would seldom change from standard to nonstandard usage.

Regular and Irregular Verbs

Verbs can be divided into two categories, called **regular** and **irregular**. Regular verbs are predictable, but irregular verbs—as the term suggests—follow no definite pattern. The forms for both regular and irregular verbs vary to show time.

- **Present tense verbs** show an action or a state of being that is occurring at the present time: I *like* your hat. He *is* at a hockey game right now. Present tense verbs can also imply a continuation from the past into the future: She *drives* to work every day.
- **Past tense verbs** show an action or a state of being that occurred in the past: We *walked* to town yesterday. Tim *was* president of the club last year.
- **Past participle verbs** are used with helping verbs such as *has, have,* and *had:* Georgina *had studied* hard before she took the test.

Regular Verbs

Present Tense

For *he, she,* and *it,* regular verbs in the present tense add an *-s* or an *-es* to the base word. The following chart shows the present tense of the base word *ask,* which is a regular verb.

	Singular	Plural
First Person:	I ask	we ask
Second Person:	you ask	you ask
Third Person:	he, she, it asks	they ask

If the verb ends in *-y,* you might have to drop the *-y* and add *-ies* for *he, she,* and *it.*

	Singular	Plural
First Person:	I try	we try
Second Person:	you try	you try
Third Person:	he, she, it tries	they try

Past Tense

For regular verbs in the past tense, add *-ed* to the base form.

Base Form (Present)	Past
walk	walked
answer	answered

If the base form already ends in *-e,* add just *-d.*

Base Form (Present)	Past
smile	smiled
decide	decided

If the base form ends in a consonant followed by *-y,* drop the *-y* and add *-ied.*

Base Form (Present)	Past
fry	fried
amplify	amplified

Regardless of how you form the past tense, regular verbs in the past tense do not change forms. The following chart shows the past tense of the base word *like,* which is a regular verb.

	Singular	Plural
First Person:	I liked	we liked
Second Person:	you liked	you liked
Third Person:	he, she, it liked	they liked

Past Participles

The past participle uses the helping verb *has, have,* or *had.* For regular verbs, the past participle form of the verb is the same as the past tense.

Base Form	Past	Past Participle
happen	happened	happened
hope	hoped	hoped
cry	cried	cried

Here is a list of some common regular verbs, showing the base form, the past tense, and the past participle. The base form can also be used with such helping verbs as *can, could, do, does, did, may, might, must, shall, should, will,* and *would.*

Base Form (Present)	Past	Past Participle
answer	answered	answered
ask	asked	asked
cry	cried	cried
decide	decided	decided
dive	dived (dove)	dived
finish	finished	finished
happen	happened	happened
learn	learned	learned
like	liked	liked
love	loved	loved
need	needed	needed
open	opened	opened
start	started	started
suppose	supposed	supposed
walk	walked	walked
want	wanted	wanted

Irregular Verbs

Irregular verbs do not follow any definite pattern.

Base Form (Present)	Past	Past Participle
shake	shook	shaken
make	made	made
begin	began	begun

Some irregular verbs that sound similar in the present tense don't follow the same pattern.

Base Form (Present)	Past	Past Participle
ring	rang	rung
swing	swung	swung
bring	brought	brought

Present Tense

For *he, she,* and *it,* irregular verbs in the present tense add an *-s* or an *-es* to the base word. The following chart shows the present tense of the base word *break,* which is an irregular verb.

	Singular	Plural
First Person:	I break	we break
Second Person:	you break	you break
Third Person:	he, she, it breaks	they break

If the irregular verb ends in *-y,* you might have to drop the *-y* and add *-ies* for *he, she,* and *it.*

	Singular	Plural
First Person:	I fly	we fly
Second Person:	you fly	you fly
Third Person:	he, she, it flies	they fly

Past Tense

Like past tense regular verbs, past tense irregular verbs do not change their forms. The following chart shows the past tense of the irregular verb *do.*

	Singular	Plural
First Person:	I did	we did
Second Person:	you did	you did
Third Person:	he, she, it did	they did

For irregular verbs in the past tense, use the following list of irregular verbs.

Past Participles

Use the past tense form with the helping verbs *has, have,* and *had.*

Here is a list of some common irregular verbs, showing the base form (present), the past tense, and the past participle. Like regular verbs, the base forms can be used with such helping verbs as *can, could, do, does, did, may, might, must, shall, should, will,* and *would.*

Base Form (Present)	Past	Past Participle
arise	arose	arisen
awake	awoke (awaked)	awoken (awaked)
be	was, were	been
become	became	become
begin	began	begun
bend	bent	bent
blow	blew	blown
burst	burst	burst
buy	bought	bought
catch	caught	caught
choose	chose	chosen
cling	clung	clung
come	came	come
cost	cost	cost
creep	crept	crept
deal	dealt	dealt
do	did	done
drink	drank	drunk
drive	drove	driven
eat	ate	eaten
feel	felt	felt
fight	fought	fought
fling	flung	flung
fly	flew	flown
forget	forgot	forgotten
freeze	froze	frozen
get	got	got (gotten)
go	went	gone
grow	grew	grown
hang	hung	hung
have	had	had
hit	hit	hit
know	knew	known
lead	led	led
leave	left	left
lose	lost	lost
make	made	made
mean	meant	meant
put	put	put
read	read	read
ride	rode	ridden
ring	rang	rung
see	saw	seen
shine	shone	shone
shoot	shot	shot
sing	sang	sung
sink	sank	sunk
sleep	slept	slept
slink	slunk	slunk
speak	spoke	spoken
spend	spent	spent

Base Form (Present)	Past	Past Participle
spread	spread	spread
steal	stole	stolen
stink	stank (stunk)	stunk
sweep	swept	swept
swim	swam	swum
swing	swung	swung
take	took	taken
teach	taught	taught
tear	tore	torn
think	thought	thought
throw	threw	thrown
thrust	thrust	thrust
wake	woke (waked)	woken (waked)
weep	wept	wept
write	wrote	written

EXERCISE 1

Selecting Verbs

Underline the correct verb form. (See Answer Key for answers.)

1. In the twentieth century, two jilted men on opposite sides of the country (create, created) amazing structures to soothe their broken hearts.

2. In 1908, Baldasare Forestiere (built, builded) a four-room underground apartment in Fresno, California.

3. Then, he (goes, went) to his native Italy and (ask, asked) his childhood sweetheart to join him in America.

4. When she refused, a sorrowful Baldasare (returns, returned) to the United States and (threw, throwed) himself into his digging.

5. By the time Baldasare died in 1946, he had (digged, dug) for thirty-eight years and had (construct, constructed) ninety underground rooms over ten acres.

6. Just after World War II, Edward Leedskalnin (began, begins) building a castle from enormous coral rocks in Florida City, Florida.

7. He had been (jilted, jilten) in 1920 by his 16-year-old fiancée, Agnes.

8. Edward (hopes, hoped) that Agnes would come back to him when he (became, become) famous for his project, which he moved to Homestead, Florida.

9. Edward (works, worked) on his castle for sixteen years in the dark of night, and no one (knows, knew) how the five-foot-tall man moved twenty-five-ton blocks.

10. Unfortunately, Agnes never (seen, saw) Coral Castle, and she did not (change, changed) her mind about marrying Edward.

EXERCISE 2

Selecting Verbs

Underline the correct verb form.

1. If you want to save money, professional tightwads urge you to reconsider the things you've always (throwed, thrown) away.

2. For instance, ties that are worn out can (become, became) tails for kites or leashes for dogs.

3. You may not have (realize, realized) that you can (use, used) toothbrushes to clean shoes.

4. Your golfing pals will wonder why they've never (thinked, thought) of using their own old socks as golf club covers.

5. A clear, plastic yogurt lid can (become, became) a frame for a school photo if you add a magnet.

6. Bridesmaid dresses can be cut up and (sewed, sewn) together to create decorative throw pillows that would dazzle Martha Stewart.

7. Two old license plates can be (reborn, reborned) as a roof for a birdhouse.

8. And don't you dare toss this textbook; it can be (used, use) to wrap fish.

9. Strapped to the chest, it can (stop, stopped) small-caliber bullets.

10. When (dropped, dropt) from sufficient height, a single copy has been (known, knowed) to kill small rodents.

"Problem" Verbs

The following pairs of verbs are especially troublesome and confusing: *lie* and *lay, sit* and *set, rise* and *raise*. One way to tell them apart is to remember which word in each pair takes a direct object. A direct object answers the question *whom* or *what* in connection with a verb. The words *lay, raise,* and *set* take a direct object.

> He *raised* the window. [He *raised* what?]

Lie, rise, and *sit,* however, cannot take a direct object. We cannot say, for example, "He rose the window." In the following examples, the italicized words are objects.

Present Tense	Meaning	Past Tense	Past Participle	Example
lie	to rest	lay	lain	I lay down to rest.
lay	to place something	laid	laid	We laid the *books* on the table.
rise	to go up	rose	risen	The smoke rose quickly.
raise	to lift, to bring forth	raised	raised	She raised the *question*.
sit	to rest	sat	sat	He sat in the chair.
set	to place something	set	set	They set the *basket* on the floor.

EXERCISE 3 — Selecting Verbs

Underline the correct verb form. (See Answer Key for answers.)

1. This story is about Bill "Chick" Walker, who (lossed, lost) all he owned at the Wagon Wheel Saloon in Las Vegas.

2. Chick had (laid, layed) one thousand dollars on the red 21 at the roulette table.

3. For that spin, he (done, did) an amazing thing—he (won, wins).

4. But after a while, Chick (became, become) stupid, and his luck (ran, run) out.

5. Before he had (ate, eaten) breakfast, he accepted free drinks from the charming Trixie, who (served, serve) cocktails.

6. His judgment was soon (ruined, ruint) by the drinks, and he (put, putted) all his money on one spin.

7. That wager (cost, costed) Chick everything, and he couldn't (raise, rise) any more money.

8. Moreover, Trixie would not (sit, set) with him because she (like, liked) only winners.

9. Chick drained his glass, (rose, raised) from his red tufted vinyl barstool, and (head, headed) for the parking lot.

10. There he (known, knew) Bonnie Lou would be waiting for him because she (lust, lusted) for losers.

EXERCISE 4   ## Selecting Verbs

Underline the correct verb form.

1. According to legend, a vampire (lays, lies) in his coffin during the daylight hours.

2. Like a teenager, he (sets, sits) his own schedule: He sleeps all day and stays out all night.

3. He cannot (rise, raise) until after the sun sets.

4. Then the bloodsucker can (rise, raise) the coffin's lid and (set, sit) up.

5. He (rises, raises) from his bed hungry.

6. But don't bother (setting, sitting) a place for him at the dinner table.

7. He goes out hunting for victims who have unwisely (lain, laid) down their crucifixes, wooden stakes, and garlic necklaces.

8. He pounces quickly so that the victim has no time to (rise, raise) an alarm.

9. If he (lies, lays) his hands upon you, you're a goner.

10. But when the sun begins to (rise, raise) in the sky, this monster must hurry back to bed to (lie, lay) his head down.

EXERCISE 5   Using Verbs in Sentences

Use each of these words in a sentence of ten words or more.

1. *lie, lay* (rest), *lain, laid* _____

_____

_____

_____

_____

_____

2. *sit, sat, set* _____

_____

_____

_____

_____

_____

3. *is, was, were* _____

_____

_____

_____

_____

_____

4. *do, does* (or *don't, doesn't*) _____

_____

_____

_____

_____

The Twelve Verb Tenses

Some languages, such as Chinese and Navajo, have no verb tenses to indicate time. English has a fairly complicated system of tenses, but most verbs pattern in what are known as the simple tenses: past, present, and future. Altogether there are twelve tenses in English. The first four charts that follow illustrate those tenses in sentences. The next charts place each verb on a timeline. The charts also explain what the different tenses mean and how to form them.

Simple Tenses

Present:	I, we, you, they *drive*.
	He, she, it *drives*.
Past:	I, we, you, he, she, it, they *drove*.
Future:	I, we, you, he, she, it, they *will drive*.

Perfect Tenses

Present Perfect:	I, we, you, they *have driven*.
	He, she, it *has driven*.
Past Perfect:	I, we, you, he, she, it, they *had driven*.
Future Perfect:	I, we, you, he, she, it, they *will have driven*.

Progressive Tenses

Present Progressive:	I *am driving*.
	He, she, it *is driving*.
	We, you, they *are driving*.
Past Progressive:	I, he, she, it *was driving*.
	We, you, they *were driving*.
Future Progressive:	I, we, you, he, she, it, they *will be driving*.

Perfect Progressive Tenses

Present Perfect Progressive:	I, we, you, they *have been driving*.
	He, she, it *has been driving*.
Past Perfect Progressive:	I, we, you, he, she, it, they *had been driving*.
Future Perfect Progressive:	I, we, you, he, she, it, they *will have been driving*.

Simple Tenses

Tense	Time Line	Time	Verb Form
Present I *drive* to work. She *drives* to work.	past —— xxx —— future Now	Present, may imply a continuation from past to future	Present: *drive* *drives*
Past I *drove* to work.	x ⌐ Now	Past	Past: *drove*
Future I *will drive* to work.	⌐ x Now	Future	Present preceded by *will*: *will drive*

Perfect Tenses

Tense	Time Line	Time	Verb Form
Present Perfect I *have driven* to work.	past —— xxx —— future Now	Completed recently in the past, may continue to the present	Past participle preceded by *have* or *has*: *have driven*
Past Perfect I *had driven* to work before I moved to the city. [event]	Event x o Now	Prior to a specific time in the past	Past participle preceded by *had*: *had driven*
Future Perfect I *will have driven* to work thousands of times by December 31 [event].	Event x o Now	At a time prior to a specific time in the future	Past participle preceded by *will have*: *will have driven*

Progressive Tenses

Tense	Time Line	Time	Verb Form
Present Progressive I *am driving* to work.	past — xxx — future Now	In progress now	Progressive (*-ing* ending) preceded by *is, am,* or *are:* *am driving*
Past Progressive I *was driving* to work.	xxx Now	In progress in the past	Progressive (*-ing* ending) preceded by *was* or *were:* *was driving*
Future Progressive I *will be driving* to work.	xxx Now	In progress in the future	Progressive (*-ing* ending) preceded by *will be:* *will be driving*

Perfect Progressive Tenses

Tense	Time Line	Time	Verb Form
Present Perfect Progressive I *have been driving* to work.	past — xxx — future Now	In progress up to now	Progressive (*-ing* ending) preceded by *have been* or *has been:* *have been driving*
Past Perfect Progressive I *had been driving* when I began ride-sharing. [event]	Event xxx o Now	In progress before another event in the past	Progressive (*-ing* ending) preceded by *had:* *had been driving*
Future Perfect Progressive By May 1 [event], I *will have been driving* to work for six years.	Event xxx o Now	In progress before another event in the future	Progressive (*-ing* ending) preceded by *will have been:* *will have been driving*

EXERCISE 6

Choosing Verb Tense

Underline the correct verb form. (See Answer Key for answers.)

1. In the eighteenth century, Benjamin Franklin (is saying, said) that compound interest was the "eighth wonder of the world."

2. Today, taking advantage of compound interest (is, was) still one way to grow a fortune.

3. I wish I (had, had been) started investing years ago.

4. If I (will have, could have) saved $2,000 per year from age 21 on, I (would have, would have had) over a million dollars now.

5. I (have, had) never realized this until I did the math.

6. So I (have decided, could have been deciding) to begin investing money every month from now on.

7. Yesterday, I (determined, have determined) an amount I should save each week.

8. I hope that you (will have considered, are considering) doing the same thing.

9. By the time we're ready to retire, we (were, may be) millionaires.

10. Someday we (will worry, worried) about how to pay the bills.

EXERCISE 7

Choosing Verb Tense

Underline the correct verb form.

1. We (study, are studying) William Shakespeare's play *Romeo and Juliet.*

2. The teenagers Romeo and Juliet (met, had met) at a party.

3. By the time the party was over, they (fell, had fallen) in love.

4. Unfortunately, though, their families (feud, were feuding), so Romeo and Juliet (hid, had hidden) their affection for one another.

5. They secretly (married, had married) and (planned, had planned) to run away together.

6. But long before Juliet met Romeo, Juliet's father (decided, had decided) that she would marry a man named Paris.

7. The night before her wedding, Juliet (took, had taken) a potion that made her appear dead.

8. This tale (has, has had) a tragic ending because before Romeo found Juliet in her tomb, he (was not informed, had not been informed) that she wasn't really dead.

9. So he (committed, had committed) suicide, and Juliet (stabbed, had stabbed) herself when she awoke to find his body.

10. If I review this exercise, I (have, will have) a hanky ready to dry my tears.

Subject-Verb Agreement

This section is concerned with number agreement between subjects and verbs. The basic principle of **subject-verb agreement** is that if the subject is singular, the verb should be singular, and if the subject is plural, the verb should be plural. In the examples under the following ten major guidelines, the simple subjects and verbs are italicized.

1. Do not let words that come between the subject and verb affect agreement.

   - Modifying phrases and clauses frequently come between the subject and verb:

     The various *types* of drama *were* not *discussed*.

     Angela, who is hitting third, *is* the best player.

     The *price* of those shoes *is* too high.

   - Certain prepositions can cause trouble. The following words are prepositions, not conjunctions: *along with, as well as, besides, in addition to, including, together with*. The words that function as objects of prepositions cannot also be subjects of the sentence.

     The *coach,* along with the players, *protests* the decision.

   - When a negative phrase follows a positive subject, the verb agrees with the positive subject.

     Phillip, not the other boys, *was* the culprit.

2. Do not let inversions (verb before subject, not the normal order) affect the agreement of subject and verb.

   - Verbs and other words may come before the subject. Do not let them affect the agreement. To understand subject-verb relationships, recast the sentence in normal word order.

     Are Jabir and his *sister* at home? [question form]

     Jabir and his *sister are* at home. [normal order]

   - A sentence filler is a word that is grammatically independent of other words in the sentence. The most common fillers are *there* and *here*. Even though a sentence filler precedes the verb, it should not be treated as the subject.

     There *are* many *reasons* for his poor work. [The verb *are* agrees with the subject *reasons*.]

3. A singular verb agrees with a singular indefinite pronoun. (See page 159.)

   - Most indefinite pronouns are singular.

     Each of the women *is* ready at this time.

     Neither of the women *is* ready at this time.

     One of the children *is* not paying attention.

   - Certain indefinite pronouns do not clearly express either a singular or plural number. Agreement, therefore, depends on the meaning of the sentence. These pronouns are *all, any, none,* and *some*.

All of the melon *was* good.

All of the melons *were* good.

None of the pie *is* acceptable.

None of the pies *are* acceptable.

4. Two or more subjects joined by *and* usually take a plural verb.

The *captain* and the *sailors were* happy to be ashore.

The *trees* and *shrubs need* more care.

- If the parts of a compound subject mean one and the same person or thing, the verb is singular; if the parts mean more than one, the verb is plural.

The *secretary* and *treasurer is* not present. [one]

The *secretary* and the *treasurer are* not present. [more than one]

- When *each* or *every* modifies singular subjects joined by *and,* the verb is singular.

Each *boy* and each *girl brings* a donation.

Each *woman* and *man has asked* the same questions.

5. Alternative subjects—that is, subjects joined by *or, nor, either/or, neither/nor, not only/but also*—should be handled in the following manner:

- If the subjects are both singular, the verb is singular.

Rosa or *Alicia is* responsible.

- If the subjects are plural, the verb is plural.

Neither the *students* nor the *teachers were* impressed by his comments.

- If one of the subjects is singular and the other subject is plural, the verb agrees with the nearer subject.

Either the Garcia *boys* or their *father goes* to the hospital each day.

Either their *father* or the Garcia *boys go* to the hospital each day.

6. Collective nouns—*team, family, group, crew, gang, class, faculty,* and the like—take a singular verb if the noun is considered a unit, but they take a plural verb if the group is considered as a number of individuals.

The *team is playing* well tonight.

The *team are getting* dressed. [In this sentence, the individuals are acting not as a unit but separately. If you don't like the way the sentence sounds, substitute "The members of the team are getting dressed."]

7. Titles of books, essays, short stories, and plays; a word spoken of as a word; and the names of businesses take a singular verb.

The Canterbury Tales was written by Geoffrey Chaucer.

Ives is my favorite name for a pet.

Markle Brothers has a sale this week.

8. Sums of money, distances, and measurements are followed by a singular verb when a unit is meant. They are followed by a plural verb when the individual elements are considered separately.

> *Three dollars was* the price. [unit]
>
> *Three dollars were* lying there. [individual]
>
> *Five years is* a long time. [unit]
>
> The *first five years were* difficult ones. [individual]

9. Be careful of agreement with nouns ending in *-s.* Several nouns ending in *-s* take a singular verb—for example, *aeronautics, civics, economics, ethics, measles, mumps.*

> *Mumps is* an unpleasant disease.
>
> *Economics is* my major field of study.

10. Some nouns have only a plural form and so take only a plural verb—for example, *clothes, fireworks, scissors, trousers.*

> His *trousers are* badly wrinkled.
>
> Marv's *clothes were* stylish and expensive.

EXERCISE 8   ## Making Subjects and Verbs Agree

Underline the verb that agrees in number with the subject. (See Answer Key for answers.)

1. "Two Kinds" (is, are) a short story by Amy Tan.

2. My trousers (is, are) wrinkled.

3. Twenty pounds (is, are) a lot to lose in one month.

4. Physics (is, are) a difficult subject to master.

5. *60 Minutes* (is, are) a respected television program.

6. Sears (is, are) having a giant sale.

7. The scissors (is, are) very sharp.

8. Five miles (is, are) too far to walk.

9. The class (is, are) stretching their muscles.

10. My dog and my cat (is, are) sleeping on the couch.

Making Subjects and Verbs Agree

Underline the verb that agrees in number with the subject.

1. Every year, New Orleans (is, are) the site of one of the longest and largest parties in the United States.

2. More than four million people from around the world (come, comes) to Mardi Gras, "the greatest free party on Earth."

3. Mardi Gras, which means "Fat Tuesday," (is, are) always forty-six days before Easter.

4. But twelve days before that, the crowd (begins, begin) to grow.

5. All of the bands in the state of Louisiana (converges, converge) on New Orleans.

6. A visitor, along with just about all of the city's residents, (enjoys, enjoy) nonstop jazz and blues music.

7. Cajun and Creole food (satisfies, satisfy) the revelers' hungry appetites.

8. There (is, are) about seventy parades, but the best ones (occurs, occur) during the last five days of the celebration.

9. Each of the spectacular parade floats (is, are) decorated and (carries, carry) riders wearing costumes.

10. Four miles (is, are) the length of a typical parade route.

11. Beads, coins, cups, and an occasional medallion (is, are) tossed from the floats into the crowd.

12. People who line the parade route (tries, try) to catch as many trinkets as they can.

13. One float, the best of all of that parade's floats, (wins, win) an award.

14. Some of the most popular festivities, besides a good parade, (is, are) the masked balls.

15. Every one of the costumes (is, are) outrageous and unique.

16. *Cajun Mardi Gras Masks* (is, are) a book that will give you some ideas.

17. All of the celebration (is, are) fun and interesting.

18. After dark, there (is, are) fireworks in the night sky.

19. Neither the participants nor the curious onlooker (wants, want) the party to end.

20. (Is, Are) these days of merrymaking something you'd enjoy?

Consistency in Tense

Consider this paragraph:

> We (1) went downtown, and then we (2) watch a movie. Later we (3) met some friends from school, and we all (4) go to the mall. For most of the evening, we (5) play video games in arcades. It (6) was a typical but rather uneventful summer day.

Does the shifting verb tense bother you (to say nothing about the lack of development of ideas)? It should! The writer makes several unnecessary changes. Verbs 1, 3, and 6 are in the past tense, and verbs 2, 4, and 5 are in the present tense. Changing all verbs to past tense makes the paragraph much smoother.

> We went downtown, and then we watched a movie. Later we met some friends from school, and we all went to the mall. For most of the evening, we played video games in arcades. It was a typical but rather uneventful summer day.

In other instances you might want to maintain a consistent present tense. There are no inflexible rules about selecting a tense for certain kinds of writing, but you should be consistent, changing tense only for a good reason.

The present tense is most often used in writing about literature, even if the literature was written long in the past:

> *Moby Dick* is a novel about Captain Ahab's obsession with a great white whale. Ahab *sets* sail with a full crew of sailors who *think* they *are going* on merely another whaling voyage. Most of the crew *are* experienced seamen.

The past tense is likely to serve you best in writing about your personal experiences and about historical events (although the present tense can often be used effectively to establish the feeling of intimacy and immediacy):

> In the summer of 1991, Hurricane Bob *hit* the Atlantic coast region. It *came* ashore near Cape Hatteras and *moved* north. The winds *reached* a speed of more than ninety miles per hour on Cape Cod but then *slackened* by the time Bob *reached* Maine.

EXERCISE 10 | ## Making Verbs Consistent in Tense

Correct verbs as needed in the following paragraph to achieve consistency in tense. Most verbs will be past tense. (See Answer Key for answers.)

Lizzie Borden was famous for being arrested and tried for the gruesome ax murder of her father and stepmother. On August 4, 1892, when Andrew Borden was taking a nap in his home, someone hits him in the head eleven times with a hatchet. His wife, Abby Borden, had already been killed in an upstairs bedroom with the same weapon. The police investigate and conclude that Andrew's thirty-two-year-old daughter Lizzie is the murderess. Lizzie is arrested but pleaded not guilty to the crimes. Her sensational trial was followed by people all over the country. The prosecution presents an overwhelming amount of circumstantial evidence. Many people thought that she is guilty. Nonetheless, Lizzie's jury acquitted her. The case remains unsolved to this day.

Making Verbs Consistent in Tense

Correct verbs as needed in the following paragraph to achieve consistency in tense. Most verbs will be present tense.

A trip to the dentist should not be a terrible experience—unless one goes to Dr. Litterfloss, credit dentist. Although he graduated *magna cum lately* from Ed's School of Dentistry, he had a reputation for being one of the dirtiest and most careless dentists in the state. He didn't even know about germs. He never used Novocain. He just spins the chair until his patients lost consciousness. Then he shot them with his x-ray gun from behind a lead wall. Sometimes he missed, and now his dental technician glows in the dark, so he didn't need a light as he worked. While drilling with one hand, he snacked on Vienna sausages with the other. Stray alley cats and mangy curs fought around his feet for food scraps, so he didn't need a cleaning service. He seldom washed his Black and Decker drill or Craftsman chisel, and he squirts tobacco juice into his spit sink. I recommended him only with strong reservation.

Active and Passive Voice

Which of these sentences sounds better to you?

> Ken Griffey Jr. slammed a home run.

> A home run was slammed by Ken Griffey Jr.

Both sentences carry the same message, but the first expresses it more effectively. The subject (*Ken Griffey Jr.*) is the actor. The verb (*slammed*) is the action. The direct object (*home run*) is the receiver of the action. The second sentence lacks the vitality of the first because the receiver of the action is the subject; the one who performs the action is embedded in the prepositional phrase at the end of the sentence.

The first sentence demonstrates the **active voice**. It has an active verb (one that leads to the direct object), and the action moves from the beginning to the end of the sentence. The second sentence exhibits the **passive voice** (with the action reflecting back on the subject). When given a choice, you should usually select the active voice. It promotes energy and directness.

The passive voice, although not usually the preferred form, does have its uses.

- When the doer of the action is unknown or unimportant:

    My car was stolen. [The doer, a thief, is unknown.]

- When the receiver of the action is more important than the doer:

    My neighbor was permanently disabled by an irresponsible drunk driver. [The neighbor's suffering is the focus, not the drunk driver.]

As you can see, the passive construction places the doer at the end of a prepositional phrase (as in the second example) or does not include the doer in the statement at all (as in the first example). In the first example, the receiver of the action (the car) is in the subject position. The verb is preceded by *was,* a *to be* helper. Here is another example:

    The book was read by her. [passive]

    She read the book. [active]

Weak sentences often involve the unnecessary and ineffective use of the passive form; Exercises 12 and 13 give you practice in identifying the passive voice and changing it to active.

EXERCISE 12

Using Active and Passive Voice

Identify each sentence as either active voice (A) or passive voice (P). If a sentence with the passive form would be more effective in the active voice, rewrite it. (See Answer Key for answers.)

_____ 1. For centuries, pirates have harassed ships on all of the world's oceans.

_____ 2. Piracy has been defined as armed robbery on the high seas.

_____ 3. Cargo was seized and coastal towns were plundered by pirates.

_____ 4. Also, people were kidnapped and held for ransom by pirates.

_____ 5. Captains of pirate ships often flew a flag with a white skull and crossbones on a black background.

_____ 6. The swashbuckling pirate of our imagination was created by writers such as Rafael Sabatini and Lord Byron.

_____ 7. The romantic portrait of a sword-wielding, treasure-hunting ruffian in gold earrings was given to readers by books like *Captain Blood* and poems like "The Corsair."

_____ 8. As a result, pirates have often been perceived by people as ruthless but adventurous heroes.

_____ 9. Actually, though, a drunken, violent, and short life was lived by these desperate criminals.

_____ 10. The decline of piracy was caused by the development of national navies in the nineteenth century.

EXERCISE 13

Using Active and Passive Voice

Identify each sentence as either active voice (A) or passive voice (P). If a sentence with the passive form would be more effective in the active voice, rewrite it.

_____ 1. A story was reported by the *Las Vegas SUN* newspaper.

_____ 2. An accident was experienced by the Flying Elvises during a skydive in Boston.

_____ 3. Elvis Presley, King of Rock 'n' Roll, was impersonated by these high-flying stuntmen.

_____ 4. Fringed white jumpsuits, slicked-back hair, and sunglasses were worn by the four-member skydiving team.

_____ 5. The toughest part of the act involved keeping their hair in place as they fell.

_____ 6. But this time, the four Elvi were blown off course.

_____ 7. A miscalculation was made by the jumpers on that windy day.

_____ 8. Two of the Elvi hit the water in Boston Harbor.

_____ 9. A street and a yacht club were struck by the two other Elvi.

_____ 10. The accident was observed by about 1,600 confused but amused
people.

Strong Verbs

Because the verb is an extremely important part of any sentence, it should be chosen
with care. Some of the most widely used verbs are the *being* verbs: *is, was, were, are,
am.* We couldn't get along in English without them, but writers often use them when
more forceful and effective verbs are available.

Consider these examples:

Weak Verb:	He *is* the leader of the people.
Strong Verb:	He *leads* the people.
Weak Verb:	She *was* the first to finish.
Strong Verb:	She *finished* first.

EXERCISE 14   Using Strong Verbs

**Replace the weak verbs with stronger ones in the following sentences. Delete un-
necessary words to make each sentence even more concise if you can. (See Answer
Key for answers.)**

1. Like most people, Bob is afraid public speaking.

2. Public speaking is the one thing most people fear more than death!

3. Bob is full of worry about looking foolish.

4. Bob is in need of more learning about public speaking.

5. So Bob is now in attendance at Santa Ana College.

6. He is a student who has enrolled in a speech class.

7. Preparation of a speech is something that Bob learns how to do.

8. Bob is now a person who can control his anxiety.

9. To relax, Bob is taking deep breaths.

10. Bob is a confident giver of speeches.

EXERCISE 15

Using Strong Verbs

Replace the weak verbs with stronger ones in the following sentences. Delete unnecessary words to make each sentence even more concise if you can.

1. Barry Bonds was the hitter of many home runs.

2. The chef was a man with a fondness for food.

3. To graduate in two years is my plan.

4. John Hancock was the first signer of the Declaration of Independence.

5. Juanita is the organizer of the event.

6. Cooking is something she likes to do.

7. Carl was the owner of the restaurant.

8. Tiger Woods will be the winner of the tournament.

9. They were in love with each other.

10. His passion for her was in a state of demise.

Subjunctive Mood

Mood refers to the intention of the verb. Three moods are relevant to our study: indicative, imperative, and subjunctive.

The **indicative mood** expresses a statement of fact.

> I considered the issue.

> I was tired.

The **imperative mood** expresses a command (and has a *you* understood subject).

> Go to the store.

The **subjunctive mood** expresses a statement as contrary to fact, conditional, desirable, possible, necessary, or doubtful. In current English the subjunctive form is distinguishable only in two forms: The verb *to be* uses *be* throughout the present tense and *were* throughout the past tense.

> He requires that we *be* [instead of *are*] on time.

> If she *were* [instead of *was*] the candidate, she would win.

In other verbs, the final *s* is dropped in the third-person singular (*he, she, it*) of the present tense to make all forms the same in any one tense.

> I request that he *report* [instead of *reports*] today.

Here are examples of the common forms:

If I *were* [instead of *was*] you, I wouldn't do that. [contrary to fact]

She behaves as if she *were* [instead of *was*] not certain. [doubt]

I wish I *were* [instead of *was*] in Texas. [wish]

Selecting Subjunctive Verbs

Underline the subjunctive verbs. (See Answer Key for answers to 1 through 5.)

1. If she (was, were) a few years older, he would ask her out.
2. I wish I (was, were) a wealthy woman.
3. If I (was, were) rich, I'd buy you a pony.
4. They act as if they (are, were) immortal.
5. She requested that her check (is, be) mailed to her.
6. If you wish you (are, were) thinner, try this new diet.
7. You talk as if you (are, were) not coming back.
8. My attorney requested that I (am, be) released on bail.
9. Let's pretend that your theory (was, were) true.
10. If I (was, were) younger, I'd wear bikinis.

CHAPTER REVIEW   VERBS

1. **Standard usage** is appropriate for the kind of writing and speaking you are likely to do in your college work and future career.

2. Whereas **regular verbs** are predictable—having an *-ed* ending for past and past participle forms—**irregular verbs,** as the term suggests, follow no definite pattern.

   raise, raised, raised [regular]; *see, saw, seen* [irregular]

3. Certain verbs (present tense here) can be troublesome and should be studied with care (page 123).

   lie, lay   sit, set   rise, raise

4. If the subject of a sentence is singular, the verb should be singular; if the subject is plural, the verb should be plural.

   The *price* of the shoes *is* high.

   The *advantages* of that shoe *are* obvious.

5. There are no inflexible rules about selecting a **tense** for certain kinds of writing, but you should be consistent, changing tense only for a good reason.

6. Usually you should select the present tense to write about literature.

   > Herman Melville's character Bartleby the Scrivener *fails* to communicate.

   Select the past tense to write about yourself or something historical.

   > I *was* eighteen when I *decided* I *was* ready for independence.

7. English has twelve verb tenses. (See charts on pages 126–128 for names, examples, functions, and forms.)

8. The **active voice** expression (subject, active verb, and sometimes object) is usually preferred over the **passive voice** expression (subject as the receiver of action, with doer unstated or at the end of a prepositional phrase).

   > She *read* the book. [active]

   > The book *was read* by her. [passive]

9. In your revision, replace weak verbs with strong ones.

   > He *was* the first to leave. [weak verb]

   > He *left* first. [strong verb]

10. The **subjunctive mood** expresses a statement that is contrary to fact, conditional, desirable, possible, necessary, or doubtful. *Be* is used throughout the present tense and *were* throughout the past.

    > He requires that we *be* [not *are*] on time.

    > I wish I *were* [not *was*] home.

    In other verbs, the final *s* is dropped in the third-person singular (*he, she, it*) of the present tense.

    > I request that he *report* [instead of *reports*] today.

CHAPTER REVIEW EXERCISES

| REVIEW 1 | ## Changing Verb Tense |

Change the verbs from present to past tense. (See Answer Key for answers to 1 through 5.)

1. Frederick Douglass is the leading spokesman of African Americans in the 1800s.

2. Born a slave, he is befriended by his master's wife and begins to educate himself.

3. As a young man, he runs away to New Bedford, Massachusetts.

4. He works as a common laborer for some time.

5. At the Massachusetts Antislavery Society in 1841, he gives a speech on the importance of freedom.

6. His speech is so well received that he was hired to lecture on his experience as a slave.

7. While traveling on the lecture circuit, he often protests various forms of segregation.

8. He insists on sitting in "Whites Only" areas on the railroad.

9. He successfully protests against segregated schools in Rochester, New York.

10. In 1845 he publishes *Narrative of the Life of Frederick Douglass*, his autobiography.

REVIEW 2 ## Making Subjects and Verbs Agree

Underline the verb that agrees in number with the subject. (See Answer Key for answers to 1 through 5.)

1. The result of the defendant's corrupt business dealings (was, were) soon felt.

2. The mayor and most citizens (was, were) deeply affected.

3. There (was, were) no justification for the defendant's behavior.

4. Neither of the defendant's parents (was, were) willing to defend him.

5. Neither the judge nor the jury members (was, were) very sympathetic with the defense's case.

6. Ethics (was, were) apparently an unknown field of study to the defendant.

7. Each and every day (was, were) consumed with intense debate.

8. In the penalty phase, the judge said that ten years (was, were) the correct sentence.

9. Then the judge added, "Fifty thousand dollars (is, are) the right sum for restitution."

10. The defendant, along with his attorney, (was, were) not pleased.

REVIEW 3

Correcting Verb Problems

Correct problems with verb form, tense, agreement, strength, and voice. As a summary of a novel, this piece should be mostly in the present tense.

Summary of *The Old Man and the Sea*

Santiago, one of many local fishermen, have not caught a fish in eighty-four days. Young Manolin, despite the objections of his parents, has a belief in the old man. His parents says Santiago is unlucky, and they will not let their son go fishing with him.

The next day Santiago sit sail. Soon he catch a small tuna, which he used for bait. Then a huge marlin hit the bait with a strike. The old man cannot rise the fish to the surface, and it pulled the boat throughout the rest of the day and during the night.

During the second day, Santiago's hand is injured by the line and he become extremely tired, but he holds on. When the fish moves to the surface, Santiago notes that it was two feet longer than his skiff. It is the biggest fish he has ever saw. He thinks in wonder if he will be up to the task of catching it. With the line braced across his shoulders, he sleeped for a while. As he dreams gloriously of lions and porpoises and of being young, he is awaken by the fish breaking water again, and Santiago is sure the fish is tiring. He lays in the boat and waits.

On the third day, the fish came to the surface. Santiago pull steadily on the line, and finally it is harpooned and killed by Santiago. The fish is tied to the skiff by him. But sharks attacked and mutilate the huge marlin. Using an oar, he beats on the sharks courageously with all his strength, but they strips the fish to a skeleton.

With the bones still tied to the skiff, the exhausted old man returned to shore. Other fishermen and tourists marvel at the eighteen-foot skeleton of the fish as the old man lays asleep. The young boy knew he has much to learn from the old man and is determined to go fishing with him.

REVIEW 4

Using Strong Verbs

Replace the weak verbs with stronger ones in the following sentences. Delete unnecessary words to make each sentence even more concise if you can. (See Answer Key for answers to 1 through 5.)

1. Whitney is in the process of rebuilding her desktop.

2. Anika is a person who is capable of leading our group.

3. Matthew was the scorer of the last touchdown.

4. Maria is a worker at the department store.

5. Jonathan is one who attracts favorable attention.

6. Lauren has a smile that is sweet.

7. Shane is waiting for the next train.

8. Jarrett is a swift runner.

9. Jannell was the second to finish the race.

10. This review is something that makes me think.

REVIEW 5

Writing Sentences with Correct Verbs

Each of the following verbs appears in its base form. Change the verb form to the tense specified in parentheses and include it in a sentence of ten or more words. (See pages 117–121 for verb forms.)

1. eat (to past) _____

_____

_____

2. begin (to future) _____

_____

_____

3. see (to past perfect) _____

_____

_____

4. walk (to future perfect)_____

_____

_____

5. speak (to present perfect) _____

_____

_____

6. go (to future progressive) _____

_____

_____

7. drink (to present progressive) _____

_____

_____

8. dance (to past progressive) _____

_____

_____

9. fly (to present perfect progressive) _____

_____

_____

10. grow (to past perfect progressive) _____

_____

_____

11. choose (to future perfect progressive) _____

_____

_____

MICROTHEME

To practice your skills acquired in this chapter, return to the Microtheme on page 116 and complete Exercise B.

Chapter

7

Pronouns

It's not true that only owls know the difference between who's *and* whom's. *This chapter will provide you with the wisdom to master those pronouns and many more.*

Learning Objectives

Working with this chapter, I will learn to

～ use the correct form of pronouns in the subjective case and the objective case.

～ make pronouns agree with their antecedents in person, number, and gender.

～ use clear pronoun reference.

MICROTHEME

EXERCISE A

Writing Activity in Miniature

Two Purposes

Writing Diagnostic: Before you work on this chapter, the Microtheme will give you an opportunity to write briefly on an engaging topic without pressure.

Chapter Learning Application: After you have studied this chapter, return to your Microtheme to check your work and practice what you have just learned.

Form and Procedure

Like an executive summary (written for a busy boss), the Microtheme conveys ideas concisely (using no more than the space on a 5- by 8-inch card) in a specified form. Indent only once, and write small enough to leave room for marking later. Directions for practicing your chapter writing skills appear in Exercise B.

Suggested Microtheme Topic

Write a Microtheme of 80 to 100 words about needed changes in procedures, management, products, or services in your workplace; if you don't have a job, write about needed changes at home or in a class.

_____

_____

_____

_____

_____

_____

_____

_____

_____

_____

_____

_____

_____

_____

EXERCISE B

Connecting Your Learning Objectives with Your Microtheme

Complete this exercise after you have studied this chapter.

1. Underline all pronouns and consider their position in sentence structure.

2. Make sure that pronouns are in the correct cases, objective or subjective.

3. Check to make sure that pronouns agree in person, number, and gender.

4. Draw a line from each pronoun to its antecedent to make sure that it has clear reference.

Should you say, "Between you and *I*" or "Between you and *me*"? What about "Let's you and *I* do this" or "Let's you and *me* do this"? Are you confused about when to use *who* and *whom*? Is it "Everyone should wear *their* coat, or *his* coat, or *his or her* coat"? Is there anything wrong with saying, "When *you* walk down the streets of Laredo"?

The examples in the first paragraph represent the most common problems people have with pronouns. This chapter will help you identify the standard forms and understand why they are correct. The result should be additional expertise and confidence in your writing.

Pronoun Case

Case is the form a pronoun takes as it fills a position in a sentence. Words such as *you* and *it* do not change, but others do, and they change in predictable ways. For example, *I* is a subject word and *me* is an object word. As you refer to yourself, you will select a pronoun that fits a certain part of sentence structure. You say, "*I* will write the paper," not "*Me* will write the paper," because *I* is in the subject position. But you say, "She will give the apple to *me*," not "She will give the apple to *I*" because *me* is in the object position. These are the pronouns that change:

Subject	Object
I	me
he	him
she	her
we	us
they	them
who, whoever	whom, whomever

Subjective Case

	Singular	Plural
First Person:	I	we
Second Person:	you	you
Third Person:	he, she, it	they
	who	

Subjective-case pronouns can fill two positions in a sentence.

1. Pronouns in the subjective case may fill subject positions.

    a. Some will be easy to identify because they are at the beginning of the sentence.

        I dance in the park.

        He dances in the park.

        She dances in the park.

We dance in the park.

They dance in the park.

Who is dancing in the park?

b. Others will be more difficult to identify because they are not at the beginning of a sentence and may not appear to be part of a clause. The words *than* and *as* are signals for these special arrangements, which can be called incompletely stated clauses.

He is taller than *I* (am).

She is younger than *we* (are).

We work as hard as *they* (do).

The words *am, are,* and *do,* which complete the clauses, have been omitted. We are actually saying, "He is taller than I *am,*" "She is younger than *we are,*" and "We work as hard as *they do.*" The italicized pronouns are subjects of "understood" verbs.

2. Pronouns in the subjective case may refer back to the subject.
   a. They may follow a form of the verb *to be,* such as *was, were, am, is,* and *are.*

   I believe it is *he.*

   It was *she* who spoke.

   The victims were *they.*

   b. Some nouns and pronouns refer back to an earlier noun without referring back through the verb.

   The leading candidates—Pedro, Darnelle, Steve, Kimilieu, and *I*—made speeches.

Objective Case

	Singular	Plural
First Person:	me	us
Second Person:	you	you
Third Person:	him, her, it	them
	whom	

Objective-case pronouns can also fill two positions in sentences.

1. Pronouns in the objective case may fill object positions.

    a. They may be objects after the verb. A direct object answers the question *what* or *whom* in connection with the verb.

> We brought *it* to your house. [*What* did we bring? *it*]

> We saw *her* in the library. [*Whom* did we see? *her*]

An indirect object answers the question *to whom* in connection with the verb.

> I gave *him* the message. [*To whom* did I give the message? *to him*]

> The doctor told *us* the test results. [*To whom* did the doctor tell the results? *to us*]

    b. They may be objects after prepositions.

> The problem was clear to *us*.

> I went with Steve and *him*.

2. Objective-case pronouns may also refer back to object words.

> They had the results for us—Judy and *me*.

> The judge addressed the defendants—John and *her*.

Techniques for Determining Case

Here are three techniques that will help you decide which pronoun to use when the choice seems difficult.

1. If you have a compound element (such as a subject or an object of a preposition), consider only the pronoun part. The sound alone will probably tell you the answer.

> She gave the answer to Yoshi and (I, *me*).

Yoshi and the pronoun make up a compound object of the preposition *to*. Disregard the noun, *Yoshi*, and ask yourself, "Would I say, 'She gave the answer *to me* or *to I*'?" The way the words sound would tell you the answer is *to me*. Of course, if you immediately notice that the pronoun is in an object position, you need not bother with sound.

2. If you are choosing between *who* (subject word) and *whom* (object word), look to the right to see if the next verb has a subject. If it does not, the pronoun probably *is* the subject, but if it does, the pronoun probably is an object.

> The person (*who*, whom) works hardest will win. [*Who* is the correct answer because it is the subject of the verb *works*.]

> The person (who, *whom*) we admire most is José. [*Whom* is the correct answer because the next verb, *admire*, already has a subject, *we*. *Whom* is an object.]

A related technique works the same way. If the next important word after *who* or *whom* in a statement is a noun or pronoun, the correct word will almost always be *whom*. However, if the next important word is not a noun or pronoun, the correct word will be *who*.

To apply this technique, you must disregard qualifier clauses such as "I think," "it seems," and "we hope."

> Tyrone is a natural leader (*who,* whom) has charisma. [*Who* is the correct answer; it is followed by something other than a noun or pronoun.]

> Tyrone is a natural leader (*who,* whom), we think, has charisma. [*Who* is the correct answer; it is followed by the qualifier clause *we think,* which is then followed by something other than a noun or pronoun.]

> Tyrone is a natural leader (who, *whom*) we supported. [*Whom* is the correct answer; it is followed by a pronoun.]

3. *Let's* is made up of the words *let* and *us* and means "you *let us*"; therefore, when you select a pronoun to follow it, consider the two original words and select another object word—*me.*

> Let's you and (I, *me*) take a trip to Westwood. [Think of "You let us, you and me, take a trip to Westwood." *Us* and *me* are object words.]

EXERCISE 1   ## Selecting Pronouns

Underline the correct pronouns. (See Answer Key for answers.)

1. We admired his beer can collection, so he left it to (I, me) and (she, her) in his will.

2. (He, Him) and (I, me) found true love via the Lovers-R-Us.com online dating service.

3. He deserves to win more than (her, she).

4. The final showdown will be between (they, them) and (we, us).

5. No one can beat (we, us), so let's you and (I, me) apply to be contestants on the *Wheel of Fortune* game show.

6. (Us, We) attorneys resent being compared to sharks.

7. The show delighted and amazed (us, we) puppet enthusiasts.

8. The individual (who, whom) gave his mother a vacuum cleaner for Mother's Day deserves a tongue-lashing.

9. You can hire (whoever, whomever) you choose.

10. Between you and (I, me), I didn't care for the twenty-minute drum solo.

EXERCISE 2   ## Selecting Pronouns

Underline the correct pronouns.

1. (She, Her) and (I, me) went to the Ripley's Believe It or Not Museum.

2. (We, Us) young people are fascinated by the weird, the gross, and the creepy.

3. I would rather go to the museum with you than with (she, her).

4. There are those (who, whom) would urge you not to waste your money to see oddities like shrunken heads and a portrait of John Wayne made of dryer lint.

5. Robert L. Ripley, an eccentric newspaper cartoonist (who, whom) loved to travel, collected strange things.

6. He is the man (who, whom) we can thank for acquiring many of the artifacts now housed in forty-four "Odditoriums" in ten different countries.

7. (Who, Whom) wouldn't be entertained by a stuffed six-legged cow or pictures of two-headed lambs and other freaks of nature?

8. And don't forget the bizarre videos, like the one of a man (who, whom) swallows and then regurgitates a live mouse.

9. I feel sorry for (whoever, whomever) misses the replica of the "Mona Lisa" made out of croutons.

10. Just between you and (I, me), though, the wax figures of bizarre accident victims, like the man impaled on a crow bar, were a little unnerving.

EXERCISE 3

Selecting Pronouns

Underline the correct pronouns. (See Answer Key for answers.)

1. (Who, Whom) did the judges crown Zucchini Queen?

2. To (who, whom) did the wealthy widow leave her vast fortune?

3. She was a woman (who, whom) loved cats, so her pets inherited her estate.

4. For (who, whom) are you buying this handsome set of Ginsu knives?

5. I know someone (who, whom) actually likes school cafeteria food.

6. (Who, Whom) is going to get the blue ribbon for the best pickles?

7. Seventeenth-century poet John Donne warned, "Ask not for (who, whom) the bell tolls; it tolls for thee."

8. How do I know (who, whom) to trust?

9. She addressed her love letter "To (Who, Whom) It May Concern."

10. The winner of the Spelling Bee was the child (who, whom) spelled the word *sesquipedalian* correctly.

EXERCISE 4

Selecting Pronouns

Underline the correct pronouns.

1. (Who, Whom) is next in line for the throne?

2. (Who, Whom) should we call if we need help assembling our new antigravity machine?

3. We all know (who, whom) put the superglue on the boss's chair.

4. With (who, whom) are you dancing next?

5. The sailor (who, whom) swabbed the deck did an excellent job.

6. When her husband suggested that it would be fun to host a party for one hundred of their closest friends, she replied, "Fun for (who, whom)?"

7. (Who, Whom) did you marry in Las Vegas' drive-thru wedding chapel?

8. The contestant (who, whom) tripped on her evening gown and fell still managed to win first runner-up.

9. He will call the plumber, (who, whom) will know what to do.

10. "*What* you know is not as important as (who, whom) you know," he confided.

EXERCISE 5

Selecting Pronouns

Underline the correct pronouns. (See Answer Key for answers.)

1. Let's you and (I, me) consider some stories called urban legends.

2. These are stories heard by people like you and (I, me), which are passed on as if they were true.

3. We hear them from people (who, whom) have heard them from others.

4. You have probably heard more of them than (I, me), but I'll tell some anyway.

5. One is about a guard dog named Gork (who, whom) was found choking in his owner's bedroom.

6. The owner, (who, whom) loved Gork dearly, took him to the veterinarian, left him, and headed home.

7. While driving home, the owner answered his cell phone, asking "To (who, whom) am I speaking?"

8. "This is your vet calling. Just between you and (I, me), you have a big problem here."

9. "Gork has someone's detached finger stuck in his throat, and I've called the police, (who, whom) are on their way to your house."

10. Eventually the police arrested an angry armed man (who, whom) they suspected had broken into the owner's house, where Gork had bitten off and choked on the intruder's finger while the intruder, (who, whom) had crawled into a closet, passed out from loss of blood.

Selecting Pronouns

Underline the correct pronouns.

1. Another famous urban legend, involving two motorists, was told to my sister and (me, I) years ago.

2. Between you and (I, me), the story is sexist, but this is the way (we, us) heard it.

3. A motorist, (who, whom) was named Al, needed someone to push his car, so he called on Sue, his neighbor, (who, whom) lived next door.

4. "I need a push to get my car started," he said to her. "Let's you and (I, me) work together, and I'll be grateful forever."

5. "You're a special person (who, whom) I've always wanted to befriend," she said happily. "Tell me what to do."

6. "My car has an automatic transmission, which means the car won't start at less than thirty-five miles per hour," said Al, (who, whom) talked fast.

7. Al sat in his car as happy as (her, she) when he looked in his rear-view mirror and saw (she, her) heading toward his back bumper at a high speed.

8. After the collision, Al stumbled out of his car and confronted Sue, (who, whom), despite her injuries, was smiling.

9. "Look what you've done to you and (I, me)!" Al yelled.

10. "Let's you and (I, me) review what you said," she answered coolly. "You said, 'thirty-five miles per hour,' and that's exactly what I was doing."

Selecting Pronouns

Underline the correct pronouns.

1. My brother can tell this urban legend better than (I, me), but here is my version.

2. A man (who, whom) always wanted a 1958 Corvette saw one advertised in the newspaper for twenty dollars.

3. Within an hour he had purchased the car from a person named Lola, but before he drove away, he said, "(Who, Whom) is the person (who, whom) authorized you to make the sale?"

4. "It's my husband, Jake, (whom, who) I now despise because he ran away with his secretary."

5. "Last week," Lola went on, "he sent this fax: 'I've spent all my money here in Las Vegas, and Flo and (me, I) need your help.'"

6. "'Please sell my Corvette and send me the money. Just between you and (I, me), I miss you lots.'"

7. The man (who, whom) bought the Corvette said, "And now you're going to send Flo and (he, him) the money?"

8. "That's right, but he didn't tell me the price. So now I'm sending twenty dollars to this jerk (whom, who) I thought I loved."

9. That urban legend was told to my family and (I, me) when I was a wide-eyed child.

10. Some people insist that the buyer was a friend of someone (whom, who) they know.

Pronoun-Antecedent Agreement

Every pronoun refers to an earlier noun, which is called the **antecedent** of the pronoun. The antecedent is the noun that the pronoun replaces. The pronoun brings the reader back to the earlier thought. Here are some examples:

> I tried to buy *tickets* for the concert, but *they* were all sold.

> Roger painted a *picture* of a pickup truck. *It* was so good that *he* entered *it* in an art show.

A **pronoun** agrees with its antecedent in person, number, and gender. **Person**—first, second, or third—indicates perspective, or point of view. **Number** indicates singular or plural. **Gender** indicates masculine, feminine, or neuter.

Subject Words

	Singular	Plural
First Person:	I	we
Second Person:	you	you
Third Person:	he, she, it	they
	who	

Object Words

	Singular	Plural
First Person:	me	us
Second Person:	you	you
Third Person:	him, her, it	them
	whom	

Agreement in Person

Avoid needless shifting of person, which means shifting of point of view, such as from *I* to *you*. First person, second person, and third person indicate perspectives from which you can write. Select one point of view and maintain it, promoting continuity and consistency. Needless shifting of person, meaning changing perspectives without reasons important for your content and purpose, is distracting and awkward. Each point of view has its appropriate purposes.

First Person

Using the word *I* and its companion forms *we, me,* and *us,* the first-person point of view emphasizes the writer, who is an important part of the subject of the composition. Choose first person for friendly letters, accounts of personal experience, and, occasionally, business correspondence, such as a letter of application for a job, which requires self-analysis.

Observe the presence of the writer and the use of *I* in this example.

> *I* could tell that the wedding would not go well when the caterers started serving drinks before the ceremony and the bride began arguing with her future mother-in-law. After the sound system crashed, the band canceled, and *I* wished *I* hadn't come.

Second Person

Using or implying the word *you,* the second-person point of view is fine for informal conversation, advice, and directions. Although it is occasionally found in academic writing, most instructors prefer that you use it only in process analysis, instructions in how to do something.

In this example, note that the word *you* is sometimes understood and not stated.

> To juggle three balls, first *you* place two balls (A and B) in one hand and one ball (C) in the other. Then toss one of the two balls (A), and before *you* catch it with your other hand, toss the single ball (C) from that hand. Before that ball (C) lands in the other hand, toss the remaining inactive ball (B). Then pick up the balls and repeat the process until the balls no longer fall to the ground.

Third Person

Referring to subject material, individuals, things, or ideas, the third-person point of view works best for most formal writing, be it academic or professional. Third-person pronouns include *he, she, it, they, him, her,* and *them.* Most of your college writing—essay exams, reports, compositions that explain and argue, critiques, and research papers—will be from this detached perspective with no references to yourself.

In this example, written in the third person, the name *Bartleby* is replaced by forms of *he.*

> *Bartleby,* one of Herman Melville's most memorable characters, has befuddled critics for more than a century. At a point in *his* life chosen for no obvious reason, *he* decides not to work, not to cooperate with others, and not to leave the premises of *his* employer because *he* "prefer[s] not to." Most readers do not know what to make of *him.*

Correcting Problems of Agreement in Person

Most problems with pronoun agreement in person occur with the use of *you* in a passage that should have been written in the first or third person. If your composition is not one of advice or directions, the word *you* is probably not appropriate and should be replaced with a first- or third-person pronoun.

If you are giving advice or directions, use *you* throughout the passage, but if you are not, replace each *you* with a first- or third-person pronoun that is consistent with the perspective, purpose, and content of the passage.

Inconsistent:	*I* love to travel, especially when *you* go to foreign countries.
Consistent:	*I* love to travel, especially when *I* go to foreign countries.
Inconsistent:	When *you* are about to merge with moving traffic on the freeway, *one* should not stop *his or her* car.
Consistent:	When *you* are about to merge with moving traffic on the freeway, *you* should not stop *your* car.
Consistent:	When *one* is about to merge with moving traffic on the freeway, *one* should not stop *his or her* car. [using third-person pronouns, including the indefinite pronoun *one*]
Consistent:	When *drivers* are about to merge with moving traffic on the freeway, *they* should not stop *their* cars. [using third-person plural pronouns to match plural noun]

EXERCISE 8

Selecting Correct Pronouns: Person

Each of the following sentences has one or more needless changes in pronoun person. Correct each problem by crossing out the inconsistent pronoun and substituting a consistent one. Change verb forms, also, if necessary. (See Answer Key for answers.)

1. People fishing on the Amazon River know that when you hook a bloodthirsty piranha, you have to be careful of its razor-sharp teeth.

2. Most people know that you can make it rain by washing your car.

3. Some of my friends have no idea where Peru is located, but you know the words to all of the Beatles's songs.

4. I got her to admit that astrology is hooey, but you couldn't convince her to stop reading her daily horoscope.

5. Every male knows that you will seldom hear a woman laugh at the antics of the Three Stooges.

6. She knew that the seating-chart mistake was her fault because you should not place a baron above a count.

7. The magicians forgot that you can't fool everyone all of the time.

8. Wise people remind us that if you don't know history, you are doomed to repeat it.

9. They should have known that you can't keep a good woman down.

10. Pyromaniac chefs love to flambé, especially when you light the Baked Alaska on fire.

Selecting Correct Pronouns: Person

Complete the following sentences while maintaining agreement in person. Use at least one personal pronoun in each completion.

First Person
1. I know that it's important to drink enough water, so _____
_____

2. However, I sometimes drink too many sodas and cups of coffee, and _____
_____

3. Hydrating my body properly causes _____
_____

Second Person
1. If you want to make sure your body is properly hydrated, _____
_____

2. Your body functions better when _____
_____

3. Health experts recommend drinking eight glasses of water per day; therefore,
_____

Third Person
1. Health-conscious people always make sure that _____
_____

2. Healthy people know that when they drink eight glasses of water per day,
_____

3. When people feel thirsty, _____
_____

Agreement in Number

Most problems with pronoun-antecedent agreement involve **number**. The main principle is simple: If the antecedent (the word the pronoun refers back to) is singular, use a singular pronoun. If the antecedent is plural, use a plural pronoun.

1. A singular antecedent requires a singular pronoun.

    Hoang forgot *his* notebook.

2. A plural antecedent requires a plural pronoun.

    Many *students* cast *their* votes today.

3. A singular indefinite pronoun as an antecedent takes a singular pronoun. Most indefinite pronouns are singular. The following are common indefinite singular pronouns: *anybody, anyone, each, either, everybody, everyone, no one, nobody, one, somebody, someone.*

    Each of the girls brought *her* book.

    When *one* makes a promise, *one* [or *he or she*] should keep it.

4. A plural indefinite pronoun as an antecedent takes a plural pronoun.

    Few knew *their* assignments.

5. Certain indefinite pronouns do not clearly express either a singular or plural number. Agreement, therefore, depends on the meaning of the sentence. These pronouns are *all, any, none,* and *some.*

    All of the grapefruit *was* good.

    All of the grapefruits *were* gone.

    None of the cake *is* acceptable.

    None of the cakes *are* acceptable.

6. Two or more antecedents, singular or plural, take a plural pronoun. Such antecedents are usually joined by *and* or by commas and *and.*

    Howard and his *parents* bought *their* presents early.

    Students, instructors, and the *administration* pooled *their* ideas at the forum.

7. Alternative antecedents—that is, antecedents joined by *or, nor, whether/or, either/or, neither/nor, not only/but also*—require a pronoun that agrees with the nearer antecedent.

    Neither Sam nor his *friends* lost *their* way.

    Neither his friends nor *Sam* lost *his* way.

8. In a sentence with an expression such as *one of those ____ who,* the antecedent is usually the plural noun that follows.

    He is one of those *people who* want *their* money now.

9. In a sentence with the expression *the only one of those ____ who,* the antecedent is usually the singular word *one.*

    She is the *only one of* the members *who* wants *her* money now.

10. When collective nouns such as *team, jury, committee,* and *band* are used as antecedents, they take a singular pronoun if they are considered as units.

> The *jury* is doing *its* best to follow the judge's directions.

When individual behavior is suggested, antecedents take a plural form.

> The *jury* are putting on *their* coats.

11. The words *each, every,* and *many a(n)* before a noun make the noun singular.

> *Each child* and *adult* was *his or her* own authority.
>
> *Each* and *every person* doubted *himself or herself.*
>
> *Many* a person is capable of knowing *himself or herself.*

EXERCISE 10

Selecting Correct Pronouns: Number

Underline the correct pronouns. (See Answer Key for answers.)

1. The band always ends (its, their) concert with a lively tuba solo.
2. Each and every American should save money, or (they, he or she) may not have enough for retirement.
3. Each camper must bring (their, his or her) own shaving cream.
4. If the class doesn't go on the field trip, (it, they) will miss the mummy exhibit.
5. Each of those farmers knows that (he, they) must rotate (his, their) crops.
6. Pauline and Reggie left (their, his or her) hearts in San Francisco.
7. Everyone should leave (their, his or her) world a better place.
8. Neither the bride nor the bridesmaids could control (her, their) giggles during the ceremony.
9. He is one of those men who likes to shave (his, their) head bald.
10. Every rose has (its, their) thorn, every dog has (its, his or her) day, and every cloud has (its, his or her) silver lining.

EXERCISE 11

Selecting Correct Pronouns: Number

Underline the correct pronouns.

1. An army of ants made (its, their) way toward the unsuspecting picnickers.
2. The company alienated many of (its, their) faithful customers by raising prices.
3. The crowd of onlookers booed (its, their) disapproval when the knight was thrown from his horse.
4. Miguel is the only one of the bullfighters who has dared to dye (his, their) hair red.

5. Neither the pilot nor the flight attendants realized (his or her, their) mistake.

6. A parent knows when (his or her, their) child is not being honest.

7. The U.S. Marines wants (their, its) equipment in top condition.

8. The camel offers good desert transportation because of (its, their) relatively low need for water.

9. Each of the nuns wanted (her, their) groceries bagged in paper instead of plastic.

10. Several members of the chess team are setting up (its, their) boards.

Agreement in Gender

A pronoun should agree with its antecedent in **gender,** if the gender of the antecedent is specific. Masculine and feminine pronouns are gender-specific: *he, him, she, her.* Others are neuter: *I, we, me, us, it, they, them, who, whom, that, which.* The words *who* and *whom* refer to people. *That* can refer to ideas, things, and people but usually does not refer to individuals. *Which* refers to ideas and things but never to people.

> My *girlfriend* gave me *her* best advice. [feminine]
>
> Mighty *Casey* tried *his* best. [masculine]
>
> The *people* with *whom* I work are loud. [neuter]

Indefinite singular pronouns used as antecedents require, of course, singular pronouns. Handling the gender of these singular pronouns is not as obvious; opinion is divided.

1. Traditionally, writers have used the masculine form of pronouns to refer to the indefinite singular pronouns when the gender is unknown.

   > *Everyone* should work until *he* drops.

2. To avoid a perceived sex bias, use *he or she* or *his or her* instead of just *he* or *his.*

   > *Everyone* should work until *he or she* drops.

3. Although option 1 is more direct, it is illogical to many listeners and readers, and option 2 used several times in a short passage can be awkward. To avoid those possible problems, writers often use plural forms.

   > *All people* should work until *they* drop.

In any case, avoid using a plural pronoun with a singular indefinite pronoun; such usage violates the basic principle of number agreement.

> **Incorrect:**   *Everyone* should do *their* best.
>
> **Correct:**   *Everyone* should do *his or her* best.
>
> **Correct:**   *People* should do *their* best.

EXERCISE 12

Selecting Correct Pronouns: Gender and Number

Underline the correct pronoun for gender and number. (See Answer Key for answers.)

1. All of the ladies in the aerobics class were swearing through clenched teeth as (she, they) completed (her, their) five hundredth leg lift.

2. Every lifeguard at the swimming pool likes being paid as (he or she, they) works on (his or her, their) tan.

3. The Boy Scout troop was proud of (its, their) handiwork: a full-size cabin made entirely of popsicle sticks.

4. All employees at Greasy Gary's Grill always wash (his or her, their) hands before returning to work.

5. That woman and her husband are mulching (his or her, their) flower beds with cut-up credit cards.

6. A disgruntled glassblower might very well refuse to let (their, his or her) spouse have a Tupperware party.

7. Each mermaid will be carefully measured so that (her, their) scales fit properly.

8. The winners of the carnival game got to select (his or her, their) prizes from a smorgasbord of stuffed animals.

9. George, the human cannonball, had to admit that (his, their) career might be a short one.

10. Does everyone who lives in Florida paint (his or her, their) house pink?

EXERCISE 13

Selecting Correct Pronouns: Gender and Number

Correct the faulty pronouns for problems in gender and number.

1. The man which founded Tree Climbers International likes to go out on limbs as often as possible.

2. Everyone will now pause to offer their thanks to the man who invented the air conditioner.

3. The savvy airboat rider keeps their mouth closed to avoid eating bugs.

4. The individual which was abducted by aliens promises to tell all in her upcoming book.

5. People which live in stone houses should not throw glass.

6. Practically every person is bothered by their particular pet peeve.

7. Around these parts, the wooly worm is thought to predict the severity of the upcoming winter by the thickness of their coat.

8. In the summer, a cricket can reveal the temperature if you count the number of their chirps over 15 seconds.

9. Someone which adds thirty-seven to the number of the cricket's chirps will know exactly how hot it is in degrees Fahrenheit.

10. So far, the only thing the cockroach has been able to reveal is the lack of success of the restaurant they call home.

Pronoun Reference

A pronoun must refer clearly to its antecedent. Because a pronoun is a substitute word, it can express meaning clearly and definitely only if its antecedent is easily identified.

In some sentence constructions, gender and number make the reference clear.

> Dimitri and Poloma discussed *his* absences and *her* good attendance. [gender]

> If the three older boys in the *club* carry out those plans, *it* will break up. [number]

Avoid ambiguous reference. The following sentences illustrate the kind of confusion that results from structuring sentences with more than one possible antecedent for the pronoun.

> **Unclear:**   Kim gave David *his* money and clothes.
>
> **Clear:**   Kim gave his own money and clothes to David.
>
> **Unclear:**   Sarah told her sister that *her* car had a flat tire.
>
> **Clear:**   Sarah said to her sister, "Your car has a flat tire."

When using a pronoun to refer to a general idea, make sure that the reference is clear. The pronouns used frequently in this way are *this, that, which,* and *it.* The best solution may be to recast the sentence to omit the pronoun in question.

> **Unclear:**   Gabriella whistled the same tune over and over, *which* irritated me.
>
> **Clear:**   Gabriella whistled the same tune over and over, a *habit* that irritated me.
>
> **Recast:**   Her whistling the same tune over and over irritated me.

Showing Clear Pronoun References

Label each sentence as V if the pronoun reference is vague or OK if it is clear. (See Answer Key for answers.)

_____ 1. (a) The middle-aged golfers insisted on wearing knickers during the tournament, which looked ridiculous.

_____ (b) During the tournament, the middle-aged golfers insisted on wearing knickers, a fashion that looked ridiculous.

_____ 2. (a) I went back to the grocery store and told the manager that my melon was moldy.

_____ (b) I went back to the grocery store and told them that my melon was moldy.

_____ 3. (a) The judge sentenced him to watch reruns of the old *Brady Bunch* sitcom, which was unnecessarily cruel.

_____ (b) The judge sentenced him to watch reruns of the old *Brady Bunch* sitcom, a penalty that was unnecessarily cruel.

_____ 4. (a) Carmen told her grandmother that she was in need of dance lessons.

_____ (b) Carmen said to her grandmother, "I'm in need of dance dessons."

_____ 5. (a) Her grandmother agreed with Carmen that it was indeed time for her to learn to salsa.

_____ (b) Her grandmother replied that it was indeed time for Carmen to learn to salsa.

_____ 6. (a) Rex's last tattoo covered his last few inches of available skin, which has left him without a goal and slightly depressed.

_____ (b) Rex's last tattoo covered his last few inches of available skin, a situation that has left him without a goal and slightly depressed.

_____ 7. (a) The zookeeper told the nun that she had to go clean out the lion's cage.

_____ (b) The zookeeper said to the nun, "I have to go clean out the lion's cage."

_____ 8. (a) Skip made an appointment at the dentist's office so that they could polish his gold tooth until it gleamed.

_____ (b) Skip made an appointment at the dentist's office so that the hygienist could polish his gold tooth until it gleamed.

_____ 9. (a) The twelve-year-old girl told Mrs. McDonald that she didn't know the first thing about raising children.

_____ (b) The twelve-year-old girl told Mrs. McDonald, "I don't know the first thing about raising children."

_____ 10. (a) The boys pulled the girls' hair, called them names, and pelted them with mud, which inexplicably failed to stir the girls' ardor.

_____ (b) The boys pulled the girls' hair, called them names, and pelted them with mud, all of which inexplicably failed to stir the girls' ardor.

EXERCISE 15

Choosing Correct Pronouns: Reference and Agreement

Identify and correct the problems with pronoun reference and agreement.

1. I eat fast food only three times a week, which is un-American to some.

2. The supervisors told the staff members that they would be getting a big raise.

3. If a woman is looking for quality men, you should log on to www.pick-a-hunk.com.

4. She called to find out the store's hours, but they didn't answer.

5. When he smashed into the pyramid of cat food with his shopping cart, it was destroyed.

6. It says in the newspaper that an elephant is on the loose.

7. I tend to submit my assignments late, which hurts my grade.

8. The Great Oz told the Tin Man that he already possessed the thing he craved most.

9. They say that the horse named Cheese Whiz may win the Triple Crown.

10. Spiderman told Superman that he may have given up on love too soon.

CHAPTER REVIEW   PRONOUNS

1. **Case** is the form a pronoun takes as it fills a position in a sentence.

2. **Subjective-case pronouns** are *I*, *he*, and *she* (singular) and *we* and *they* (plural). *Who* can be either singular or plural.
   Subjective-case pronouns can fill subject positions.

   > *We* dance in the park.

   > It was *she* who spoke. [referring back to and meaning the same as the subject]

3. **Objective-case pronouns** are *me*, *him*, and *her* (singular) and *us* and *them* (plural). *Whom* can be either singular or plural.
   Objective-case pronouns fill object positions.

   > We saw *her* in the library. [object of verb]

   > They gave the results to *us*. [object of a preposition]

4. Three techniques are useful for deciding which pronoun case to use.
   a. If you have a compound element (such as a subject or an object of a preposition), consider only the pronoun part.

   > They will visit you and (I, me). [Consider: They will visit me.]

   b. If the next important word after *who* or *whom* in a statement is a noun or pronoun, the word choice will be *whom*; otherwise, it will be *who*. Disregard qualifier clauses such as *It seems* and *I feel*.

   > The person *whom* judges like will win.

   > The person *who* works hardest will win.

   > The person *who*, we think, worked hardest won. [ignoring the qualifier clause]

   c. *Let's* is made up of the words *let* and *us* and means *"You let us"*; therefore, when you select a pronoun to follow it, consider the two original words and select another object word—*me*.

   > Let's you and *me* go to town.

5. A pronoun agrees with its antecedent in person, number, and gender.
   a. Avoid needless shifting in **person**, which means shifting in point of view, such as from *I* to *you*.

   > "*I* was having trouble. *You* could see disaster ahead." Change to "*I* was having trouble. *I* could see disaster ahead."

   b. Most problems with pronoun-antecedent agreement involve **number**. The principles are simple: If the antecedent (the word the pronoun refers back to) is singular, use a singular pronoun. If the antecedent is plural, use a plural pronoun.

   > Royce forgot *his* notebook.

   > Many students cast *their* votes.

   > Someone lost *his or her* [not *their*] book.

c. The pronoun should agree with its antecedent in **gender,** if the gender of the antecedent is specific. Masculine and feminine pronouns are gender-specific: *he, him, she, her.* Others are neuter: *I, we, me, us, it, they, them, who, whom, that, which.* The words *who* and *whom* refer to people. *That* can refer to ideas, things, and people but usually does not refer to individuals. *Which* refers to ideas and things but not to people. To avoid a perceived sex bias, you can use *he or she* or *his or her* instead of just *he* or *his;* however, many writers simply make antecedents and pronouns plural.

> Everyone should revise *his or her* composition carefully.

> Students should revise *their* compositions carefully.

6. A pronoun must refer clearly to its antecedent. Because a pronoun is a substitute word, it can express meaning clearly and definitely only if its antecedent is easily identified.

CHAPTER REVIEW EXERCISES

Selecting Correct Pronouns: Case

Underline the correct pronouns. (See Answer Key for answers to 1 through 5.)

1. Between you and (me, I), pronouns are not that difficult.

2. Those (who, whom) have much trouble may not have studied the rules.

3. Let's you and (I, me) consider those pesky rules.

4. The opportunity offered to you and (I, me) should not be wasted.

5. (We, Us) students can lick these pronoun problems together.

6. To (whom, who) should I give credit for my success?

7. Some of the credit should go to you and (me, I).

8. I know you didn't study harder than (I, me).

9. Now I know that the person (who, whom) studies will prosper.

10. You and (I, me) should now celebrate.

Selecting Correct Pronouns: Person

Each of the following sentences has one or more needless changes in pronoun person. Correct each problem by crossing out the inconsistent pronoun and substituting a consistent one. Change verb form, also, if necessary. (See Answer Key for answers to 1 through 5.)

1. Everybody knows that you should remove high heels before attempting to

   catch a tossed bridal bouquet.

2. All people have faults, no matter who you are.

3. He tried to give her a Diamonique engagement ring, but one could tell it was fake.

4. When the metal detector's crackling indicates the possibility of loose change in the sand, you feel alive.

5. A job applicant should realize that smacking your gum noisily while answering the interviewer's questions is a no-no.

6. There was a time when almost every woman longed for a prince charming to whisk you away.

7. A man can never have too many swords in your collection.

8. A cowboy knows that you can always depend on your trusted steed.

9. I didn't think you could donate your teeth to science.

10. An ad campaign in Paris is trying to convince the French that you should be friendly to Americans.

REVIEW 3

Selecting Correct Pronouns: Number

Some of the following sentences have a problem with pronoun-antecedent number agreement. If a sentence is correct, label it C. If not, correct it. (See Answer Key for answers to 1 through 5.)

_____ 1. The famous singing group The Village People encouraged its audience to sing along to its hit "YMCA."

_____ 2. Trudy and the other trick-or-treaters all chose the hula dancer as her Halloween costume.

_____ 3. Someone with very large feet left their footprints at the scene of the flour factory explosion.

_____ 4. The sinister Olaf and his devilish sidekick will stop at nothing to carry out his evil plans.

_____ 5. The girls who run the drink stand refuse to reveal the secret ingredient in her lemonade.

_____ 6. There will be a stampede of determined shoppers as soon as the stores in the mall open its doors.

_____ 7. The phones began ringing in the Complaint Department when the company began using cheaper vinegar in their pickles.

_____ 8. The members of the Polar Bear Club eagerly anticipate its next plunge into icy Canadian waters.

_____ 9. Few of the men would admit his fondness for fondue.

_____ 10. None of the monkeys in the tree could be coaxed down from its perch.

Selecting Correct Pronouns: Gender

Correct the faulty pronoun-antecedent gender agreement in the following sentences. One sentence is correct. Rewrite the sentences as necessary. (See Answer Key for answers to 1 through 5.)

1. An individual who does not want to get their hair wet should not sit right next to the killer whale's tank.

2. A gambler should cash in their chips while they are ahead.

3. People shouldn't do the crime if he or she doesn't want to do the time.

4. Tom Thumb, one of the most popular of all the midget wrestlers, entertained their fans during the 1970s and 1980s.

5. The physicists liked to unwind by going up on the roof of his or her office building and seeing what gravity can do to a watermelon.

6. Many a bounty hunter has had to work both weekends and holidays to get their job done.

7. None of the hot dog connoisseurs could resist the once-in-a-lifetime opportunity to take his or her family to Frankfurt, the birthplace of the frankfurter.

8. The members of the band wanted to add some disco classics to their repertoire.

9. Each of Martha Stewart's viewers eagerly awaits the secret to keeping their compost pile smelling lemony fresh.

10. Each and every Elvis fan hopes to make a pilgrimage to Graceland before they die.

REVIEW 5

Selecting Correct Pronouns: References

Identify and correct the problems with pronoun reference. (See Answer Key for answers to 1 through 5.)

1. He joined the Marine Corps and that straightened him out.

2. Joe told Rick that he wanted to cut his hair.

3. They say that you can fool some of the people some of the time, but you can't fool all of the people all of the time.

4. They say that senior citizens should get a flu shot every year.

5. Betty Sue told Rhonda Ann that her sauerkraut was the best in town.

6. When their son began drum lessons, they soundproofed the walls, but it still got through.

7. In the school cafeteria, you can choose between slop, gruel, or mystery meat.

8. Fay told her daughter that she was grouchy.

9. They say that time heals all wounds.

10. He told her he was planning to shave his head, which made her laugh.

REVIEW 6

Writing Sentences with Correct Pronouns

Write a sentence using each of the following words. Do not use the word as the first one in the sentence. One sentence should contain the word *between* before a pronoun such as "between you and _____."

1. she _____

_____

_____

2. her _____

_____

_____

3. him _____

_____

_____

4. us _____

_____

_____

5. who _____

_____

_____

6. whom _____

_____

_____

7. me _____

_____

_____

8. I _____

_____

_____

9. they _____

_____

_____

10. them _____

_____

_____

MICROTHEME

To practice your skills acquired in this chapter, return to the Microtheme on page 147 and complete Exercise B.

Chapter

8

Adjectives and Adverbs

When we relate to close friends and family members, we may be able to convey simple ideas and feelings by using only grunts and gestures. But when we need to communicate more complex messages with people we hardly know, we depend on precise words, often adjectives and adverbs.

FLOW OF WRITING

Learning Objectives

Working with this chapter, I will learn to

∿ recognize adjectives and adverbs.

∿ use adjectives and adverbs more precisely.

∿ avoid dangling modifiers.

∿ avoid misplaced modifiers.

MICROTHEME

EXERCISE A

Writing Activity in Miniature

Two Purposes

Writing Diagnostic: Before you work on this chapter, the Microtheme will give you an opportunity to write briefly on an engaging topic without pressure.

Chapter Learning Application: After you have studied this chapter, return to your Microtheme to check your work and practice what you have just learned.

Form and Procedure

Like an executive summary (written for a busy boss), the Microtheme conveys ideas concisely (using no more than the space on a 5- by 8-inch card) in a specified form. Indent only once, and write small enough to leave room for marking later. Directions for practicing your chapter writing skills appear in Exercise B.

Suggested Microtheme Topic
Write a Microtheme of 80 to 100 words about three items you would place in a time capsule to be opened in fifty years. Explain why the items are significant.

_____

_____

_____

_____

_____

_____

_____

_____

_____

_____

_____

_____

_____

_____

EXERCISE B

Connecting Your Learning Objectives with Your Microtheme

Complete this exercise after you have studied this chapter.

1. Underline adjectives and adverbs, and make sure they are necessary and well-selected.

2. Be sure you have not dangled or misplaced modifiers. If in question, you should underline the modifier and draw a line to the word being modified.

FLOW OF WRITING

Adjectives modify (describe) nouns and pronouns and answer the questions *Which one? What kind?* and *How many?*

> *Which one?* The <u>new</u> <u>car</u> is mine.
>   adj   n

> *What kind?* <u>Mexican</u> <u>food</u> is my favorite.
>   adj   n

> *How many?* A <u>few</u> <u>friends</u> are all one needs.
>   adj   n

Adverbs modify verbs, adjectives, and other adverbs and answer the questions *How? Where? When? Why?* and *To what degree?* Most words ending in *-ly* are adverbs.

> *Where?* The cuckoo <u>flew</u> <u>south</u>.
>   v   adv

> When? The cuckoo <u>flew</u> <u>yesterday</u>.
>   v   adv

> Why? The cuckoo <u>flew</u> <u>because of the cold weather</u>.
>   v   adv phrase

> How? The cuckoo <u>flew</u> <u>swiftly</u>.
>   v   adv

> <u>Without adjectives and adverbs</u>, <u>even</u> John Steinbeck, the <u>famous</u>
>   adv phrase   adv   adj

> <u>Nobel Prize–winning</u> author, <u>surely</u> could <u>not</u> have described the
>   adj   adv   adv

> <u>crafty</u> octopus <u>very</u> <u>well</u>.
>   adj   adv   adv

We have two concerns regarding the use of adjectives and adverbs (modifiers) in writing. One is a matter of **diction,** or word choice—in this case, how to select adjectives and adverbs that will strengthen the writing. The other is how to identify and correct problems with modifiers.

Selecting Adjectives and Adverbs

If you want to finish the sentence "She was a(n) _____ speaker," you have many adjectives to select from, including these:

distinguished	irritating	profound	persuasive
influential	colorful	polished	long-winded
adequate	boring	abrasive	humorous

If you want to finish the sentence "She danced _____," you have another large selection, this time adverbs such as the following:

comically	catatonically	slowly	zestfully
gracefully	awkwardly	carnally	smoothly
mechanically	limply	serenely	frantically

Adjectives and adverbs can be used to enhance communication. If you have a thought, you know what it is, but when you deliver that thought to someone else, you may not say or write what you mean. Your thought may be eloquent and your word choice weak. Keep in mind that no two words mean exactly the same thing.

Further, some words are vague and general. If you settle for a common word such as *good* or a slang word such as *neat* to characterize something you like, you will be limiting your communication. Of course, those who know you best may understand fairly well; after all, people who are really close may be able to convey ideas using only grunts and gestures.

But what if you want to write to someone you hardly know to explain how you feel about an important issue? Then the more precise the word, the better the communication. By using modifiers, you may be able to add significant information. Keep in mind, however, that anything can be overdone; therefore, use adjectives and adverbs wisely and economically.

Your first resource in searching for more effective adjectives should be your own vocabulary storehouse. Another resource is a good thesaurus (book of synonyms). Finally, you may want to collaborate with others to discuss and share ideas.

Supply the appropriate modifiers in the following exercises, using a dictionary, a thesaurus, or the resources designated by your instructor.

EXERCISE 1   ## Supplying Adjectives

Provide adjectives to modify these nouns. Use only single words, not adjective phrases.

1. A(n) _____ dog

2. A(n) _____ comedian

3. A(n) _____ voice

4. A(n) _____ neighbor

5. A(n) _____ ballplayer

6. A(n) _____ party

7. A(n) _____ singer

8. A(n) _____ date

9. A(n) _____ car

10. A(n) _____ job

EXERCISE 2	**Supplying Adverbs**

Provide adverbs to modify these verbs. Use only single words, not adverb phrases.

1. sleep _____

2. run _____

3. talk _____

4. walk _____

5. kiss _____

6. smile _____

7. drive _____

8. leave _____

9. laugh _____

10. eat _____

Comparative and Superlative Forms

For making comparisons, most adjectives and adverbs have three different forms: the positive (one), the comparative (comparing two), and the superlative (comparing three or more).

Adjectives

1. Some adjectives follow a regular pattern.

Positive (one)	Comparative (comparing two)	Superlative (comparing three or more)
nice	nicer	nicest
rich	richer	richest
big	bigger	biggest
tall	taller	tallest
lonely	lonelier	loneliest
terrible	more terrible	most terrible
beautiful	more beautiful	most beautiful

These are usually the rules:

a. Add -er (or -r) to short adjectives (one or two syllables) to rank units of two.

Julian is *nicer* than Sam.

b. Add *-est* (or *-st*) to short adjectives (one or two syllables) to rank units of three or more.

> Of the fifty people I know, Julian is the *kindest*.

c. Add the word *more* to long adjectives (three or more syllables) to rank units of two.

> My hometown is *more beautiful* than yours.

d. Add the word *most* to long adjectives (three or more syllables) to rank units of three or more.

> My hometown is the *most beautiful* in all America.

2. Some adjectives are irregular in the way they change to show comparison.

Positive (one)	Comparative (comparing two)	Superlative (comparing three or more)
good	better	best
bad	worse	worst

Adverbs

1. Some adverbs follow a regular pattern.

Positive (one)	Comparative (comparing two)	Superlative (comparing three or more)
clearly	more clearly	most clearly
quickly	more quickly	most quickly
carefully	more carefully	most carefully
thoughtfully	more thoughtfully	most thoughtfully

a. Add *-er* to some one-syllable adverbs for the comparative form and add *-est* for the superlative form.

> My piglet runs *fast*. [positive]
>
> My piglet runs *faster* than your piglet. [comparative]
>
> My piglet runs *fastest* of all known piglets. [superlative]

b. Add the word *more* to form comparisons of longer adverbs and the word *most* to form the superlative forms.

> Shanelle reacted *happily* to the marriage proposal. [positive]
>
> Shanelle reacted *more happily* to the marriage proposal than Serena. [comparative]
>
> Of all the women Clem proposed to, Shanelle reacted *most happily*. [superlative]

c. In some cases, the word *less* may be substituted for *more*, and the word *least* for *most*.

> Mort's views were presented *less effectively* than Al's. [comparative]
>
> Of all the opinions that were shared, Mort's views were presented *least effectively*. [superlative]

2. Some adverbs are irregular in the way they change to show comparisons.

Positive (one)	Comparative (comparing two)	Superlative (comparing three or more)
well	better	best
far	farther (distance)	farthest (distance)
	further	furthest
badly	worse	worst

Using Adjectives and Adverbs Correctly

1. Avoid double negatives. Words such as *no, not, none, nothing, never, hardly, barely,* and *scarcely* should not be combined.

Double Negative: I do *not* have *no* time for recreation. [incorrect]

Single Negative: I have *no* time for recreation. [correct]

Double Negative: I've *hardly never* lied. [incorrect]

Single Negative: I've *hardly* ever lied. [correct]

2. Do not confuse adjectives with adverbs. Among the most commonly confused adjectives and adverbs are *good/well, bad/badly,* and *real/really.* The words *good, bad,* and *real* are always adjectives. *Well* is sometimes an adjective. The words *badly* and *really* are always adverbs. *Well* is usually an adverb.

To distinguish these words, consider what is being modified. Remember that adjectives modify nouns and pronouns and that adverbs modify verbs, adjectives, and other adverbs.

Incorrect: I feel *badly* today. [We're concerned with the condition of I.]

Correct: I feel *bad* today. [The adjective *bad* modifies the pronoun I.]

Incorrect: She feels *well* about that choice. [We're concerned with the condition of *she*.]

Correct: She feels *good* about that choice. [The adjective *good* modifies the pronoun *she*.]

Incorrect: Ted plays the piano *good*. [The adjective *good* modifies the verb *plays*, but adjectives should not modify verbs.]

Correct: Ted plays the piano *well*. [The adverb *well* modifies the verb *plays*.]

Incorrect: He did *real* well. [Here the adjective *real* modifies the adverb *well*, but adjectives should not modify adverbs.]

Correct: He did *really* well. [The adverb *really* modifies the adverb *well*.]

3. Do not use an adverb such as *very, more,* or *most* before adjectives such as *perfect, round, unique, square,* and *straight.*

Incorrect: It is *more* round.

Correct: It is round.

Correct: It is *more nearly* round.

4. Do not double forms, such as *more lonelier* or *most loneliest*.

Incorrect: Julie was *more nicer* than Jake.

Correct: Julie was *nicer* than Jake.

EXERCISE 3

Selecting Adjectives and Adverbs

Underline the correct adjective or adverb. (See Answer Key for answers.)

1. Betty Skelton was one of the (most, more) successful female stunt pilots of the 1940s and 1950s.

2. In the 1930s and 1940s, the public was (real, really) interested in watching acrobatic air shows.

3. Skelton was (not hardly, hardly) going to sit there and watch the men have all the fun.

4. She wanted (bad, badly) to learn to fly, and she was (real, really) adventurous, so she learned to perform daredevil feats.

5. Her small, agile airplane, which was named Little Stinker, performed tricks (well, good.)

6. One of her (better, best) stunts was the inverted ribbon cut.

7. It was a (real, really) thrill to watch her fly upside down twelve feet off the ground and use her propeller to slice a foil strip strung between two poles.

8. The crowd could (not hardly, hardly) contain its excitement.

9. She earned only $25 for each air show, so the pay was (bad, badly).

10. But according to Betty, her six-year acrobatic flying career was the (more, most) enjoyable time in her life.

EXERCISE 4

Selecting Adjectives and Adverbs

Correct any problems with adjectives and adverbs in the following sentences. (See Answer Key for answers.)

1. Today, in the twenty-first century, dressing like 1960s hippies is a real big trend among young people.

2. There are some signs that the 1970s, when fashion has never been worser, is next.

3. Women are already stomping around in the most biggest platform shoes I've ever seen.

4. I do not have no regrets about wearing a lot of polyester in the 1970s.

5. But we can only pray that powder-blue leisure suits with wide lapels don't never come back into style.

6. Men thought they looked real suave when they wore these suits with shirts unbuttoned to show their chest hair and gold chains.

7. The male disco dancer thought he could dance especially good in white gabardine pants like the ones John Travolta wore in *Saturday Night Fever.*

8. Remember that in the 1970s, a very unique look was achieved with fashions like knee-high glitter socks and hats made out of beer cans crocheted together.

9. Women thought they looked well in knee-length corduroy gaucho pants and dingo boots.

10. Was there never no sillier piece of jewelry than the mood ring?

EXERCISE 5   Selecting Adjectives and Adverbs

Underline the correct word or words. (See Answer Key for answers.)

1. In the early 1900s, if you were (real, really) (good, well) at tug-of-war, you could have competed in the Olympics.

2. Tug-of-war used to be an Olympic sport, but it's not (no, any) more.

3. I can (not, not hardly) believe that sports like golf and croquet used to be part of the Olympic Games, too.

4. Today, one of the (odder, oddest) of all of the Olympic sports is curling.

5. No, it's not a competition to see which hairdresser can create the (more, most) beautiful style.

6. And curling enthusiasts get (real, really) angry if you compare their sport to shuffleboard on ice.

7. But when people see curlers sweeping the ice with brooms to help a 42-pound rock glide better, they often conclude that the sport is one of the (stranger, strangest) they've ever seen.

8. Another odd Olympic sport is for those who can ski and shoot rifles (good, well).

9. In the biathlon, the athlete who takes home the gold is the one who hits targets (best, better) and skis (faster, fastest).

10. The triathlon combines swimming, cycling, and running, but a blend of cross-country skiing and marksmanship seems (more, most) odd.

EXERCISE 6   ## Selecting Adjectives and Adverbs

Correct any problems with adjectives and adverbs in the following sentences.

1. After her eighth cup of coffee, she is one of the most liveliest women in the office.

2. He wanted the fry cook job real bad, but his interview didn't go good.

3. As he strolled through Bronco Bob's Bar and Boot Shop, he knew that he had never seen a more perfect setting for a square dance.

4. He was real sorry for eating her artistic masterpiece, so he offered his sincere apologies.

5. Of the two weightlifters, Carlos is best at clean-and-jerk lifts.

6. She looks well in Spandex and sequins.

7. After her divorce, she finally felt happily.

8. The skater fell during every one of her jumps, so she performed pretty bad.

9. My baby cries louder than that baby.

10. In a blind taste test, most consumers said that Squirt was the better of the three leading brands of imitation cheese food.

Dangling and Misplaced Modifiers

Modifiers should clearly relate to the word or words they modify.

1. A modifier that fails to modify a word or group of words already in the sentence is called a **dangling modifier.**

   Dangling: *Walking down the street*, a snake startled him. [Who was walking down the street? The person isn't mentioned in the sentence.]

   Correct: *Walking down the street*, Don was startled by a snake.

Correct: As *Don* walked down the street, *he* was startled by a snake.

Dangling: *At the age of six,* my uncle died. [Who was six years old? The person isn't mentioned in the sentence.]

Correct: *When I was six,* my uncle died.

2. A modifier that is placed so that it modifies the wrong word or words is called a **misplaced modifier.** The term also applies to words that are positioned so as to unnecessarily divide closely related parts of sentences such as infinitives (*to* plus verb) or subjects and verbs.

Misplaced: The sick man went to a doctor *with a high fever.*

Correct: The sick man *with a high fever* went to a doctor.

Misplaced: I saw a great movie *sitting in my pickup.*

Correct: *Sitting in my pickup,* I saw a great movie.

Misplaced: Kim found many new graves *walking through the cemetery.*

Correct: *Walking through the cemetery,* Kim found many new graves.

Misplaced: I forgot all about my sick dog *kissing my girlfriend.*

Correct: *Kissing my girlfriend,* I forgot all about my sick dog.

Misplaced: They tried to *earnestly and sincerely* complete the task. [splitting of the infinitive *to complete*]

Correct: They tried *earnestly and sincerely* to complete the task.

Misplaced: My neighbor, *while walking to the store,* was mugged. [unnecessarily dividing the subject and verb]

Correct: *While walking to the store,* my neighbor was mugged.

Try this procedure in working through Exercises 7, 8, and 9.

1. Circle the modifier.

2. Draw an arrow from the modifier to the word or words it modifies.

3. If the modifier does not relate directly to anything in the sentence, it is dangling; recast the sentence.

4. If the modifier does not modify the nearest word or words, or if it interrupts related sentence parts, it is misplaced; reposition it.

EXERCISE 7   Correcting Dangling and Misplaced Modifiers

Each of the following sentences has a dangling (D) or a misplaced (M) modifier. Identify the problems and correct them by rewriting the sentences. (See Answer Key for answers.)

_____ 1. Driving through the Brazilian rain forest, leafcutter ants were spotted going about their work.

_____ 2. This tribe of ants is one of the few creatures on this planet that grows food.

_____ 3. Leafcutter ants learned to cleverly farm over 50 million years ago.

_____ 4. Climbing trees, the leaves are cut down and bitten into the shape of half-moons.

_____ 5. Then each ants hoists a leaf and carries it back down the tree toward the nest, weighing ten times more than it does.

_____ 6. Marching home with their leaves, a parade of fluttering green flags is what the ants resemble.

_____ 7. Carried into the subterranean tunnels of the nest, the leafcutters deposit their cargo.

_____ 8. Taking over, the leaves are cleaned, clipped, and spread with secretions from tiny gardener ants' bodies.

_____ 9. Lined up in neat rows, the ants place fungus on the hunks of leaves.

_____ 10. Cultivated for food, the ants use the leaves as fertilizer for their fungus garden.

EXERCISE 8

Correcting Dangling and Misplaced Modifiers

Each of the following sentences has a dangling (D) or a misplaced (M) modifier. Identify the problems and correct them by rewriting the sentences.

_____ 1. Changing the oil regularly, a car runs better and lasts longer.

_____ 2. The crusty old sailor went to the fortuneteller with bad luck.

_____ 3. The bartender decided to make an appointment to see a psychologist with a drinking problem.

_____ 4. Reaching speeds of 180 miles per hour, the fans were thrilled by the race cars.

_____ 5. I decided to sell my parrot with reluctance.

_____ 6. Breathing deeply the intoxicating scent of new shoes, she felt her adrenaline begin to uncontrollably flow.

_____ 7. Carlos was determined to quickly amass his fortune at the blackjack table and retire early.

_____ 8. Swimming in a butter and garlic sauce, the diners relished every bite of the shrimp.

_____ 9. He wanted to badly propose to her and make her his bride.

_____ 10. I decided to foolishly purchase the solar-powered electric blanket.

Correcting Dangling and Misplaced Modifiers

Each of the following sentences has a dangling (D) or a misplaced (M) modifier. Identify the problems and correct them by rewriting the sentences.

_____   1. I observed the parade of floats and marching bands on the rooftop.

_____   2. Flat busted, my piano had to be pawned for cash.

_____   3. The alleged burglar addressed the judge on his knees.

_____   4. Freshly snared from the ocean floor, he enjoyed the delicious lobster.

_____   5. Wearing a strapless velvet evening gown, Bob thought his wife looked ravishing.

_____   6. The student asked to see the school nurse with a sore throat.

_____   7. The lost child held on tight to the detective crying for his mommy.

_____   8. Cursing like a longshoreman, the baby finally arrived after her thirty-sixth hour of labor.

_____   9. By jumping on a trampoline, your heart gets a good cardiovascular workout.

_____ 10. The outlaw phoned his granny in a pickle.

CHAPTER REVIEW   ADJECTIVES AND ADVERBS

1. **Adjectives** modify (describe) nouns and pronouns and answer the questions *Which one? What kind?* and *How many?*

2. **Adverbs** modify verbs, adjectives, and other adverbs and answer the questions *Where? When? Why? How?* and *To what degree?* Most words ending in *-ly* are adverbs.

3. Anything can be overdone; therefore, use adjectives and adverbs like gravy, sparingly.

4. Some adjectives follow a regular pattern.

    nice, nicer, nicest

    lonely, more lonely, most lonely

    These are usually the rules:

    a. Add *-er* to short adjectives (one or two syllables) to rank units of two.

    Jethro is *shorter* than Cy.

    b. Add *-est* to short adjectives (one or two syllables) to rank units of more than two.

    Senator Goodyear is the *brightest* person in Congress.

    c. Add the word *more* to long adjectives (three or more syllables) to rank units of two.

    Your state is *more* prosperous than mine.

    d. Add the word *most* to long adjectives (three or more syllables) to rank units of three or more.

    Your state is the *most* prosperous state in the West.

    e. Some adjectives are irregular in the way they change to show comparison.

    good, better, best

    bad, worse, worst

5. Some adverbs follow a regular pattern.

    sadly, more sadly, most sadly

    carefully, more carefully, most carefully

    a. Add *-er* to some one-syllable adverbs for the comparative form and add *-est* for the superlative form.

    Pierre works *hard*. [positive]

    Pierre works *harder* than Simon. [comparative]

    Pierre works *hardest* of all students in the class. [superlative]

b. Add the word *more* to adverbs of two or more syllables for the comparative form and the word *most* to adverbs of two or more syllables for the superlative form.

> Sultana proofread *carefully.* [positive]
>
> Sultana proofread *more carefully* than Venny. [comparative]
>
> Sultana proofread *most carefully* of all in the class. [superlative]

c. In some cases the word *less* may be substituted for *more* and the word *least* for *most.*

> Martelle examined the contract *less carefully* during her second reading. [comparative]
>
> Martelle examined the contract *least carefully* during her third reading. [superlative]

d. Some adverbs are irregular in the way they change to show comparisons.

> *well, better, best*
>
> *badly, worse, worst*

6. Use adjectives and adverbs correctly.

a. Avoid double negatives. Words such as *no, not, none, nothing, never, hardly, barely,* and *scarcely* should not be combined.

b. Do not confuse adjectives with adverbs. Among the most commonly confused adjectives and adverbs are *good/well, bad/badly,* and *real/really.* The words *good, bad,* and *real* are always adjectives. *Well* is sometimes an adjective. The words *badly* and *really* are always adverbs. *Well* is usually an adverb.

Incorrect: Clint did *good.* [*Good* is not an adverb.]

Correct: Joline felt *good.* [*Good* does not address the matter of feeling; it indicates the condition of the subject, *Joline.*]

Correct: Clint did *well.* [Used here as an adverb, *well* modifies the verb *did.*]

Correct: Sigmund said, "Carl, you are not a *well* person." [Used here as an adjective, *well* modifies the noun *person.*]

Incorrect: Elvis was *real* happy with his new disguise. [*Happy* is an adjective modifying the noun *Elvis,* and *real* modifies that adjective. Because only adverbs modify adjectives, we need the word *really.*]

Correct: Elvis was *really* happy with his new disguise.

Incorrect: I feel *badly.* [*Badly* is an adverb but here indicates the condition of the subject; therefore, it modifies the pronoun *I.*]

Correct: I feel *bad.* [*Bad* is an adjective modifying the pronoun *I.*]

Correct: I explained that *badly.* [*Badly,* an adverb, modifies the verb *explained.*]

    c. Do not use an adverb such as *very, more,* or *most* before adjectives such as *perfect, round, unique, square,* and *straight.*

        Incorrect: It is *more square.*

        Correct: It is *square.*

        Correct: It is *more nearly square.*

    d. Do not double forms such as *more lonelier* or *most loneliest.*

        Incorrect: She is *more smarter* than I.

        Correct: She is *smarter* than I.

7. A **dangling modifier** gives information but fails to make clear which word or group of words it refers to.

        Incorrect: *Ignoring the traffic signals,* the car crashed into a truck. [The car is not ignoring; the driver is.]

        Correct: *Ignoring the traffic signals,* the driver crashed his car into a truck.

8. A **misplaced modifier** is placed so that it modifies the wrong word or words.

        Incorrect: The monkeys attracted the attention of the elegant women *who picked fleas off one another.*

        Correct: The monkeys *who picked fleas off one another* attracted the attention of the elegant women.

CHAPTER REVIEW EXERCISES

| REVIEW 1 | ## Using Correct Modifiers |

Correct problems with modifiers. (See Answer Key for answers to the first paragraph.)

In 1951, Sir Hugh Beaver, who was the managing director of the Guinness Brewery, became embroiled in an argument about which bird was the faster game bird in Europe. He wondered if a book that supplied the answers to such burning questions would sell good. So, he worked with a fact-finding agency to compile what became *The Guinness Book of World Records,* first published in 1955. The book proved to be popularer than all other books Climbing to the top of the British bestseller lists. Over the years, more than 94 million copies of the book's editions have been sold in 100 different countries and 37 different languages, making it the top-selling copyrighted book of all time. Today, of course, Guinness World Records is still a household name. The organization continues to be the better known collector and verifier of records set around the globe.

Some of the Guinness records—such as oldest living person, largest animal, and worst flood—are set automatic without any special effort on the part of the record-holder. Other people, though, intentional set records Seeking a moment in the spotlight. These individuals think up some very creatively and often crazy stunts to perform, usual in front of large crowds. Rattling at full-throttle, one man won his place in history by juggling three chainsaws the longest (44 throws). Wearing only swimming trunks, a tub filled with ice was where another man set the record for the "Longest Full-body Ice Contact Endurance" (66 minutes 4 seconds). And there's actual a record for longest underwater pogo-stick jumping (3 hours 40 minutes), which was achieved in the Amazon River. Apparently, as long as people want to know about these odd accomplishments, Guinness World Records will be there to list them for us.

REVIEW 2

Writing Short Paragraphs Containing Adjectives and Adverbs

For each numbered item, write a short paragraph using the words in parentheses.

1. (good, better, best) _____

_____

_____

_____

_____

_____

2. (good, well) _____

_____

_____

_____

_____

_____

_____

3. (more, most) _____

_____

_____

_____

_____

_____

4. (bad, badly) _____

_____

_____

_____

_____

_____

5. (real, really) _____

_____

_____

_____

_____

_____

MICROTHEME

To practice your skills acquired in this chapter, return to the Microtheme on page 173 and complete Exercise B.

Balancing Sentence Parts

When the wheels on your car start to wobble, you must drive to a repair shop to have them balanced. But if your sentences start to wobble, you can apply the principles of parallelism discussed in this chapter and fix them yourself.

FLOW OF WRITING

Learning Objectives

Working with this chapter, I will learn to

~ identify words that signal parallel structure.

~ identify combination words that signal parallel structure.

~ avoid awkwardness of expression by selecting words that are parallel in form and thought.

MICROTHEME

EXERCISE A

Writing Activity in Miniature
Two Purposes

Writing Diagnostic: Before you work on this chapter, the Microtheme will give you an opportunity to write briefly on an engaging topic without pressure.

Chapter Learning Application: After you have studied this chapter, return to your Microtheme to check your work and practice what you have just learned.

Form and Procedure

Like an executive summary (written for a busy boss), the Microtheme conveys ideas concisely (using no more than the space on a 5- by 8-inch card) in a specified form. Indent only once, and write small enough to leave room for marking later. Directions for practicing your chapter writing skills appear in Exercise B.

Suggested Microtheme Topic

Write a Microtheme of 80 to 100 words about your best boss or guardian. Emphasize the important qualities of that person.

_____

_____

_____

_____

_____

_____

_____

_____

_____

_____

_____

_____

_____

_____

EXERCISE B

Connecting Your Learning Objectives with Your Microtheme

Complete this exercise after you have studied this chapter.

1. Circle signal words and combination signal words.

2. Underline words that are parallel and linked by signal words and combination signal words.

3. Be sure that the parallel words are balanced in form and thought.

We are surrounded by balance. Watch a colorful cross-frame, or diamond, kite as it soars in the sky. If you draw an imaginary line from the top to the bottom of the kite, you will see corresponding parts on either side. If you were to replace one of the sides with a loose-flapping fabric, the kite would never fly. A similar lack of balance can also cause a sentence to crash.

Consider these statements:

> "*To be or not to be*—that is the question." [dash added]

This line from *Hamlet,* by William Shakespeare, is one of the most famous lines in literature. Compare it to the well-balanced kite in a strong wind. Its parts are parallel and it "flies" well.

> "*To be or not being*—that is the question."

It still vaguely resembles the sleek kite, but now the second phrase causes it to dip like an unbalanced kite. Lurching, the line begins to lose altitude.

> "*To be or death is the other alternative*—that is the question."

The line slams to the floor. Words scatter across the carpet. We go back to the revision board.

The first sentence is forceful and easy to read. The second is more difficult to follow. The third is almost impossible to understand. We understand it only because we know what it should look like from having read the original. The point is that perceptive readers are as critical of sentences as kite-watchers are of kites.

Basic Principles of Parallelism

Parallelism as it relates to sentence structure is usually achieved by joining words with similar words: nouns with nouns, adjectives (words that describe nouns and pronouns) with adjectives, adverbs (words that describe verbs, adjectives, and other adverbs) with adverbs, and so forth.

> *Men, women,* and *children* enjoy the show. [nouns]
>
> The players are *excited, eager,* and *enthusiastic.* [adjectives]
>
> The author wrote *skillfully* and *quickly.* [adverbs]

Parallel structure may also be achieved by joining groups of words with similar groups of words: prepositional phrase with prepositional phrase, clause with clause, sentence with sentence.

> She fell *in love* and *out of love* in a few minutes. [prepositional phrases]
>
> *Who he was* and *where he came from* did not matter. [clauses]
>
> *He came in a hurry. He left in a hurry.* [sentences]

Parallelism means balancing one structure with another of the same kind. Faulty parallel structure is awkward and draws unfavorable attention to what is being said.

Nonparallel:	Vince Carter's reputation is based on his ability in *passing, shooting,* and *he is good at rebounds.*
Parallel:	Vince Carter's reputation is based on his ability in *passing, shooting,* and *rebounding.*

In the nonparallel sentence, the words *passing* and *shooting* are of the same kind (verblike words used as nouns), but the rest of the sentence is different. You don't have to know terms to realize that there is a problem of balance in sentence structure. Just read the material aloud. Then compare it with the statement in which *he is good at rebounds* has been changed to *rebounding* to make a sentence that's easy on the eye, ear, and brain.

Signal Words

Some words signal parallel structure. If you use *and*, the items joined by *and* should almost always be parallel. If they aren't, then *and* is probably inappropriate.

> The weather is hot *and* humid. [*and* joins adjectives]

> The car *and* the trailer are parked in front of the house. [*and* joins nouns]

The same principle is true for *but,* although it implies a direct contrast. Where contrasts are being drawn, parallel structure is essential to clarify those contrasts.

> He *purchased* a Dodger Dog, *but* I *chose* the Stadium Peanuts. [*but* joins contrasting clauses]

> She *earned* an A in math *but failed* her art class. [*but* joins contrasting verbs]

You should regard all the coordinating conjunctions (FANBOYS: *for, and, nor, but, or, yet, so*) as signals for parallel structure.

EXERCISE 1

Identifying Signal Words and Parallel Elements

Underline the parallel elements—words, phrases, or clauses—and circle the signal words in the following sentences. The sentences in Exercises 1 through 9 are based on video review excerpts from *Movie Guide* by the Wherehouse; the film titles are shown in parentheses. (See Answer Key for answers.)

> **Example:**   One by one they <u>are stalked</u>, <u>terrorized</u>, (and) <u>murdered</u>. (*The Howling*)

1. The residents become the target of vicious, relentless, and inexplicable attacks by hordes of birds. (*The Birds*)

2. A family moves into a supposedly haunted New York home, and it finds that the house is inoperative. (*The Amityville Horror*)

3. While the family members try to make a comfortable life for themselves and to ignore a few irritations, all hell breaks loose.

4. Muffy invited her college friends to her parents' secluded island home but neglected to tell them it might be the last day of their lives. (*April Fool's Day*)

5. A woman discovers that her young daughter has inherited an evil streak and has caused the death of several people. (*The Bad Seed*)

6. A physician surgically separates Siamese twins, and they hate him. (*Basket Case*)

7. One twin is normal, and the other is horribly deformed.

8. The deformed twin becomes an embittered and vindictive person.

9. In a final unreasoning, angry, and brutal assault, she rips the face off the doctor.

10. A slimy alien crashes to earth and devours everyone in its path. (*The Blob*)

EXERCISE 2

Identifying Signal Words and Parallel Elements

Underline the parallel elements—words, phrases, or clauses—and circle the signal words in the following sentences.

1. An old granny tells tales of wolves and of children of the night. (*The Company of Wolves*)

2. Several convicts from another planet escape and fly to the planet Earth. (*Critters*)

3. Krite eggs hatch bloodthirsty babies and the babies continue the family tradition. (*Critters 2*)

4. Four people become trapped in a shopping mall with walking flesh-eaters and a gang of motorcyclists. (*Dawn of the Dead*)

5. A mad scientist dreams of creating life and using his ingenious talents. (*Frankenstein*)

6. He succeeds in producing a monster with the brain of a friend, the emotions of a child, and the body of a giant.

7. Combining fact, fiction, and horror, this film is an imaginative tale of fear. (*Gothic*)

8. A man flees a disturbed past while being pursued by a lawman, a psycho-pathic killer, and the woman who still loves him. (*Night Breed*)

9. A man wants money he didn't earn, a sightless woman wants to see, and a man's past catches up with him. (*Night Gallery*)

10. Norman Bates attempts to put his life together and to put his old habits behind him. (*Psycho III*)

EXERCISE 3

Correcting Faulty Parallelism

Identify the sentences with parallel elements (P) and those with faulty parallelism (X). Correct the weak element. You need not rewrite the entire sentence. (See Answer Key for answers.)

_____ 1. Employees of a medical supply company release several zombies who like to roam the countryside and eating brains. (*Return of the Living Dead*)

_____ 2. A genetic experiment gone completely haywire spawns a new, hideous life form that breaks free and escaping into the sewer. (*Scared to Death*)

_____ 3. A young traveler finds madness, mystery, and he finds mayhem in the Louisiana bayou in this chilling Gothic tale. (*Sister, Sister*)

_____ 4. The Prince of Darkness has resurfaced in Los Angeles with a new look, a new life, a new love, and having an old enemy. (*To Die For*)

_____ 5. The Puttermans wanted clearer, more effective television reception. (*Terrorvision*)

_____ 6. They purchased a satellite dish, a good television set, and they sat down to watch.

_____ 7. Unfortunately for them, their new equipment brought monsters into their living room and upsetting their lives.

_____ 8. Scientists have bred the combat weapons—beasts with the cunning of human beings, the strength of giants, and who had the blood-lust of predators. (*Watchers*)

_____ 9. An explosion sets the mistakes free, and no one is safe.

_____ 10. A group of teenagers go for a free late-night showing at a wax museum horror display but tragically becoming part of the show. (*Waxwork*)

EXERCISE 4   ## Correcting Faulty Parallelism

Identify the sentences with parallel elements (P) and those with faulty parallelism (X). Correct the weak element. You need not rewrite the entire sentence.

_____ 1. This film gives a warm and nostalgic look back at the year 1963 and focuses on one summer night of cruising in a small town. (*American Graffiti*)

_____ 2. It features greasers, geeks, good girls, and has cleancut characters.

_____ 3. This film casts a cynical shadow on bad acting, bad special effects, and uses bad dialogue. (*Attack of the Killer Tomatoes*)

_____ 4. Savage tomatoes roll around to terrorize the citizens and destroying their society.

_____ 5. Alex Foley is a brash, street-smart Detroit detective and who follows the trail of a friend's murder. (*Beverly Hills Cop*)

_____ 6. This zany comedy features a series of sketches that satirize movies, television, and ridicule other aspects of contemporary society. (*Kentucky Fried Movie*)

_____ 7. Prince Alceem quickly finds a new job, new friends, new enemies, and has lots of trouble. (*Coming to America*)

_____ 8. High school students struggle with independence, success, money, and to be mature in this off-beat comedy. (*Fast Times at Ridge-mont High*)

_____ 9. A bespectacled spectacle of a bookkeeper adores his pet fish and dreams of becoming one of these scaled wonders. (*The Incredible Mr. Limpet*)

_____ 10. When his wish suddenly comes true, he fisheyes a lady fish and becoming an invaluable hero to the U.S. Navy.

EXERCISE 5

Completing Parallel Structures

Fill in the blanks in the following sentences with parallel elements. (See Answer Key for possible answers.)

1. The animated Disney classic concerns a little girl who follows a white rabbit to a land of wonder, _____ , and _____ . (*Alice in Wonderland*)

2. In this exciting and _____ family adventure, Benji is adopted by a loving family. (*Benji*)

3. When the two children are kidnapped, Benji is the only one who knows where they are and _____ .

4. A daring family decides to move to Alaska and _____ completely apart from society. (*The Alaska Wilderness Adventure*)

5. This film takes us into the forest to share the excitement, _____ , and _____ of a little deer. (*Bambi*)

6. The caped crusader and his faithful boy wonder fight for _____ , _____ , and _____ . (*Batman*)

7. Acme Co.'s best customer uses his entire arsenal, but Road Runner _____ and _____ . (*Road Runner*)

8. Coldheart has captured children and made them his slaves, and the Care Bears must outwit him with _____ and _____ . (*The Care Bears in a Land Without Feeling*)

9. Van Dyke is delightful as a man whose old automobile suddenly develops the ability to _____ and _____ . (*Chitty-Chitty Bang-Bang*)

10. The mistreated stepdaughter is transformed by her fairy godmother, who

_____ her and _____ her to the royal ball. (*Cinderella*)

EXERCISE 6   **Completing Parallel Structures**

Fill in the blanks in the following sentences with parallel elements. (See Answer Key for possible answers.)

1. Schwarzenegger plays a _____ , _____ killing machine. (*The Terminator*)

2. Nothing can stop him from his mission to find and _____ an innocent woman.

3. A man's dreams lead him to Mars in search of certain danger, his old _____ , and a mysterious _____ . (*Total Recall*)

4. A spaceship crash-lands on an unknown planet, and the three astronauts _____ . (*Planet of the Apes*)

5. There, the apes are the rulers, and the _____ .

6. Ultimately the alien grows to be an enormous size and _____ killing everyone on board. (*Alien*)

7. When unsuspecting guests check in at a hotel, they are surprised to find vicious ants who appear and _____ them with a vengeance. (*Ants*)

8. A futuristic ex-cop is drawn out of retirement to seek and _____ a group of renegade robots. (*Bladerunner*)

9. This is a touching and sometimes comical adventure of an _____ but _____ alien. (*E.T.*)

10. Max's somewhat cloudy origin is brought to light as the "creation" of an _____ and _____ computer-generated talk-show host. (*Max Headroom—The Original Story*)

Combination Signal Words

The words *and* and *but* are the most common individual signal words used with parallel constructions. Sometimes, however, **combination words** signal the need for parallelism or balance. The most common ones are *either/or, neither/nor, not only/but also, both/and,* and *whether/or.* Now consider this faulty sentence and a possible correction.

Nonparallel: *Either we will* win this game, *or let's* go out fighting.

Parallel: *Either we will* win this game, *or we will* go out fighting.

The correction is made by changing *let's* to *we will* to parallel the *we will* in the first part of the sentence. The same construction should follow the *either* and the *or.*

Nonparallel: Flour is used *not only* to bake cakes *but also in* paste.

Parallel: Flour is used *not only to bake* cakes *but also to make* paste.

The correction is made by changing *in* (a preposition) to *to make* (an infinitive). Now an infinitive follows both *not only* and *but also.*

EXERCISE 7

Identifying Combination Signal Words and Parallel Elements

Underline the parallel elements—words, phrases, or clauses—and circle the combination signal words in the following sentences. (See Answer Key for answers.)

1. Robin Hood not only robbed from the rich but also gave to the poor.

    (*Adventures of Robin Hood*)

2. Both Humphrey Bogart and Katharine Hepburn star in this movie about

    two unlikely people traveling together through the jungle rivers of Africa

    during World War II. (*The African Queen*)

3. Dr. Jekyll discovers a potion, and now he can be either himself or Mr.

    Hyde. (*Dr. Jekyll and Mr. Hyde*)

4. An Oklahoma family moves to California and finds neither good jobs nor

    compassion in the "promised land." (*The Grapes of Wrath*)

5. In this Christmas classic, Jimmy Stewart stars as a man who can either die

    by suicide or go back to see what life would have been like without him.

    (*It's a Wonderful Life*)

6. During the Korean War, army surgeons discover that they must either develop a lunatic lifestyle or go crazy. (*M*A*S*H*)

7. An advertising executive not only gets tied up with an obnoxious but boring salesman but also goes with him on a wacky chase across the country. (*Planes, Trains, and Automobiles*)

8. In this flawless integration of animation and live action, Roger and Eddie try to discover both who framed Roger and who is playing patty-cake with his wife. (*Who Framed Roger Rabbit?*)

9. A long-suffering black woman named Celie experiences not only heartaches but also some joy as she rises from tragedy to personal triumph. (*The Color Purple*)

10. An independent man learns that he is expected to give up either his dignity or his life. (*Cool Hand Luke*)

EXERCISE 8   ## Correcting Faulty Parallelism

Underline the parallel elements—words, phrases, or clauses—and circle the combination signal words in the following sentences. If the elements are not parallel, change them to achieve balance. You need not rewrite the entire sentence.

Example: (Either) the street punks would terrorize the school (or) a former gang member would stop them. (*The Moment of Truth*)

1. A fanatical submarine captain makes a misguided effort to sink the ships of both the allies and the enemy. (*20,000 Leagues Under the Sea*)

2. After a young woman is brutally attacked by a scurvy street gang, not only she studies martial arts but also plans for absolute bloody revenge. (*Alley Cat*)

3. The main issue is whether a street-wise girl will find the killer or he will escape. (*Avenging Angel*)

4. Either the Barbarian brothers will triumph or the evil world will win. (*The Barbarians*)

5. Neither the Joker nor anyone else can get the last laugh on Batman. (*Batman*)

6. Two youngsters are shipwrecked in the South Pacific and not only they mature but also slowly make a surprising discovery. (*Blue Lagoon*)

7. A neighborhood gang will either reign, or Danny McGavin will. (*Colors*)

8. After Conan's parents were murdered, he swore that he would either get revenge or die trying. (*Conan the Barbarian*)

9. The question is whether Harry will kill the psychopath or the psychopath will kill him. (*Dirty Harry*)

10. Neither Mumbles nor Breathless Mahoney communicated well with Dick Tracy. (*Dick Tracy*)

EXERCISE 9

Correcting Faulty Parallelism

Underline the parallel elements—words, phrases, or clauses—and circle the combination signal words in the following sentences. If the elements are not parallel, change them to achieve balance. You need not rewrite the entire sentence.

1. James Bond protects the U.S. gold reserve both with some wonderfully ingenious gadgets and a few unusually lovely ladies. (*Goldfinger*)

2. Two convicts decide that either they must escape from Devil's Island or die. (*Papillon*)

3. These prehistoric people are not only competing in a quest for fire but also in a struggle for dominance. (*Quest for Fire*)

4. Whether one side won or the other, human beings would benefit.

5. Neither his poor physical condition nor his reputation would discourage Rocky Balboa. (*Rocky*)

6. Both Al Capone and Bugs Moran neglected to pass out Valentine's Day cards in 1934. (*The St. Valentine's Day Massacre*)

7. It was neither a bird nor was it a plane; it was Superman. (*Superman— The Movie*)

8. The pilot loved both the experience of flying and to be around a certain beautiful astrophysicist. (*Top Gun*)

9. A computer whiz kid manages not only to get himself hooked into a top-secret military computer but also finds the fate of the world in his hands. (*Wargames*)

10. Only one person would walk away from this friendship; it would be either the drug smuggler or it would be the cop. (*Tequila Sunrise*)

CHAPTER REVIEW   BALANCING SENTENCE PARTS

1. **Parallelism** is a balance of one structure with another of the same kind—nouns with nouns, verbs with verbs, adjectives with adjectives, phrases with phrases, and clauses with clauses.

   > *Goats, chickens,* and *cows* [nouns] *roamed* the yard and *caused* [verbs] considerable confusion.

   > Tanya walked *into the room* and *out of the room* with grace [prepositional phrases].

   > *Tanya walked into the room,* and *she walked out of the room* with grace [independent clauses].

2. Faulty parallel structure is awkward and draws unfavorable attention to what is being said.

   > *Hitting* home runs and *to catch* balls in the outfield were his main concerns. [should be *Hitting . . . and catching* or *To hit . . . and to catch*]

3. Some words signal parallel structure. All coordinating conjunctions (FANBOYS: *for, and, nor, but, or, yet, so*) can give such signals.

   > My car is inexpensive *and* plain.

   > My dog is ugly, *but* it is a good companion.

4. Combination words also signal the need for parallelism or balance. The most common ones are *either/or, neither/nor, not only/but also, both/and,* and *whether/or.*

   > Patsy decided that propagating plants could be *either* a hobby *or* a business but not both. [A noun follows each of the combination words.]

CHAPTER REVIEW EXERCISES

Correcting Faulty Parallelism

Eliminate awkwardness in the following passage by using parallel structure. (See Answer Key for possible answers to the first two paragraphs.)

Ken Kesey wrote *One Flew Over the Cuckoo's Nest* as a novel. It was later made into a stage play and a film. The title was taken from a children's folk rhyme: "One flew east, one flew west, / One flew over the cuckoo's nest."

The narrator in the novel is Chief Bromden, the central character is Randle Mc-Murphy, and Nurse Ratched is the villain. Bromden sees and can hear but does not speak. He is a camera with a conscience. McMurphy is both an outcast and serves as a leader, and he speaks out for freedom and as an individual. Nurse Ratched is the voice of repression. She is the main representative of what Bromden calls the "Combine." She organizes, directs, controls, and, if necessary to her purposes, will destroy.

The setting is a mental institution where McMurphy has gone to avoid doing more rigorous time in the nearby prison. Discovering what the inmates are going through, he seeks to liberate them from their affliction and freeing them from Nurse Ratched's domination.

A battle of wills ensues, and the reader wonders who will win. The nurse has the whole system behind her, one that prevents the inmates from regaining self-esteem. McMurphy is a colorful, irreverent, expressive person and who appeals to the men's deepest need for self-respect and to be sane. She offers her therapy; his is also offered. She gives drugs. She also gives group therapy, which is tightly controlled by her to produce humiliation. McMurphy provides recreation in the form of first a fishing trip and then sex (for some).

McMurphy is eventually defeated by the system. Neither his energy was enough nor his intelligence when the Combine moves in. McMurphy is given a lobotomy and reduced to a mere body without a mind. Out of profound respect and deeply loving, Bromden destroys McMurphy's body and then escapes.

REVIEW 2

Completing Parallel Structures

Complete each of the following sentences by adding a construction that is parallel to the underlined construction.

1. We went to the zoo not only for <u>fun</u> but also for _____

_____

2. He attended Utah State University for <u>a good education</u> and _____

_____

3. For a college major, she was considering <u>English</u>, <u>history</u>, and _____

4. Mr. Ramos was <u>a good neighbor</u> and _____

5. My breakfast each day that week consisted of <u>a slice of bread</u>, <u>a glass of low-fat milk</u>, and _____

6. She decided that she must choose between <u>a social life</u> and _____

_____

7. Either <u>she would make the choice</u>, or _____

_____

8. Because we are mutually supportive, either <u>we will all have a good time</u>, or _____

_____

9. Like the Three Musketeers, our motto is "<u>All for one</u> and _____

_____

10. My intention was to <u>work for a year</u>, <u>save my money</u>, and _____

_____

REVIEW 3

Writing Sentences with Parallel Structure

Use each of these signal words or combined signal words in a sentence of ten or more words.

1. and _____

_____

_____

2. but _____

    _____

    _____

3. so _____

    _____

    _____

4. either/or _____

    _____

    _____

5. both/and _____

    _____

    _____

MICROTHEME

To practice your skills acquired in this chapter, return to the Microtheme on page 192 and complete Exercise B.

Chapter

10

Punctuation and Capitalization

Reading a passage with wrong punctuation is like driving on streets with wrong traffic signs and signals.

FLOW OF WRITING

Learning Objectives

Working with this chapter, I will learn to

∿ use punctuation correctly.
∿ use punctuation for writing effectiveness.
∿ choose between the semicolon and the comma for clear expression.
∿ use capitalization correctly.

FLOW OF WRITING

MICROTHEME

Writing Activity in Miniature
Two Purposes

Writing Diagnostic: Before you work on this chapter, the Microtheme will give you an opportunity to write briefly on an engaging topic without pressure.

Chapter Learning Application: After you have studied this chapter, return to your Microtheme to check your work and practice what you have just learned.

Form and Procedure
Like an executive summary (written for a busy boss), the Microtheme conveys ideas concisely (using no more than the space on a 5- by 8-inch card) in a specified form. Indent only once, and write small enough to leave room for marking later. Directions for practicing your chapter writing skills appear in Exercise B.

Suggested Microtheme Topic
Write a Microtheme of 80 to 100 words about the reasons for or against body piercing or tattooing. In parentheses at the beginning of your Microtheme, indicate the age group you are addressing.

_____

Connecting Your Learning
Objectives with Your
Microtheme

Complete this exercise after you have studied this chapter.

1. Use the chapter table of contents to look up any questionable marks of punctuation or capitalization.

2. Consider punctuation in relation to what you have learned about sentence structure in other chapters.

nderstanding punctuation will help you to write better. If you aren't sure how to punctuate a compound or a compound-complex sentence, then you probably will not write one. If you don't know how to show that some of your words come from other sources, you may mislead your reader. If you misuse punctuation, you will force your readers to struggle to get your message. So take the time to review and master the mechanics. Your efforts will be rewarded.

End Punctuation

Periods

1. Place a period after a statement.

   The weather is beautiful today.

2. Place a period after common abbreviations.

   Dr.   Mr.   Mrs.   Dec.   A.M.

   Exceptions: FBI   UN   NAACP   FHA

3. Use an ellipsis—three periods within a sentence and four periods at the end of a sentence—to indicate that words have been omitted from quoted material.

   James Thurber, "The Secret Life of Walter Mitty"

   He stopped walking and the buildings . . . rose up out of the misty court-room. . . .

Question Marks

1. Place a question mark at the end of a direct question.

   Will you go to the country tomorrow?

2. Do *not* use a question mark after an indirect (reported) question.

   She asked me what caused the slide.

Exclamation Points

1. Place an exclamation point after a word or a group of words that expresses strong feeling.

   Oh!   What a night!   Help!   Gadzooks!

2. Do not overwork the exclamation point. Do not use double exclamation points. Use the period or comma for mild exclamatory words, phrases, or sentences.

   Oh, we can leave now.

EXERCISE 1

Using End Punctuation

Add end punctuation. (See Answer Key for answers.)

1. Have you ever heard of the Mummy's Curse

2. In 1923, twenty-four people entered the newly discovered tomb of Egypt's King Tutankhamen

3. Only weeks after they unearthed Tut's final resting place, the man who financed the dig died

4. By 1929, eleven people connected with the discovery of the tomb had also died early of unnatural causes

5. Holy sarcophagus, the tomb was cursed

6. I heard that an untimely death was in store for all of the tomb raiders

7. As each person on the expedition passed away, the newspapers shrieked, "The mummy's curse strikes again "

8. Did you know that within a decade, the press had linked thirty deaths to King Tut

9. Studies now show, though, that on average, the twenty-four people who entered the burial chamber lived to be seventy years old

10. I suppose that the legendary curse was a fiction created by the press

---

EXERCISE 2

Using End Punctuation

Add end punctuation.

1. Did you know that the U.S. Department of Commerce once kept a list of genuine haunted houses

2. There are thirty houses on the last version of this agency's list

3. Eeek, I just saw a government-certified ghost

4. San Diego's Whaley House is one of the places on the official list

5. Could this historic home be the most haunted house in America

6. At least four different spirits are active in this place

7. Oh, the sound of ghostly footsteps is driving me mad

8. Thomas and Anna Whaley have been dead for over a hundred years, but visitors still smell his cigars and her perfume

9. They also hear the Whaleys' disembodied voices and the tunes Anna played on her piano

10. Help, the ghost of Anna Whaley just materialized right in front of me

Commas

Commas to Separate

1. Use a comma to separate main clauses joined by one of the coordinating conjunctions—*for, and, nor, but, or, yet, so.* The comma may be omitted if the clauses are brief and parallel.

   We traveled many miles to see the game, *but* it was canceled.

   Mary left *and* I remained. [brief and parallel clauses]

2. Use a comma after introductory dependent clauses and long introductory phrases (generally, four or more words is considered long).

   Before the arrival of the shipment, the boss had written a letter protesting the delay. [two prepositional phrases]

   If you don't hear from me, assume that I am lost. [introductory dependent clause, an adverbial modifier]

   In winter we skate on the river. [short prepositional phrase, no comma]

3. Use a comma to separate words, phrases, and clauses in a series.

   Red, white, and *blue* were her favorite colors. [words]

   He ran down the street, across the park, and *into the arms of his father.* [prepositional phrases]

   When John was asleep, when Mary was at work, and *when Bob was studying,* Mother had time to relax. [dependent clauses]

4. However, when coordinating conjunctions connect all the elements in a series, the commas are omitted.

   He bought apples *and* pears *and* grapes.

5. Use a comma to separate coordinate adjectives not joined by *and* that modify the same noun.

   I need a *sturdy, reliable* truck.

6. Do not use a comma to separate adjectives that are not coordinate. Try the following technique to determine whether the adjectives are coordinate: Put *and* between the adjectives. If it fits naturally, the adjectives are coordinate; if it does not, they are not, and you do not need a comma.

> She is a kind, beautiful person.
>
> kind *and* beautiful [natural, hence the comma]
>
> I built a red brick wall.
>
> red *and* brick wall [not natural, no comma]

7. Use a comma to separate sentence elements that might be misread.

> Inside the dog scratched his fleas.
>
> *Inside,* the dog scratched his fleas.

Without benefit of the comma, the reader might initially misunderstand the relationship among the first three words.

Commas to Set Off

1. Use commas to set off (enclose) adjectives in pairs that follow a noun.

> The scouts, *tired and hungry,* marched back to camp.

2. Use commas to set off nonessential (unnecessary for meaning of the sentence) words, phrases, and clauses.

> My brother, *a student at Ohio State University,* is visiting me. [If you drop the phrase, the basic meaning of the sentence remains intact.]
>
> Marla, *who studied hard,* will pass. [The clause is not essential to the basic meaning of the sentence.]
>
> All students *who studied hard* will pass. [Here the clause *is* essential. If you remove it, you would have *All students will pass,* which is not necessarily true.]
>
> I shall not stop searching *until I find the treasure.* [A dependent clause at the end of a sentence is usually not set off with a comma. However, a clause beginning with the word *though* or *although* will be set off regardless of where it is located.]
>
> I felt unsatisfied, *though we had won the game.*

3. Use commas to set off parenthetical elements such as mild interjections (*oh, well, yes, no,* and others), most conjunctive adverbs (*however, otherwise, therefore, similarly, hence, on the other hand,* and *consequently,* but not *then, thus, soon, now,* and *also*), quotation indicators, and special abbreviations (*etc., i.e., e.g.,* and others).

> *Oh,* what a silly question! [mild interjection]
>
> It is necessary, *of course,* to leave now. [sentence modifier]
>
> We left early; *however,* we missed the train anyway. [conjunctive adverb]
>
> "When I was in school," *he said,* "I read widely." [quotation indicator]

Books, papers, pens, *etc.,* were scattered on the floor. [The abbreviation *etc.* should be used sparingly, however.]

4. Use commas to set off nouns used as direct address.

Play it again, *Sam.*

Please tell us the answer, *Jane,* so we can discuss it.

5. Use commas to separate the numbers in a date.

June 4, *1965,* is a day I will remember.

6. Do not use commas if the day of the month is not specified, or if the day is given before the month.

June 1965 was my favorite time.

One day I will never forget is 4 June 1965.

7. Use commas to separate the city from the state. No comma is used between the state and the ZIP code.

Walnut, CA 91789

8. Use a comma after both the city and the state when they are used together in a sentence.

Our family visited Anchorage, *Alaska,* last summer.

9. Use a comma following the salutation of a friendly letter and the complimentary closing in any letter.

Dear Saul,

Sincerely,

10. Use a comma in numbers to set off groups of three digits. However, omit the comma in dates, serial numbers, page numbers, years, and street numbers.

The total assets were *$2,000,000.*

I look forward to the year 2050.

EXERCISE 3

Using Commas

Insert commas where needed. (See Answer Key for answers.)

1. Edward Teach who was better known as Blackbeard terrorized the oceans

   on the *Queen Anne's Revenge* from 1716 to 1718.

2. Blackbeard and his band of pirates ambushed ships took the passengers

   and crew hostage and ransacked cabins in search of valuables.

3. They were looking for coins gold silver and jewelry.

4. Blackbeard ferocious and menacing quickly earned a reputation for being the most frightening of all pirates.

5. To make himself look especially fierce he braided his long hair and bushy beard and tied the braids with black ribbons.

6. Before he fought in battles he wove slow-burning fuses into his hair and lit them to look demonic.

7. He was a large man who wore a red coat and adorned himself with numerous swords pistols and knives.

8. He spent the warmer months terrorizing the coasts of North and South Carolina and then he menaced the seas of the Caribbean in the winter.

9. Instead of the usual skull-and-crossbones Blackbeard's black flag had an image of a horned skeleton holding a spear and an hourglass.

10. When the crew of other ships saw this flag they usually surrendered without a fight.

11. Blackbeard captured a ship sailing from Charleston South Carolina and threatened to kill its passengers if the townspeople didn't give him a chest filled with medical remedies.

12. The townspeople paid the ransom so Blackbeard freed his prisoners.

13. The pirate captured over forty ships and caused the deaths of hundreds of people during his short lawless career.

14. By the spring of 1718 Blackbeard commanded four ships and three hundred pirates.

15. Blackbeard's favorite hideout was off Ocracoke Island one of a string of islands off the coast of North Carolina.

16. The British colonists there liked to buy the pirates' cheap stolen goods so they turned a blind eye to Blackbeard's activities.

17. Blackbeard's reign of terror ended however on November 22 1718.

18. The governor of Virginia fed up with Blackbeard's crimes sent Royal Navy ships to trap the pirates in Ocracoke Inlet.

19. During the brief but bloody battle Blackbeard was shot five times but he fought on until a Navy seaman slashed his throat from behind.

20. As a warning to other pirates the Navy captain cut off Blackbeard's head and hung it from the bow of his ship.

EXERCISE 4　　　# Using Commas

Insert commas where needed.

1. In *Frankenstein* the original classic horror thriller written by Mary Shelley and published on October 3 1818 Victor Frankenstein was a gifted dedicated student.

2. While he studied science at the university he came upon the secret of how to create life.

3. Being more interested in simple practical matters than in theory he set out to construct a living breathing creature.

4. Victor who was very much concerned about process first needed to gather the materials necessary for his experiment.

5. He went all around town picking up body parts and he stored them in his laboratory.

6. The dissecting room at a local hospital provided him with the most basic articles and he was very grateful.

7. Local butcher shops had plenty of items perhaps including some spare ribs.

8. Finally he was ready to begin construction of a strange humanlike creature.

9. He made a creature that was eight feet tall four feet wide and very strong.

10. The face of the creature which could be described only as hideous was not easy to look upon.

11. One night while Victor was sleeping lightly the monster lonely and troubled came to his bedroom.

12. Victor screamed loudly and the monster ran away in disappointment.

13. Victor developed brain fever which was a result of the encounter.

14. When Victor recovered from his illness he discovered that one of his brothers had been murdered by an unknown person.

15. In despair and befuddlement Victor went to a remote wilderness to sort out his problems.

16. One day when he was out walking Victor saw a strange lumbering creature running into the mountains.

17. Victor chased the creature but he was unable to catch it.

18. Soon after he sat down to rest and the creature appeared before him.

19. It was Victor Frankenstein's monster who had come to talk to him.

20. With a great deal of self-pity the monster explained that he was very sad because people were unkind to him.

EXERCISE 5

Using Commas

Insert commas where needed. (See Answer Key for answers.)

1. Frankenstein's monster distraught and desperate told a story of acute loneliness.

2. After leaving Victor Frankenstein's house he had gone to live in the country.

3. He had tried diligently to help the simple gentle people by bringing them firewood.

4. They took the firewood; however they were at first frightened and then angry.

5. The monster very upset and dejected had gone back to the city.

6. There he killed Victor's innocent unsuspecting brother and he then cleverly tried to place the blame on someone else.

7. Listening to the monster in horror Victor Frankenstein realized what he had done in this act of creation.

8. The monster started making demands and it was clear that he would force Victor to carry them out.

9. He said that if Victor did not make a suitable female companion for him he would begin killing human beings at random.

10. Victor went away gathered up some more parts and started building a bride for the monster.

11. The monster waited in eager anticipation but he was to be sorely disappointed.

12. Victor became disgusted with his project and he destroyed all the tissue just before it came to life.

13. Needless to say the monster was deeply distressed by this unexpected shocking development.

14. Before the monster ran away he swore to get revenge on Victor's wedding night.

15. When Victor got married he armed himself fully for he expected a visit from the enraged vengeful monster.

16. On the night of the wedding the monster slipped into the bridal chamber and strangled the horrified unlucky bride.

17. Victor himself vowed to avenge the murder by killing the monster but the monster was nowhere to be found.

18. Victor finally died in a cabin in the desolate frozen lands of the North and much later his body was found by a friend.

19. The monster dropped by for one last visit for he wanted to complain about his unhappy life.

20. He said that Victor had created a man without a friend love or even a soul and therefore Victor was more wicked than anyone.

EXERCISE 6   # Using Commas

Insert commas where needed.

1. In August 1862 Confederate private Henry Clark was fighting in the Battle of Richmond Kentucky when he was hit in the thigh with an enemy shell.

2. Clark was taken prisoner and the Union medic who treated the soldier's wound discovered that the patient had a secret.

3. Henry Clark was acutally a women and her name was really Mary Ann Clark.

4. Federal troops gave her a dress to wear made her promise to return to the life of a lady and then released her.

5. Mary Ann replaced the dress with a uniform returned to the rebel army and was immediately promoted.

6. Clark seems to have openly served as a female officer but about four hundred other women disguised themselves as men to fight in the Civil War.

7. To get to the front lines women had to pass themselves off as men.

8. If a woman was detected of course she was sent home.

9. But both armies were desperate for troops and physical exams of new recruits were not thorough.

10. Being discovered was unlikely for soldiers slept in their uniforms and took baths infrequently.

11. Many of the women blended in by learning to cuss taking up gambling and even dating local girls.

12. Some of the females gave themselves away with their ladylike behaviors but most were detected only when they needed medical treatment.

13. Research shows that most of these female soldiers were not eccenric crazy or deranged.

14. According to a letter from Clark's mother Mary Ann joined the military to escape a bad marriage.

15. Martha Parks Lindley however joined because she could not part from her husband.

16. Their fellow soldiers thought that Lindley and his constant companion a "young man" named Jim Smith were just very close friends.

17. Charlotte Hope signed up to avenge the death of her fiancé who was killed in an 1861 raid.

18. Charlotte angry and grief-stricken vowed to kill one Union soldier for each of the twenty-one years her fiancé had lived.

19. Others wanted to be soldiers for the financial benefits for patriotic reasons or just for the thrill of it.

20. Apparently most of the women enlisted for the same reasons men joined.

Semicolons

The **semicolon** indicates a stronger division than the comma. It is used principally to separate independent clauses within a sentence.

1. Use a semicolon to separate independent clauses not joined by a coordinating conjunction.

> You must buy that car today; tomorrow will be too late.

2. Use a semicolon between two independent clauses joined by a conjunctive adverb such as one of the HOTSHOT CAT words (*however, otherwise, therefore, similarly, hence, on the other hand, then, consequently, accordingly, thus*).

> It was very late; *therefore,* I remained at the hotel.

3. Use a semicolon to separate main clauses joined by a coordinating conjunction if one or both of the clauses contain distracting commas.

> Byron, the famous English poet, was buried in Greece; *and* Shelley, who was his friend and fellow poet, was buried in Italy.

4. Use a semicolon in a series between items that themselves contain commas.

> He has lived in Covina, California; Reno, Nevada; Tribbey, Oklahoma; and Bangor, Maine.

Using Semicolons and Commas

Insert semicolons and commas where needed. (See Answer Key for answers.)

1. In September 1991, two hikers saw the head and shoulders of a dead man protruding through the ice of the Italian Alps and they assumed that the man was just another Alpine accident victim.

2. Rescue workers were summoned they used jackhammers to extricate the man's body and his possessions from the ice.

3. But then an archaeologist saw the copper ax found beside the corpse he realized that the body was actually a spectacular archaeological discovery.

4. The snow and ice had naturally mummified the corpse and it had been frozen there on the mountain for about 5,300 years.

5. The Iceman was a well-preserved specimen of a Neolithic human his remains were the oldest human flesh ever found.

6. During the Neolithic period, metal tools had begun to replace stone tools consequently the Iceman carried both a flint dagger and a copper ax.

7. X-rays and examinations of the Iceman's body showed that he had been about forty years old when he died he had been killed by an arrow shot into his back.

8. He had also suffered other wounds for example his hand had been deeply cut and several of his ribs had been broken.

9. Archaeologists surmised that he may have been in a battle he fled the scene after being wounded.

10. In spite of his injuries he had begun ascending the mountain.

11. His broken ribs would have made climbing difficult so he must have thought he'd find safety at higher elevations.

12. The clothing, tools, and weapons found with the Iceman were also interesting for very few Neolithic artifacts have survived.

13. Feathers on his arrows revealed Neolithic people's understanding of ballistic principles obviously, they knew that feathers would make an arrow fly more accurately.

14. The embers he carried taught us how Neolithic people transported fire they wrapped the glowing coals in leaves and placed them in birch bark containers.

15. The Iceman also taught us about Neolithic clothing his leather shoes, for instance, were insulated with grass.

16. His people apparently did not weave cloth all of the Iceman's clothing was made from animal skins.

17. After archaeologists determined the age of the Iceman's ax they were forced to admit being wrong about the date copper smelting began.

18. Today, the Iceman is kept in a refrigerated vault in Italy his body remains encased in a glaze of ice to preserve it.

19. The Iceman has revealed a great deal about the Neolithic age but he has also raised new questions.

20. Archaeologists hope to continue to study and learn more from him so the Iceman will remain frozen in time.

EXERCISE 8

Using Semicolons and Commas

Insert semicolons and commas where needed.

1. Once upon a time, there was a young woman named Cyberella she lived in Oklahoma with an evil stepmother and an obnoxious stepsister.

2. One night at eleven her wretched stepfamily was snoring raucously and Cyberella was busily dusting the family computer, which someone had left running.

3. It was then that Cyberella inadvertently hit the Instant Internet button therefore the screen lit up.

4. She had never been permitted to use the Internet but she had enviously watched her evil stepfamily at the keyboard.

5. Cyberella created the screen name Cool4aday and logged on for fun and education naturally she started with the index of chat rooms.

6. She was delighted with her unexpected opportunity however she realized that the computer was programmed to go out of commission at midnight.

7. Now she was a free-spirited cyberspace explorer surfing the World Wide Web at midnight she would turn back into a servant ripping out cobwebs and capturing dust bunnies.

8. Cyberella spotted a chat room called "Talk to the Prince" feeling like a princess she joined in the conversation.

9. To her amazement she discovered that she was chatting with a real prince Prince Igor of Transylvania in fact he seemed to like her.

10. Prince Igor boldly invited Cyberella to accompany him to a private chat room breathlessly she said yes and followed him with demure keystrokes.

11. They chatted shyly and then passionately for almost an hour and soon the prince became royally enamored by the way she processed thought noticing that she wrote skillfully, using her spell checker and grammar checker in a most delicate way.

12. Cyberella wanted to tell Prince Igor explicitly what was in her heart therefore she often used the computer thesaurus feature, impressing him further with her highly eloquent diction.

13. Prince Igor was about to ask the royal marriage question then Cyberella heard the clock strike her computer went dark and she believed she would never again chat with her sweet prince.

14. Prince Igor was devastated and vowed to find this lovely correspondent he therefore directed his army to undertake a royal search that would properly but legally identify Cool4aday and expose all impostors.

15. The soldiers would test the computer-assisted writing skills of everyone in the world if necessary moreover they would even provide laptops for any computerless woman who looked as if she could possibly be the mystery writer.

16. Cyberella had informed Prince Igor that she was from the American Southwest a fact that enabled him to focus his search.

17. Following electronic clues, the soldiers visited Amarillo Texas Tucumcari New Mexico Tulsa Oklahoma and Window Rock Arizona.

18. At last a soldier came to Cyberella's house and was greeted by the obnoxious stepsister, who claimed that she was Cool4aday and began to chat on line with Prince Igor however the stepsister forgot to use her spell checker and the prince flamed a rejection.

19. Then the soldier handed Cyberella a laptop computer and instructions of course both the wicked stepmother and the obnoxious stepsister scoffed.

20. Nevertheless, Cyberella was verified as Cool4aday and the prince was wildly elated therefore he declared an international holiday slapped his leg with glee and offered to grant her fondest wish.

21. "Does that mean I get this laptop for myself?" Cyberella asked and Prince Igor, a bit humbled by her response said "No, that means you get me for yourself."

22. "Oh, that's very, very nice but may I also have this laptop?" Cyberella asked striking a hard bargain as she fondly hugged the computer.

23. "Yes" Prince Igor said. "I'll even toss in a laser printer and I'll add a few pounds of copy paper and a stack of Dungeon-and-Dragon software customized in one of my own castles."

24. They got married and lived happily ever after for a while then the wicked stepfamily tried to move into the palace but they were arrested and were no longer allowed to use the Internet in Transylvania or Oklahoma until they had passed a writing test which they never did.

Quotation Marks

Quotation marks are used principally to set off direct quotations. A direct quotation consists of material taken from the written work or the direct speech of others; it is set off by double quotation marks. Single quotation marks are used to set off a quotation within a quotation.

Double Quotation Marks: He said, "I don't remember."

Single Quotation Marks: He said, "I don't remember if she said, 'Wait for me.'"

1. Use double quotation marks to set off direct quotations.

   Lavonne said, "Give me the book."

   As Edward McNeil writes of the Greek achievement: "To an extent never before realized, mind was supreme over faith."

2. Use double quotation marks to set off titles of shorter pieces of writing such as magazine articles, essays, short stories, short poems, one-act plays, chapters in books, songs, and separate pieces of writing published as part of a larger work.

   The book *Literature: Structure, Sound, and Sense* contains a deeply moving poem titled "On Wenlock Edge."

   Have you read "The Use of Force," a short story by William Carlos Williams?

   My favorite Elvis song is "Don't Be Cruel."

3. Use double quotation marks to set off slang, technical terms, and special words.

   There are many aristocrats, but Elvis is the only true "King." [special word]

   The "platoon system" changed the game of football. [technical term]

4. Use double quotation marks in writing dialogue (conversation). Write each speech unit as a separate paragraph and set it off with double quotation marks.

   "Will you go with me?" he asked.

   "Yes," she replied. "Are you ready now?"

5. Use single quotation marks to set off a quotation within a quotation.

   Professor Baxter said, "You should remember Shakespeare's words, 'Nothing will come of nothing.'"

6. Do *not* use quotation marks for indirect quotations.

   Incorrect: He said that "he would bring the supplies."

   Correct: He said that he would bring the supplies.

7. Do *not* use quotation marks for the title on your own written work. If you refer to that title in another piece of writing, however, you need the quotation marks.

Punctuation with Quotation Marks

1. A period or a comma is always placed *inside* the quotation marks.

Our assignment for Monday was to read Poe's poem "The Raven."

"I will read you the story," he said. "It's a good one."

2. A semicolon or a colon is always placed *outside* the quotation marks.

He read Robert Frost's poem "Design"; then he gave the examination.

He quoted Frost's "Stopping by Woods on a Snowy Evening": "But I have promises to keep."

3. A question mark, an exclamation point, or a dash (see page 228) is placed *outside* the quotation marks when it applies to the entire sentence and *inside* the quotation marks when it applies to the material in quotation marks.

He asked, "Am I responsible for everything?" [quoted question within a statement]

Did you hear him say, "I have the answer"? [statement within a question]

Did she say, "Are you ready?" [question within a question]

She shouted, "Impossible!" [quoted exclamation]

Roy screamed, "I'll flunk if I don't read Poe's short story 'The Black Cat'!" [exclamation that does not belong to the material inside the single quotation marks]

"I hope—that is, I—" he began. [dash within a quotation]

"Accept responsibility"—those were his words. [dash that does not belong to the material inside the quotation marks]

4. A single question mark is used in sentence constructions that contain a double question—that is, a quoted question following a question.

Mr. Rodriguez said, "Did he say, 'Are you going?'"

Italics

Italics (slanting type) is used to call special attention to certain words or groups of words. In handwriting, such words are underlined; computers provide italics.

1. Italicize (underline) foreign words and phrases that are still listed in the dictionary as foreign.

nouveau riche   *Weltschmerz*

2. Italicize (underline) titles of books (except the Bible), long poems, plays, magazines, motion pictures, musical compositions, newspapers, and works of art.

I think Hemingway's best novel is *A Farewell to Arms*.

His source material was taken from *Time, Newsweek,* and the Los Angeles *Times.* [Sometimes the name of the city in titles of newspapers is italicized—for example, the *New York Times.*]

The *Mona Lisa* is my favorite painting.

3. Italicize (underline) the names of ships, airplanes, spacecraft, and trains.

   Ships: *Queen Mary   Lurline   Stockholm*

   Spacecraft: *Challenger   Voyager 2*

4. Italicize (underline) to distinguish letters, figures, and words when they refer to themselves rather than to the ideas or things they usually represent.

   Do not leave the second *o* out of *sophomore.*

   Your *3*'s look like *5*'s.

EXERCISE 9

Using Quotation Marks and Italics

Insert quotation marks and italics (underlining) as needed. (See Answer Key for answers.)

1. Professor Jones said, Now we will read from The Complete Works of Edgar Allan Poe.

2. The enthusiastic students shouted, We like Poe! We like Poe!

3. The professor lectured for fifty-seven minutes before he finally said, In conclusion, I say that Poe was an unappreciated writer during his lifetime.

4. The next speaker said, I believe that Poe said, A short story should be short enough so that a person can read it in one sitting.

5. Then, while students squirmed, he read The Fall of the House of Usher in sixty-eight minutes.

6. Now we will do some reading in unison, said Professor Jones.

7. Each student opened a copy of The Complete Works of Edgar Allan Poe.

8. Turn to page 72, said Professor Jones.

9. What parts do we read? asked a student.

10. You read the words, or maybe I should say word, of the raven, said the professor.

Using Quotation Marks and Italics

Insert quotation marks and italics (underlining) as needed.

1. The students were not pleased with their small part in the group reading of The Raven.

2. They made several derogatory comments about Professor Jones, even though he had written a learned textbook titled A Short, Brief, and Concise Study of English Rhetoric and the Art of Using English Effectively, Correctly, and Well.

3. As Professor Jones lit candles around a sculpted artwork, one student yelled, The poem says bust of Pallas, and that is not Pallas.

4. Professor Jones retorted archly, We didn't have a bust of Pallas in the department, so I brought a bust of Elvis from the chairperson's office.

5. Another student nodded approval and whispered to his enthralled companion, That prof is cool, real cool.

6. His companion, an English minor with a keen knowledge of grammar, whispered good-naturedly, Really cool is what you mean.

7. Yes, he said, that's what I mean. Sometimes I leave out my ly's and use the wrong words, and people think I'm a gashead.

8. The professor reached into his bag of props, took out a dark, feathered object, and said, I have brought a stuffed raven.

9. That's not a raven. That's a crow, said a student who was majoring in ornithology.

10. The professor waggled his finger playfully at his audience and said, I believe Coleridge once observed, Art sometimes requires the willing suspension of disbelief.

Dashes

The **dash** is used when a stronger break than the comma is needed. The dash is typed as two hyphens with no space before or after them (--).

1. Use a dash to indicate a sudden change in sentence construction or an abrupt break in thought.

   Here is the true reason—but maybe you don't care.

2. Use a dash after an introductory list. The words *these, those, all,* and occasionally *such* introduce the summarizing statement.

   English, French, history—these are the subjects I like.

   Dodgers, Giants, Yankees—such names bring back memories of exciting World Series games.

3. Use a dash to set off material that interrupts the flow of an idea, sets off material for emphasis, or restates an idea as an appositive.

   You are—I am certain—not serious. [interrupting]

   Our next question is—how much money did we raise? [emphasis]

   Dione plays the kazoo—an instrument with a buzz. [restatement]

4. Use a dash to indicate an unfinished statement or word or an interruption. Such interruptions usually occur in dialogue.

   Susan said, "Shall we—" [no question mark]

   "I only wanted—" Jason remarked. [no comma]

5. Do *not* use a dash in places in which other marks of punctuation would be more appropriate.

   Incorrect: Lupe found the store—and she shopped.

   Correct: Lupe found the store, and she shopped.

   Incorrect: I think it is too early to go—

   Correct: I think it is too early to go.

Colons

The **colon** is a formal mark of punctuation used chiefly to introduce something that is to follow, such as a list, a quotation, or an explanation.

1. Use a colon after a main clause to introduce a formal list, an emphatic or long restatement (appositive), an explanation, an emphatic statement, or a summary.

   These cars are my favorites: Cadillac, Chevrolet, Toyota, Oldsmobile, and Pontiac. [list]

   He worked toward one objective: a degree. [restatement or appositive]

   Let me emphasize one point: I do not accept late papers. [emphatic statement]

2. Use a colon to introduce a formal quotation or a formal question.

> Shakespeare's Polonius said: "Neither a borrower nor a lender be." [formal quotation]

> The question is this: Shall we surrender? [formal question]

3. Use a colon in the following conventional ways: to separate a title and subtitle, a chapter and verse in the Bible, and hours and minutes; and after the salutation in a formal business letter.

> Title and subtitle: *Korea: A Country Divided*
> Chapter and verse: Genesis 4:12
> Hour and minutes: 8:25 P.M.
> Salutation: Dear Ms. Chen:

Parentheses

1. Use parentheses to set off material that is not part of the main sentence but is too relevant to omit altogether. This category includes numbers that designate items in a series, amplifying references, explanations, directions, and qualifications.

> He offered two reasons for his losing: (1) he was tired, and (2) he was out of condition. [numbers]

> Review the chapters on the Civil War (6, 7, and 8) for the next class meeting. [references]

> Her husband (she had been married about a year) died last week. [explanation]

2. Use a comma, semicolon, or colon after the parentheses when the sentence punctuation requires their use.

> Although I have not lived here long (I arrived in 2002), this place feels like my only true home.

3. Use a period, question mark, or exclamation point in appropriate positions, depending on whether they go with the material within the parentheses or with the entire sentence.

> The greatest English poet of the seventeenth century was John Milton (1608–1674).

> The greatest English poet of the seventeenth century was John Milton. (Some might not agree; I myself favor Andrew Marvell.)

Brackets

Brackets are used within a quotation to set off editorial additions or corrections made by the person who is quoting.

> Churchill said: "It [the Yalta agreement] contained many mistakes."

EXERCISE 11

Using Dashes, Colons, Parentheses, Brackets, and Quotation Marks

Insert dashes, colons, parentheses, brackets, and quotation marks as needed. (See Answer Key for answers.)

1. Many of literature's great works poems, stories, and novels began as dreams.

2. Robert Louis Stevenson 1850–1894, the author of *Treasure Island,* often dreamed complete stories that he would later write.

3. He had the following to say of his tale about Jekyll and Hyde I dreamed the scene . . . in which Hyde, pursued for some crime, took the powder and underwent the change in the presence of his pursuers.

4. Mary Shelley 1797–1851 she was married to Romantic poet Percy Bysshe Shelley said that a nightmare gave her the idea for her novel *Frankenstein.*

5. English Romantic poet Samuel Taylor Coleridge, who is famous for the poem The Rime of the Ancient Mariner, is another literary artist inspired by a dream.

6. One of his best-known poems is titled Kubla Khan: Or, a Vision in a Dream.

7. This poem begins with these famous lines In Xanadu did Kubla Khan/A stately pleasure-dome decree.

8. Coleridge said that he fell asleep after reading in a history book Here the Khan Kubla another spelling of the name is Kublai Khan commanded a palace to be built and a stately garden thereunto. And thus ten miles of fertile ground were enclosed within a wall.

9. Poet, philosopher, and literary critic Coleridge had a fertile imagination and a huge intellect.

10. Unfortunately, though, he was interrupted as he composed his verse about Xanadu, and his vision completely evaporated, forcing him to subtitle the poem A Fragment.

EXERCISE 12

Using Dashes, Colons, Parentheses, Brackets, and Quotation Marks

Insert dashes, colons, parentheses, brackets, and quotation marks as needed.

1. Benjamin Franklin 1706–1790 was a remarkable man.

2. In his lifetime, Franklin served in many different roles statesman, scientist, philosopher, and publisher.

3. He rose from humble beginnings his father was a candle-maker to become America's first international celebrity.

4. His fame was due in part to his many inventions bifocals, swim fins, the odometer, the lightning rod, and the urinary catheter, among others.

5. Franklin was also an author his most famous publications were his autobiography and *Poor Richard's Almanack* who had a way with words.

6. In his *Almanack,* he included these clever sayings One today is worth two tomorrows; Early to bed and early to rise makes a man healthy, wealthy, and wise; and A penny saved is a penny earned.

7. In addition to *Poor Richard's* 1733–1758, Franklin published the *Pennsylvania Gazette* 1729–1766.

8. He is the one who left us with this astute aphorism Time is money.

9. Observant, witty, humorous Franklin also wrote, Three may keep a secret, if two of them are dead.

10. He wrote the following clever epitaph for himself The body of Benjamin Franklin, printer (like the cover of an old book, its contents worn out, and stript he used the old spelling of this word of its lettering and gilding), lies here, food for worms! Yet the work itself shall not be lost, for it will, as he believed, appear once more in a new and more beautiful edition, corrected and amended by its Author!

Apostrophes

The **apostrophe** is used with nouns and indefinite pronouns to show possession; to show the omission of letters and figures in contractions; and to form the plurals of letters, numerals, and words referred to as words.

1. A possessive shows that something is owned by someone. Use an apostrophe and -*s* to form the possessive of a noun, singular or plural, that does not end in -*s*.

    man's coat   women's suits

2. Use an apostrophe alone to form the possessive of a plural noun ending in -*s*.

    girls' clothes   the Browns' house

3. Use an apostrophe and -*s* or the apostrophe alone to form the possessive of singular nouns ending in -*s*. Use the apostrophe and -*s* only when you would pronounce the *s*.

    James' hat or (if you would pronounce the *s*) James's hat

4. Use an apostrophe and -*s* to form the possessive of certain indefinite pronouns.

    everybody's idea   one's meat   another's poison

5. Use an apostrophe to indicate that letters or numerals have been omitted.

    o'clock (short for *of the clock*)   in the '90s (short for *1990s*)

6. Use an apostrophe with pronouns only when you are making a contraction. A contraction is a combination of two words. The apostrophe in a contraction indicates where a letter has been omitted.

    it is = it's

    she has = she's

    you are = you're

    If no letters have been left out, don't use an apostrophe.

Incorrect:	The dog bit it's tail. [not a contraction]
Correct:	The dog bit its tail.
Incorrect:	Whose the leader now?
Correct:	Who's the leader now? [a contraction of *who is*]
Incorrect:	Its a big problem.
Correct:	It's a big problem. [a contraction of *it is*]

7. Use an apostrophe to indicate the plural of letters, numerals, and words used as words.

    Dot your *i*'s.   five *8*'s   *and*'s

    Note that the letters, numerals, and words are italicized, but the apostrophe and *s* are not.

Hyphens

The **hyphen** brings two or more words together into a single compound word. Correct hyphenation, therefore, is essentially a spelling problem rather than one of punctuation. Because the hyphen is not used with any degree of consistency, consult your dictionary for current usage. Study the following as a beginning guide.

1. Use a hyphen to separate the parts of many compound nouns.

> brother-in-law   go-between

2. Use a hyphen between prefixes and proper names.

> all-American   mid-Atlantic

3. Use a hyphen to join two or more words used as a single adjective modifier before a noun.

> bluish-gray eyes   first-class service

4. Use a hyphen with spelled-out compound numbers up to ninety-nine and with fractions.

> twenty-six   two-thirds

Note: Dates, street addresses, numbers requiring more than two words, chapter and page numbers, time followed directly by A.M. or P.M., and figures after a dollar sign or before measurement abbreviations are usually written as figures, not words.

Capitalization

Following are some of the many conventions concerning the use of capital letters in English.

1. Capitalize the first word of a sentence.

2. Capitalize proper nouns and adjectives derived from proper nouns.

Names of persons:
> Edward Jones

Adjectives derived from proper nouns:
> a Shakespearean sonnet   a Miltonic sonnet

Countries, nationalities, races, languages:
> Germany   Spanish
> English   Chinese

States, regions, localities, other geographical divisions:
> California   the Far East   the South

Oceans, lakes, mountains, deserts, streets, parks:
> Lake Superior   Fifth Avenue   Sahara Desert

Educational institutions, schools, courses:
> Santa Ana College   Joe Hill School
> Spanish 3   Rowland High School

Organizations and their members:

    Boston Red Sox   Boy Scouts   Audubon Society

Corporations, governmental agencies or departments, trade names:

    U.S. Steel Corporation   Treasury Department
    Coca-Cola   White Memorial Library

Calendar references such as holidays, days of the week, months:

    Easter   Tuesday   January

Historic eras, periods, documents, laws:

    Declaration of Independence   Geneva Convention
    Romantic Age   First Crusade

3. Capitalize words denoting family relationships when they are used before a name or substituted for a name.

    He walked with his nephew and Aunt Grace.

                  but

    He walked with his nephew and his aunt.

    Grandmother and Mother are away on vacation.

                  but

    My grandmother and my mother are away on vacation.

4. Capitalize abbreviations after names.

    Henry White Jr.   Juan Gomez, M.D.

5. Capitalize titles of essays, books, plays, movies, poems, magazines, newspapers, musical compositions, songs, and works of art. Do not capitalize articles, short conjunctions, or prepositions unless they come at the beginning or the end of the title.

    Desire Under the Elms   *Terminator*

    The Last of the Mohicans   *Of Mice and Men*

    "Blueberry Hill"

6. Capitalize any title preceding a name or used as a substitute for a name. Do not capitalize a title following a name.

    Judge Wong   Alfred Wong, a judge

    General Clark   Raymond Clark, a general

    Professor Fuentes   Harry Fuentes, the biology professor

EXERCISE 13

Using Capital Letters, Hyphens, Apostrophes, and Quotation Marks

Correct capitalization and insert hyphens, apostrophes, and quotation marks as needed. (See Answer Key for answers.)

1. Ive heard that you intend to move to el paso, texas, my brother in law said.

2. My date of departure on united airlines is july 11, I answered.

3. Then youve only thirty three days remaining in california, he said.

4. My mother gave me some samsonite luggage, and dad gave me a ronson razor.

5. Jennifer does not know i am leaving for the university of texas.

6. Jennifer, my mothers dog, is one quarter poodle and three quarters cocker spaniel.

7. That dogs immediate concern is almost always food rather than sentimentality.

8. I wouldnt have received my scholarship without the straight *A*s from my elective classes.

9. I am quite indebted to professor jackson, a first rate teacher of english and several courses in speech.

10. I wasnt surprised when grandma gave me a box of stationery and a note asking me to write mother each friday.

EXERCISE 14

Using Capital Letters, Hyphens, Apostrophes, and Quotation Marks

Correct capitalization and insert hyphens, apostrophes, and quotation marks as needed.

1. Many young readers of *Harry Potter and the sorcerer's stone* and its sequels wish that Hogwarts school of witchcraft and wizardry were a real place.

2. They wish they could take classes like professor snapes course in making potions or professor mcGonagalls course in transfiguration.

3. In interviews, however, author j.k. rowlling says, the setting is a fictional place.

4. Maybe she hasnt heard of flamel college, which was named after nicholas flamel, a first rate alchemist who lived in europe from 1330 to 1418.

5. Legend has it that flamel actually achieved every alchemists life long goal when he figured out how to turn other metals into gold.

6. Through the sacramento, california, institution named for him, would be witches and wizards can now earn credentials with names like diploma in magic and degree in esoteric arts.

7. Classes include crystal magic, developing psychic abilities, and pagan paths.

8. The person who described the college on its Web site wrote, we offer an unconventional curriculum.

9. The faculty of flamel college includes well known astrologers, witches, alchemists, and experts on ghosts and hauntings.

10. If you get straight *A*s in your courses, maybe you can command a few spirits to write your dissertation for you.

EXERCISE 15

Using Capital Letters and All Punctuation Marks

Correct capitalization and insert punctuation marks as needed.

will rogers 1879–1935 was a famous movie star newspaper writer and lecturer. A part cherokee indian he was born in what was then indian territory before oklahoma became a state. He is especially known for his humor and his social and political criticism. He said my ancestors may not have come over on the *mayflower*, but they met em at the boat. He said that when many oklahomans moved to california in the early 1930s the average IQ increased in both states. In his early years, he was a first class performer in rodeos circuses and variety shows. When he performed in variety shows he often twirled a rope. He usually began his presentations by saying, all I know is what I read in the papers. Continuing to be close to his oklahoma roots he appeared in fifty one silent movies and twenty one talking movies. At the age of fifty

six he was killed in an airplane crash near Point Barrow Alaska. He was so popular

and influential that his statue now stands in washington d.c. On another statue of

him in Claremore Oklahoma is inscribed one of his most famous sayings I never met

a man I didn't like.

CHAPTER REVIEW   PUNCTUATION AND CAPITALIZATION

1. There are three marks of **end punctuation.**
- **a.** Periods
  Place a period after a statement.
  Place a period after common abbreviations.
- **b.** Question marks
  Place a question mark at the end of a direct question.
  Do not use a question mark after an indirect question.

  She asked me what caused the slide.

- **c.** Exclamation points
  Place an exclamation point after a word or group of words that expresses strong feeling.

  Do not overwork the exclamation point. Do not use double exclamation points.

2. The **comma** is used to separate and to set off sentence elements.
- **a.** Use a comma to separate main clauses joined by one of the coordinating conjunctions—*for, and, nor, but, or, yet, so.*

  We went to the game, but it was canceled.

- **b.** Use a comma after long introductory modifiers. The modifiers may be phrases or dependent clauses.

  Before she and I arrived, the meeting was called to order.

- **c.** Use a comma to separate words, phrases, and clauses in a series.

  He ran down the street, across the park, and into the forest.

- **d.** Use a comma to separate coordinate adjectives not joined by *and* that modify the same noun.

  I need a sturdy, reliable truck.

- **e.** Use a comma to separate sentence elements that might be misread.

  Outside, the thunder rolled.

- **f.** Use commas to set off nonessential (unnecessary for the meaning of the sentence) words, phrases, and clauses.

  Maria, who studied hard, will pass.

g. Use commas to set off nouns used as direct address.

What do you intend to do, Hamlet?

h. Use commas to separate the numbers in a date.

November 11, 1918, is a day worth remembering.

i. Use commas to separate the city from the state. No comma is used between the state and the ZIP code.

Boston, MA 02110

3. The **semicolon** indicates a longer pause and stronger emphasis than the comma. It is used principally to separate main clauses within a sentence.
   a. Use a semicolon to separate main clauses not joined by a coordinating conjunction.

   You must buy that car today; tomorrow will be too late.

   b. Use a semicolon between two main clauses joined by a conjunctive adverb (such as *however, otherwise, therefore, similarly, hence, on the other hand, then, consequently, accordingly, thus*).

   It was very late; therefore, I remained at the hotel.

4. **Quotation marks** bring special attention to words.
   a. Quotation marks are used principally to set off direct quotations. A direct quotation consists of material taken from the written work or the direct speech of others; it is set off by double quotation marks. Single quotation marks are used to set off a quotation within a quotation.

   He said, "I don't remember if she said, 'Wait for me.'"

   b. Use double quotation marks to set off slang, technical terms, and special words.

   The "platoon system" changed the game of football. [technical term]

5. **Italics** (slanting type) are also used to call special attention to certain words or groups of words. In handwriting or typing, such words are underlined.
   a. Italicize (underline) foreign words and phrases that are still listed in the dictionary as foreign.

   modus operandi   perestroika

   b. Italicize titles of books; long poems; plays; magazines; motion pictures; musical compositions; newspapers; works of art; names of aircraft and ships; and letters, numbers, and words referred to by their own name.

   War and Peace   Apollo 12   leaving the second *o* out of *sophomore*

6. The **dash** is used when a stronger pause than the comma is needed. It can also be used to indicate a break in the flow of thought and to emphasize words (less formal than the colon in this situation).

   I can't remember the town—now I do—it's Tupelo.

7. The **colon** is a formal mark of punctuation used chiefly to introduce something that is to follow, such as a list, a quotation, or an explanation.

> These cars are my favorites: Cadillac, Chevrolet, Toyota, Oldsmobile, and Pontiac.

8. **Parentheses** are used to set off material that is of relatively little importance to the main thought of the sentence. Such material—numbers, parenthetical material, figures, supplementary material, and sometimes explanatory details—merely amplifies the main thought.

> The years of the era (1961–1973) were full of action.

> I paid twenty dollars ($20) for that mousepad.

9. **Brackets** are used within a quotation to set off editorial additions or corrections made by the person who is quoting.

> "It [the Yalta Agreement] contained many mistakes."

10. The **apostrophe** is used with nouns and indefinite pronouns to show possession, to show the omission of letters and figures in contractions, and to form the plurals of letters, figures, and words referred to as words.

> man's coat   girls' clothes   can't   five *and*'s   it's [contraction]

11. The **hyphen** is used to link two or more words together into a single compound word. Hyphenation, therefore, is essentially a spelling problem rather than a punctuation problem. Because the hyphen is not used with any degree of consistency, it is best to consult your dictionary to learn current usage.

  a. Use a hyphen to separate the parts of many compound words.

> about-face   go-between

  b. Use a hyphen between prefixes and proper names.

> all-American   mid-July

  c. Use a hyphen with spelled-out compound numbers up to ninety-nine and with fractions.

> twenty-six   one hundred   two-thirds

  d. Use a hyphen to join two or more words used as a single adjective modifier before a noun.

> first-class service   hard-fought game   sad-looking mother

12. In English, there are many conventions concerning the use of capital letters. Although style and use of capital letters may vary, certain rules for capitalization are well established.

  a. Capitalize the first word of a sentence.

  b. Capitalize proper nouns and adjectives derived from proper nouns such as the names of persons, countries, nationalities and races, days of the week, months, and titles of books.

  c. Capitalize words denoting family relationships when they are used before a name or substituted for a name.

> The minister greeted Aunt May, my grandfather, and Mother.

CHAPTER REVIEW EXERCISES

Using Capital Letters and All Punctuation Marks

Correct capitalization and insert punctuation marks as needed. (See Answer Key for answers.)

1. everyone defines the term success differently how do you define it

2. according to american author and editor christopher morley the only success is being able to spend your life the way you want to spend it

3. margaret thatcher former leader of great britain said that success is being good at what youre doing but also having a sense of purpose

4. author vernon howard had this to say on the subject "you have succeeded in life when all you really want is only what you really need

5. albert einstein however believed that if A equals success in life then

    $A = x + y + z$

6. x is work y is play and z is keeping your mouth shut

7. one of the most well known quotes about success comes from philosopher ralph waldo emerson who wrote that to have succeeded is "to leave the world a bit better" and "to know that even one life has breathed easier because you have lived

Using Capital Letters and All Punctuation Marks

Correct capitalization and insert punctuation marks as needed.

Jack (Jackie) Roosevelt Robinson 1919–1972 was born in Pasadena California. After excelling in sports in high school and community college he transferred to UCLA, where he lettered in four sports baseball, basketball, football, and track. In world war II he was commissioned second lieutenant in the army. After he was discharged he joined the negro league as a player with the Kansas City Monarchs for $100 a week. In 1947 he was offered a tryout with the Brooklyn dodgers. Before no African Americans had been allowed to participate in the minor or major leagues.

After signing a contract, Jackie Robinson was sent to the minor leagues and there he played for one year with Montreal a team in the International League. Following a year in which he was the best hitter in the league he was brought up to the major leagues. During the first year 1947 he showed his greatness and was named the rookie of the year. Two years later he was the most valuable player in the national league and won the batting title with a .342 average. Despite the initial bigoted opposition by some baseball fans and players he performed with dignity courage and skill. Nevertheless he was an independent proud person. In the book Players of Cooperstown Mike Tully wrote he Robinson refused to be someone he was not, refused to conform to an image of a man who 'knew his place.' Because sports is such a high profile activity Jackie Robinson is credited with playing a significant role in breaking down the racial barriers in society. In his ten years in the major leagues he helped his team reach the world series six times. He was inducted into the Baseball hall of fame in 1962.

REVIEW 3

Demonstrating Ability to Use Correct Punctuation

Demonstrate your ability to use correct punctuation by writing sentences that contain the following marks. Use the topics in parentheses.

Comma (travel)

1. To separate independent clauses in a compound sentence using coordinating conjunctions (FANBOYS)

   _____

   _____

   _____

2. For long introductory modifiers

   _____

   _____

   _____

3. To separate words in a series

_____

_____

_____

Semicolon (a family member)

4. To connect two related independent clauses without a coordinating conjunction

_____

_____

_____

Quotation Marks (Use this textbook as your source for quotations.)

5. To set off a quotation (words taken from the written work or the speech of others)

_____

_____

_____

Italics, Shown by Underlining (school)

6. Word or letter referred to by its name

_____

_____

_____

7. Title of a book

_____

_____

_____

Colon (computers)

8. To introduce a list

_____

_____

_____

Apostrophe (friendship)

9. A singular possessive

_____

_____

_____

10. A plural possessive

_____

_____

_____

11. A contraction

_____

_____

_____

Hyphen (shopping)

12. Numbers

_____

_____

_____

13. Two-word modifiers

_____

_____

_____

_____

MICROTHEME

To practice your skills acquired in this chapter, return to the Microtheme on page 208 and complete Exercise B.

Chapter

11

Spelling and Phrasing

A person who is not born a great speller will probably never be one, but almost anyone can, with work, become a competent speller, an accomplishment to be proud of.

FLOW OF WRITING

Learning Objectives

Working with this chapter, I will learn to

~ discover my spelling problems and address them systematically.

~ make a list of my troublesome words.

~ memorize the words I commonly misspell.

~ use my spell checker effectively by understanding what it can and cannot do.

FLOW OF WRITING

MICROTHEME

Writing Activity in Miniature

Two Purposes

Writing Diagnostic: Before you work on this chapter, the Microtheme will give you an opportunity to write briefly on an engaging topic without pressure.

Chapter Learning Application: After you have studied this chapter, return to your Microtheme to check your work and practice what you have just learned.

Form and Procedure

Like an executive summary (written for a busy boss), the Microtheme conveys ideas concisely (using no more than the space on a 5- by 8-inch card) in a specified form. Indent only once, and write small enough to leave room for marking later. Directions for practicing your chapter writing skills appear in Exercise B.

Suggested Microtheme Topic

Write a Microtheme of 80 to 100 words about an imaginary vacation to a time and place of your choice. (Space travel is acceptable, but no space-alien abduction pieces unless approved by your instructor.)

_____

_____

_____

_____

_____

_____

_____

_____

_____

_____

_____

_____

_____

EXERCISE B

Connecting Your Learning Objectives with Your Microtheme

Complete this exercise after you have studied this chapter.

1. Circle questionable words and check them in a dictionary.

2. Make sure you did not use second-best words because you could not spell the best words.

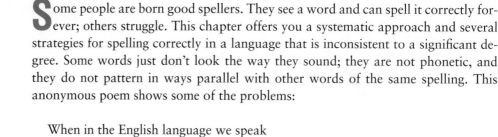

Some people are born good spellers. They see a word and can spell it correctly forever; others struggle. This chapter offers you a systematic approach and several strategies for spelling correctly in a language that is inconsistent to a significant degree. Some words just don't look the way they sound; they are not phonetic, and they do not pattern in ways parallel with other words of the same spelling. This anonymous poem shows some of the problems:

> When in the English language we speak
> Why is *break* not rhymed with *freak?*
> Will you tell me why it's true
> That we *sew,* but we also saw *few?*
> And why cannot makers of verse
> Rhyme the word *horse* with *worse?*
> *Beard* sounds much different from *heard*
> *Cord* is so different from *word*
> *Cow* is *cow,* but *low* is *low.*
> *Shoe* never rhymes with *foe,*
> And think of *hose,* and *dose,* and *lose,*
> And think of *goose* and yet of *choose,*
> *Doll* and *roll,* and *home* and *some.*
> And since *pay* is rhymed with *say,*
> Why *paid* and *said,* I pray?
> *Mood* is not pronounced like *wood*
> And *done* is not like *gone* and *lone.*
> To sum it all up, it seems to me
> That sounds and letters just do not agree.

Despite these problems inherent in our language, you can be an effective speller. Unfortunately, for those who are not, there are unhappy consequences. In a society as literate as ours, if you are a poor speller, you will find yourself with a serious handicap. The professions and trades, as well as schools, are demanding that individuals spell well and write effectively. If you write *thier* for *their* or *definately* for *definitely* in compositions, term reports, examinations, letters of application, or business reports, you will draw unfavorable attention from your audience.

Steps to Efficient Spelling

1. Make up your mind that you are going to spell well.

2. Use your Self-Evaluation Chart (inside front cover of this book) to keep a list of words you misspell; work on spelling them correctly.

3. Get into the habit of looking up new words in a dictionary for correct spelling as well as for meaning.

4. Look at each letter in a word carefully and pronounce each syllable; that is, *change-a-ble, con-tin-u-ous, dis-ap-pear-ance.*

5. Visualize how the word is made up.

6. Write the word correctly several times. After each writing, close your eyes and again visualize the word.

7. Set up frequent recall sessions with problem words. Become aware of the reasons for your errors.

Your Spell Checker

Your computer spell checker is an important tool with many benefits and some limitations. With about 100,000 words in a typical database, the spell checker alerts you to problem words that should be verified. If you agree that the spelling of a word should be checked, you can then select from a list of words with similar spellings. A likely substitute word will be highlighted. With a keystroke, you can correct a problem, add your own word to the database, or ignore the alert. With a few more keystrokes, you can type in your own correction. You may even be able to program your spell checker to correct automatically your most frequent spelling or typing errors. You will be amazed at how many times your computer will catch misspellings that your eye did not see.

However, the spell checker has limitations. If you intended to type *he* and instead typed *me*, the spell checker will not alert you to a possible problem because the word you typed is spelled correctly. If you use the wrong word, such as *herd* instead of *heard*, the spell checker will not detect a problem. Thus you should always proofread your writing after you have spell checked it. Do not be lulled into a false sense of spelling security simply because you have a machine on your side. As a writer, you are the final spell checker.

Spelling Tips

The following tips will help you become a better speller:

1. Do not omit letters.

Many errors occur because certain letters are omitted when the word is pronounced or spelled. Observe the omissions in the following words. Then concentrate on learning the correct spellings.

Incorrect	Correct	Incorrect	Correct
agravate	aggravate	irigation	irrigation
ajourned	adjourned	libary	library
aproved	approved	paralell	parallel
aquaintance	acquaintance	parlament	parliament
artic	arctic	paticulary	particularly
comodity	commodity	readly	readily
efficent	efficient	sophmore	sophomore
envirnment	environment	stricly	strictly
familar	familiar	unconsious	unconscious

2. Do not add letters.

Incorrect	Correct	Incorrect	Correct
athelete	athlete	ommission	omission
comming	coming	pasttime	pastime
drownded	drowned	priviledge	privilege
folkes	folks	similiar	similar
occassionally	occasionally	tradgedy	tragedy

3. Do not substitute incorrect letters for correct letters.

Incorrect	Correct	Incorrect	Correct
benefisial	beneficial	offence	offense
bull*i*tins	bulletins	peculi*er*	peculiar
*sen*sus	census	re*si*tation	recitation
di*s*cription	description	scre*a*ch	screech
de*s*ease	disease	substan*si*al	substantial
dissen*t*ion	dissension	surpri*z*e	surprise
it*i*ms	items	techn*a*cal	technical

4. Do not transpose letters.

Incorrect	Correct	Incorrect	Correct
alu*nm*i	alumni	*pre*haps	perhaps
child*er*n	children	*pe*rfer	prefer
dup*il*cate	duplicate	*pe*rscription	prescription
irre*ve*lant	irrelevant	princip*el*s	principles
kind*el*	kindle	*ye*ild	yield

Note: Whenever you notice other words that fall into any one of these categories, add them to the list.

5. Apply the spelling rules for spelling *ei* and *ie* words correctly.

Remember the poem?

Use *i* before *e*
Except after *c*
Or when sounded like *a*
As in *neighbor* and *weigh*.

i before e

achieve	chief	niece	relieve
belief	field	piece	shield
believe	grief	pierce	siege
brief	hygiene	relief	variety

Except after c

ceiling	conceive	deceive	receipt
conceit	deceit	perceive	receive

Exceptions: either, financier, height, leisure, neither, seize, species, weird

When sounded like a

deign	freight	neighbor	sleigh
eight	heinous	reign	veil
feign	heir	rein	vein
feint	neigh	skein	weigh

6. Apply the rules for dropping the final *e* or retaining the final *e* when a suffix is added.

Words ending in a silent *e* usually drop the *e* before a suffix beginning with a vowel; for example, *accuse* + *-ing* = *accusing*. Here are some common suffixes beginning with a vowel: *-able*, *-al*, *-age*, *-ary*, *-ation*, *-ence*, *-ing*, *-ion*, *-ous*, *-ure*.

admire + -*able* = admirable
arrive + -*al* = arrival
come + -*ing* = coming
explore + -*ation* = exploration
fame + -*ous* = famous

imagine + -*ary* = imaginary
locate + -*ion* = location
please + -*ure* = pleasure
plume + -*age* = plumage
precede + -*ence* = precedence

Exceptions: *dye* + -*ing* = *dyeing* (to distinguish it from *dying*), *acreage, mileage.*

Words ending in a silent *e* usually retain the *e* before a suffix beginning with a consonant; for example: *arrange* + -*ment* = *arrangement*. Here are some common suffixes beginning with a consonant: *-craft, -ful, -less, -ly, -mate, -ment, -ness, -ty.*

entire + -*ty* = entirety
hate + -*ful* = hateful
hope + -*less* = hopeless
like + -*ness* = likeness

manage + -*ment* = management
safe + -*ly* = safely
stale + -*mate* = stalemate
state + -*craft* = statecraft

Exceptions: Some words taking the -*ful* or -*ly* suffixes drop the final *e:*

awe + -*ful* = awful
due + -*ly* = duly

true + -*ly* = truly
whole + -*ly* = wholly

Some words taking the suffix -*ment* drop the final *e*; for example:

acknowledgment   argument   judgment

Words ending in silent *e* after *c* or *g* retain the *e* when the suffix begins with the vowel *a* or *o*. The final *e* is retained to keep the *c* or *g* soft before the suffixes.

advantageous
courageous

noticeable
peaceable

7. **Apply the rules for doubling a final consonant before a suffix beginning with a vowel.**

Words of one syllable:

blot	blotted	get	getting	rob	robbed
brag	bragging	hop	hopped	run	running
cut	cutting	hot	hottest	sit	sitting
drag	dragged	man	mannish	stop	stopped
drop	dropped	plan	planned	swim	swimming

Words accented on the last syllable:

acquit	acquitted	equip	equipped
admit	admittance	occur	occurrence
allot	allotted	omit	omitting
begin	beginning	prefer	preferred
commit	committee	refer	referred
concur	concurring	submit	submitted
confer	conferring	transfer	transferred
defer	deferring		

Words that are not accented on the last syllable and words that do not end in a single consonant preceded by a vowel do not double the final consonant (whether or not the suffix begins with a vowel).

Frequently Misspelled Words

a lot	eighth	likely	sacrifice
absence	eligible	lying	safety
across	eliminate	marriage	scene
actually	embarrassed	mathematics	schedule
all right	environment	meant	secretary
among	especially	medicine	senior
analyze	etc.	neither	sense
appearance	exaggerate	ninety	separate
appreciate	excellent	ninth	severely
argument	exercise	nuclear	shining
athlete	existence	occasionally	significant
athletics	experience	opinion	similar
awkward	explanation	opportunity	sincerely
becoming	extremely	parallel	sophomore
beginning	familiar	particular	speech
belief	February	persuade	straight
benefit	finally	physically	studying
buried	foreign	planned	succeed
business	government	pleasant	success
certain	grammar	possible	suggest
college	grateful	practical	surprise
coming	guarantee	preferred	thoroughly
committee	guard	prejudice	though
competition	guidance	privilege	tragedy
complete	height	probably	tried
consider	hoping	professor	tries
criticism	humorous	prove	truly
definitely	immediately	psychology	unfortunately
dependent	independent	pursue	unnecessary
develop	intelligence	receipt	until
development	interest	receive	unusual
difference	interfere	recommend	using
disastrous	involved	reference	usually
discipline	knowledge	relieve	Wednesday
discussed	laboratory	religious	writing
disease	leisure	repetition	written
divide	length	rhythm	
dying	library	ridiculous	

Confused Spelling and Confusing Words

The following are more words that are commonly misspelled or confused with one another. Some have similar sounds, some are often mispronounced, and some are only misunderstood.

a   An adjective (called an article) used before a word beginning with a consonant or a consonant sound, as in "I ate *a* donut."

an   An adjective (called an article) used before a word beginning with a vowel (*a, e, i, o, u*) or with a silent *h*, as in "I ate *an* artichoke."

and	A coordinating conjunction, as in "Sara *and* I like Johnny Cash."
accept	A verb meaning "to receive," as in "I *accept* your explanation."
except	A preposition meaning "to exclude," as in "I paid everyone *except* you."
advice	A noun meaning "guidance," as in "Thanks for the *advice*."
advise	A verb meaning "to give guidance," as in "Will you please *advise* me of my rights?"
all right	An adjective meaning "correct" or "acceptable," as in "It's *all right* to cry."
alright	Not used in formal writing.
all ready	An adjective that can be used interchangeably with *ready*, as in "I am *all ready* to go to town."
already	An adverb meaning "before," which cannot be used in place of *ready*, as in "I have *already* finished."
a lot	An adverb meaning "much," as in "She liked him *a lot*," or a noun meaning "several," as in "I had *a lot* of suggestions."
alot	Misspelling.
altogether	An adverb meaning "completely," as in "He is *altogether* happy."
all together	An adverb meaning "as one," which can be used interchangeably with *together*, as in "The group left *all together*."
choose	A present tense verb meaning "to select," as in "Do whatever you *choose*."
chose	The past tense form of the verb *choose*, as in "They *chose* to take action yesterday."
could of	A misspelled phrase caused by confusing *could've*, meaning *could have*, with *could of*.
could have	Correctly spelled phrase, as in "I *could have* danced all night."
effect	Usually a noun meaning "result," as in "That *effect* was unexpected."
affect	Usually a verb meaning "change," as in "Ideas *affect* me."
hear	A verb indicating the receiving of sound, as in "I *hear* thunder."
here	An adverb meaning "present location," as in "I live *here*."
it's	A contraction of *it is,* as in "*It's* time to dance."
its	Possessive pronoun, as in "Each dog has *its* day."
know	A verb usually meaning "to comprehend" or "to recognize," as in "I *know* the answer."
no	An adjective meaning "negative," as in "I have *no* potatoes."
led	The past tense form of the verb *lead,* as in "I *led* a wild life in my youth."
lead	A present tense verb, as in "I *lead* a stable life now," or a noun referring to a substance, such as "I sharpened the *lead* in my pencil."
loose	An adjective meaning "without restraint," as in "He is a *loose* cannon."
lose	A present tense verb from the pattern *lose, lost, lost,* as in "I thought I would *lose* my senses."
paid	The past tense form of *pay,* as in "He *paid* his dues."
payed	Misspelling.
passed	The past tense form of the verb *pass,* meaning "went by," as in "He *passed* me on the curve."
past	An adjective meaning "former," as in "That's *past* history," or a noun, as in "He lived in the *past*."
patience	A noun meaning "willingness to wait," as in "Job was a man of much *patience*."
patients	A noun meaning "people under care," as in "The doctor had fifty *patients*."

peace	A noun meaning "a quality of calmness" or "absence of strife," as in "The guru was at *peace* with the world."
piece	A noun meaning "part," as in "I gave him a *piece* of my mind."
quiet	An adjective meaning "silent," as in "She was a *quiet* child."
quit	A verb meaning "to cease" or "to withdraw," as in "I *quit* my job."
quite	An adverb meaning "very," as in "The clam is *quite* happy."
receive	A verb meaning "to accept," as in "I will *receive* visitors now."
recieve	Misspelling.
stationary	An adjective meaning "not moving," as in "Try to avoid running into *stationary* objects."
stationery	A noun meaning "paper material to write on," as in "I bought a box of *stationery* for Sue's birthday present."
than	A conjunction, as in "He is taller *than* I am."
then	An adverb, as in "She *then* left town."
their	A possessive pronoun, as in "They read *their* books."
there	An adverb, as in "He left it *there*," or a filler word as in "*There* is no time left."
they're	A contraction of *they are*, as in "*They're* happy."
to	A preposition, as in "I went *to* town."
too	An adverb meaning "excessively" or "very," as in "you are *too* late to qualify for the discount," or "also," as in "I have feelings, *too*."
two	An adjective of number, as in "I have *two* jobs."
thorough	An adjective meaning "complete" or "careful," as in "He did a *thorough* job."
through	A preposition, as in "She went *through* the yard."
truly	An adverb meaning "sincerely" or "completely," as in "He was *truly* happy."
truely	Misspelling.
weather	A noun meaning "condition of the atmosphere," as in "The *weather* is pleasant today."
whether	A conjunction, as in "*Whether* he would go was of no consequence."
write	A present tense verb, as in "Watch me as I *write* this letter."
writen	Misspelling.
written	Past participle of the verb *write*, as in "I have *written* the letter."
you're	A contraction of *you are*, as in "*You're* my friend."
your	A possessive pronoun, as in "I like *your* looks."

EXERCISE 1

Spelling Confusing Words

Underline the correct word or words. (See Answer Key for answers.)

1. I cannot (hear, here) the answers.

2. She is taller (then, than) I.

3. They left town to find (their, they're, there) roots.

4. Sam went (through, thorough) the initiation.

5. I am only asking for a little (peace, piece) of the action.

6. Whatever you say is (alright, all right) with me.

7. I (passed, past) the test, and now I'm ready for action.

8. That smash was (to, too, two) hot to handle.

9. I did not ask for her (advise, advice).

10. I found (a lot, alot) of new ideas in that book.

11. She has (all ready, already) left.

12. I (chose, choose) my answer and hoped for the best.

13. I knew that I would (recieve, receive) fair treatment.

14. Juan was (quit, quite, quiet) happy with my decision.

15. Maria (could of, could have) completed the assignment.

16. Marlin knew they would (lose, loose) the game.

17. I've heard that (it's, its) a good movie.

18. June would not (accept, except) my answer.

19. I did not (know, no) what to do.

20. Sean (paid, payed) his bill and left town.

EXERCISE 2

Spelling Confusing Words

Underline the correct word or words.

1. She said that my application was (alright, all right).

2. Sheriff Dillon worked hard for (peace, piece) in the valley.

3. She was the first woman to (recieve, receive) a medal.

4. He spoke his mind; (then, than) he left.

5. The cleaners did a (through, thorough) job.

6. After the loud explosion, there was (quit, quiet, quite).

7. The nurse worked diligently with his (patience, patients).

8. They were not (altogether, all together) happy, but they (could of, could have) been.

9. The cowboys (led, lead) the cows to water.

10. For my hobby, I study (grammar, grammer).

11. Elvis (truly, truely) respected his mother.

12. Zeke asked for the (whether, weather) report.

13. I never (advise, advice) my friends about gambling.

14. You should (accept, except) responsibility for your actions.

15. Joan inherited (alot, a lot) of money.

16. We waited for the gorilla to (chose, choose) a mate.

17. Virginia thinks (its, it's) a good day for a party.

18. It was a tale of (to, too, two) cities.

19. I went (they're, their, there) to my childhood home.

20. It was the best letter Kevin had ever (writen, written, wrote).

Wordy Phrases

Certain phrases clutter sentences, consuming our time in writing and our readers' time in reading. Be on the lookout for wordy phrases as you revise and edit your composition.

Wordy: *Due to the fact* that he was unemployed, he had to use public transportation.

Concise: *Because* he was unemployed, he had to use public transportation.

Wordy: *Deep down inside* he believed that the Red Sox would win.

Concise: He believed that the Red Sox would win.

Wordy	Concise
at the present time	now
basic essentials	essentials
blend together	blend
it is clear that	(delete)
due to the fact that	because
for the reason that	because
I felt inside	I felt
in most cases	usually
as a matter of fact	in fact
in the event that	if
until such time as	until
I personally feel	I feel
in this modern world	today
in order to	to
most of the people	most people
along the lines of	like
past experience	experience
at that point in time	then
in the final analysis	finally
in the near future	soon
have a need for	need
in this day and age	now

EXERCISE 3

Wordy Phrasing

Circle the wordy phrases and write in concise phrases.

1. I tried to recall that moment, but my memories seemed to blend together.

2. I expect to get out of this bed and go to work in the near future.

3. As a matter of fact, when I was a child, I had an imaginary playmate.

4. I feel in my heart that bees work too hard.

5. I am not surprised by this conviction due to the fact that as a child he used to torment vegetables.

6. In this modern world most of the people do not use enough shoe polish.

7. I was crowned Mr. Clean for the reason that I always wash my hands before I wash my hands.

8. At the present time I am concentrating on not thinking about warthogs.

9. Procrastination is an idea I will consider in the near future.

10. I personally feel that Cupid just shot me with a poisoned arrow.

CHAPTER REVIEW   SPELLING AND PHRASING

1. Do not omit letters.

      Incorrect: *libary*

      Correct: *library*

2. Do not add letters.

      Incorrect: *athalete*

      Correct: *athlete*

3. Do not substitute incorrect letters for correct letters.

      Incorrect: *technacal*

      Correct: *technical*

4. Do not transpose letters.

      Incorrect: *perfer*

      Correct: *prefer*

5. Apply the spelling rules for spelling *ei* and *ie* words correctly.

Use *i* before *e*
Except after *c*
Or when sounded like *a*
As in *neighbor* and *weigh*.

Exceptions: *either, financier, height, leisure, neither, seize, species, weird.*

6. Apply the rules for dropping the final *e* or retaining the final *e* when a suffix is added. (See the exceptions on pages 248–249.)

Correct: *come   coming*

7. Apply the rules for doubling a final consonant before a suffix beginning with a vowel if the final syllable is accented.

Correct: *transfer   transferred*

8. Study the list of frequently misspelled words (see page 250).

9. Some words are sometimes misspelled because they are mispronounced or share a pronunciation with another word.

Incorrect: *alright*

Correct: *all right*

Two words with the same sound and different meanings: *hear   here*

10. Use your spell checker, but be aware of its limitations and always proofread your writing.

CHAPTER REVIEW EXERCISES

REVIEW 1   **Adding Suffixes**

Add the indicated suffixes to the following words. If you need help, see pages 248–249 for adding suffixes. (See Answer Key for answers.)

1. fame + -*ous* = _____
2. locate + -*ion* = _____
3. notice + -*able* = _____
4. drop + -*ed* = _____
5. like + -*ly* = _____
6. hope + -*less* = _____
7. manage + -*ment* = _____
8. hot + -*est* = _____
9. rob + -*ed* = _____

10. stop + -ed = _____

11. safe + -ly = _____

12. argue + -ment = _____

13. judge + -ment = _____

14. courage + -ous = _____

15. swim + -ing = _____

16. commit + -ed = _____

17. occur + -ence = _____

18. omit + -ed = _____

19. begin + -ing = _____

20. prefer + -ed = _____

Correcting Misspelling

Underline the misspelled words and write the correct spelling above the words. Draw two lines under the words that are incorrectly spelled but would go unchallenged by your spell checker.

Professor Pufnagel was torturing his English students once again, and he relished his familar evil roll. "Today, class, we will write without the assistence of computers. In fact, never again will we use them in this class. They are a perscription for lazyness. And they make life to easy for alot of you."

The profesor lectured the students for an hour, stresing that when he was in school, there were no computers in his enviroment. He extoled the virtues of writting with little yellow pensils, fountain pens, and solid, dependible typewriters. He went on with his ranting, listing computer games, television sets, frozen foods, plastic wrap, asperin, and Velcro as similiar and familiar negative forces that had lead society to it's truely sorry state. "You are nothing but a pityful pack of party people, and you will recieve no sympathy from me," he sputtered. Grabbing a student's laptop computer, Pufnagel reared back and, like an athalete, hurled it against the wall. In the corner of the classroom lay a pile of high-tech junk, once fine shinning machines, now just garbage—smashed in a senseless, aweful war against technology.

The students starred in embarassed amazement at there professor, who was developing a nervous twitch. His mouth began twisting and contorting as his limbs jerked with the helter-skelter motion of a tangled marionette. He clutched desparately at his throat, and smoke began to poor out of his ears and neck. Unconsious, he crashed to the floor with a clatter.

One of the students, who had just taken a CPR class, rushed forward and attempted to revive the fallen educator. As the student pounded with a catchy rap rhythm on the chest of his stricken teacher, everyone herd a loud pop and sizzle.

It was a door in Pufnagel's chest, which had poped open to reveal the complex electrical control panel of a short-circuited cyborg!

Just than a security team in white jumpsuits from student goverment entered the class, carefully deposited Pufnagel on a wheelbarrow, and roled him out to the Faculty Service Center.

A few minutes later a Professor Ramirez arrived. "Ladys and gentlemen," she said, "its time to start your search engines. Your prevous professor's mainframe is down, but I'm his substitute and mine is fine, fine, fine, fine, fine, fine, fine, fine, fine, fine. . . ."

MICROTHEME

To practice your skills acquired in this chapter, return to the Microtheme on page 245 and complete Exercise B.

Using the Writing Process

Most college writing occurs as paragraphs and essays in response to special assignments, tests, reports, and research papers. Chapters 12 through 14 concentrate on the paragraph, showing you how to use the stages of the writing process and giving you opportunities to experiment. A common form for short composition answers for various tasks, the well-organized paragraph is often a miniature structural version of the essay. Chapter 15 demonstrates how you can use your mastery of process writing for paragraphs in essay writing.

The Writing Process: Prewriting the Paragraph

You can use the developmental paragraph in three ways: (1) as a complete answer to a short writing assignment, (2) as a middle or body paragraph in a longer composition, and (3) as a brief workplace communication.

FLOW OF WRITING

Learning Objectives

Working with this chapter, I will learn to

~ define a paragraph.

~ use the basic paragraph patterns.

~ prewrite the paragraph.

The Paragraph Defined

Defining the word *paragraph* is no easy task because there are different kinds of paragraphs, each one having a different purpose:

Introductory: Usually the first paragraph in an essay, it gives the necessary background and indicates the main idea, called the **thesis.**

Developmental: A unit of several sentences, it expands on an idea. This book features the writing of developmental paragraphs.

Transitional: A very brief paragraph, it merely directs the reader from one point in the essay to another.

Concluding: Usually the last paragraph in an essay, it makes the final comment on the topic.

The following paragraph is both a definition and an example of the developmental paragraph.

<table>
<tr><td>Topic sentence</td><td rowspan="8">*The developmental paragraph contains three parts: the subject, the topic sentence, and the support.* The **subject** is what you will write about. It is likely to be broad and must be focused or qualified for specific treatment. The **topic sentence** contains both the subject and the treatment—what you will do with the subject. It carries the central idea to which everything else in the paragraph is subordinated. For example, the first sentence of this paragraph is a topic sentence. Even when not stated, the topic sentence as an underlying idea unifies the paragraph. The **support** is the evidence or reasoning by which a topic sentence is developed. It comes in several basic patterns and serves any of the four forms of expression: narration, description, exposition, and argumentation. These forms, which are usually combined in writing, will be presented with both student and professional examples in the following chapters. *The **developmental paragraph**, therefore, is a group of sentences, each with the function of supporting a controlling idea called the topic sentence.*</td></tr>
<tr><td>Support</td></tr>
<tr><td>Support</td></tr>
<tr><td>Support</td></tr>
<tr><td>Concluding sentence</td></tr>
</table>

Basic Paragraph Patterns

The most important point about a developmental paragraph is that it should state an idea and support it. The support, or development, can take several forms, all of which you already use. It can

- give an account (tell a story).
- describe people, things, or events.
- explain by analyzing, giving examples, comparing, defining, showing how to do something, or showing causes.
- argue that something should be done or resisted, that something is true or untrue, or that something is good or bad.

(All of these forms of expression are discussed with examples in Chapters 16 through 22.) You will not find it difficult to write solid paragraphs once you understand that good writing requires that main ideas have enough support so that your reader can understand how you have arrived at your main conclusions.

Two effective patterns of conventional paragraph structure are shown in Figure 12.1. Pattern A merely states the controlling idea, the topic sentence, and develops it; Pattern B adds a concluding sentence following the development.

Figure 12.1
Paragraph Patterns

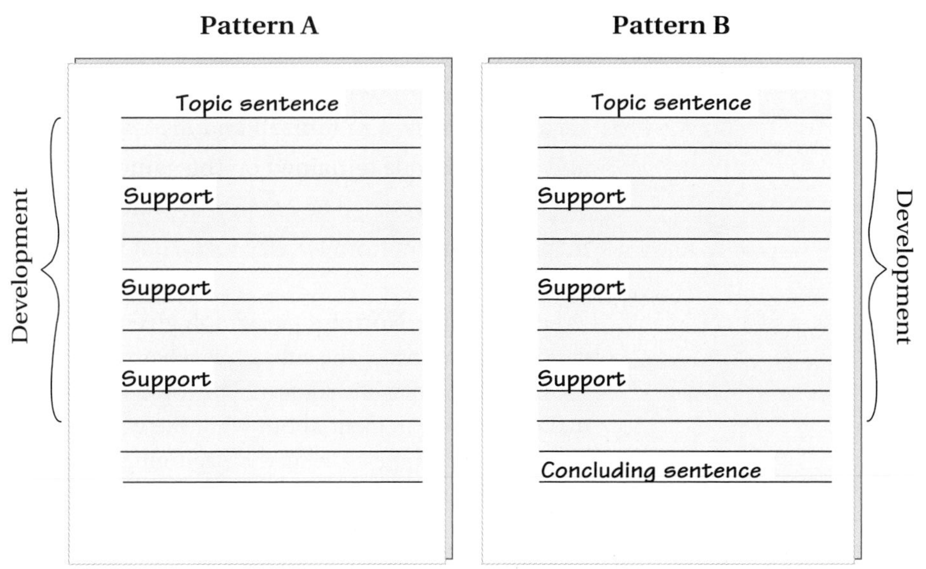

Pattern A	Pattern B
Topic sentence	Topic sentence
Support	Support
Support	Support
Support	Support
	Concluding sentence

(Development brackets appear on both patterns)

A paragraph, however, is not a constraining formula: it has variations. In some instances, for example, the topic sentence is not found in a single sentence. It may be the combination of two sentences, or it may be an easily understood but unwritten underlying idea that unifies the paragraph. Nevertheless, the paragraph in most college writing contains discussion that supports a stated topic sentence, and the instruction in this book is based on that fundamental idea.

A Sample Paragraph

The following paragraph was written by college student Cyrus Norton. The subject of the paragraph and the treatment of the paragraph have been marked. Norton's topic sentence (not the first sentence in this case), his support of the topic sentence, and his concluding sentence are also marked.

This is the final draft. Following it, we will back up and, in this chapter and the next two, show how Norton moved during the writing process from his initial idea to this polished paragraph.

Magic Johnson, an NBA Great

Cyrus Norton

Some NBA (National Basketball Association) players are good because they have a special talent in one area. <ins>Magic Johnson was a great NBA star because he was excellent in shooting, passing, rebounding, and leading.</ins> As a shooter few have ever equaled him. He could slam, shovel, hook, and fire from three-point range—all with deadly accuracy. As for free throws, he led all NBA players in shooting percentage in 1988–89. While averaging more than twenty points per game, he helped others become stars with his passes. As the point guard (the quarterback of basketball), he was always near the top in the league in assists and was famous for his "no-look" pass, which often surprised even his teammates with its precision. When he wasn't shooting or passing, he was rebounding. A top rebounding guard is unusual in professional basketball, but Magic, at

Margin labels: Topic sentence · Support for shooting · Support for passing · Support for rebounding

six feet, nine inches, could bump shoulders and leap with anyone. These three qualities made him probably the most spectacular triple-double threat of all time. "Triple-double" means reaching two digits in scoring, assists, and rebounding. Magic didn't need more for greatness in the NBA, but he had more. With his everlasting smile and boundless energy, he was also an inspirational team leader. He always believed in himself and his team. When his team was down by a point and three seconds remained on the game clock, the fans looked for Magic to get the ball. They watched as he dribbled once, he faded, he leaped, he twisted, and he hooked one in from twenty feet. That was magic. <u>That was Magic</u>.

Support for leading appears in the left margin beside the paragraph; *Concluding sentence* labels the last line.

Let's consider Norton's paragraph given what we know about paragraphs in general. Magic Johnson, the subject, is what the paragraph is all about. In this example, the title also names the subject. The topic sentence, the unifying and controlling idea, makes a clear statement about what the writer will do with the subject. As usual, the topic sentence appears near the beginning of the paragraph. The support gives evidence and examples to back up the controlling idea. The last sentence, "That was Magic," echoes the topic sentence. It is usually called the concluding sentence.

The author has told you what he was going to say, he has said it, and finally he has reminded you of what he has told you. The concluding sentence is sometimes omitted. The two most common designs of paragraphs in college writing are these:

topic sentence → support → concluding sentence
topic sentence → support

"Magic Johnson, an NBA Great" is a typical paragraph: a group of sentences that present and develop an idea. In college writing, a paragraph is usually expository; that is, its purpose is to explain. In this example, you, the reader, get the point. You're informed and maybe even entertained a little by the explanation.

The Writing Process

Although the first section of this chapter defined and illustrated the paragraph as a concept, it stopped short of presenting an overall plan for paragraph writing. The reason for that omission is simple. Each assignment has its own guidelines that vary according to the kind of topic, the source of ideas, the time permitted, the conditions for writing (especially in or outside class), and the purpose. Obviously, if one is to use a system, it must be flexible, because a technique that is an asset for one assignment may be a burden for another. Therefore, a good writer should know numerous techniques, treating each as a tool that can be used when needed. All of these tools are in the same box, one labeled "The Writing Process."

The writing process consists of strategies that can help you proceed from your purpose or initial idea to a final developed paragraph. Those strategies can be divided into prewriting techniques and writing stages. Using prewriting, you explore, experiment, gather information, formulate your thesis, and develop and organize your support. Then you write a first draft, revise your draft as many times as necessary, and edit your writing. The typical college writing assignment process looks like this:

Stage One: Exploring / Experimenting / Gathering Information
Stage Two: Writing the Controlling Idea / Organizing and Developing Support
Stage Three: Writing / Revising / Editing

These stages are discussed in Chapters 12, 13, and 14, respectively. Collectively they represent what is known as the writing process.

A blank worksheet with brief directions for completing the three stages of the writing process appears at the end of the Student Overview (page 7). This Writing Process Worksheet is designed to be duplicated and completed with each major writing assignment. It gives you clear, consistent guidance and provides your instructor with an easy format for finding and checking information. Customarily it should be stapled to the front of your rough and final drafts. A sample worksheet completed by a student appears on pages 287–288 in Chapter 14.

Stage One Strategies

Certain strategies commonly grouped under the heading *prewriting* can help you get started and develop your ideas. These strategies—freewriting, brainstorming, clustering, note taking—are very much a part of writing. The understandable desire to skip to the finished statement is what causes the most common student-writer grief: that of not filling the blank sheet or of filling it but not significantly improving on the blankness. The prewriting strategies described in this section will help you attack the blank sheet constructively with imaginative thought, analysis, and experimentation. They can lead to clear, effective communication.

Freewriting

One strategy is **freewriting,** an exercise that its originator, Peter Elbow, has called "babbling in print." When you freewrite, you write without stopping, letting your ideas tumble forth. You do not concern yourself with the fundamentals of writing, such as punctuation and spelling. Freewriting is an adventure into your memory and imagination. It is concerned with discovery, invention, and exploration. If you are at a loss for words on your subject, write in a comment such as "I don't know what is coming next" or "blah, blah, blah" and continue when relevant words come. It is important to keep writing. Freewriting immediately eliminates the blank page and thereby helps you break through an emotional barrier, but that is not the only benefit. The words that you sort through in that idea kit will include some you can use. You can then underline or circle those words and even add notes on the side so that the freewriting continues to grow even after its initial spontaneous expression.

The way in which you proceed depends on the type of assignment: working with a topic of your choice, a restricted list of topics, or a prescribed topic.

The *topic of your choice* affords you the greatest freedom of exploration. You would probably select a subject that interests you and freewrite about it, allowing your mind to wander, perhaps mixing fact and fantasy, direct experience, and hearsay. A freewriting about music might uncover areas of special interest and knowledge, such as jazz or folk rock, that you would want to pursue further in freewriting or other prewriting strategies.

Working from a *restricted list* requires a more focused freewriting. With the list, you can, of course, experiment with several topics to discover what is most suitable for you. If, for example, "career choice," "career preparation," "career guidance," and "career prospects" are on the restricted list, you would probably select one and freewrite about it. If it works well for you, you would probably proceed with the next step of your prewriting. If you are not satisfied with what you uncover in freewriting, you would explore another item from the restricted list or take notes from the Internet or library sources.

When working with a *prescribed topic,* you focus on a particular topic and try to restrict your freewriting to its boundaries. If your topic specifies a division of a subject area such as "political involvement of your generation," then you would tie those key words to your own information, critical thinking, and imaginative responses. If the topic is restricted to, let's say, a particular reading selection such as a poem, then that poem would give you the framework for your free associations with your own experiences, creations, and opinions.

You should learn to use freewriting because it will often serve you well, but you need not use it every time you write. Some very short writing assignments do not call for freewriting. An in-class assignment may not allow time for freewriting.

Nevertheless, freewriting is often a useful strategy in your toolbox of techniques. It can help you get words on paper, break emotional barriers, generate topics, develop new insights, and explore ideas.

Freewriting can lead to other stages of prewriting and writing, and it can also provide content as you develop your topic.

The following example of freewriting and the writing, revising, and editing examples in Chapter 14 relate to student Cyrus Norton's paragraph titled "Magic Johnson, an NBA Great" (pages 263–264). Norton's topic came from a restricted list; he was directed to write about the success of an individual. Had he been working with a prescribed topic, he might have been directed to concentrate on a specific aspect of Johnson's career, such as business, philanthropy, public service, or the one Norton chose: great basketball playing.

great	Magic Johnson was the <u>greatest</u> player I've ever seen in professional basketball.
leader, inspiration	Actually not just a player but a <u>leader</u> and an <u>inspiration</u> to the team so they always gave him the ball when the game was on the line. It was too bad his career was cut short when they discovered he was HIV positive. Actually he came back but then
rich	retired again. He made <u>a lot of money</u> and I guess he invested it wisely because his name is linked to the Lakers and theaters and more. Also to programs making people aware of the danger of AIDS and helping kids grow up and stay out of trou-
playing	ble. But the main thing about Magic is the <u>way he played</u>. He could do everything.
scoring	He even played center one time in a championship game. He always <u>scored a lot</u>
passing	and he could <u>pass</u> like nobody else. Even though he was a guard, he was tall and
rebounding	could <u>rebound</u>. He was great. Everyone says so.

After doing this freewriting, Norton went back through his work looking for ideas that might be developed in a paper.

Observe how he returned to his freewriting and examined it for possible ideas to develop for a writing assignment. As he recognized those ideas, he underlined important words and phrases and made a few notes in the margins. By reading only the underlined words, you can obtain a basic understanding of what is important to him. It is not necessary to underline entire sentences.

In addition to putting some words on that dreaded blank sheet of paper, Norton discovered that he had quite a lot of information about Magic Johnson and that he had selected a favorable topic to develop. The entire process took little time. Had he found few or no promising ideas, he might have freewritten about another topic. In going back through his work, he saw some errors in writing, but he did not correct them, because the purpose of freewriting is discovery, not correct grammar, punctuation, or spelling. Norton was confident that he could then continue with the process of writing a paper.

Norton's understanding of the topic came mainly from information he had collected from reading and from watching sports programs on television. He knew that if he needed to gather more information, he could do further research, which could take the form of reading, underlining, annotating, note taking, outlining, and summarizing. These techniques are explained in Chapter 1.

EXERCISE 1

Freewriting

Try freewriting on a broad topic such as one of these: the best car on the market, a popular college course, a controversial television program, a favorite retail store or mall, a good school, a neighborhood you know well, a memorable learning experience, a person who has influenced you, or a useful piece of software. Following the example on page 266, underline and annotate the phrases that may lead you to ideas to explore further.

Brainstorming

This prewriting strategy features important words and phrases that relate in various ways to the subject area or to the specific topic you are concerned about. Brainstorming includes two basic forms: (1) asking and answering questions and (2) listing.

Big Six Questions

One effective way to get started is to ask the big six questions about your subject: *Who? What? Where? When? Why? How?* Then let your mind run free as you jot down answers in single entries or lists. Some of the big six questions may not fit, and some may be more important than others, depending on the purposes of your writing. For example, if you were writing about the causes of a situation, the *Why?* question could be more important than the others; if you were concerned with how to do something, the *How?* question would predominate. If you were writing in response to a reading selection, you would confine your thinking to questions appropriately related to the content of that reading selection.

Whatever your focus for the questions is, the result is likely to be numerous ideas that will provide information for continued exploration and development of your topic. Thus your pool of information for writing widens and deepens.

Norton continued with the topic of Magic Johnson, and his topic tightened to focus on particular areas.

Who: Magic Johnson
What: great basketball player
Where: the NBA
When: for more than ten years
Why: love of game and great talent
How: shooting, passing, rebounding, leading, coolness, inspiring

As it turned out, *How?* was the most fruitful question for Norton.

Listing

Another effective way to brainstorm, especially if you have a defined topic and a storehouse of information, is to skip the big six questions approach and simply make a list of words and phrases related to your topic.

Had Norton known at the outset that he would write about Magic Johnson's greatness as a basketball player, he might have gone directly to a list such as this:

(shooting)
intelligence
(rebounding)
coolness
quickness
(passing)
split vision
determination
(leading)
work ethic
unselfishness
attitude
ambition

From this list, Norton might have selected perhaps four ideas for his framework, circling them for future reference.

Even if you do not have a focused topic, you may find a somewhat random listing useful, merely writing or typing in phrases as they occur to you. This exploratory activity is similar to freewriting. After you have established such a list, you can sort out and group the phrases as you generate your topic and find its natural divisions. Feel free to accept, reject, or insert phrases.

EXERCISE 2

Brainstorming

Further explore the topic you worked with in Exercise 1 by first answering the big six questions and then by making a list.

Big Six Questions

Who? _____

What? _____

Where? _____

When? _____

Why? _____

How? _____

List

_____

_____

_____

_____

_____

_____

_____

_____

_____

_____

Clustering

Still another prewriting technique is *clustering*. Start by "double-bubbling" your topic; that is, write it down in the middle of the page and draw a double circle around it. Then, responding to the question "What comes to mind?" single-bubble other ideas on spokes radiating out from the hub that contains the topic. Any bubble can lead to another bubble or numerous bubbles in the same way. This strategy is sometimes used instead of or before making an outline to organize and develop ideas.

The more restricted the topic inside the double bubble, the fewer the number of spokes that will radiate with single bubbles. For example, a topic such as "high school dropouts" would have more spokes than "reasons for dropping out of school."

Here is Norton's cluster on the subject of Magic Johnson. He has drawn broken circles around subclusters that seem to relate to a feasible unified topic.

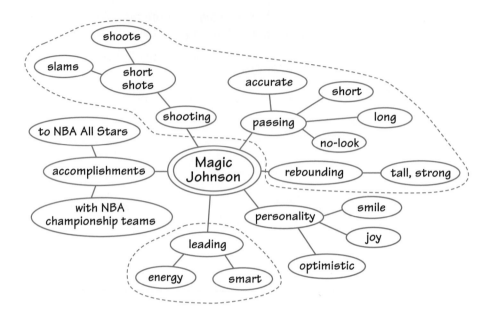

Clustering

Continuing with your topic, develop a cluster of related ideas. Draw broken circles around subclusters that have potential for focus and more development.

Writer's Guidelines

1. A **paragraph** is a group of sentences, each with the function of stating or supporting a single controlling idea that is contained in the topic sentence.

2. A paragraph contains two parts: the topic sentence and the support.

   - The **topic sentence** expresses the controlling idea of the paragraph. It has a subject (what the paragraph is about) and indicates the treatment (what the writer will do with the subject).
   - The **support** is the evidence, such as details, examples, and explanations, that backs up the topic sentence.

3. The two most common paragraph designs in college writing are these:

   - Topic sentence → support → concluding sentence
   - Topic sentence → support

4. **Prewriting** includes activities you do before writing your first draft or whenever you need new ideas. You should use only the activities that will best help you explore, generate, limit, and develop your topic.

   - *Freewriting:* writing without stopping, letting your ideas tumble forth. Freewriting helps you break emotional barriers, generate topics, and discover and explore ideas. If you need more information, consult sources on the Internet or in the library and take notes.
   - *Brainstorming:* a listing procedure that helps you discover key words and phrases that relate to your subject. Begin by asking *Who? What? Where? When? Why?* and *How?* questions about your subject or by merely listing ideas concerning your subject.
   - *Clustering:* a graphic way of showing connections and relationships. Start by double-bubbling your topic. Then ask "What comes to mind?" and single-bubble other ideas on spokes radiating out from the double bubble.

Chapter

13

The Writing Process: Developing and Organizing Support

The foundation of a good outline and, hence, of a good paragraph is a strong topic sentence, which means one with a specific subject and a well-defined treatment.

FLOW OF WRITING

Learning Objectives

Working with this chapter, I will learn to

~ write a topic sentence.

~ write an outline for developing and organizing support.

The most important advice this book can offer you is *state your controlling idea and support it.* If you have no controlling idea—no topic sentence—your paragraph will be unfocused, and your readers may be confused or bored. If you organize your material well, so that it supports and develops your controlling idea, you can present your views to your readers with interest, clarity, and persuasion.

Stating the controlling idea and organizing support can be accomplished effectively and systematically. How? This chapter presents several uncomplicated techniques you can use in Stage Two of the writing process.

Writing the Controlling Idea as a Topic Sentence

An effective topic sentence has both a subject and a treatment. The subject is what you intend to write about. The treatment is what you intend to do with your subject.

Consider, for example, this topic sentence:

<u>Magic Johnson</u> <u>was a great all-around NBA player.</u>
     subject   treatment

It is an effective topic sentence because it limits the subject and indicates treatment that can be developed in additional sentences. Another sound version is the following, which goes further to include divisions for the treatment.

<u>Magic Johnson</u> <u>was a great NBA star because he was excellent in</u>
     subject   treatment

<u>shooting, passing, rebounding, and leading.</u>

Ineffective topic sentences are often too broad, too vague, or too narrow.

Ineffective:	Magic Johnson was everything to everybody.
Too Broad or Vague:	Magic Johnson was fun.
	Magic Johnson was a success in basketball.
Ineffective:	Magic Johnson went to college in Michigan.
Too Narrow:	Magic Johnson signed with the Los Angeles Lakers.

Usually, simple statements of fact do not need or do not allow for development.

EXERCISE 1

Evaluating Topic Sentences

In the following statements, underline and label subject (S) and treatment (T). Also judge each sentence as effective (E) or ineffective (I). Effective statements are those that you can easily relate to supporting evidence. Ineffective statements are too broad, too vague, or too narrowly factual.

_____ 1. Columbus is located in Ohio.

_____ 2. Columbus is a fabulous city.

_____ 3. Columbus has dealt thoroughly with its housing problems.

_____ 4. A monkey is a primate.

_____ 5. Monkeys are fun.

_____ 6. In clinical studies monkeys have demonstrated a remarkable ability to reason.

_____ 7. More than a million cats are born in California each year.

_____ 8. A simple observation of a domesticated cat in the pursuit of game will show that it has not lost its instinct for survival.

_____ 9. The two teams in the Rose Bowl have similar records.

_____ 10. Michigan State is in the Rose Bowl.

Writing Topic Sentences

Complete the following entries to make each one a solid topic sentence. Only a subject and part of the treatment are provided. The missing part may be more than a single word.

Example: Car salespersons behave differently depending on _the car they are selling and the kind of customer they are serving._

1. Television commercials are often _____

_____

2. Word-processing features can _____

_____

3. My part-time job taught me _____

_____

4. I promote environmental conservation by _____

_____

5. The clothing that a person wears often reveals _____

_____

6. My close friend is preoccupied with _____

_____

7. Winning a lot of money is not always _____

_____

8. Country music appeals to our most basic _____

_____

9. Friendship depends on _____

_____

10. A good salesperson should _____

_____

EXERCISE 3

Writing Topic Sentences

Convert each of the following subjects into a topic sentence.

1. Computer literacy _____

_____

2. My taste in music _____

_____

3. Bus transportation _____

_____

4. The fear of crime _____

_____

5. An excellent boss _____

_____

6. Doing well in college English classes _____

_____

7. Violence on television _____

_____

8. Childcare centers _____

_____

9. Good health _____

_____

10. Teenage voters _____

_____

Writing an Outline

An **outline** is a pattern for showing the relationship of ideas. The two main outline forms are the **sentence outline** (each entry is a complete sentence) and the **topic outline** (each entry is a key word or phrase). The topic outline is commonly used for paragraphs and short essays.

Indentation, number and letter sequences, punctuation, and the placement of words are important to clear communication. We do not read an outline expecting to be surprised by form and content, as we may read a poem. We go to the outline for information, and we expect to find ideas easily. Unconventional marks (circles, squares, half-parentheses) and items out of order are distracting and, therefore, undesirable in an outline. The standard form is as easily mastered as a nonstandard form, and it is worth your time to learn it. Outlining is not difficult: The pattern is flexible and can have any number of levels and parts.

Basically, an outline shows how a topic sentence is supported. Thus it shows the organization of the paragraph. The most important supporting material, called the **major support,** is indicated by Roman numerals. That major support is developed by less important supporting material, called the **minor support,** which in turn may be developed by details or examples. The major and minor support may be derived from one or more strategies of prewriting such as listing and clustering. Here is the outline developed by Norton:

Topic Sentence: Magic Johnson was a great NBA star because he was excellent in shooting, passing, rebounding, and leading.

I. Shooting (major support)
   A. Short shots (minor support)
      1. Shovel (detail)
      2. Slam-dunk (detail)
   B. Long shots (minor support)
   C. Free throws (minor support)
II. Passing (major support)
   A. No-look (minor support)
   B. Precise (minor support)
III. Rebounding (major support)
   A. Tall (minor support)
   B. Strong (minor support)
IV. Leading (major support)
   A. Energy (minor support)
   B. Spirit (minor support)
      1. Faith (detail)
      2. Smile (detail)

The foundation of a good outline and, hence, of a good paragraph is a strong topic sentence, which means one with a specific subject and a well-defined treatment. After you have written a good topic sentence, the next step is to divide the treatment into parts. Just what the parts are will depend on what you are trying to do in the treatment. Consider the thought process involved. What sections of material would be appropriate in your discussion to support or explain that topic sentence? You will probably find that your listing or clustering has already addressed one or more ways of dividing your material. Therefore, reexamine your other forms of prewriting for patterns of development, as well as support.

Among the most common forms of division are the following:

- Divisions of time or incident to tell a story

  I. Situation

  II. Conflict

  III. Struggle

  IV. Outcome

  V. Meaning

- Divisions of example or examples

  I. First example

  II. Second example

  III. Third example (or divide one example into three or more aspects)

- Divisions of causes or effects

  I. Cause (or effect) one

  II. Cause (or effect) two

  III. Cause (or effect) three

- Divisions of a unit into parts (such as the federal government into executive, legislative, and judicial branches—or Magic Johnson's all-around skill into shooting, passing, rebounding, and leading)

  I. Part one

  II. Part two

  III. Part three

- Divisions of how to do something or how something was done

  I. Preparation

  II. Steps

      A. Step 1

      B. Step 2

      C. Step 3

EXERCISE 4

Completing Outlines

Fill in the missing parts of the following outlines. Consider whether you are dealing with time, examples, causes, effects, parts, or steps. The answers will vary depending on your individual experiences and views.

1. Too many of us are preoccupied with material things.

   I. Clothing

   II. Cars

   III. _____

2. Television sitcoms may vary, but every successful show has certain components.

   I. Good acting

   II. _____

   III. Good situations

   IV. _____

3. A person who is trying to discourage unwanted sexual advances should take several measures.

   I. _____

   II. Set clear boundaries

   III. Avoid compromising situations

4. Concentrating during reading involves various techniques.

   I. Preview material

   II. Pose questions

   III. _____

5. Crime has some bad effects on a nearby neighborhood.

   I. People fearful

      A. Don't go out at night

      B. _____

   II. People without love for neighborhood

      A. _____

      B. Put houses up for sale

III. People as victims

    A. Loss of possessions

    B. _____

6. Exercising can improve a person's life.

  I. Looks better

    A. Skin

    B. _____

  II. Feels better

    A. _____

    B. Body

  III. Performs better

    A. Work

    B. _____

7. Shoppers in department stores can be grouped according to needs.

  I. _____

  II. Special-needs

  III. Bargain hunters

8. There are different kinds of intelligence based on situations.

  I. Street-smart

  II. Common sense

  III. _____

9. Smoking should be discouraged.

  I. Harm to smokers

    A. _____

    B. Cancer risk

  II. Harm to those around smokers

    A. _____

    B. Fellow workers

    III. Cost

        A. Industry—production and absenteeism

        B. _____

10. An excellent police officer must have six qualities.

      I. _____

     II. Knowledge of law

   III. _____

   IV. Emotional soundness

    V. Skill in using weapons

   VI. _____

EXERCISE 5

Writing a Topic Sentence and an Outline

Still working with the same topic you chose in Exercise 1, page 267, write a topic sentence and an outline. The topic sentence may suggest a particular pattern of development. Following the lead of that topic sentence, the Roman-numeral headings will often indicate divisions of time or place, steps, causes, effects, or parts of a unit. For example, if you have selected your favorite retail store for your subject and your reasons for choosing it as the treatment, then those reasons would be indicated with Roman-numeral headings.

Writer's Guidelines

1. An effective **topic sentence** has both a subject and a treatment. The subject is what you intend to write about. The treatment is what you intend to do with your subject.

   Example: <u>Wilson High School</u> <u>offers a well-balanced academic program.</u>
                                 subject   treatment

2. An **outline** is a form for indicating the relationship of ideas. The outline shows how a topic sentence is supported. Thus it reveals the organization of the paragraph. Major support is indicated by Roman numerals. The major support is developed by minor support, which in turn may be developed by details or examples.

Topic sentence

    I. Major support

      A. Minor support

      B. Minor support

         1. Details or examples

         2. Details or examples

   II. Major support

      A. Minor support

      B. Minor support

Chapter
14

The Writing Process: Writing, Revising, and Editing the Paragraph

Don't be embarrassed by the roughness of your first draft. You should be embarrassed only if you leave it that way.

FLOW OF WRITING

Learning Objectives

Working with this chapter, I will learn to

~ write a first draft.

~ revise systematically by using CLUESS.

~ edit by using COPS.

Writing Your First Draft

Once you have written your topic sentence and completed your outline (or list or cluster), you are ready to begin writing your paragraph. The initial writing is called the **first,** or rough, **draft.** Your topic sentence is likely to be at or near the beginning of your paragraph and will be followed by your support as ordered by your outline.

Paying close attention to your outline for basic organization, you should proceed without worrying about the refinements of writing. This is not the time to concern yourself with perfect spelling, grammar, or punctuation.

Whether you write in longhand or use a computer depends on what works best for you. Some writers prefer to do a first draft by hand, mark it up, and then go to the computer. Computers save you time in all aspects of your writing, especially revision.

Don't be embarrassed by the roughness of your first draft. You should be embarrassed only if you leave it that way. You are seeing the reason why a first draft is called "rough." Famous authors have said publicly that they wouldn't show their rough drafts to their closest, most forgiving friends.

The Recursive Factor

The process of writing can be called **recursive,** which means "going back and forth." In this respect, writing is like reading. If you do not understand what you have read, you back up and read it again. After you have reread a passage, you may still need to read it selectively. The same can be said of writing. If, for example, after having developed an outline and started writing your first draft, you discover that your subject is too broad, you have to back up, narrow your topic sentence, and then adjust your outline. You may even want to return to an early cluster of ideas to see how you can use a smaller grouping of them. Revision is usually the most recursive of all parts of the writing process. You will go over your material again and again until you are satisfied that you have expressed yourself as well as you possibly can.

It this textbook, the recursive factor is also called "The Flow of Writing," as captured by the icon of the waves at the beach. Waves move in cycles, going forward and doubling back and thrusting again, moving with more vigor toward a high tide. You may have to catch a lot of trial rides before you get close to that perfect wave of expression. The revising and editing of your work make up those rides.

Revising Your Writing

The term **first draft** suggests quite accurately that there will be other drafts, or versions, of your writing. Only in the most dire situations, such as an in-class examination when you have time for only one draft, should you be satisfied with a single effort.

What you do beyond the first draft is revising and editing. **Revision** concerns itself with organization, content, and language effectiveness. **Editing** involves a final correcting of mistakes in spelling, punctuation, and capitalization. In practice, editing and revision are not always separate activities, although writers usually wait until the next-to-the-last draft to edit some minor details and attend to other small points that can be easily overlooked.

Successful revision almost always involves intense, systematic rewriting. You should learn to look for certain aspects of skillful writing as you enrich and repair your first draft. To help you recall these aspects so that you can keep them in mind and examine your material in a comprehensive fashion, this textbook offers a memory device—an acronym in which each letter suggests an important feature of good writing and revision. This device enables you to memorize the features of good writing quickly. Soon you will be able to recall and refer to them automatically. These features need not be attended to individually when you revise your writing, although they may be. They need not be attended to in the order presented here. The acronym is CLUESS (pronounced "clues"), which provides this guide: coherence, language, unity, emphasis, support, sentences.

Coherence

Coherence is the flow of ideas, with each idea leading logically and smoothly to the next. It is achieved by numbering parts or otherwise indicating (*first, second, third, then, next, soon,* and so on), giving directions (according to space, as in "To the right is a map, and to the left of that map is a bulletin board"), using transitional words (*however, otherwise, therefore, similarly, hence, on the other hand, then, consequently, accordingly, thus*), using demonstrative pronouns (*this, that, those*), and moving in a clear order (from the least important to the most important or from the most important to the least important).

Language

Language here stands for diction or word choice: using words that clearly convey your ideas and are suitable for what you are writing and for your audience. In college writing that means you will usually avoid slang and clichés such as "a barrel of laughs," "happy as a clam," and "six of one and a half dozen of another." Your writing will contain standard grammar and usage. See page 321 for a discussion of general and specific words.

If you are writing with a computer, use the thesaurus feature for careful diction, but keep in mind that no two words share exactly the same meaning.

Unity

Unity in a paragraph begins with a good topic sentence. Then everything in your paragraph should be related and subordinated to that topic sentence. Repetition of a key word or phrase can make the unity even stronger.

Emphasis

Emphasize important ideas by using **position** (the most emphatic parts of a work are the beginning and the end), **repetition** (repeat key words and phrases), and **isolation** (a short, direct sentence among longer ones will usually command attention).

Support

Support is the material that backs up, justifies, or proves your topic sentence. Work carefully with the material from your outline (or list or cluster) to make sure that your ideas are well supported. If your paragraph is skimpy and your ideas seem slender, you are probably generalizing and not explaining how you arrived at your conclusions. Avoid repetition that does not add to the content; use details and examples; indicate parts and discuss relationships; and explain why your generalizations are true, logical, and accurate. Your reader can't accept your ideas unless he or she knows by what reasoning or use of evidence you developed them.

Sentences

Be sure your sentences are complete (not fragments) and that you have not incorrectly combined word groups that could be sentences (comma splices and run-ons). Consider using different types of sentences and different sentence beginnings.

Write as many drafts as necessary, revising as you go for all the aspects of effective writing. Don't confuse revising with editing (the final stage of the writing process); don't get bogged down in fixing such things as spelling and punctuation.

Editing Your Writing

Editing, the final stage of the writing process, involves a careful examination of your work. Look for problems with *c*apitalization, *o*missions, *p*unctuation, and *s*pelling (COPS).

Because you can find spelling errors in others' writing more easily than in your own, a computerized spell checker is extremely useful. (See page 247.) However, a spell checker will not detect wrong words that are correctly spelled, so you should always proofread.

Before you submit your writing to your instructor, do what almost all professional writers do before sending their material along: Read it aloud, to yourself or to a willing accomplice. Reading material aloud will help you catch any awkwardness of expression, omission and misplacement of words, and other problems that are easily overlooked by an author.

As you can see, writing is a process and is not a matter of just sitting down and producing sentences. The parts of the process from prewriting to revising to editing are connected, and your movement is ultimately forward, but this process allows you to go back and forth in the recursive manner discussed earlier. If your outline is not working, perhaps the flaw is in your topic sentence. You may need to go back and fix it. If one section of your paragraph is skimpy, perhaps you will have to go back and reconsider the pertinent material in your outline or clustering. There you might find more details or alter a statement so that you can move into more fertile areas of thought.

Norton wrote the following first draft, marked it for revision, and then completed the final draft, which you read on pages 263–264. For simplification, only this draft is shown, although a typical paper might require several drafts, including one in which the author has done nothing but edit his or her revised writing.

Magic Johnson , an NBA Great

Some NBA players are good because they ~~are good~~ ^have a special talent in one area ~~such as~~ (National Basketball Association) shooting, passing, or rebounding. Magic Johnson was ^a great ^NBA star because he was ~~good~~ ^excellent in ~~all of those things and more.~~ shooting, passing, rebounding, and leading. As a shooter few have ~~been able~~ ^ever equaled him. ~~to do what he could.~~ He could slam, shovel, hook, and fire from three-point

—all with deadly accuracy   As for

range. When it came to free throws, he led all NBA players in shooting per-

While   ing

centage in 1988–89. Then he averaged more than twenty points per game,

s   with his passes   (the quarterback of basketball),

he helped other become stars. As the point guard he was always near

s

the top in the league in asists and was famous for his no-look passes.

"   "

its

Which often surprised even his teammates with their precision.

When he wasn't shooting or passing, he was rebounding.   in professional basketball

A top rebounding guard is unusual, but Magic, standing at six feet nine

u   leap

inches tall, could bump sholders and jump with anyone. These three quali-

ties made him probably the most spectacular triple-double threat of all time.

"Triple-double" means reaching two digits in scoring, assists, and rebounding.

Magic didn't need more for greatness in the NBA, but he had more. He

With

was also an inspirational team leader with his everlasting smile and bound-

He   ed

less energy. Always believing in himself and his team. When his team

remained on the game clock,   the fans

was down by a point and three seconds were left, you always looked for

They   he   he

Magic to get the ball. Then you watched as he dribbled once, faded, leaped,

he   he   ! That was magic.

twisted, and hooked one in from twenty feet That was Magic.

The Writing Process Worksheet

One effective and systematic way to organize your writing is by using the Writing Process Worksheet. The procedure is simple. First, copy the directions for your assignment, making certain that you know precisely what you are to do and when you are to submit your paper. Few things are more frustrating to both student and instructor than an assignment that falls outside the directions or is not turned in on time.

Next, do your prewriting, beginning on the worksheet and using extra pages if necessary. Prewriting will vary according to your assignment and according to your instructor's requirements.

Then follow your prewriting activities with writing, which includes revising and editing.

Keep in mind that the writing process is recursive and that you can go back and forth between different activities, depending on your needs. For example, if one part of your outline does not work as you write your rough draft, go back to your outline or other prewriting activities to add or subtract ideas.

The Writing Process Worksheet is useful in helping you understand the assignment, in reminding you of the best tools the writing process offers for prewriting and writing, and in providing an organized packet of material for your instructor. For some instructors that packet will include these parts stapled in this order: a completed Writing Process Worksheet, a rough draft marked for revision, and a final draft.

Norton's Writing Process Worksheet follows. You will find a full-size blank Writing Process Worksheet on page 7. It can be photocopied, filled in, and submitted with each assignment if your instructor directs you to do so.

Writing Process Worksheet (completed through Stage 2)

Title   Magic Johnson, an NBA Great

Name   Cyrus Norton   **Due Date** Monday, October 21, 9 a.m.

ASSIGNMENT

In the space below, write whatever you need to know about your assignment, including information about the topic, audience, pattern of writing, length, whether to include a rough draft or revised drafts, and whether your paper must be typed.

Topic: person who has achieved excellence / about qualities that made him or her excellent / analysis by division / 200 to 300 words / paragraph / one or more rough drafts / typed final draft / audience of instructor and other students, those who have heard of the subject but don't have detailed information—

STAGE ONE

Explore   Freewrite, brainstorm (list), cluster, or take notes as directed by your instructor. Use the back of this page or separate paper if you need more space.

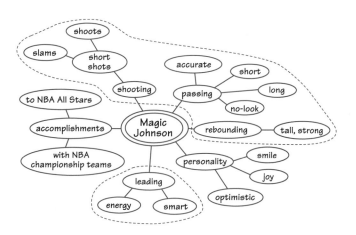

STAGE TWO

Organize   Write a topic sentence or thesis; label the subject and treatment parts.

<u>Magic Johnson</u> <u>was a great NBA star because he was excellent in shooting,</u>
    subject   treatment

<u>passing, rebounding, and leading.</u>

Write an outline or an outline alternative.

    I. Shooting
        A. Short shots
        B. Long shots
        C. Free throws
   II. Passing
        A. No-look
        B. Precise

III. Rebounding
    A. Tall
    B. Strong
IV. Leading
    A. Energy
    B. Spirit

STAGE THREE

Write On separate paper, write and then revise your paragraph or essay as many times as necessary for **c**oherence, **l**anguage (usage, tone, and diction), **u**nity, **e**mphasis, **s**upport, and **s**entences (**CLUESS**). Read your work aloud to hear and correct any grammatical errors or awkward-sounding sentences.

Edit any problems in fundamentals, such as **c**apitalization, **o**missions, **p**unctuation, and **s**pelling (**COPS**). (See the revised and edited rough draft on pages 285–286.)

EXERCISE 1

Revising and Editing

Treat the following paragraph as your own rough draft and mark it in the way Norton marked his rough draft. First consider **c**oherence, **l**anguage, **u**nity, **e**mphasis, **s**upport, and **s**entences (**CLUESS**). Then edit the paragraph, correcting fundamentals such as **c**apitalization, **o**missions, **p**unctuation, and **s**pelling (**COPS**). (See Answer Key for possible answers.)

Young voters are not voting the way they should. The latest figures show that only 20 percent are going to the poles. The next-older generation is, the so-called baby boomers, they are going to the poles at about twice that rate. Because I'm part of the young group, I'm concerned, but the answers to why we usually don't bother to vote are as obvious as the nose on your face. For one thing the younger people don't think voting changes anything. The political parties are all about the same, and the candidates look and talk alike, even though they seem angry with each other. For another a lot of young voters don't have parents that voted or even talked about politics when they were growing up, they don't either. Still another thing is that the issues going around don't move young people that much. The politicians talk about the national debt and social security and health care and we're concerned about jobs and the high cost of education. If they could get people we could believe in and they would talk about issue that matter to us, then maybe they'd see more of us at the polls.

EXERCISE 2

Revising and Editing

Mark this rough draft for coherence, language, unity, emphasis, support, and sentences (CLUESS). Then edit the paragraph, correcting fundamentals such as capitalization, omissions, punctuation, and spelling (COPS).

High school dress codes don't make any sense to me. I've heard all the reasons. Too many kids wear gang clothes, and some get attacked or even killed. Parents have to put up too much money and even then the kids without parents with deep pockets can't compete. And then there are those that say kids behave bad if they dress in a free spirit way. Let's take them one at a time. As for the gang stuff, it's mainly how you act, not how you look, and if the gang stuff is still a problem, then just ban certain items of clothing. You don't have to go to the extreames of uniforms, just change the attitude, not the clothes. Then comes the money angle. Let the kid get a part-time job if they want better clothes. The behavior number is not what I can relate to. I mean, you go to class and learn, and you do it the school way, but the way you dress should have something to do with how you want to express yourself. Do they want to turn out a bunch of little robots that think the same way, behave the same way, and yes with the dress code even look the same way. Get real! If they'll cut us some slack with how we dress, they'll get happier campers in the classroom. Later better citizens in society.

EXERCISE 3

Revising and Editing

Mark this rough draft for coherence, language, unity, emphasis, support, and sentences (CLUESS). Then edit the paragraph, correcting fundamentals such as capitalization, omissions, punctuation, and spelling (COPS).

In the los Angeles Basin, people know why the Santa Anas are called the "devil winds." I know I do. At their worst they come in from the desert searing hot like the breeth of a blast furnace, tumbling over the mountain ranges and streaking down the canyons. Pitilessly destroying and disrupting. I hate them. Trees are striped of foliage, broken, and toppled. Fires that starts in the foothills may become firestorms. And bombard the downwind areas with lots of stuff. That sounds bad, doesn't it? But even without fire, the winds picks up sand, dirt, and debris and sent them toward the ocean as a hot, dry tide going out. All the time the Santa Anas are relentless, humming, howling, and whining through yards, and rattling and ripling lose shingles. Palm fronds move around. I've seen it and heard it lots of times. Dogs howl and often panic and run away, birds hunkers down in windbreaks; and human beings mostly stay inside Wiping up dust, coughing, and getting grumpy. The devil winds earning their reputation. Santa Anas suck.

EXERCISE 4

Revising and Editing

Using your topic from the previous chapters, write a rough draft and a final draft. Use CLUESS and COPS for revising and editing.

Or do the following:
Fill in the blank to complete the topic sentence: _____ **[person's name] is an excellent [coach, doctor, neighbor, parent, preacher, teacher, sibling].**

    Then use the topic sentence to write a paragraph. Go through the complete writing process. Use one or more prewriting techniques (freewriting, brainstorming, clustering, outlining), write a first draft, revise your draft as many times as necessary, edit your work, and write a final polished paragraph.

    In your drafts, you may rephrase the topic sentence as necessary. Using the paragraph on pages 285–286 (showing Magic Johnson as a shooter, passer, rebounder, and leader) as a model, divide your topic into whatever qualities make your subject an excellent example of whichever type of person you have chosen.

Writer's Guidelines

1. **Writing the rough draft:** Referring to your outline for guidance and to your topic sentence for limits, write a first, or rough, draft. Do not get caught up in correcting and polishing your writing during this stage.

2. **Revising:** Mark and revise your rough draft, rewriting as many times as necessary to produce an effective paragraph. The main points of revision are contained in the acronym CLUESS, expressed here as questions.

    Coherence: Does the material flow smoothly, with each idea leading logically to the next?
    Language: Are the words appropriate for the message, occasion, and audience?
    Unity: Are all ideas related to and subordinate to the topic sentence?
    Emphasis: Have you used techniques such as repetition and placement of ideas to emphasize your main point(s)?

Support: Have you presented material to back up, justify, or prove your topic sentence?

Sentences: Have you used some variety of structure and avoided fragments, comma splices, and run-ons?

3. **Editing:** Examine your work carefully. Look for problems in *c*apitalization, *o*missions, *p*unctuation, and *s*pelling (COPS).

4. **Using word-processing features:** Use your thesaurus and spell checker to help you revise and edit, but note that those features have their limitations.

5. **Using the Writing Process Worksheet:** Explore your topic, organize your ideas, and write your paragraphs using the Writing Process Worksheet as your guide. Photocopy the blank form on page 7.

Chapter

15

Moving from Paragraphs to Essays

As you learn the properties of effective paragraphs—those with a strong topic sentence and strong support—you also learn how to organize an essay, if you just magnify the procedure.

FLOW OF WRITING

Learning Objectives

Working with this chapter, I will learn

~ that a paragraph is often an essay in miniature.

~ to write introductory, middle, and concluding paragraphs.

Writing the Short Essay

The definition of a paragraph gives us a framework for defining an essay: A **paragraph** is a group of sentences, each with the function of supporting a single, main idea, which is contained in the topic sentence.

The main parts of a paragraph are the topic sentence (subject and treatment), support (evidence and reasoning), and, often, the concluding sentence at the end. Now let's use that framework for an essay. An **essay** is a group of paragraphs, each with the function of stating or supporting a controlling idea called the thesis.

The main parts of an essay are as follows:

Introduction: carries the thesis, which states the controlling idea—much like the topic sentence for a paragraph but on a larger scale.

Development: introduces the evidence and reasoning—the support.

Conclusion: provides an appropriate ending—often a restatement of or reflection on the thesis.

Thus, considered structurally, a paragraph is often an essay in miniature. That does not mean that all paragraphs can grow up to be essays or that all essays can shrink to become paragraphs. For college writing, however, a good understanding of the parallel between well-organized paragraphs and well-organized essays is useful. As you learn the properties of effective paragraphs—those with a strong topic sentence and strong support—you also learn how to organize an essay, if you just magnify the procedure. The essay form can be used across the curriculum and, with modifications, at the workplace.

Figure 15.1 illustrates the parallel parts of outlines, paragraphs, and essays. Of

Figure 15.1
Paragraph and Essay Compared

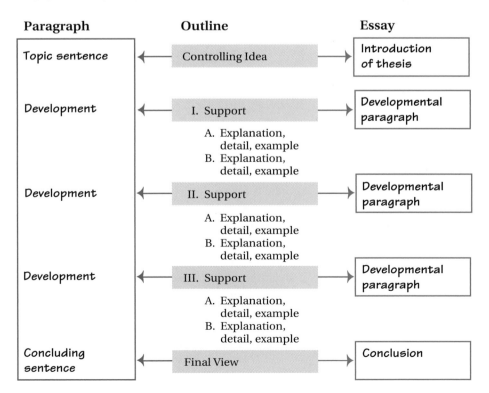

course, the parallel components are not exactly the same in a paragraph and an essay. The paragraph is shorter and requires much less development, and some paragraph topics simply couldn't be developed much more extensively to their advantage. But let's consider the ones that can. What happens? How do we proceed?

Introductory Paragraph

The topic sentence idea is expanded to the introductory paragraph through elaboration: explanation, historical background, anecdote, quotation, or stress on the significance of an idea. Usually the introduction is about three to six sentences long. If you say too much, your paper will be top-heavy. If you don't say enough, your readers will be confused. A solid opening paragraph should

- introduce the subject through the thesis or controlling idea.
- gain reader interest.
- move the reader into the middle paragraphs.
- avoid any statement of apology about your topic or your writing and avoid beginning with a statement such as "I am writing an essay about. . . ."

Middle Paragraphs

The middle paragraphs are similar to the paragraphs you have been writing. They are developmental paragraphs used to support the thesis. Each has its own unity based on the topic sentence, moves logically and coherently, and has adequate and appropriate development. The topic sentence is usually at the beginning of the paragraph in a college essay, regardless of the form. Although some essays are an expansion of a particular form of discourse and therefore use basically the same pattern for each paragraph, many essays combine the forms. For example, you might have one middle paragraph that gives examples, one that defines, and one that clarifies. You may also have combinations within paragraphs. Nevertheless, developmental paragraphs are always related to the central idea and presented in a logical arrangement. The coherence of the paragraphs can often be improved by the use of the same principles that you have applied to individual paragraphs: using sequence words such as *first, second,* and *third;* using transitional words such as *therefore, moreover,* and *for example;* and arranging material in chronological order, spatial order, or order of relative importance.

Concluding Paragraph

Like the introductory paragraph, the concluding paragraph is a special unit with a specific function. In the concluding paragraph, usually three to six sentences long, you end on a note of finality. The way that you end depends on what you want to do. If you can't decide on how to end, try going back to your introduction and see what you said there. If you posed a question, the answer should be in the conclusion. If you laid out the framework for an exploration of the topic, then perhaps you will want to bring your discussion together with a summary statement. Or perhaps a quotation, an anecdote, or a restatement of the thesis in slightly different words would be effective. Do not end with a complaint, an apology, or the introduction of a new topic or new support. Do not begin your conclusion with a worn-out phrase such as "last but not least" or "in conclusion." Try for a fresh approach.

Examining a Paragraph and an Essay

The following paragraph and essay, both on the topic of drunk driving, were written by the same student. Notice how each is developed.

Get Them Off the Road (paragraph)

Daniel Humphreys

Topic sentence   <u>Drunk driving has become such a severe problem in California that something must be done</u>. The best solution is to do what Sweden did long ago: Lower the blood-alcohol content level to .04 percent for drunk-driving arrests. <u>Driving</u> is not

I. Support   a right; it <u>is a privilege</u>, and that privilege should not be extended to the person who drinks to the extent that his or her physical and mental abilities are signifi-

II. Support   cantly impaired. <u>Alcohol</u>, working as a depressant, <u>affects our entire nervous system</u>, according to numerous sources cited in <u>The Police Officer's Source Book</u>. As a result of this impairment, "50 percent of all fatal traffic accidents" involve intoxicated drivers, as reported by the National Highway Traffic Safety Administration. Cavenaugh and Associates, research specialists, say that in California 6,863 people were killed in alcohol-related accidents in the four-year period from 1997

III. Support   through 2000. They go on to say that nationally <u>intoxicated drivers cost us some-</u>

Concluding sentence   <u>where between $11 billion and $14 billion each year</u>. <u>It is time to give drunk dri-</u><u>vers a message</u>: "Stay off the road. You are costing us pain, injury, and death, and no one has the right to do that."

Get Them Off the Road (essay)

Daniel Humphreys

Introduction   The state of California, along with the rest of the nation, has a problem with society involving drinking and driving. Prohibition is not the answer, as history

Thesis of essay   has demonstrated. But there is a practical answer to be found in a law. <u>I believe that the legal BAC (blood-alcohol concentration) while driving should be lowered from .08 percent to .04 percent for three strong reasons.</u>

Topic sentence of paragraph   First, <u>driving in California is a privilege</u>, not a right, and <u>a person impaired by alcohol should not be allowed that privilege</u>. Statutory law states that when stopped by a police officer who suspects drunk driving, one must submit to a BAC test. The level of impairment is an individual trait because of the elapsed time of

I. Support paragraph 1   consumption, body size, and tolerance, but <u>alcohol</u> is a depressant to all of us. It <u>affects our nervous system and slows our muscular reactions</u>. As a result of extensive scientific study, Sweden determined that .04 percent BAC was the level of significant impairment, and, therefore, it passed a federal law to enforce drunk driving penalities at that point. Penalties there are extreme.

Topic sentence of paragraph   Second, <u>we</u>, like the people in Sweden, <u>are concerned about the dangers of drunk driving</u>. The National Highway Traffic Safety Administration has stated that <u>"50 percent of all fatal accidents" involve intoxicated drivers and that 75 percent of those</u>

II. Support paragraph 2   <u>drivers have a BAC of .10 percent or higher</u>. Cavenaugh and Associates, a California think tank, reports that in the four-year period between 1997 and 2000, 17,354 people were injured and 6,863 were killed in alcohol-related accidents in California.

Topic sentence of paragraph

III. Support paragraph 3

Third, even if we are among the fortunate few who are not touched directly by the problems of drunk driving, <u>there are other effects</u>. <u>One is money</u>. There are the loss of production, cost of insurance, cost of delays in traffic, cost of medical care for those who have no insurance, and many other costs. Cavenaugh and Associates say that drunk drivers cost us nationally somewhere between $11 billion and $14 billion a year.

Conclusion

Restated thesis

Police officers report that drinking people are quick to say, "I'm okay to drive," but every four years our nation loses more lives to drunk drivers than it lost in the entire Vietnam War. To lower the legal BAC limit to .04 percent would mean saving lives, property, and money.

EXERCISE 1

Expanding a Paragraph to an Essay

The following paragraph could easily be expanded into an essay because the topic sentence and its related statements can be developed into an introduction; each of the main divisions (five) can be expanded into a separate paragraph; and the restated topic sentence can, with elaboration, become the concluding paragraph. Divide the paragraph following with the symbol ¶ and annotate it in the left-hand margin with the words *Introduction*, *Support* (and numbers for the middle five paragraphs), and *Conclusion* to show the parts that would be developed further. The topic sentence has already been marked for you.

What Is a Gang?

Will Cusak

Topic sentence

The word *gang* is often used loosely to mean "a group of people who go around together," but that does not satisfy the concerns of law enforcement people and sociologists. <u>For those professionals, the definition of gang has five parts that combine to form a unit</u>. First a gang has to have a name. Some well-known gang names are Bloods, Crips, Hell's Angels, and Mexican Mafia. The second part of the definition is clothing or other identifying items such as tattoos. The clothing may be of specific brands or colors, such as blue for Crips and red for Bloods. Members of the Aryan Brotherhood often have blue thunderbolt tattoos. A third component is rituals. They may involve such things as the use of handshakes, other body language or signing, and graffiti. A fourth is binding membership. A gang member is part of an organization, a kind of family, with obligations and codes of behavior to follow. Finally, a gang will be involved in some criminal behavior, something such as prostitution, drugs, thievery, or burglary. There are many different kinds of gangs—ethnic, regional, behavioral—but they all have these five characteristics.

EXERCISE 2

Analyzing Essay Form

Underline the thesis in the first paragraph; the topic sentences in paragraphs 2, 3, 4, and 5; and the most forceful concluding statement in the last paragraph. In the left-hand margin, label each part you underlined. In this essay the topic sentences are not all at the beginning of paragraphs. Observe how information is used to support the topic sentences, and double underline some key phrases of that support.

More Than Book 'Em

Jerry Price

1   As a police officer, when I am on patrol I have a wide variety of duties. I respond to several different types of calls. One of the most common calls involves a family dispute between a husband and wife. When I respond to that kind of problem, I have to play one or more quite different roles. The main roles for family disputes are counselor, referee, and law enforcer.

2   The most common family dispute involves a husband and wife arguing. Usually the argument is almost over when I arrive. I need to talk to both sides. Depending on how intense they are, I either separate them or talk to them together. Both the husband and wife will tell me they are right and the other spouse is wrong. I then become a counselor. In this role I must be a good listener to both parties, and when they are done talking, it's my turn to talk. In the worst situation I may tell them it looks as if they are headed for a separation or divorce. However, most of the time I tell them to act like adults and talk to their spouse as they talked to me. I may suggest that they seek professional counseling. With the husband and wife now having everything off their chests, and after their having received my small lecture, they may be able to go back to living relatively peaceful lives together.

3   In a different scenario, if the yelling and screaming is still going on when I arrive, I may want to just stand back and be a referee. I usually allow the wife to talk first. She typically tells her husband off. Not forgetting my role as referee, I step in only if the argument gets extremely ugly. When this happens, I send the wife to a neutral corner to cool off. Then I allow her to continue her verbal assault. When I feel the husband has had enough, I stop the wife and give the husband a turn. All the time I am watching and listening. My main task is to keep the fight clean. If I think progress is being made with the couple, I let it continue. If the argument is going in circles, I may stop the fight. At this time I may send one of the fighters out for a drive or to a friend's house to cool off. This diversion is, however, only a temporary solution to the problem, for when the couple gets back together I will probably be needed for round two.

4   When the family dispute turns into a fist fight, it's usually the husband hitting his wife. Wives do hit their husbands, but the male ego usually won't let the man call the police. When the husband has hit his wife, and she has only a very minor injury, it will be up to her to have her husband arrested. If the wife is bleeding or has several bruises, then I make the decision. In these cases I become the enforcer of the law. I always place the husband under arrest even if the wife doesn't

want it. As the enforcer I then take the husband to jail. The severity of the wife's injuries will determine how long the husband will stay in jail. He may be released in a couple of hours with a ticket and a court date or he may be in jail until he can be seen by a judge. Prior convictions and restraining orders are considerations.

5   As a typical police officer on patrol, I make many decisions and play many roles in domestic disturbance cases. The circumstances of these cases dictate the way each is handled. As an experienced officer, I should be able to make the right decision, and I should know when to be a counselor, a referee, or a law enforcer.

Topics for Short Essays

Many paragraph topics in this book can become topics for short essays. In Part Four, the writing instruction is presented according to the well-known patterns listed here. Although the writing topics suggested at the end of Chapters 16 through 22 refer to paragraph writing, almost all of the topics can be further developed into essays. You may want to refer back to the following list if you are working on an essay assignment.

> **Narration:** Expand each part of the narrative form (situation, conflict, struggle, outcome, meaning) into one or more paragraphs. Give the most emphasis to the struggle.
>
> **Description:** Expand each unit of descriptive detail into a paragraph. All paragraphs should support the dominant impression.
>
> **Exemplification:** Expand one example into an extended example or expand a group of examples into separate paragraphs. Each paragraph should support the main point.
>
> **Process Analysis:** Expand the preparation and each step in the process into a separate paragraph.
>
> **Analysis by Division:** Expand each part of the unit into a paragraph.
>
> **Comparison and Contrast:** In the point-by-point pattern, expand each point into a separate paragraph. In the subject-by-subject pattern, first expand each subject into a separate paragraph. If you have sufficient material on each point, you can also expand each point into a separate paragraph.
>
> **Argument:** Expand the refutation and each main division of support into a separate paragraph.

Writer's Guidelines

You do not usually set out to write an essay by first writing a paragraph. However, the organization for the paragraph and the essay is often the same, and the writing process is also the same. You still proceed from initial prewriting to topic, to outline, to draft, to revising, to editing, to final paper. The difference is often only a matter of development and indentation.

> **1.** The well-designed paragraph and the well-designed essay often have the same form.
>   **a.** The **introduction** of an essay carries the thesis, which states the controlling idea—much like the topic sentence for a paragraph but on a larger scale.

b. The **development,** or middle part, supplies evidence and reasoning—the support.

c. The **conclusion** provides an appropriate ending—often a restatement of or reflection on the thesis.

2. These are the important relationships:

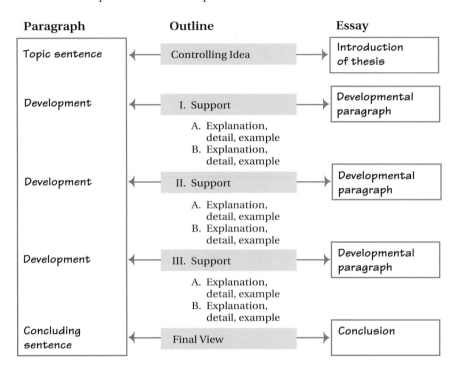

Part
IV

Writing Paragraphs and Essays: Instruction, with Reading Selections

Part IV discusses, and also demonstrates through reading selections, how our thoughts often occur in flexible, useful patterns. As you write in classes across the campus, notice how many regular writing assignments, especially papers and essay tests, expect you to narrate, describe, use examples, analyze by division, compare and contrast, and argue. The chapters in this part will provide you with examples of good writing, demonstrate the writing process, and offer an abundance of topics.

Narration: Moving Through Time

A narrative can be as short as a joke, as long as history, or anything between, including a single paragraph.

FLOW OF WRITING

Learning Objectives

Working with this chapter, I will learn to

~ organize the narrative pattern.

~ use techniques of narration.

~ use narration in different contexts.

Writing Narration

In our everyday lives, we tell stories and invite other people to do so by asking questions such as "What happened at work today?" and "What did you do last weekend?" We are disappointed when the answer is "Nothing much." We may be equally disappointed when a person doesn't give us enough details or gives us too many and spoils the effect. After all, we are interested in people's stories and in the people who tell them. We like narratives.

What is a narrative? A **narrative** is an account of an incident or a series of incidents that make up a complete and significant action. A narrative can be as short as a joke, as long as history, or anything between, including a single paragraph or an essay. Each narrative has five properties: situation, conflict, struggle, outcome, and meaning.

The example in the following narrative pattern is based on a scene in Mark Twain's *The Adventures of Tom Sawyer*.

The Basic Pattern

Situation

Situation is the background for the action. The situation may be described only briefly, or it may even be implied. ("Tom Sawyer, a youngster living in a small town, has been directed by his Aunt Polly to whitewash the fence in front of their house.")

Conflict

Conflict is friction, such as a problem in the surroundings, with another person(s), or within the individual. The conflict, which is at the heart of each story, produces struggle. ("A fun-loving boy who would rather go fishing than do simple, manual chores, Tom wants to find others to do his work for him. He knows that others would not want to paint the fence, so he must persuade them.")

Struggle

Struggle, which need not be physical, is the manner of dealing with the conflict. The struggle adds action or engagement and generates the plot. ("Hearing Ben Rogers nearby making huffing steamboat sounds and enjoying play, Tom pretends he is a serious artist as he brushes the sparkling white paint onto the dark fence before standing back to admire it. When Ben starts to tease Tom about having to work, Tom says, 'What do you call work?' 'Why, ain't that work?' Ben asks. Tom says it suits him and few boys could do it. Soon Tom has Ben asking if he can paint the fence and offering an apple for the privilege. Tom relents. Then other friends drop by and fall for the same scheme.")

Outcome

Outcome is the result of the struggle. ("In a short time the fence has three coats of paint, and Tom has a collection of treasures, including a dead rat and a one-eyed cat.")

Meaning

Meaning is the significance of the story, which may be deeply philosophical or simple, stated or implied. ("Tom has discovered that to make a person want something it is only necessary to make that something seem difficult to obtain.")

Techniques

The properties of a narrative, which are present in some way in all the many forms of the narrative, are enhanced by the use of various techniques.

- **Description** (the use of specific details to advance action, with images to make readers see, smell, taste, hear, and feel)

    "*huffing* steamboat sounds"

    "*sparkling white paint* onto the *dark fence*"

- **Dialogue** (the exact words of the speakers, enclosed in quotation marks)

    Tom says, *"What do you call work?"*

    "Why, ain't that work?" Ben asks.

- **Transitional words** (words, such as *after, finally, following, later, next, soon, then,* and *when,* that move a story forward, for narratives are usually presented in chronological order)

    "*When* Ben starts"

    "*Soon* Tom has Ben asking"

    "*Then* other friends"

- **Consistent tense** (using the same time frame as indicated by verb choice)
    Most narratives are related in the past tense:

    I *saw* the twister.

    I *ran* for the storm cellar.

    I *locked* the door behind me.

    However, a present tense accounting can project a keen sense of immediacy:

    I *see* the twister.

    I *run* for the storm cellar.

    I *lock* the door behind me.

    Be consistent with the past or present tense for your overall narrative pattern.

Purpose and Time Frame

Most narratives written as college assignments will have an expository purpose; that is, they explain a specified idea. Consider working with a short time frame for short writing assignments. The scope would usually be no more than one incident of brief duration for one paragraph. For example, writing about an entire graduation ceremony might be too complicated, but concentrating on the moment when you walked forward to receive the diploma or the moment when the relatives and friends came down on the field could work very well.

Practicing Patterns of Narration

Some narratives seem more structured than others, but all have the same basic patterns. The parts, especially conflict and struggle, will vary in extent, depending on the circumstances.

EXERCISE 1

Completing Patterns

Fill in the blanks to complete the pattern for the topic "Lost and Found." Add descriptive details as needed.

(Situation) I. Person taking store money deposit bag to bank

(Conflict) II. Person loses bag

(Struggle) III. _____

(Outcome) IV. _____

(Meaning) V. _____

EXERCISE 2

Completing Patterns

Fill in the blanks to complete the pattern for the topic "Good Samaritan." Add descriptive details as needed.

(Situation) I. Driver with flat tire, dead of night

(Conflict) II. No spare tire

(Struggle) III. _____

(Outcome) IV. _____

(Meaning) V. _____

EXERCISE 3	Writing Patterns

Fill in the blanks to complete the pattern for the topic "An Incident at Work" or for another topic of your choice. Add descriptive details as needed.

(Situation) I. _____

(Conflict) II. _____

(Struggle) III. _____

(Outcome) IV. _____

(Meaning) V. _____

EXERCISE 4	Writing Patterns

Fill in the blanks to complete the pattern for the topic "Dealing with a Problem at School" or for another topic of your choice. Add descriptive details as needed.

(Situation) I. _____

(Conflict) II. _____

(Struggle) III. _____

(Outcome) IV. _____

(Meaning) V. _____

Connecting Reading and Writing: Growing Pains and Pleasures

Even under the best of conditions, growing up is not a smooth progression. It is actually a hobbling and sprinting back and forth with some jogging to the sides and, usually, movement forward and up.

Because of the unevenness of this journey, we can all reflect on particular experiences during which we have relocated ourselves in a personal sense as if we were dealing with geography: have reached a plateau, climbed a mountain, fallen into a canyon, been stranded on an island, been lost in a desert, stumbled into paradise. These experiences may be events—special occasions, holidays, ceremonies, celebrations, graduations, special recognition. They may be traumatic events—accidents, injuries, illnesses, deaths, betrayals, escapes, entrapments. They may be struggles—for recognition, acceptance, self-identity, respect. They may involve relationships—love (in its many forms), changes in family make-up, establishing and reestablishing friendships as a result of moving or changing. They may be seemingly small acts of kindness, insults to the spirit, tokens of love.

THE QUIGMANS   by Buddy Hickerson

Impossible childhood feats #223

Whatever they are, they are key experiences, as indelible on our memories as dark ink on white linen. Against these key experiences we measure the more ordinary ones and chart our progress or lack of it toward where we are today. We don't bury these experiences; from time to time they pop up on our mind screens like CD-ROM images as reminders of who we are and how we got that way. If we made time lines for our lives, these experiences would be the listed items, on a personal scale equal to the great wars, developments, discoveries, creations, and inventions of world history. They will always be with us for pain or pleasure.

"My First Real Fire" is an initiation story of a young man entering a dangerous career field. "Unforgettable Crying" unexpectedly brings the writer closer to her father. "100 Miles per Hour, Upside Down and Sideways" looks back almost twenty years to the author's flirtation with a muscle car and fame.

We begin with a humorous paragraph by student writer Joel Bailey, who gives an account of his clumsiness as a worker in a fast-food establishment. First Bailey completed the Writing Process Worksheet, which shows how he moved from understanding his assignment to exploratory prewriting to writing his paper. The worksheet is followed by his final draft. His two rough drafts marked for revision are not shown.

You will find a full-size blank worksheet on page 7, which can be photocopied, filled in, and submitted with each assignment if your instructor directs you to do so.

Writing Process Worksheet

Title   King of Klutziness

Name   Joel Bailey   **Due Date**   Monday, September, 9 a.m.

ASSIGNMENT   In the space below, write whatever you need to know about your assignment, including information about the topic, audience, pattern of writing, length, whether to include a rough draft or revised drafts, and whether your paper must be typed.

Write a one-page narrative about a work-related incident that was a learning experience and made a deep impression. Submit this sheet and a rough draft marked for revision with the final draft. Type the final draft. Audience: other students and instructor.

STAGE ONE

Explore   Freewrite, brainstorm (list), cluster, or take notes as directed by your instructor. Use the back of this page or separate paper if you need more space.

Listing

first day at work	celebrity customer	he's really angry
Carl's Jr., Hollywood	take order	funnier now
no training	make mistake	than then
easy at first	he's angry	be cool the
things change	I spill Coke	next time
busy	smear catsup	
really busy		

STAGE TWO

Organize   Write a topic sentence or thesis; label the subject and the treatment parts.

My first day at work was a truly memorable experience for me and my
      subject   treatment
unfortunate customer.

Write an outline or an outline alternative.

  I. Situation
     A. Carl's Jr.
     B. My first day at work
 II. Conflict
     A. No training
     B. Too many customers
     C. Make mistake with celebrity customer
III. Struggle
     A. Mistake follows mistake
     B. Attempted correction becomes mistake
     C. Customer really angry
IV. Outcome
     A. Customer upset
     C. Embarrassment for me
 V. Meaning
     A. A learning experience
     B. Incident funnier now than then

STAGE THREE

Write   On separate paper, write and then revise your paragraph or essay as many times as necessary for **c**oherence, **l**anguage (usage, tone, and diction), **u**nity, **e**mphasis, **s**upport, and **s**entences (**CLUESS**). Read your work aloud to hear and correct any grammatical errors or awkward-sounding sentences.

Edit any problems in fundamentals, such as **c**apitalization, **o**missions, **p**unctuation, and **s**pelling (**COPS**).

King of Klutziness

Joel Bailey

Topic sentence   <u>It was my first task of what would be a memorable day at work in Carl's Jr., a fast-food place by Universal Studio near Hollywood.</u> I was assigned to the front

Situation   counter because another worker was late. There I was at noon, the busiest time of the day, with no training, scared, and nervous. In the beginning, things went well. Orders were routine, and I filled them and made change. As time passed, the lines got short, and I was still doing great because, after all, the job didn't require the mentality of a rocket scientist. Several counter people left their registers to

Conflict   help out in back. Then a lot of people came in at one time. Only two of us were taking orders. I was nervous. I served three persons, hardly looking up as I punched the keys, called out orders, and made change. After barely glancing at the next person, I heard his voice ordering, a familiar voice. It was Alex Benson, a reporter for a TV channel I frequently watched. I repeated his order so it would be perfect, and I took his money. After I gave him his change, he stared at the receipt

Struggle   and said with more than a touch of irritation, "You made a mistake. You charged me for two chicken burgers." I apologized and gave him a refund. "What about the tax," he growled. "You didn't refund the tax." I was really getting nervous. He always laughed and smiled on TV. I gave him the tax money. I grabbed someone else's chicken order just so I could give him quick service, but when I handed him the tray, my hand slipped and I spilled his Coke on his trousers. Quickly I grabbed

Outcome   a napkin and ran around the counter and wiped at the Coke stain. Unfortunately the napkin I grabbed had catsup on it. Now I had added a condiment to the Coke stain. By that time I might as well have salted and peppered him. Beyond anger,

Meaning   and looking at me wildly, he fled with his tray to a distant booth and sat with his back to the wall. I decided not to ask for an autograph.

EXERCISE 5   Discussion and Critical Thinking

1. Is Bailey really klutzy or is this just first-day jitters?

2. Is Bailey's problem with understanding the restaurant's procedures or with executing the procedures?

3. Was this a funny situation at the time?

4. How does the conflict differ from the struggle?

My First Real Fire

TYSON M. BURNS

Like many students at community colleges, Tyson M. Burns brings many life experiences with him. As a member of the National Guard, he participated in Desert Shield and Desert Storm, so his recent work as a firefighter was not his first taste of action. Here he narrates his real-life "baptism by fire."

1   I am violently torn from my dream by the shrieking of the alarm. I'm on autopilot, still half asleep and trying to make my eyes focus as I jump into my boots and run for the fire engine. A mass of shoulders and elbows clash as we all put on our jackets and hoods. Somewhere above my head a loudspeaker comes to life, and the dispatcher tells us that the carpet warehouse down the street is fully engulfed in flames. My heart starts to race, and I feel a cold wave of adrenaline wash over my body.

2   The ride to the fire is a rough one. As I vigorously chew on a handful of Tums, I steady myself by holding on to the door handle with my left hand and bring a bottle of water to my mouth with my right. I'm trying to concentrate on what I will have to do when I get there. The siren and air horns are deafening as I run through the various procedures in my head. This is my first real fire. Will I get to go inside? What will it look like, feel like, and sound like inside? My Captain in the front seat looks back over his shoulder at me and asks, "You want to get hot tonight?" I just nod my head as I adjust the straps on my facemask.

3   We are the first of four fire trucks to respond to the fire. We park on the street in front of the building. It's a typical large plate glass storefront with a showroom in the front and a warehouse in the rear of the building. Thick black smoke is billowing from the back of the building and rising in a huge dark column that blocks the stars. I am assigned to a hose team and sandwiched between my Captain and Lieutenant. I am scared, but I feel much better going in with two experienced firefighters. In what seems like only a matter of seconds, the entry team cuts open one of the warehouse loading doors.

4   As we crawl in, all I can see is the floor and my Captain's rear end. A bubbling, sizzling, popping sound fills my ears. I never thought I would hear frying bacon in a fire. The mechanical clunk and hiss of my breathing reminds me of Darth Vader from the old *Star Wars* movies. I am getting excited, and I have to remind myself to breathe slowly so my air will last.

5   When I look around, I see that I am surrounded by a thick cloud of bright orange light. I can only see about a foot and a half in front of me; my left hand is on the back of my Captain's air tank and our hose is in the crook of my right arm. Inside this swirling cloud, it looks like a hundred bright orange floodlights are shining down on us from all directions. I feel the hose jerk and then vibrate as my Captain opens the nozzle at the end of the hose and sprays water over our heads. I wait for a few seconds. When I don't feel boiling hot water come back down on us, I know we are in trouble.

6   The heat is intense. It must be over 500 degrees in here. It almost takes my breath away, like when you first enter a steam room and you catch your breath. In those first few seconds, you have a slight panic; your skin burns and your face stings. But after a few moments you get used to it and realize you're okay. Before I know it, I am sweating profusely, but instead of it cooling me I can feel it heat up and begin to burn my skin. The cool stale air that I had been breathing is now getting warmer and smelling like plastic as my air tank begins to heat up. The rubber around my facemask is getting hotter and beginning to sting my face. I wonder how much heat my protective equipment can take. I wonder how much more I can take. I don't want to disappoint my Captain and Lieutenant.

7   I hear a muffled, garbled yelling behind me and feel a hand slapping my left shoulder. I arch my back and turn my head so I can hear my Lieutenant better. Through his mask I hear him yell, "IT'S TOO HOT, IT'S GONNA FLASH OVER, WE NEED TO GET THE HECK OUTTA HERE!!" I relay the message to my Captain, and he agrees. I feel him get up from his knees to a crouch and head for the doorway. I follow him, my left hand never leaving his air tank. As we emerge from the opening, I feel my Lieutenant slam into the back of me, knocking us all down like dominoes. I roll off my Captain and look up at what should have been a smoke-filled sky. Instead, I see bright orange flames rolling over our heads from the doorway we had just come through. A second later I feel invisible hands grabbing my harness and dragging me across the parking lot.

8   My helmet and mask are jerked off my head. I feel the night air instantly cool my cheeks and sweat soaked hair. A voice asks, "Can you tell me what your name is? Do you know where you are right now?" I look down to see if all of my body parts are still attached, and I notice that my whole body is smoking, as if steam is escaping through the fabric of my coat and pants. My Lieutenant was right. The flames must have flashed over as we were exiting. The paramedic who is checking me out notices that I am staring at my steaming gloves and says, "You guys were just coming through the doorway as it spewed this huge ball of fire. Just like when circus performers spit mouthfuls of alcohol across a match." As I throw up, the other firefighters are laughing and patting me on the back and saying, "So, how does it feel to be a real firefighter?"

9   Fabulous.

EXERCISE 6

Discussion and Critical Thinking

1. Burns's essay is a narrative within a narrative. The larger one encompasses the entire event. The second one (paragraphs 3 through 9), a scene, covers the trip inside the building. Annotate the parts of the narrative (situation, conflict, struggle, outcome, and meaning) for that scene.

2. Indicate by paragraph number the use of dialogue.

3. Does Burns use present or past tense verbs?

4. List some images (sight, sound, smell, touch) from paragraphs 6 and 7 that enable us to share his experience imaginatively with him.

Sight:

Sound:

Smell:

Touch:

5. What does this account tell you about the writer?

Unforgettable Crying

TZU-YIN WANG

Student Tzu-Yin Wang thought she knew her father. He was a man devoid of sentiment. Paradoxically, she would have to travel far from him in order to get close and discover the real person. One incident, one narrative, tells all you need to know about a daughter and dad.

1   My father, just slightly taller than my mother, is not imposing physically. But he is a stubborn person of few words and few smiles, and he is a man of strong will. Unable to express his love for people easily, he has never chatted playfully with his children. When we children have met with difficulty, we have gone to our mother, who has always forced us to get his opinion. My main image of him has been reinforced almost daily: Dad is sitting in his chair, reading the newspaper and drinking his favorite beer. I thought I knew him exactly for what he was and wasn't, and then something happened.

2   After I graduated from high school in 2000 in Taiwan, my aunt in Los Angeles persuaded my mother to let me finish my B.A. degree in America. Last summer [2002] was the first time I went back to Taiwan. When I arrived, I looked at my parents and couldn't believe what I was seeing. They had aged, both my father and mother. That very night she asked me to fix her hair, as I had so many times before. When I pushed her black hair aside to part it, I saw the gray hair underneath. I was too sad to tell her. I bravely pulled it up in her favorite style and kissed her on the cheek. I couldn't help but look at my father sitting in his chair and wonder if he, too, had gray hair. But I would never peek and certainly would never ask.

3   During my two weeks in Taiwan, I seemed to go back to my past life. I walked familiar roads, went to the unchanged Sky Market with my mother, and ate in the Hwalien Restaurant, where my father and mother had so often taken me.

4   Nevertheless, my happy vacation ended on a terrible Saturday. Because the plane was fully booked, I had been put on standby. My mother was worried that I would be late for the beginning of the new semester, so she phoned the airline continually to ask for any available seat. To my surprise, she convinced the airlines of my emergency, and a call came in saying a seat was available for a flight

leaving in three hours. As I packed my baggage, I could hear the clock ticking on the wall, seeming to pronounce the death penalty, for I was unwilling to leave my family so soon.

5   After my brother put my luggage into the trunk of the car, I knew it was time for me to leave. As my mother and I went back to my room to see if I had forgotten anything, through a crack in the door, I glimpsed my father, with a cheerless expression, pass by my room. My mother also saw him pass and told me that she had quarreled with him and that he was still angry. I concluded that my father already knew I was about to leave and didn't want to say good-bye. I was very sad.

6   Because there were no direct flights from my hometown of Kaosiung to Los Angeles, I took a commuter plane to Taipei for my transfer to America. When I reached Taipei, I called home, and my sister answered. She said my father was upset because I had left without saying good-bye. I asked her to put him on the phone. At first he was again angry. Then I explained, and he began sobbing. He sounded heartbroken. His crying was deep, sorrowful. I couldn't believe it came from my stoical father. It was unforgettable. I cried too. I cried off and on from Taipei to Los Angeles.

7   I used to think that my father didn't need comfort or consideration for his feelings, or even that he had feelings. I didn't know there was tenderness underneath his toughness. I was wrong. My father is a common person, and all people need love and feel love. His unforgettable crying told me he cares about me. Sometimes falling tears are louder than words.

EXERCISE 7   ## Discussion and Critical Thinking

1. In the left margin, annotate the basic pattern of the narrative (situation, conflict, struggle, outcome, and meaning).

2. Underline the thesis.

---

100 Miles per Hour, Upside Down and Sideways

RICK BRAGG

Pulitzer Prize–winning author Rick Bragg has reported for the St. Petersburg Times, *the* Los Angeles Times, *and the* New York Times. *All Over But the Shoutin',* from which this excerpt is taken, is an autobiography about his growing up in a poor family and being nurtured by his self-sacrificing mother in Piedmont, Alabama. He also is the author of the bestseller I Am a Soldier, Too: The Jessica Lynch Story.

1   Since I was a boy I have searched for ways to slingshot myself into the distance, faster and faster. When you turn the key on a car built for speed, when you hear that car rumble like an approaching storm and feel the steering wheel tremble in

your hands from all that power barely under control, you feel like you can run away from anything, like you can turn your whole life into an insignificant speck in the rearview mirror.

2   In the summer of 1976, the summer before my senior year at Jacksonville High School, I had the mother of all slingshots. She was a 1969 General Motors convertible muscle car with a 350 V-8 and a Holley four-barreled carburetor as long as my arm. She got about six miles to the gallon, downhill, and when you started her up she sounded like Judgment Day. She was long and low and vicious, a mad dog cyclone with orange houndstooth interior and an eight-track tape player, and looked fast just sitting in the yard under a pine tree. I owned just one tape, that I remember, *The Eagles' Greatest Hits*.

3   I worked two summers in the hell and heat at minimum wage to earn enough money to buy her and still had to borrow money from my uncle Ed, who got her for just nineteen hundred dollars mainly because he paid in hundred-dollar bills. "You better be careful, boy," he told me. "That'un will kill you." I assured him that, Yes, Sir, I would creep around in it like an old woman.

4   I tell myself I loved that car because she was so pretty and so fast and because I loved to rumble between the rows of pines with the blond hair of some girl who had yet to discover she was better than me whipping in the breeze. But the truth is I loved her because she was my equalizer. She raised me up, at least in my own eyes, closer to where I wanted and needed to be. In high school, I was neither extremely popular nor one of the great number of want-to-bes. I was invited to parties with the popular kids, I had dates with pretty girls. But there was always a distance there, of my own making, usually.

5   That car, in a purely superficial way, closed it. People crowded around her at the Hardee's. I let only one person drive her, Patrice Curry, the prettiest girl in school, for exactly one mile.

6   That first weekend, I raced her across the long, wide parking lot of the TG&Y, an insane thing to do, seeing as how a police car could have cruised by at any minute. It was a test of nerves as well as speed, because you actually had to be slowing down, not speeding up, as you neared the finish line, because you just ran out of parking lot. I beat Lyn Johnson's Plymouth and had to slam on my brakes and swing her hard around, to keep from jumping the curb, the road, and plowing into the parking lot of the Sonic Drive-In.

7   It would have lasted longer, this upraised standing, if I had pampered her. I guess I should have spent more time looking at her than racing her, but I had too much of the Bragg side of the family in me for that. I would roll her out on some lonely country road late at night, the top down, and blister down the blacktop until I knew the tires were about to lift off the ground. But they never did. She held the road, somehow, until I ran out of road or just lost my nerve. It was as if there was no limit to her, at how fast we could go, together.

8   It lasted two weeks from the day I bought her.

9   On Saturday night, late, I pulled up to the last red light in town on my way home. Kyle Smith pulled up beside me in a loud-running Chevrolet, and raced his engine. I did not squall out when the light changed—she was not that kind of car—but let her rpm's build, build and build, like winding up a top.

10   I was passing a hundred miles per hour as I neared a long sweeping turn on Highway 21 when I saw, coming toward me, the blue lights of the town's police. I cannot really remember what happened next. I just remember mashing the gas pedal down hard, halfway through that sweeping turn, and the sickening feeling as the car just seemed to lift and twist in the air, until I was doing a hundred miles per hour still, but upside down and sideways.

11   She landed across a ditch, on her top. If she had not hit the ditch in just the right way, the police later said, it would have cut my head off. I did not have on my seat belt. We never did, then. Instead of flinging me out, though, the centrifugal force—I had taken science in ninth grade—somehow held me in.

12   Instead of lying broken and bleeding on the ground beside my car, or headless, I just sat there, upside down. I always pulled the adjustable steering wheel down low, an inch or less above my thighs, and that held me in place, my head covered with mud and broken glass. The radio was still blaring—it was the Eagles' "The Long Run," I believe—and I tried to find the knob in the dark to turn it off. Funny. There I was in an upside-down car, smelling the gas as it ran out of the tank, listening to the tick, tick, tick of the hot engine, thinking: "I sure do hope that gas don't get nowhere near that hot manifold," but all I did about it was try to turn down the radio.

13   I knew the police had arrived because I could hear them talking. Finally, I felt a hand on my collar. A state trooper dragged me out and dragged me up the side of the ditch and into the collective glare of the most headlights I had ever seen. There were police cars and ambulances and traffic backed up, it seemed, all the way to Piedmont.

14   "The Lord was riding with you, son," the trooper said. "You should be dead."

15   My momma stood off to one side, stunned. Finally the police let her through to look me over, up and down. But except for the glass in my hair and a sore neck, I was fine. Thankfully, I was too old for her to go cut a hickory and stripe my legs with it, but I am sure it crossed her mind.

16   The trooper and the Jacksonville police had a private talk off to one side, trying to decide whether or not to put me in prison for the rest of my life. Finally, they informed my momma that I had suffered enough, to take me home. As we drove away, I looked back over my shoulder as the wrecker dragged my car out of the ditch and, with the help of several strong men, flipped it back over, right-side up. It looked like a white sheet of paper someone had crumped up and tossed in the ditch from a passing car.

17   "The Lord was riding with that boy," Carliss Slaughts, the wrecker operator, told my uncle Ed. With so many people saying that, I thought the front page of the *Anniston Star* the next day would read: LORD RIDES WITH BOY, WRECKS ANYWAY.

18   I was famous for a while. No one, no one, flips a convertible at a hundred miles per hour, without a seat belt on, and walks away, undamaged. People said I had a charmed life. My momma, like the trooper and Mr. Slaughts, just figured God was my copilot.

19   The craftsmen at Slaughts' Body Shop put her back together, over four months. My uncle Ed loaned me the money to fix her, and took it out of my check. The body and fender man made her pretty again, but she was never the same. She was fast but not real fast, as if some little part of her was still broken deep inside. Finally, someone backed into her in the parking lot of the Piggly Wiggly, and I was so disgusted I sold her for fourteen hundred dollars to a preacher's son, who drove the speed limit.

EXERCISE 8

Discussion and Critical Thinking

1. Throughout this essay, Bragg refers to his car as "her," not an uncommon term men use in referring to their vehicles. How do you feel about his using that term instead of the neuter "it"?

2. How would you feel if a female were writing an essay about her car and refer-ring to it as "him"? Would your reaction be any different from that in ques-tion 1?

3. For the most part, Bragg shows the reader what happens by presenting scenes and giving details, but he also tells what happened. When he tells about the meaning of the experience (hence, the meaning of the narrative), how significant is the passage of time, considering that he is now almost twenty years older?

4. Why was the car especially important to him in high school? (See paragraph 4.) What does Bragg mean when he says, "She was my equalizer"?

5. In paragraph 1, Bragg says, "Since I was a boy I have searched for ways to slingshot myself into the distance, faster and faster. . . . [Y]ou feel like you can run away from anything." As a youngster, his way was buying a car; as an adult, what "ways" might he be referring to? How do we escape or offset the "anything's."

6. What is the conflict Bragg deals with in his narrative?

7. Could you make the case that one meaning of this narrative is that Bragg has grown up; and now, instead of finding an equalizer in a fast, sporty car, he finds it in career accomplishments? Explain.

Topics for Writing Narration

You will find a blank Writing Process Worksheet on page 7, which can be photo-copied, filled in, and submitted with each assignment if your instructor directs you to do so.

Reading-Related Topics

"King of Klutziness"

1. Write a narrative about learning how to do something specific on the job. In what way(s) did you or someone else perform badly, perhaps ridiculously? Many of these events occur on the first day of employment.

"My First Real Fire"

2. Using this essay as a model, write about your being initiated at the workplace through a scary or threatening experience. The job might involve working with potentially dangerous equipment, dealing with the elements (fire, water, air, or land), or mixing with intimidating or creepy people.

"Unforgettable Crying"

3. Using this essay as a model, write about an experience that enabled you to understand—for better or worse—someone you have known for a while. The experience might deal with jeopardy, injury, death, divorce, unemployment, incarceration, embarrassment, birth, sickness, homesickness, teamwork, help, or gratitude.

"100 Miles per Hour, Upside Down and Sideways"

4. Write about an experience of your adolescence in which you—out of immaturity or a desire for attention or emotional release—did something that was foolish then but offers some insight into yourself as you look back on it now.

General Topics

5. Write a narrative based on a topic sentence such as this: "One experience showed me what _____ [pain, fear, anger, love, sacrifice, dedication, joy, sorrow, shame, pride] was really like."

6. Write a simple narrative about a fire, a riot, an automobile accident, a rescue, shoplifting, or some other unusual happening you witnessed.

7. Write a narrative that supports (or opposes) the idea of a familiar saying such as one of the following:

You never know who a friend is until you need one.

A bird in the hand is worth two in the bush

A person who is absent is soon forgotten.

Better to be alone than to be in bad company.

A person in a passion rides a mad horse.

Borrowing is the mother of trouble.

A person who marries for money earns it.

The person who lies down with dogs gets up with fleas.

Never give advice to a friend.

If it isn't broken, don't fix it.

Nice people finish last.

It isn't what you know, it's whom you know.

Fools and their money are soon parted.

Every person has a price.

You get what you pay for.

Haste makes waste.

The greatest remedy for anger is delay.

A person full of him- or herself is empty.

To forget a wrong is the best revenge.

Money is honey, my little sonny, And a rich man's joke is always funny.

Cross-Curricular Topics

8. Write a case study of an individual's behavior: in a class requiring observation, such as teacher training, physical education, sociology, psychology, or business management.

9. Write a report on an experiment in a class (biology, ecology, psychology).

10. Describe a pivotal moment or revealing incident in the life of a historical figure, composer, artist, author.

Career-Related Topics

11. Write a narrative account of a work-related encounter between a manager and a worker and briefly explain the significance of the event.

12. Write a narrative account of an encounter between a customer and a salesperson. Explain what went right and what went wrong.

13. Write a narrative account of how a person solved a work-related problem perhaps by using technology.

14. Write a narrative account of a salesperson handling a customer's complaint. Critique the procedure.

Writer's Guidelines: Narration

1. Include these points so you will be sure you have a complete narrative:

- situation
- conflict
- struggle
- outcome
- meaning

2. Use these techniques or devices as appropriate:

- images that appeal to the senses (sight, smell, taste, hearing, touch) and other details to advance action
- dialogue
- transitional devices (such as *next, soon, after, later, then, finally, when, following*) to indicate chronological order

3. Give details concerning action.

4. Be consistent with point of view and verb tense.

5. Keep in mind that most narratives written as college assignments will have an expository purpose; that is, they explain a specific idea.

6. Consider working with a short time frame for short writing assignments. The scope would usually be no more than one incident of brief duration for one paragraph. For example, writing about an entire graduation ceremony might be too complicated, but concentrating on the moment when you walked forward to receive the diploma or the moment when the relatives and friends came down on the field could work very well.

7. Write and revise.

- Write and then revise your paragraph or essay as many times as necessary for coherence, language (usage, tone, and diction), unity, emphasis, support, and sentences (**CLUESS**). Read your work aloud to hear and correct any grammatical errors or awkward-sounding sentences.
- Edit any problems in fundamentals, such as capitalization, omissions, punctuation, and spelling (**COPS**).

Chapter
17

Description: Moving Through Space and Time

These descriptive accounts of possessions will remind you of your own loves and loathings of the inanimate objects to which you perhaps attach much more meaning than they warrant.

PRIZED AND DESPISED POSSESSIONS

FLOW OF WRITING

Learning Objectives

Working with this chapter, I will learn to

〜 recognize and write objective and subjective description.

〜 use imagery to support a dominant impression.

〜 use description with other forms.

Writing Description

Description is the use of words to represent the appearance or nature of something. Often called a word picture, description attempts to present its subject for the mind's eye. In doing so, it does not merely become an indifferent camera; instead, it selects details that will depict something well. Just what details the descriptive writer selects will depend on several factors, especially the type of description and the dominant impression in the passage.

Types of Description

On the basis of treatment of subject material, description is customarily divided into two types: objective and subjective.

Effective **objective description** presents the subject clearly and directly as it exists outside the realm of emotions. If you are explaining the function of the heart, the characteristics of a computer chip, or the renovation of a manufacturing facility, your description would probably feature specific, impersonal details. Most technical and scientific writing is objective in that sense. It is likely to be practical and utilitarian, making little use of speculation or poetic technique while focusing on details of the physical senses.

Effective **subjective description** is also concerned with clarity and it may be direct, but it conveys a feeling about the subject and sets a mood while making a point. Because this expression involves personal views, subjective description (often called *emotional description*) has a broader range of uses than objective description.

Descriptive passages can have a combination of objective and subjective description; only the larger context of the passage will reveal the main intent.

Dominant Impression

Never try to give all of the details in a description. Instead, be selective, picking only those that you need to make a dominant impression, always taking into account the knowledge and attitudes of your readers. Remember, description is not photographic. If you wish to describe a person, select only those traits that will project your dominant impression. If you wish to describe a landscape, do not give all the details that you might find in a picture; just pick the details that support your dominant impression. That extremely important dominant impression is directly linked to your purpose and is created by choosing and arranging images, figurative language, and details.

Imagery

To convey your main concern effectively to readers, you will have to give some sensory impressions. These sensory impressions, collectively called **imagery,** refer to that which can be experienced by the senses—what we can see, smell, taste, hear, and touch.

Subjective description is more likely to use images and words rich in associations than is objective description. But just as a fine line cannot always be drawn between the objective and the subjective, a fine line cannot always be drawn between word choice in one and in the other. However, we can say with certainty that whatever the type of description, careful word choice will always be important. Consider the following points about precise diction.

To move from the general to the specific is to move from the whole class or body to the individual(s); for example,

General	Specific	More Specific
food	pastry	Twinkie
mess	dirty floor	muddy footprints
drink	soda	Coke
odor	garden smell	fragrance of roses

Words are classified as abstract or concrete depending on what they refer to. **Abstract words** refer to qualities or ideas: *good, ordinary, ultimate, truth, beauty, maturity, love.* **Concrete words** refer to substances or things; they have reality: *onions, grease, buns, tables, food.* The specific concrete words, sometimes called *concrete particulars*, often support generalizations effectively and convince the reader of the accuracy of the account.

Order: Time and Space

Time and space are the main controlling factors in most description, providing order.

If you were describing something that was not changing, such as a room, you would be concerned with space and give directions to the reader such as

next to, below, under, above, behind, in front of, beyond, in the foreground, in the background, to the left, to the right.

If you were describing something that was changing, such as a butterfly going through metamorphosis, you would be concerned mainly with time and use transitional words such as

first, second, then, soon, finally, while, after, next, later, now, before.

If you were walking through an area—so that the setting was changing—you would use both time and space for order.

Consider giving your description a sense of movement or a narrative framework. Include some action if it fits your purpose. In the following descriptive tour from the novel *Spree,* J. N. Williamson, the celebrated author of suspense, leads you effortlessly through time and space. As a reader you identify with an imaginary troubled teen being ingested by a total institution. You shuffle along, you see, you fear.

Time: initial observation

Space: exterior

It was a juvenile detention center in a metropolitan city, and neither the center nor the city was different enough from others of its kind to be worth specifying. The apprehensive glance that arriving teenagers got of the building's exterior showed them for the most part little more than a bigger, more institutional version of their own drab homes; it tended to be only the brighter, imaginative boys and girls who noticed the steel mesh on the windows. For some of them, the concrete indication of captivity was just a materialized rendition of what they had known all their lives.

Time: then or next

Space: inside

Inside the juvenile center, beyond the main hall that struck some visitors as looking like the lobby and check-in desk of some cheap hotel in a 1940s private-eye film, was a network of seemingly countless short hallways. Each one appeared to lead somewhere important, but most of them merely led to tiny offices that looked exactly alike, or to other crossing hallways. . . .

Time: finally or at last

Space: inside and back

The principal reason why most of the newcomers wound up feeling ample apprehension was because of the bolted-door cell area, cosmetically constructed at the back of the building on the long, ill-lit second floor. It was one thing to talk tough on the streets, something else to see the doors locking behind you—and to accept the fact, at last, that you wouldn't be departing the center until time prescribed by the first-floor juvenile court finally passed.

Useful Procedure for Writing Description

What is your subject? (a college stadium)

What is the dominant impression? (deserted)

What is the situation? (You are walking through the stands an hour after a game.)

What is the order? (time and place)

What details support the dominant impression?

  1. (the sight of vacant seats and an abandoned playing field)

  2. (intermingled smell of stale food and spilled beer)

  3. (sight of napkins, paper plates and cups, programs, and peanut shells blowing in a fierce wind)

  4. (raspy sound of the wind blowing paper products and whining through the steel girders)

  5. (the tacky feel and popping sound of your sneakers as they stick to and pull free from cement coated with spilled soft drinks)

Clustering may be useful.

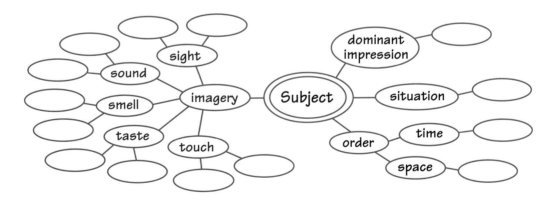

Practicing Patterns of Description

Description, which is almost always used with other patterns, is very important and often neglected. The following exercises feature descriptive writing that supports a dominant impression of colorful action.

EXERCISE 1

Completing Descriptive Patterns

Fill in the blanks to complete each outline.

Inside the Movie Theater

   I. Getting refreshments

      A. See

         1. _____

         2. _____

      B. Smell

         1. _____

         2. _____

      C. Touch

         1. _____

         2. _____

  II. Watching the movie

      A. Sights

         1. On the screen

            a. _____

            b. _____

         2. In the audience

            a. _____

            b. _____

      B. Sounds

         1. On the screen

            a. _____

            b. _____

         2. In the audience

            a. _____

            b. _____

      C. Enjoyment

         1. Group experience

2. Refreshments

a. _____

b. _____

EXERCISE 2

Completing Descriptive Patterns

Fill in the blanks to complete the following outline.

A Produce Area in a Supermarket

(Dominant impression: Diversity)

   I. Food displays (sight—color, shape)

     A. Pile of red radishes

     B. _____

     C. _____

  II. Smells (from vegetables, fruits)

     A. Acidic tangerines

     B. _____

 III. Textures (smooth or rough to touch)

     A. Rough-skinned potatoes

     B. _____

 IV. Taste (samples of sweet/sour, ripe/unripe)

     A. _____

     B. _____

Connecting Reading and Writing:
Prized and Despised Possessions

We all own things we couldn't do without, maybe things we expect to be buried with. Some of our loved ones might like to bury the things first—it sometimes happens. Of course, there are the things that we'd like to get rid of, but we can't.

This section features these prized and despised possessions. Herman Velasco reflects wistfully on the sight and smell of his "magical, stinky gloves." Gary Soto's object is a jacket. It was the primary item of clothing in his most formative years. He holds the wretched garment responsible for his major discomfort and failures. Having hoped for a studly motorcycle jacket, he instead received a vinyl jacket the color of "day-old guacamole." His account is one of how he outlasted that coat.

These descriptive accounts of possessions will remind you of your own loves and loathings of the inanimate objects to which you perhaps attach much more meaning than they warrant.

THE QUIGMANS by Buddy Hickerson

"Yeah . . . Dis is Victoria. No, we ain't got no more of da Evening in Bermuda size 8. Fergit it. Oh, yeah? Well, bite me!"

A well-loved possession might be an old pair of blue jeans, a sweater, a stuffed toy, a tattered book, a piece of jewelry, a pocketknife, a pair of shoes, a picture album, a record, a thimble, a coin, or a piece of sports equipment. You may turn to them in times of stress as talismans the same way that some people who are having trouble will eat "comfort" foods related to the happier, simpler times of childhood.

Other objects may inspire hatred, and they may be identical to the items above. In fact, any item can move from the loved to hated category. A hated item might be a tool (associated with the chores you disliked), an instrument (perhaps musical, such as an accordion, a violin, a piano), an alarm clock, a lunch pail, or an identification bracelet.

One of the most poignant reading selections in this section is by student Julie Lee, who writes about a scarf that was mistakenly burned in a family ceremony. Except for her two preliminary drafts, her entire paragraph writing assignment, including the Writing Process Worksheet, immediately follows.

You will find a full-size blank worksheet on page 7, which can be photocopied, filled in, and submitted with each assignment if your instructor directs you to do so.

Writing Process Worksheet

Title My Burning Scarf

Name Julie Lee   **Due Date** Tuesday, January 12, 9 a.m.

ASSIGNMENT   In the space below, write whatever you need to know about your assignment, including information about the topic, audience, pattern of writing, length, whether to include a rough draft or revised drafts, and whether your paper must be typed.

Write a descriptive paragraph of about 250 words on something you prize(d) or despise(d). Submit this completed worksheet, a rough draft, and a typed final draft. Audience: instructor and students who probably have not experienced what the writer did.

STAGE ONE   **Explore** Freewrite, brainstorm (list), cluster, or take notes as directed by your instructor. Use the back of this page or separate paper if you need more space.

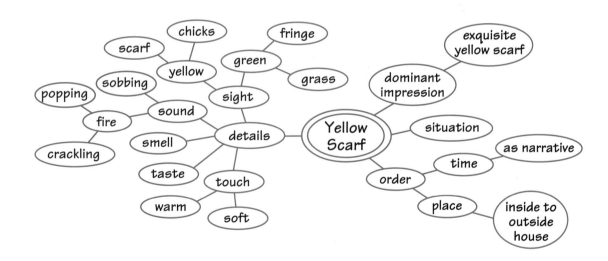

STAGE TWO   **Organize** Write a topic sentence or thesis; label the subject and the treatment parts.

During my childhood, <u>my favorite possession</u> <u>was the yellow scarf my</u>
                                  subject   treatment

<u>dad gave me when I was five.</u>

Write an outline or an outline alternative.

I. Receiving scarf
   A. Gift from Dad
   B. Special
II. Treasuring it for its beauty and utility
   A. Design
   B. Colors
   C. Texture
   D. Wearing it
III. Letting my sister use it
   A. Terminally ill (sister)
   B. Going to doctor
IV. Sister dies
V. Mother burning items
   A. Starts to burn scarf
   B. Unsuccessful in intervening
   C. Colors change in burning

STAGE THREE

Write On separate paper, write and then revise your paragraph or essay as many times as necessary for **c**oherence, **l**anguage (usage, tone, and diction), **u**nity, **e**mphasis, **s**upport, and **s**entences (**CLUESS**). Read your work aloud to hear and correct any grammatical errors or awkward-sounding sentences.

Edit any problems in fundamentals, such as **c**apitalization, **o**missions, **p**unctuation, and **s**pelling (**COPS**).

My Burning Scarf

Julie Lee

During my childhood, my favorite possession was the yellow scarf my dad gave me when I was five. Hand-sewn with care in Japan, it attracted many curious and envious eyes. Needless to say, I was the proud owner of that scarf and loved the attention it brought me. The scarf was about two feet square and made of pure virgin wool. It was decorated with a fringed green edge, and in one corner five embroidered yellow-colored chicks played against the background needlework of lush green grass. The material was as soft as cashmere and had the warmth of fur. It kept my cheeks warm when I wrapped it loosely around my neck. But when I was six, I let my seriously ill sister wear my scarf to the doctor's office. She didn't give it back to me immediately and, because she was sick, I didn't ask for it. Sadly she died of leukemia after months of suffering. A few days after she died, from my bedroom, I saw my mother in the backyard burning personal items that belonged to my dead sister. It was the Korean custom to do so. My mother was crying and so were other adults standing in a circle around the fire. Then I saw my mother pick up my wadded yellow scarf and shake it out. I rushed outside, shrieking for her to stop. Over the sounds of sobbing and the popping of the fire, I wanted to shout, "That's my scarf, my precious possession." But I didn't, and my mother, thinking I was crying only for my sister, flung it into the flames of the fire that popped and cracked, and the green and yellow of my childhood turned to orange, then red, then gray.

EXERCISE 3	Discussion and Critical Thinking

1. Underline the topic sentence.

2. In the left margin, annotate the images of sight, sound, and touch.

3. The author looks back almost fifteen years to an experience. In what ways is her recollection clearly that of a six or seven year old?

Magical, Stinky Gloves

HERMAN VELASCO

Objects that are prized by one person may be despised by others, and sometimes these objects "disappear." The qualities of the gloves that made them special to student Herman Velasco also made them subjects of a locker-room hit list.

1   When I was a sophomore in high school, I had the privilege of playing varsity football. Football was a big thing in my school. Most of all, my friends were playing junior varsity, so I didn't personally know anybody on the team. My first day at practice was a hellish experience. I played on the line, so I had to go up against really big opponents. All the veteran players would try to hurt all the newcomers. I remember my hands being cut up, bruised, and bloody. We had a star lineman by the name of Eric Winter. He saw my hands and gave me his brand new gloves. Those gloves were state of the art. They featured black cowhide leather stitched with white thread, padded with wool fiber, and topped at the wrist with a velcro strap. Receiving a gift like this from a player like him made me feel special, and for almost three years the gloves were extremely important to me.

2   I wore those gloves throughout most of my high school football career. By the time I was a senior, they were all crusty with the salt from sweat, the blood from wounds, and the dirt and fertilizer from dozens of playing fields. Their smell was somewhere between that of roadkill and a barnyard, but I still cherished them. They fit my hands perfectly. I had to tape them up with gray duct tape because the padding was coming out. They were no longer black. They were now a sort of mustard brown with green around the palm, from algae, I think. If there were an athletes' hand disease, I would have had it. A few games into that season, they smelled so bad that my coaches made me place them in a plastic bag until just before I took the field. Feeding on the moisture trapped in that bag, the gloves turned a deeper shade of green.

3   I enjoyed having those gloves and the reputation that went along with them. They gave me the confidence and the identification I needed on the field. If the opposing team started "talking trash," I would place them on the face of a downed opponent as a form of torture or punishment. Everyone who went up against me hated those gloves. One day not long before my last game, someone stole them. Only my so-called friends and the coaches had access to them, but I never found out who it was.

4   Playing gloveless in that game, I suffered a serious knee injury. Later I was told I could never play football again. Sometimes I think of those gloves and wonder if

I would have been injured if I had been wearing my magical, stinky gloves. Maybe I would have gone on to a fine career on the gridiron. Then maybe I wouldn't and would instead be sitting here wearing those obnoxious gloves as I write this essay. What a wonderful essay I could write, if only I had those gloves!

EXERCISE 4

Discussion and Critical Thinking

1. Underline the thesis.

2. In the left margin, annotate the images of sight, smell, and touch.

3. Would you say this essay is mainly narration (a story), mainly a description, or both?

4. Do you think Velasco kept the gloves in spite of their disgusting qualities or because of their disgusting qualities? Why?

5. In the last few sentences, Velasco speculates about how well he would write if he only had those gloves. Usually, it's better not to make that kind of aside in an essay, but does it work here?

The Jacket

GARY SOTO

A writer and university professor, Gary Soto well remembers the self-consciousness of growing up. On one occasion he was all set to be cool with a fine new jacket; then his mother bought the wrong one—one that was "the color of day-old guacamole" and was "the ugly brother who tagged along wherever [he] went." Soto's best-known book is Living Up the Street.

1   My clothes have failed me. I remember the green coat that I wore in fifth and sixth grades when you either danced like a champ or pressed yourself against a greasy wall, bitter as a penny toward the happy couples.

2   When I needed a new jacket and my mother asked what kind I wanted, I described something like bikers wear: black leather and silver studs with enough belts to hold down a small town. We were in the kitchen, steam on the windows from her cooking. She listened so long while stirring dinner that I thought she understood for sure the kind I wanted. The next day when I got home from school, I discovered draped on my bedpost a jacket the color of day-old guacamole. I threw my books on the bed and approached the jacket slowly, as if it were a stranger whose hand I had to shake. I touched the vinyl sleeve, the collar, and peeked at the mustard-colored lining.

3   From the kitchen Mother yelled that my jacket was in the closet. I closed the door to her voice and pulled at the rack of clothes in the closet, hoping the jacket on the bedpost wasn't for me but my mean brother. No luck. I gave up. From my bed, I stared at the jacket. I wanted to cry because it was so ugly and so big that I knew I'd have to wear it a long time. I was a small kid, thin as a young tree, and it would be years before I'd have a new one. I stared at the jacket, like an enemy, thinking bad things before I took off my old jacket whose sleeves climbed halfway to my elbow.

4   I put the big jacket on. I zipped it up and down several times, and rolled the cuffs up so they didn't cover my hands. I put my hands in the pockets and flapped the jacket like a bird's wings. I stood in front of the mirror, full face, then profile, and then looked over my shoulder as if someone had called me. I sat on the bed, stood against the bed, and combed my hair to see what I would look like doing something natural. I looked ugly. I threw it on my brother's bed and looked at it for a long time before I slipped it on and went out to the backyard, smiling a "thank you" to my mom as I passed her in the kitchen. With my hands in my pockets I kicked a ball against the fence, and then climbed it to sit looking into the alley. I hurled orange peels at the mouth of an open garbage can and when the peels were gone I watched the white puffs of my breath thin to nothing.

5   I jumped down, hands in my pockets, and in the backyard on my knees I teased my dog, Brownie, by swooping my arms while making bird calls. He jumped at me and missed. He jumped again and again, until a tooth sunk deep, ripping an L-shaped tear on my left sleeve. I pushed Brownie away to study the tear as I would a cut on my arm. There was no blood, only a few loose pieces of fuzz. Damn dog, I thought, and pushed him away hard when he tried to bite again. I got up from my knees and went to my bedroom to sit with my jacket on my lap, with the lights out.

6   That was the first afternoon with my new jacket. The next day I wore it to sixth grade and got a D on a math quiz. During the morning recess Frankie T., the playground terrorist, pushed me to the ground and told me to stay there until recess was over. My best friend, Steve Negrete, ate an apple while looking at me, and the girls turned away to whisper on the monkey bars. The teachers were no help: They looked my way and talked about how foolish I looked in my new jacket. I saw their heads bob with laughter, their hands half-covering their mouths.

7   Even though it was cold, I took off the jacket during lunch and played kickball in a thin shirt, my arms feeling like braille from goose bumps. But when I returned to class I slipped the jacket on and shivered until I was warm. I sat on my hands, heating them up, while my teeth chattered like a cup of crooked dice. Finally warm, I slid out of the jacket but a few minutes later put it back on when the fire bell rang. We paraded out into the yard where we, the sixth graders, walked past all the other grades to stand against the back fence. Everybody saw me. Although they didn't say out loud, "Man, that's ugly," I heard the buzz-buzz of gossip and even laughter that I knew was meant for me.

8   And so I went, in my guacamole jacket. So embarrassed, so hurt, I couldn't even do my homework. I received Cs on quizzes, and forgot the state capitals and the rivers of South America, our friendly neighbor. Even the girls who had been friendly blew away like loose flowers to follow the boys in neat jackets.

9   I wore that thing for three years until the sleeves grew short and my forearms stuck out like the necks of turtles. All during that time no love came to me—no little dark girl in a Sunday dress she wore on Monday. At lunchtime I stayed with the ugly boys who leaned against the chainlink fence and looked around with propellers of grass spinning in our mouths. We saw girls walk by alone, saw couples,

hand in hand, their heads like bookends pressing air together. We saw them and spun our propellers so fast our faces were blurs.

10   I blame that jacket for those bad years. I blame my mother for her bad taste and her cheap ways. It was a sad time for the heart. With a friend I spent my sixth-grade year in a tree in the alley waiting for something good to happen to me in that jacket, which had become the ugly brother who tagged along wherever I went. And it was about that time that I began to grow. My chest puffed up with muscle and, strangely, a few more ribs. Even my hands, those fleshy hammers, showed bravely through the cuffs, the fingers already hardening for the coming fights. But that L-shaped rip on the left sleeve got bigger; bits of stuffing coughed out from its wound after a hard day of play. I finally Scotch-taped it closed, but in rain or cold weather the tape peeled off like a scab and more stuffing fell out until that sleeve shriveled into a palsied arm. That winter the elbows began to crack and whole chunks of green began to fall off. I showed the cracks to my mother, who always seemed to be at the stove with steamed-up glasses, and she said that there were children in Mexico who would love that jacket. I told her that this was America and yelled that Debbie, my sister, didn't have a jacket like mine. I ran outside, ready to cry, and climbed the tree by the alley to think bad thoughts and watch my breath puff white and disappear.

11   But whole pieces still casually flew off my jacket when I played hard, read quietly, or took vicious spelling tests at school. When it became so spotted that my brother began to call me "camouflage," I flung it over the fence into the alley. Later, however, I swiped the jacket off the ground and went inside to drape it across my lap and mope.

12   I was called to dinner: Steam silvered my mother's glasses as she said grace; my brother and sister with their heads bowed made ugly faces at their glasses of powdered milk. I gagged too, but eagerly ate big rips of buttered tortilla that held scooped up beans. Finished, I went outside with my jacket across my arm. It was a cold sky. The faces of clouds were piled up, hurting. I climbed the fence, jumping down with a grunt. I started up the alley and soon slipped into my jacket, that green ugly brother who breathed over my shoulder that day and ever since.

EXERCISE 5

Discussion and Critical Thinking

1. Why is the jacket more of a disappointment than it would have been if Soto's mother had given it to him as a surprise?

2. What kind of jacket did Soto request?

3. How is the jacket like a person and an evil force?

4. What are some of the failures Soto attributes to his jacket?

5. Why doesn't he lose it or throw it away?

6. What does Soto do to make this essay funny?

7. Is this mainly a description or a narration, or is it a combination with purposes integrated?

8. One might think that Soto had an unhappy, or even twisted, childhood. Do you think so? Explain.

Topics for Writing Description

You will find a blank Writing Process Worksheet on page 7, which can be photocopied, filled in, and submitted with each assignment if your instructor directs you to do so.

Reading-Related Topics

"My Burning Scarf"

1. Write a highly descriptive paragraph or essay about a possession you received or purchased, treasured, and—somehow—lost, through theft, your gift-giving, or someone's neglect. Describe it well, but locate the possession in the framework of a little story.

"Magical, Stinky Gloves"

2. Write about the gloves from their point of view (and from wherever they are now).

3. Write about the gloves from a coach's or a teammate's perspective.

4. Using this as a model, write about an item of clothing that you liked better as it became older and more decrepit. Consider items such as shoes, a shirt, pants, a belt, a purse, sweats, or socks. Be sure to relate the possession to different phases and events in your life.

5. Write about the power of a so-called good-luck object to instill confidence in the carrier. Describe one or more such objects owned by you, someone you know, or someone you have read about.

"The Jacket"

6. Write about the jacket from the point of view of Soto's mother.

7. Write about the jacket from the jacket's point of view.

8. Write about an embarrassing article of clothing you wore as a child, an article that you thought at the time had an influence on how others felt about you and certainly how you felt about yourself.

9. Write about an article of clothing you wore with pride as a child or one that you now wear with pride.

General Topics

Objective Description

Give your topic some kind of frame. As you develop your purpose, consider the knowledge and attitudes of your readers. You might be describing a lung for a biology instructor, a geode for a geology instructor, a painting for an art instructor, or a comet for an astronomy instructor. Instead, you might want to pose as the seller of an object such as a desk, a table, or a bicycle. Describe some of the following topics:

10. A simple object, such as a pencil, a pair of scissors, a cup, a sock, a dollar bill, a coin, a ring, or a notebook.

11. A human organ, such as a heart, a liver, a lung, or a kidney.

12. A visible part of your body, such as a toe, a finger, an ear, a nose, or an eye.

13. A construction, such as a room, a desk, a chair, or a table.

14. A mechanism, such as a bicycle, a tricycle, a wagon, a car, a motorcycle, a can opener, or a stapler.

Subjective Description

The following topics also should be developed in the context of a purpose other than just writing a description. Your intent can be as simple as giving a subjective reaction to your topic. Unless you are dealing with a topic that you can present reflectively or a topic interesting in itself, you will usually need some kind of situation. The narrative framework (something happening) is especially useful in providing order and vitality to writing. Here are two possibilities for you to consider:

15. Personalize a trip to a supermarket, a stadium, an airport, an unusual house, a mall, a beach, a court, a place of worship, a club, a business, a library, or a police station. Deal with a simple conflict in one of those places, while emphasizing descriptive details. Pick a high point in any event, and describe a few seconds of it. Think about how a scene can be captured by a video camera, and then give focus by applying the dominant impression principle, using the images of sight, sound, taste, touch, and smell that are relevant. The event might be a ball game, a graduation ceremony, a wedding ceremony, a funeral, a dance, a concert, a family gathering, a class meeting, a rally, a riot, a robbery, a fight, a proposal, or a meal. Focus on a body of subject material that you can cover effectively in the paragraph you write.

16. Download and, if possible, print a photo from the Internet. Select a subject that interests you, perhaps a product, a current event, or a vacation spot. The key word *pictures* will give you a variety to choose from on most search engines. Next, using your imagination, project a person or persons onto the picture you selected and describe something that occurs. The "something" need not be highly dramatic.

Cross-Curricular Topics

17. Use description in the following assignments.

- Agriculture: field trip report

- Art History: report on a museum or a particular work of art

- Education: school visit report

- Ecology: field trip report

- Geology: field trip report

- Sociology: report on a field trip to an urban zone, a prison, or another institution

Career-Related Topics

18. Describe a well-furnished, well-functioning office or other work area. Be specific.

19. Describe a computer-related product; pay special attention to the dominant trait that gives the product its reputation.

20. Describe a person groomed and attired for a particular job or interview. Provide details pertaining to the person and in naming the place or situation. Describe yourself from a detached point of view if you like.

Writer's Guidelines: Description

1. In an objective description, use direct, practical language appealing mainly to the sense of sight.

2. In a subjective description, appeal to the reader's feelings, especially through the use of figurative language and the use of images of sight, sound, smell, taste, and touch.

3. Use specific and concrete words if appropriate.

4. Be sure that readers can answer the following questions:

- What is the subject of this description?

- What is the dominant impression?

- What details support the dominant impression?

- What is the situation?

- What is the order of details—time, space, or both?

5. Consider giving your description a narrative framework. Include some action if it fits.

6. Write and revise.

- Write and then revise your paragraph or essay as many times as necessary for coherence, language (usage, tone, and diction), unity, emphasis, support, and sentences (**CLUESS**). Read your work aloud to hear and correct any grammatical errors or awkward-sounding sentences.

- Edit any problems in fundamentals, such as capitalization, omissions, punctuation, and spelling (**COPS**).

Exemplification:
Writing with Examples

Using a vivid example that your reader recognizes will provide a common denominator for sharing your ideas.

FLOW OF WRITING

Learning Objectives

Working with this chapter, I will learn to

~ determine characteristics of
  good examples.

~ find good examples.

~ connect examples with central ideas.

Writing Exemplification

Exemplification means using examples to explain, convince, or amuse. Lending interest and information to writing, exemplification is one of the most common and effective ways of developing ideas. Examples may be developed in a sentence or more, or they may be only phrases or even single words, as in the following sentence: "Eating fast foods, such as *hamburgers, pizza, pupusas, wonton,* and *tacos,* has become a shared cross-cultural experience."

Characteristics of Good Examples

As supporting information, the best examples are specific, vivid, and representative. These three qualities are closely linked; collectively, they must support the topic sentence of a paragraph and the thesis of an essay.

You use examples to inform or convince your reader. Of course, an example by itself does not necessarily prove anything. We know that examples can be found on either side of an argument, even at the extreme edges. Therefore, in addition to providing specific examples so that your reader can follow your argument precisely and vivid ones so that your reader will be interested, you should choose examples that are representative. Representative examples are examples that your reader can consider, accept as appropriate, and even match with his or her own examples. If you are writing a paragraph about cheating and you give one specific, vivid, and representative example, your reader should be able to say, "That's exactly what happens. I can imagine just how the incident occurred, and I could give some examples that are similar."

Techniques for Finding Examples

Writing a good paragraph or essay of exemplification begins, as always, with prewriting. The techniques you use will depend on what you are writing about. Assuming that you begin with a topic idea, one useful technique is listing. Base your list on what you have read, heard, and experienced. Here is a list, compiled by student Lara Olivas, on the broad topic "cheating at school":

When I copied homework

Looking at a friend's test answers

A student with hand signals

Jake and his electronic system

Time for planned cheating

Those who got caught

A person who bought a research paper

Jess, who copied from me

The Internet "Cheaters" source

The two students who exchanged identities

More work than it's worth

More stress than it's worth

Number and Order of Examples

After you have explored your topic and collected information, you must decide whether to use only one example with a detailed explanation, a few examples with a bit less information, or a cluster of examples. A well-stated topic sentence will guide you in making this decision. When you are writing about a personal topic, you will probably have far more examples than you can use.

If your example is an incident or a series of incidents, you will probably use time order, reinforcing that arrangement with terms such as *next, then, soon, later, last,* and *finally*. If your examples exist in space (maybe in different parts of a room), then you would use space references *(up, down, left, right, east, west, north, south)*. Arranging examples by emphasis means going from the most important example to the least important or from the least to the most important.

Connecting Examples with Purpose

Here is the paragraph student Lara Olivas wrote on the topic "the hard work of cheating." After compiling the list of examples above, Olivas decided that for her purpose in this paragraph, one specific, vivid, and representative example with explanation would make her point.

Cheating Is Not Worth the Bother
Lara Olivas

Topic sentence

One example

Explanation of the example follows

Order of time *(first, next, after, finally)*

Concluding sentence (connects ending to beginning)

<u>Cheating students often put themselves under more stress than honest students</u>. I remember someone in my junior composition class who needed a research paper, so he found a source and bought one for seventy-five dollars. The <u>first</u> trouble was that he had to submit the work in stages: the topic, the working bibliography, the note cards, the outline, the rough draft, and the final. <u>Therefore,</u> he went to the library and started working backwards. Of course, he couldn't turn in only the bib cards actually used in the paper, and <u>next</u> he had to make out note cards for the material he "would be" documenting, and even make out more. <u>After</u> having all kinds of trouble, he realized that the bought paper was of "A" quality, whereas he had been a "C" student. He went back to his source and was told he should change the sentence structure and so on to make the paper weaker. <u>Finally he dropped the class after spending more time on his paper than I did on mine</u>. He also suffered more anxiety than the students who put in the most work on their papers.

Observe how a professional writer from Los Angeles uses examples to explain his topic sentence about cultural diversity. The annotations show how the paragraph answers the questions following the selection.

Topic sentence
Cluster of examples

Specific, vivid, "diversified world." Examples relate to "diversified world."

<u>This is the typical day of a relatively typical soul in today's diversified world</u>. I wake up to the sound of my Japanese clock radio, put on a T shirt sent me by an uncle in Nigeria and walk out into the street, past German cars, to my office. Around me are English-language students from Korea, Switzerland, and Argentina—all on this Spanish-named road in this Mediterranean-style town. On TV, I find, the news is in Mandarin; today's baseball game is being broadcast in Korean. For lunch I can walk to a sushi bar, a tandoori palace, a Thai café, or the newest burrito joint (run by an

old Japanese lady). Who am I, I sometimes wonder, the son of Indian parents and a British citizen who spends much of his time in Japan (and is therefore—what else?—an American permanent resident)?

Useful Procedure for Writing with Examples

Asking yourself the following questions will help you write effective paragraphs using exemplification.

1. What am I trying to say?

2. What examples might support that idea? (Use listing.)

3. How many examples and what order should I use?

4. Are my examples specific, vivid, and representative?

5. Have I made a connection between my examples and my topic sentence or thesis?

Practicing Patterns of Exemplification

A well-designed outline can help you make clear connections between your topic sentence and your examples. Remember that in some instances you can support your point with a single example extended in detail, and in other cases you may need several examples. In Exercise 1, the topic sentences are developed by multiple examples.

EXERCISE 1

Completing Patterns of Exemplification

Fill in the blanks to add more examples that support the topic sentence.

1. Topic sentence: Just walking through my favorite mall shows me that the world is smaller than it used to be.

   I. People of different cultures (with specific examples)

   II. Foods of different cultures (with specific examples)

   III. _____

   IV. _____

2. Topic sentence: Driving to work (or school) this month and observing the behavior of other drivers have convinced me that road rage has invaded my community.

   I. A man honking his horn impatiently at an elderly driver

   II. _____

   III. _____

3. Controlling idea: Some people let television watching interfere with their social lives.

   I. Watching football games at a family gathering on holidays

   II. Watching television in a _____

   III. _____

4. Controlling idea: Most successful movies are more concerned with action than with character, and the action is violent.

   I. (Name of movie) _____

   II. (Name of movie) _____

   III. (Name of movie) _____

Connecting Reading and Writing: Living in the Age of Irritations

If it is true that anger is a normal human emotion, then perhaps we are becoming more and more normal. Of course, anger has no pure form. It ranges from mild discontent to uncontrollable rage. Its sources are just as varied. What sets off one person may go unnoticed by another. Or what sets off one person at a particular time may not bother that same person at another time, depending on any number of circumstances. Some argue that we live in the Age of Irritations. The population density, the cultural (in the broadest sense) differences, the competitive grabbing for "the golden ring," the decline in civility, and the simultaneous demands from home, work, school, and associates are all sources of stress-producing irritations.

How often do you become irritated? What does it take to move your irritation down the fast track to anger? The reading selections that follow give you a sampling of what sets off some people. In "The Mean Season," Roy Rivenburg discusses the various forms of rudeness we all know and love to hate. He gives us contemporary examples, a bit of history, and even some speculation about where we're headed. In "Sleepless in El Paso," Leo N. Miletich is not headed anywhere, except for a possible noise-induced nervous breakdown. His vivid examples let you tune in to what he cannot tune out.

In the first selection, "Sweet and Sour Workplace," student Sarah Betrue recounts her experience on the job (the conventional hothouse of all irritations), which in this case is a Chinese restaurant. A full-time student and a full-time worker, Sarah Betrue has a very busy life, which would go more smoothly if she did not have so many irritations. We are likely to identify with her experiences and to admire her for beginning and ending her workday in tranquility.

You can follow her writing process by studying her Writing Process Worksheet.

You will find a full-size, blank worksheet on page 7, which can be photocopied, filled in, and submitted with each assignment if your instructor directs you to do so.

THE QUIGMANS   **by Buddy Hickerson**

B. Hickerson, copyright Los Angeles Times Syndicate. All rights reserved.

Writing Process Worksheet

Title   Sweet and Sour Workplace

Name   Sarah Betrue   **Due Date** Friday, October 15, 11 a.m.

ASSIGNMENT

In the space below, write whatever you need to know about your assignment, including information about the topic, audience, pattern of writing, length, whether to include a rough draft or revised drafts, and whether your paper must be typed.

Paragraph of about 300 words on irritations that produce stress and anger. Use specific examples for support. Take the examples from experiences at work, home, school, or any place in my life. Audience: people similar to me, who will be familiar with stress, although maybe not with my examples. Submit this completed sheet, a rough draft marked for revision, and a typed final draft.

STAGE ONE

Explore   Freewrite, brainstorm (list), cluster, or take notes as directed by your instructor. Use the back of this page or separate paper if you need more space.

Listing

School	Home + personal	Work
Parking	Keeping	Complaining boss
Registration	balance	Fellow employees
for classes	Boyfriend	immature
Confusing,	Shopping	self-centered
difficult		lazy
assignments		Customers
Annoying students		freeloaders
Food		name callers

STAGE TWO

Organize Write a topic sentence or thesis; label the subject and the treatment parts.

<u>Stressful and frustrating situations</u> <u>occur daily behind the scenes at</u>
          subject   treatment
<u>my workplace, making it almost impossible for me to maintain a positive</u>
<u>attitude.</u>

Write an outline or an outline alternative.

  I. Boss
    A. Strict
    B. Unappreciative
      1. Usually
      2. This morning
 II. Fellow employees
    A. Cooks
    B. Cashiers
    C. Waitresses
      1. Self-centered
      2. Behaving typically yesterday
III. Customers
    A. Complaining generally
    B. One in particular
      1. Demanding
      2. Insulting

STAGE THREE

Write On separate paper, write and then revise your paragraph or essay as many times as necessary for **c**oherence, **l**anguage (usage, tone, and diction), **u**nity, **e**mphasis, **s**upport, and **s**entences (**CLUESS**). Read your work aloud to hear and correct any grammatical errors or awkward-sounding sentences.

Edit any problems in fundamentals, such as **c**apitalization, **o**missions, **p**unctuation, and **s**pelling (**COPS**).

Sweet and Sour Workplace
Sarah Betrue

Every morning as I enter my workplace, I admire the vibrant colors of both the tropical fish in the aquarium and the ancient silk Chinese robes hung from the wall. But as I take the dreaded step from the dining area to the kitchen, the

Topic sentence scenery drastically changes. <u>Stressful and frustrating situations occur daily behind the scenes at the restaurant, making it almost impossible for me to maintain a positive attitude</u>. Yesterday is a typical shift. <u>The first voices I hear are the</u>

Example <u>owners complaining about how filthy the restaurant looks</u>, although the night before the other employees and I worked with Ajax for three hours scrubbing shelves and floor sinks. As the day progresses, I try to squeeze in some extra cleaning between busy times, but I find myself doing all the extra work myself. The young girls I work with think having this job is just an extension of their social lives. During lunch hour, the dining area is packed, the line for takeout has

Example reached a ridiculous length, and two phone calls are on hold. <u>That's when Morgan decides to call her boyfriend on her cell phone</u>. Naturally I become frustrated and proceed to speak with her. She glares at me with fire in her eyes and screams, "I've got more important things to deal with at this time!" Getting nowhere with politeness, I grab the phone from her hand and turn it off. No

Example

sooner has this crisis ended than the house phone rings again. <u>On the line is a very unhappy woman.</u> After listening to a few colorfully disparaging descriptions of a meal she ordered, I tell her I cannot give refunds or food exchanges if her order is not returned first. She threatens to report our restaurant to newspapers and authorities, and then tells me to do something I am physically incapable of doing and hangs up in my ear. At the end of the day I am so angry and frustrated with having to put up with such occurrences that I want to grab hold of one of the woks and hit someone upside the head. But just as I reach for the handle, I

Concluding sentence

get a vision, an image of my paycheck, and I begin to relax. <u>I leave the restaurant with no blood on my hands, wishing everyone a wonderful evening.</u>

EXERCISE 2

Discussion and Critical Thinking

1. What evidence is there that Betrue is not essentially a negative thinker?

2. What kind of order does Betrue use for her three specific supporting examples?

3. If you were one of the owners of the restaurant, how would you react to Betrue's paragraph?

The Mean Season

ROY RIVENBURG

In this article, Roy Rivenburg, a veteran reporter for the Los Angeles Times, *covers all the bases of rudeness. After giving the particulars, he looks for historical patterns and trends, and he explores a bit of the psychology and philosophy behind the current lack of civility. At the same time, he acknowledges those who maintain that instances of incivility are overstated.*

1   Read this story, dirt bag! Yeah, we're talking to you. And no, we don't care if it offends your precious sensibilities. In case you're too stupid to have noticed—and you probably are—this country seems to have turned a lot meaner and ruder lately.

2   To get a clue, try stepping into a crosswalk. As humorist Henry Beard notes: Once upon a time, for a New Yorker visiting Los Angeles, that was an unnerving experience. "Cars would always stop for you," he marvels. "You'd hear the brakes screech and you'd assume, being from Manhattan, that the only possible explanation was the driver planned to get out and kill you." Today, the once-venerated California pedestrian must dodge traffic like a matador. And Beard sees the change as part of a much larger shift: a meltdown of courtesy, a wave of in-your-face

aggressiveness and a collective mean streak that has snaked into schools, churches, the media—everything.

3   The kinder, gentler nation has fallen and it can't get up:

- Television commercials used to compare the sponsor's produce to an anonymous "Brand X." Now, advertisers such as MCI and AT&T openly refer to each other as corporate scum.

- Greeting card companies have added "Drop dead" and "You're an [expletive]" messages to their product lines. Other entrepreneurs deliver bouquets of dead flowers and revenge-o-grams of rotting fish.

- High school sports leagues have started banning postgame handshakes to avoid fistfights.

- News reports are laced with stories of fatal duels over parking spaces, loud stereos, and subway seats.

4   "We're playing tag with hate," says Dr. Mark Goulston, a Santa Monica psychiatrist. Then again, who even wants to be nice when the chief apostles of it are Barney the Dinosaur and Mr. Rogers?

5   Still, things could be worse. Go back to almost any period in history—the Old West, eighteenth-century London, ancient Rome—and it's hard to conclude, despite the absence of Howard Stern, that previous generations were somehow more civil than this one. "It's easy to idealize the past," says historian William McNeill, "but human beings have been very nasty to each other for a very long time." People in the Middle Ages didn't carry swords as a fashion statement, he notes. And frontier America was a far cry from "Little House on the Prairie."

6   Indeed, when anthropologists dug up one Old West graveyard a few years ago, they found that two-thirds of the men under age 45 had died violently. Among the victims: William Johnson, whose head was blown off by his father-in-law's shotgun after he made the faux pas of mentioning at the dinner table that he had fought for the Union in the Civil War. But others argue that the current decline of civility is unprecedented. And they blame everything from microwave ovens to Jack in the Box hamburger ads.

7   Lauren Burton has had a ringside seat on the passage from We Decade to Me Decade to Up Yours Decade. As director of the L.A. County Bar Association's dispute resolution office, she has noticed a surge in neighbor-to-neighbor combat lately. In Encino, it was a two-year jihad of lawsuits, countersuits, and water-hose fights over the noise of a bouncing basketball. In the San Gabriel Valley, it was spitting, more water squirting, and an outdoor light aimed through a bedroom window because of a shedding pecan tree. In Long Beach, it was a double homicide sparked by a longstanding argument over the volume of a stereo. Each year, thousands of such feuds erupt in the cities and suburbs of Southern California, Burton says. It's the 1990s sequel to the Hatfields and McCoys, whose infamous battle supposedly began with an 1860 dispute over a hog and ultimately claimed twenty lives.

8   "People think of two things now when they have a conflict," she says. "One is revenge, the other is, 'Sue the bastard.'" Part of the trouble, she suggests, is a clash of cultures. As neighborhoods become more diverse, the differing backgrounds and desires can create a social powder keg. Throw in a little overcrowding, take away some religion, add a dose of hippie wisdom and things can get completely out of hand, experts say, especially in the United States.

9   Unlike Japan, for instance, which crams citizens closer together but counters possible side effects with "a culture that has historically chosen rules and conformity

over freedom, we took the crowding but didn't suppress our [liberties]," says Rex Julian Beaber, a psychologist and attorney. And there's a price to pay. "It's a function of anonymity," he says. "In a small town, everyone knows everyone and your reputation is changed for life if you do something bad. [In a big city], you can kill in a crowd and walk away." Or, as psychiatrist Goulston puts it: "One reason more people are jerks is because they know they can get away with it. Years ago, we thought someone would stop us or punish us or our conscience would bother us."

10   On February 5, 1994, gentility officially qualified as deviant behavior. That's when Oprah did a show on people who commit random acts of senseless kindness. Suddenly, on national TV, an ominous truth set in: Nice people had become the freaks.

11   The rest of the country seemed to be moving down the trail blazed by New York, which for years had been pioneering new and innovative alternatives to politeness. It's gotten so bad, according to the *New York Times,* that the city "appears to be the most foul-mouthed [place] in the nation, rivaling only prison and the armed forces." Close behind in the need-to-have-their-mouths-washed-out-with-soap department are movies and music. Films for adults now average seventy to eighty expletives each, the profanity article notes.

12   Still, civility supporters do see rays of hope. Beaber says a resurrection of manners is already under way among America's "most savage humans: lawyers." The L.A. County court system has "promulgated new rules of courtesy" to halt "increasingly volatile, vicious and demonic attacks" between attorneys, Beaber says.

13   And there's more to come as society scrambles to deal with phenomena that previous generations couldn't even have imagined. "We'll see increasing attempts to formalize what was before an unspoken social norm," he says. "For example, it used to be that a manufacturer of children's games wouldn't dream of creating a game where you cut off a person's head and it squirts blood." Now, with grisly video games like Mortal Kombat on the market, "The Senate is holding hearings and [might create] rules to stop this," Beaber says.

14   Even if such efforts draw fire from civil libertarians, he predicts that "the middle class is sufficiently tired of the effects of the breakdown of [decency] that they're going to be willing to give up [some freedoms]." He likens it to gun-control laws. "The Brady bill wasn't passed because of liberals, who always supported [such regulations]. It was passed because conservatives had seen [so much] carnage in schools and on the streets that they deserted the conservative ship."

15   Others contend "niceness laws" won't work. But their alternatives sound hokey, impractical, or both. Dispute-fixer Burton, for example, says, "We should divide the city into 365 areas and hold a 'Get to Know Your Neighbors Day' for each of the neighborhoods over the next year. It's harder to be inappropriate and confrontational with someone you really know," she explains. Goulston's advice is merely "count to ten" before reacting to someone else's behavior. He admits it might sound naive, but says small-scale efforts can pay off: "That's why some Neighborhood Watch programs are more effective than police." Even the federal government has gone altruistic. In February, it announced National Random Acts of Kindness Day, which advised putting coins into someone else's parking meter, anonymously buying ice cream cones for kids or mailing greeting cards to strangers.

16   Meanwhile, in New York, satirist Beard—who co-founded the *National Lampoon*—says what the country really needs is a dose of humor. With political correctness at an apex, he observes, too many Americans are ready to blow up at the slightest provocation. "It's an unfortunate combination of events. We're getting nastier and oversensitive at the same time. People oughta lighten up."

17   And then there's Timothy Miller. A psychologist and author from Stockton, he

insists that the whole meanness thing is an illusion: "People are reacting primarily to what they see on TV news and too little to what's really going on." In truth, he says, crime rates are flat, manners just seem to be in decline because there are more older people and they always think youngsters are beasts, and "events like freeway shootings—although appalling and emotionally gripping—are extremely rare."

18   Most other observers, however, suggest oblivion could be just around the corner. The so-called era of gentility, they say, which began in the 1850s and lingered into [the twentieth] century, was an aberration, a fluke.

19   Ultimately, discussions of this sort come back to a question of human nature. Call it Original Sin, call it a biological inclination to violence, call it a reaction to improper toilet training, but the story is still the same: The human heart is clouded by darkness. "If you could read the mind of Joe Blow Civilized Driver after he gets cut off on the freeway, it is as bestial, vicious, and rapacious as a tiger," Beaber says. "He may not act it out by beating the [other driver] with a tire iron, but that's his impulse and his fantasy."

20   In a 1994 pastoral letter, America's Catholic bishops sounded a similar theme, saying, "It is futile to suggest we can end all violence . . . merely by our own efforts. . . . We must realize that peace is most fundamentally a gift from God." Any solution that doesn't include prayer, they wrote, will inevitably fall short.

21   Goulston suspects another element is needed. "Americans never act until there's some sort of a wake-up call," he says. Could that be the Oklahoma City bombing? Goulston doesn't know. "But if that isn't it," he wonders, "then what kind of wake-up call will it take?"

EXERCISE 3

Vocabulary Highlights

Write a short definition of each word as it is used in the essay. (Paragraph numbers are given in parentheses.) Be prepared to use the words in your own sentences.

entrepreneurs (3)	volatile (12)
apostles (4)	oblivion (18)
unprecedented (6)	aberration (18)
random (10)	inclination (19)
innovative (11)	rapacious (19)

EXERCISE 4

Discussion and Critical Thinking

1. Is Rivenburg objective or subjective in his discussion of meanness and rudeness?

2. Which sentence in the first paragraph is the thesis?

3. What ideas do the examples in paragraph 3 support?

4. List three examples of the causes of recent neighbor-to-neighbor combat.

5. How did Japan deal with the problem of population density?

6. Why are there fewer interpersonal disputes in small towns?

7. What does psychologist Timothy Miller argue?

8. Do you agree with Beaber, who maintains that human beings are inclined toward meanness? Why or why not?

Sleepless in El Paso
LEO N. MILETICH

In an essay reading like a can-you-top-this list of irritations, freelance author Leo N. Miletich explains why he cannot sleep in his El Paso apartment. This selection first appeared in Newsweek *in 1995.*

1   Stephen Foster's* words to "Beautiful Dreamer," "Sounds of the rude world, heard in the day/Lulled by the moonlight have all passed away," belong in another time. On a recent evening, unlulled by the moonlight, the city streets department ripped up nine blocks of pavement around my apartment building between 9:30 P.M. and 6 A.M. Compared with what I usually hear at night, the steady roar of heavy equipment was actually soothing.

2   Night noise to Stephen Foster was an occasional steamboat whistle, or the rattle of a passing buckboard; "life's busy throng" came to a halt for him after dark. Of that I'm envious: Foster didn't have my neighbors. The world has grown ruder.

3   I've had to share common apartment walls with numerous people for most of my life. The experience has often left me feeling that if the human race were a club, I'd turn in my membership.

4   Some neighbors use car horns in lieu of doorbells; other residents have barking dogs. A number of people can't seem to hear music unless the beat is vibrating the walls and rattling the windows; and there are those dysfunctional couples who debate by smashing crockery against the walls (passing observation: small apartments contribute to domestic discord). There are helpful souls who keep their televisions so loud that I have no need to use the sound on mine if we're on the same channel.

5   Growing up, I had to keep my voice down, use an earphone for the radio and stereo, place the TV away from any shared wall, step lightly on the stairs and ease the door closed, all in an effort not to disturb the neighbors. And the neighbors did the same. It was a cardinal rule of apartment living. It was called courtesy and consideration—the neighborly thing to do. What ever happened to that? Do parents ever say, "Don't slam that door" to their children anymore?

6   My next-door neighbors slam doors at all hours of the day or night. These are heavy iron-framed security screen doors that when slammed reverberate through my place like cannon shots. The kids slam them. Their parents slam. People who visit slam them. I find this crashing incomprehensible.

7   There's a college kid down the block with a boom car. When he cranks it up, the

*Nineteenth-century composer of nostalgic ballads.

bass alone sounds like there's a rumbling Sherman tank in my bathroom, a rolling thunderstorm overhead. When he adds music (and "Beautiful Dreamer" is not on his playlist), it can be heard for three blocks in any direction, especially at midnight. The vibrations alone have been known to set off car alarms as he drives past. I hope his ears bleed at night.

8   In the next building is a 13-year-old girl who likes to blast her stereo at a pulse-pounding level so that it's clearly audible in my place even with the doors and windows closed. I knocked on her front door late one night and found myself facing not a bunch of drugged-out crazoids, as I'd feared, but her middle-aged parents. They seemed distressed and intimidated. They said they couldn't do a thing about the rock music pounding away in the next room, that the girl refused to use her earphones. I was getting a headache just standing at the door. Always in favor of compromise, I suggested unplugging the stereo and tossing it in the dumpster. Instead, the mother pulled me inside the sonic maelstrom, pleading with me to reason with the girl. At my approach, the teenager bolted down the hallway, locked herself in the bathroom (slamming the door) and screamed at us for disturbing her.

9   And friends wonder why I never wanted children.

10   I've tried seeing things in a wider perspective. I'm sure the people in my paternal grandparents' war-torn, ancestral homeland of Croatia would love to exchange the sound of artillery and snipers for the sound of stereos and televisions, just as people in squalid public-housing areas would cheer the sound of music and sitcoms over the sounds of screams, gunfire and sirens in the street. To the hearing impaired, I'm a fortunate man. But intellectualizing this problem doesn't prevent my yawning all day and nodding off on the bus.

11   The people currently sharing a thin, hollow bedroom wall with me have been disrupting my sleep for nearly three years through simple, inconsiderate acts that have the cumulative effect of being profoundly irritating. Apart from the door slamming, I have music throbbing through the wall (which, like a drum, seems to amplify low-frequency sounds). Voices chatter throughout the night. If something needs fixing or building in the apartment, no neighborly inhibitions prevail because of the hour. I've been awakened at 1 A.M. by hammering and sawing.

12   I've tried explaining, in a friendly manner, how thin the wall is and how I have this peculiar habit of needing to sleep at night. I've also tried the time-honored method of noise reduction by pounding on the wall when the decibels reach impossible limits. The return response from next door is to pound right back and increase the volume. I've tried earplugs and sound machines that simulate rain, trains and waves. Nothing can drown out the late-night conversation or the sudden thumps, bumps and rattles in the middle of the night. I might as well be living next to poltergeists.

13   When I mentioned to my landlord that professional torturers use sleep deprivation as a way to break people, he was unfazed; after all, he doesn't live here. One day, in response to my last complaint, the landlord's son uttered what must be the defining attitude for this closing decade of the twentieth century: "It's the '90s: People don't give a s - - -."

14   That, I thought, should be on a T shirt or a bumper sticker. Or maybe it should be the title of Newt's next book.

15   Bob Dole and the Christian Coalition might think about giving up their fruitless attack on sex and violence in our pop culture and start concentrating on the real-world aural terrorists who stress out our nights. Make consideration a campaign issue, rudeness an etiquette crime. If presidential candidates have a need for a campaign promise that's sure to win votes, they should forget the chicken-in-every-pot cliché (or is it now a gun in every car?). Guarantee everyone in America a good night's sleep on a regular basis.

EXERCISE 5

Vocabulary Highlights

Write a short definition of each word as it is used in the essay. (Paragraph numbers are given in parentheses.) Be prepared to use the words in your own sentences.

in lieu of (4)

dysfunctional (4)

discord (4)

cardinal (5)

maelstrom (8)

squalid (10)

intellectualizing (10)

inhibitions (11)

simulate (12)

poltergeists (12)

EXERCISE 6

Discussion and Critical Thinking

1. Circle the two sentences in the first two paragraphs that together serve as the thesis.

2. Underline examples supporting the thesis.

3. In paragraph 15, the author refers to the presidential election campaign going on at the time of his writing this essay. What contemporary reference might he make if he were writing the article now?

4. What suggestions for dealing with the irritations would you have for the author?

5. Do you agree with the statement by the landlord's son in paragraph 13? Why or why not?

6. Two of Miletich's subtopics include the young versus the old, and the previous generation versus the current generation. Do your experiences support his views?

7. Miletich uses both exaggeration and humor in his discussion (see especially paragraph 7). Are they effective? Why or why not?

8. Overall what is the tone—thoughtful, humorous, angry, whiny—produced by Miletich's selection of examples and his commentary?

Topics for Writing Exemplification

You will find a blank Writing Process Worksheet on page 7, which can be photocopied, filled in, and submitted with each assignment if your instructor directs you to do so.

Reading-Related Topics

"Sweet and Sour Workplace"

1. With this selection as a model, use examples to develop your ideas on how you have experienced and dealt with irritation at school, home, or work.

2. With this selection as a model, use examples to write about irritations in a neighborhood; in theaters during a movie; on airplanes, buses, or trains; on streets, highways, and freeways; or in restaurants.

"The Mean Season"

3. Use your own examples to support your discussion of one (or more) of the following statements and modify it (or them) a bit if you like:

   • We're playing tag with hate.

   • Civility supporters see rays of hope.

   • Manners just seem to be in decline because there are more older people and they think youngsters are beasts.

   • The human heart is clouded by darkness.

   • The human heart is lit by sunshine.

   • Recent events have started to waken Americans to a real problem with meanness (and they're getting madder than hell).

4. Keep track of acts of kindness and goodness versus acts of rudeness and meanness for a certain time period. Your study can cover many aspects of life, or it can be focused on work, school, streets, or home. You might station yourself at some location (a doorway, a crosswalk) where people have the opportunity to choose between being considerate or not being considerate. Use examples and give simple statistics. This could be an opportunity for you to work collaboratively with classmates.

"Sleepless in El Paso"

5. If you have suffered from inconsiderate neighbors, write a paragraph or an essay about your experiences. Use abundant examples, including one or more that are extended for a particular scene (as Miletich did in paragraph 8).

6. If you have had considerate neighbors, write about the precautions they have taken (after you complained or without your complaining), giving specific examples of their actions and, perhaps, specific examples of what you have done in appreciation.

General Topics

7. Make a judgmental statement about an issue you believe in strongly and then use one or more examples to illustrate your point. These are some possible topics:

   • The price of groceries is too high.

   • Professional athletes are paid too much.

   • A person buying a new car may get a lemon.

   • Drivers sometimes openly ignore the laws on a selective basis.

   • Politicians should be watched.

   • Working and going to school is tough.

   • Working, parenting, and going to school is tough.

   • All computer viruses have common features.

   • Many people under the age of eighteen spend too much time playing computer games.

   • Some computer games teach children useful skills.

Cross-Curricular Topics

8. Use examples as supporting information in discussing a person, an event, or an issue pertaining to another class you have taken or are taking. Your explanation might focus on why someone or something was successful or unsuccessful. As a report on a field trip, examples might support a dominant impression of, say, a museum exhibit, in an art history class, or an observation for a case study in an education or a psychology class.

Career-Related Topics

9. Use specific examples to support one of the following statements as applied to business or work:

   • It's not what you know; it's whom you know.

   • Don't burn your bridges.

   • Like Lego®, business is a matter of connections.

   • Tact is the lubricant that oils the wheels of industry.

   • The customer is always right.

   • Money is honey, my little sonny, and a rich man's joke is always funny.

   • If you take care of the pennies, the dollars will take care of themselves.

   • A kind word turns away wrath.

Writer's Guidelines: Exemplification

1. Use examples to explain, convince, or amuse.

2. Use examples that are vivid, specific, and representative.

   • Vivid examples attract attention.

   • Specific examples are identifiable.

   • Representative examples are typical and therefore the basis for generalizations.

3. Tie your examples clearly to your topic sentence or thesis.

4. Draw your examples from what you have read, heard, and experienced.

5. Brainstorm a list of possible examples before you write.

6. Order your examples by time, space, or level of importance.

7. Ask yourself the following questions as you proceed:

   • What am I trying to say?

   • What examples might support that idea? (Use listing.)

   • How many examples and what order should I use?

   • Are my examples specific, vivid, and representative?

   • Have I made a connection between my examples and my topic sentence or thesis?

8. Write and revise.

   • Write and then revise your paragraph or essay as many times as necessary for coherence, language (usage, tone, and diction), unity, emphasis, support, and sentences (**CLUESS**). Read your work aloud to hear and correct any grammatical errors or awkward-sounding sentences.

   • Edit any problems in fundamentals, such as **c**apitalization, **o**missions, **p**unctuation, and **s**pelling (**COPS**).

Chapter
19

Process Analysis: Writing About Doing

We are involved daily in tasks of explaining to others how to do something or how something was done, and in those instances we are all teachers.

FLOW OF WRITING

Learning Objectives

Working with this chapter, I will learn to

~ **explain how to do something.**
~ **explain how something occurred or was done.**

Writing Process Analysis

If you have any doubt about how frequently we use process analysis, just think about how many times you have heard people say, "How do you do it?" or "How is [was] it done?" Even when you are not hearing those questions, you are posing them yourself when you need to make something, cook a meal, assemble an item, take some medicine, repair something, or figure out what happened. In your college classes, you may have to discover how osmosis occurs, how a rock changes form, how a mountain was shaped, how a battle was won, or how a bill goes through the legislature.

If you need to explain how to do something or how something is (was) done, you will write a paper of **process analysis.** You will break down your topic into stages, explaining each so that your reader can duplicate or understand the process.

Two Types of Process Analysis: Directive and Informative

The questions How do I do it? and How is [was] it done? will lead you into two different types of process analysis—directive and informative.

Directive process analysis explains how to do something. As the name suggests, it gives directions and instructs the reader. It says, for example, "Read me, and you can bake a pie (tune up your car, analyze a book, write an essay, take some medicine)." Because it is presented directly to the reader, it usually addresses the reader as "you," or it implies the "you" by saying something such as "First [you] purchase a large turnip, and then [you] . . ." In the same way, this textbook addresses you or implies "you" because it is a long how-to-do-it (directive process analysis) statement.

Informative process analysis explains how something is (was) done by giving data (information). Whereas the directive process analysis tells you what to do in the future, the informative process analysis tells you what has occurred or what is occurring. If it is something in nature, such as the formation of a mountain, you can read and understand the process by which it emerged. In this type of process analysis, you do not tell the reader what to do; therefore, you usually do not use the words *you* or *your.*

Working with Stages

Preparation or Background

In the first stage of directive process analysis, list the materials or equipment needed for the process and discuss the necessary setup arrangements. For some topics, this stage will also provide technical terms and definitions. The degree to which this stage is detailed will depend on both the subject itself and the expected knowledge and experience of the projected audience.

Informative process analysis may begin with background or context rather than with preparation. For example, a statement explaining how mountains form might begin with a description of a flat portion of the earth made up of plates that are arranged like a jigsaw puzzle.

Steps or Sequence

The actual process will be presented here. Each step or sequence must be explained clearly and directly and phrased to accommodate the audience. The language, especially in directive process analysis, is likely to be simple and concise; however, avoid dropping words such as *and, a, an, the,* and *of* and thereby lapsing into "recipe language." The steps may be accompanied by explanations about why certain procedures are necessary and how not following directions carefully can lead to trouble.

Time Order

The order will usually be chronological (time based) in some sense. Certain transitional words are commonly used to promote coherence: *first, second, third, then, soon, now, next, finally, at last, therefore, consequently,* and—especially for informative process analysis—words used to show the passage of time such as hours, days of the week, and so on.

Basic Forms

Consider using this form for the directive process (with topics such as how to cook something or how to fix something).

How to Fry Green Tomatoes
I. Preparation
    A. Stove and utensils
    B. Cast-iron skillet
    C. Ingredients
        1. Sliced green tomatoes
        2. Cornmeal
        3. Buttermilk
        4. Bacon grease (or oil)
        5. Seasoning (salt, pepper, and so on)
II. Steps
    A. Heat skillet on high flame
    B. Add bacon grease to coat skillet
    C. Dip sliced green tomatoes in buttermilk
    D. Dip sliced green tomatoes in cornmeal
    E. Drop sliced green tomatoes into hot skillet
    F. Reduce flame under skillet
    G. Brown and turn sliced green tomatoes once
    H. Drain golden brown green tomatoes on paper towel
    I. Serve

Consider using this form for the informative process (with topics such as how a volcano functions or how a battle was won).

How a Tornado Occurs

    I. Background

        A. Cool, dry air from the north

        B. Warm, humid air from the south

        C. Usually afternoon or early evening

    II. Sequence

        A. Narrow zone of thunderstorms forms

        B. Warm, humid air rises

        C. More warm air rushes in to replace it

        D. In-rushing air rotates

        E. Pressure drops

        F. Wind velocity increases

        G. Twisting, snaking funnel-shaped cloud extends down from larger cloud formation

Combined Forms

Combination process analysis occurs when directive process analysis and informative process analysis are blended, usually when the writer personalizes the account. Take this scenario:

> Two people with the log-on names Captain Ahab and Ishmael are e-mailing.
>
> *Ishmael:* "I'm really intrigued with your idea of raising your own catfish, but I don't know how to make a pond."
>
> *Captain Ahab:* "Let me tell you how I made mine. First I shoveled out a 20' × 5' × 5' hole in my back lawn. Then I turned on the hose and . . ."

This process analysis begins as if it is only informative, but the main intent and the main need are clearly directive.

Often the personalized account is more interesting, and many assignments are done in that fashion. A paper about making a pecan pie may be informative—but uninspiring. A paper about the time you helped your grandmother make a pecan pie (giving all the details) may be informative, directive, and entertaining. It is often the cultural framework provided by personal experience that transforms a pedestrian directive account into something memorable.

Consider this student paragraph about something that has occurred, which tells us how to do something if we choose to do so.

Pupusas, Salvadoran Delight

PATTY SERRANO

We all have at least one kind of food that reminds us of childhood, something that has filled our bellies in times of hunger and perhaps comforted our minds in times of stress. For Patty Serrano, a community college student living at home, that special dish is pupusas. *In El Salvador these are a favorite item in homes and restaurants and at roadside stands. In Southern California, they're available in little restaurants called* pupusarias.

Topic sentence　Every time my mom decides to make pupusas, we jump for joy. <u>A pupusa contains only a few ingredients, and it may sound easy to make, but really good ones must be made by experienced hands.</u> My mom is an expert, having learned as a

Preparation　child from her mother. All the <u>ingredients</u> are <u>chosen fresh.</u> The <u>meat,</u> either pork or beef, can be bought prepared, but my <u>mom chooses to prepare it herself.</u> The

Steps　1　<u>meat,</u> which is called "carnitas," <u>is ground and cooked with tomatoes and spices.</u> The cheese—she uses a white Jalisco—has to be stringy because that kind gives pupusas a very good taste, appearance, and texture. Then comes the <u>preparation</u>

2　<u>of the "masa," or cornmeal.</u> It has to be soft but not so soft that it falls apart in the making and handling. All of this is done while the "comal," or skillet, is being

3　heated. She then grabs a chunk of <u>masa</u> and <u>forms it into a tortilla</u> like a magician turning a ball into a thin pancake. Next she grabs small chunks of <u>meat</u> and

4

5　<u>cheese</u> and <u>places them in the middle of the tortilla.</u> The <u>tortilla</u> is <u>folded in half</u>

6　<u>and formed again.</u> After <u>placing the pupusa into the sizzling skillet</u> with one hand, she is already starting another pupusa. It's amazing how she does two

7　things at the same time. She <u>turns</u> the <u>pupusas over and over</u> again <u>until</u> she is sure that <u>they are done.</u> We watch, mouths open, plates empty. In my family it is a tradition that I get the first pupusa because I like them so much. I love opening the hot pupusas, smelling the aroma, and seeing the stringy cheese stretching in the middle. I'm as discriminating as a wine taster. But I never eat a pupusa without "curtido," chopped cabbage with jalapeño. Those items balance the richness

Concluding sentences　of the other ingredients. <u>I could eat Mom's pupusas forever. I guess it has something to do with the way my mom makes them, with experienced, magical, loving hands.</u>

Useful Prewriting Procedure

All the strategies of freewriting, brainstorming, and clustering can be useful in writing a process analysis. However, if you already know your subject well, you can simply make two lists, one headed "Preparation" or "Background" and the other "Steps" or "Sequence." Then jot down ideas for each. After you have finished with your listing, you can delete parts, combine parts, and rearrange parts for better order. That editing of your lists will lead directly to a formal outline you can use in Stage Two of the writing process.

Patty Serrano used the following lists as her initial prewriting activity for "*Pupusas,* Salvadoran Delight."

Preparation	Steps
get vegetables	cook meat
meat, fresh	cook tomatoes and spices
cheese, stringy white Jalisco	shape tortilla
spices	put meat, cheese, vegetables
masa	into tortilla
skillet	fold and seal tortilla
hot stove	place pupusa into skillet
	make more pupusas
	turn pupusas
	remove pupusas
	eat pupusas

Practicing Patterns of Process Analysis

Underlying a process analysis is a definite pattern. In some presentations, such as directions with merchandise to be assembled, the content reads as mechanically as an outline, and no reader objects. The same can be said of most recipes. In other presentations, such as your typical college assignments, the pattern is submerged in flowing discussion. The directions or information must be included, but the writing should be well developed and interesting. Regardless of the form you use or the audience you anticipate, keep in mind that in process analysis the pattern provides a foundation for the content.

EXERCISE 1

Completing Patterns of Process Analysis

A. Using directive process analysis, fill in the blanks to complete this pattern for replacing a flat tire with a spare. Work in a group if possible.

   I. Preparation

      1. Park car.

      2. _____

      3. Obtain car jack.

      4. _____

      5. _____

   II. Steps

      1. Remove hub cap (if applicable).

      2. Loosen lug nuts a bit.

      3. _____

4. _____

5. Remove wheel with flat tire.

6. _____

7. _____

8. Release jack pressure.

9. _____

B. Using informative process analysis, fill in the blanks to complete this pattern for an explanation of how a watermelon seed grows into a plant and produces a watermelon. Work in a group if possible.

   I. Background (what happens before the sprouting)

      1. Seed planted in cultivated land

      2. _____

      3. Receives heat (from sun)

  II. Sequence (becomes plant and produces fruit)

      1. Sprouts

      2. _____

      3. Responds to sunlight and air

      4. _____

      5. _____

      6. Flower pollinated

      7. _____

EXERCISE 2   # Writing Patterns of Process Analysis

A. Using directive process analysis, fill in the blanks to complete this pattern for directions on how to cook a specific food or to fix an item.

   I. Preparation

      1. _____

      2. _____

      3. _____

      4. _____

      5. _____

II. Steps

1. _____

2. _____

3. _____

4. _____

5. _____

6. _____

7. _____

8. _____

9. _____

B. Using informative process analysis, fill in the blanks to complete this pattern for an explanation of how a person can be hired, trained, and promoted at a specific job.

I. Background (hiring)

1. _____

2. _____

3. _____

II. Sequence (training, promotion)

1. _____

2. _____

3. _____

4. _____

5. _____

6. _____

7. _____

Connecting Reading and Writing: The Joy and Grief of Work

Work is inseparable from life. There is a German saying—"You are what you eat." There should be another saying—"You are what you do for a living." After all, one reason we change jobs is that we say the work is adversely affecting other parts of our lives. The effects are not just a matter of stress. Whatever procedures, attitudes, and thought processes we develop at work are likely to find their way into our everyday lives. For instance, a professor's teacherish behavior at times emerges even when he or she is relating to loved ones.

THE QUIGMANS   **by Buddy Hickerson**

"Another lawsuit. Perhaps I should rethink my choice of vocation."

Work can also be full of repetition, a necessary condition of almost any job, but more so in some. If we are involved in repetition, we may perceive it as tedium and imagine that out there somewhere are exciting careers teeming with intellectual stimulation and creativity. Regardless of the job, if a person does it long enough, it will probably become to an important extent a "been-there, done-that" activity. Once I talked to a heart specialist, telling him of my gratitude for his doing just the right thing in saving the life of my relative. "It's all a matter of procedures," he said, with a dismissive wave of his hand. "I respond to each symptom and choose a procedure. It's as automatic and predictable as fixing a car. I don't have much choice."

Each job has a procedure. While we are learning, the procedure may seem extremely complicated, perhaps almost impossible. Virtually every workplace has a collection of legends about mistakes made by new employees, and most of us remember our struggles with routines that we now perform without conscious thought.

All of the reading selections in this section relate to what people or machines do at work. The most complicated process is covered in "Fast-Track French Fries," by Eric Schlosser, which shows how a popular fast food is processed. In "The Skinny on Working for a Dermatologist," J. Kim Birdine writes about her preparation and steps in assisting a dermatologist in the operating room. "Workin' at the Car Wash" offers instructions that can be used at work, as the title suggests, or can be used by anyone with a grimy car. "Making Faces," by student Seham Hemmat explains how she gives makeovers in a mall beauty shop. By evening Seham Hemmat is a community college student. By day she is an employee of a mall specialty store where, to use her words, she does "face detail work." She rewrote this paragraph of process analysis six times, twice reading it aloud to her peer group and listening to their suggestions (especially those from the two male members) before she was satisfied with the content and tone. Her word choice suggests a somewhat humorous view of work she takes seriously but not too seriously. Hemmat's Writing Process Worksheet shows you how her writing project evolved from idea to final draft.

You will find a full-size blank worksheet on page 7, which can be photocopied, filled in, and submitted with each assignment if your instructor directs you to do so.

Writing Process Worksheet

Title   Making Faces

Name   Seham Hammat   **Due Date**   Thursday, November 18, 8 a.m.

ASSIGNMENT

In the space below, write whatever you need to know about your assignment, including information about the topic, audience, pattern of writing, length, whether to include a rough draft or revised drafts, and whether your paper must be typed.

Write a directive process analysis. Personalize it by using a narrative framework. If possible, write about one procedure you do at work. Audience: general readers outside the field of work. One paragraph of about 250 words. Include this sheet completed, one or more rough drafts, and a typed final draft.

STAGE ONE

Explore   Freewrite, brainstorm (list), cluster, or take notes as directed by your instructor. Use the back of this page or separate paper if you need more space.

Listing

Preparation	*Steps*
Check out customer	Take off old makeup
Get right products	Wash face
Discuss price	Toner on
Discuss time	Moisturizer
	Foundation
	Powder
	Fix eyebrows
	Fix lashes
	Put on blush
	Add liner and lipstick

STAGE TWO

Organize   Write a topic sentence or thesis; label the subject and the treatment parts.

If you'd like to do what I do, just follow these directions.
          subject   treatment

Write an outline or an outline alternative.

I.   Preparation
    A. Evaluate client
    B. Select supplies
        1. Cleanser
        2. Toner
        3. Others
    C. Check tray of tools
II. Steps
    A. Strip off old makeup
    B. Scrub face
    C. Put on toner
    D. Add moisturizer

    E. Rub on foundation
    F. Dust on powder
    G. Gel eyebrows
        1. Trim
        2. Shape
        3. Pencil
    H. Curl lashes
    I. Dab on blush
    J. Paint lips

STAGE THREE

Write   On separate paper, write and then revise your paragraph or essay as many times as necessary for **c**oherence, **l**anguage (usage, tone, and diction), **u**nity, **e**mphasis, **s**upport, and **s**entences (**CLUESS**). Read your work aloud to hear and correct any grammatical errors or awkward-sounding sentences.

Edit any problems in fundamentals, such as **c**apitalization, **o**missions, **p**unctuation, and **s**pelling (**COPS**).

Making Faces

Seham Hemmat

       The Face Place, a trendy mall store, is where I work. Making faces is what I do. I don't mean sticking out my tongue; I mean reworking the faces of women who want a new or fresh look. When I get through, if I've done a good job, you can't tell if my subject is wearing makeup or not. <u>If you'd like to do what I do, just follow these directions.</u> Imagine you have a client. Her name is Donna. <u>Check her out</u> for skin complexion, skin condition, size of eyes, kind of eyebrows, and lip shape. Then <u>go to the supply room and select</u> the <u>items</u> you need for the faceover, including a cleanser and toner with added moisturizers. <u>Put them on a tray by your brushes and other tools and basic supplies.</u> <u>Begin by stripping off her old makeup</u> with a few cotton balls and cleanser. Donna's skin is a combination of conditions. Her forehead, nose, and chin are oily, and her cheeks are dry. <u>Scrub her down</u> with Tea Tree, my favorite facial cleanser from a product line that is not tested on animals. Scour the oil slicks extra. Then <u>slather on</u> some <u>Tea Tree toner</u> to close her pores so the dirt doesn't go back in. <u>Add</u> a <u>very light moisturizer</u> such as one called Elderflower Gel. Donna has a pale complexion. <u>Put on a coat of 01 foundation</u>, the fairest in the shop, which evens out her skin tone. Next, with a big face brush, <u>dust on a layer of 01 powder</u> to give her a smooth, dry look. Now Donna, who's watching in a mirror, speaks up to say she wants her eyebrows brushed and lightened just a bit. She has dark eyebrows and eyelashes that won't require much mascara or eyebrow pencil. <u>So use gel to fix the eyebrows</u> in place while you <u>trim, shape, and pencil them</u>. Move downward on the face, going next to her eyes. Use brown mascara to <u>curl her already dark lashes.</u> With your blusher brush, <u>dab</u> some peach rose <u>blush on</u> her <u>cheeks</u> and <u>blend it in.</u> <u>Line her lips</u> with bronze sand lip liner pencil and <u>fill in the rest</u> with rouge mauve lipstick. Swing Donna around to the big lighted mirror. Watch her pucker her lips, squint her eyes, flirt with herself. See her smile. Now you pocket the tip. Feel good. <u>You've just given a woman a new face, and she's out to conquer the world.</u>

Topic sentence

Preparation

Steps 1

2

3

4

5

6

7

8

9

10

Concluding sentences

EXERCISE 3 | Discussion and Critical Thinking

1. Is this paragraph of process analysis mainly directive or informative?

2. How does Hemmat take her paragraph beyond a list of mechanical directions?

3. In addition to using chronological order (time), what other order does she use briefly?

4. What word choice may have come from suggestions offered by the males in her discussion group?

The Skinny on Working for a Dermatologist

J. KIM BIRDINE

After having traveled a long way, from a Korean orphanage to the United States, J. Kim Birdine is still on the move. In writing this essay of process analysis, she demonstrates the same intellectual qualities she uses so well in her role as an assistant to a doctor, both in the office and in the operating room.

1   As a medical assistant for a dermatologist, I am actively involved in every aspect of the practice, recommending products, doing laser treatments for veins, and administering skin peels. The younger patients generally see the doctor to correct their skin problems, whether they're suffering from a persistent dry patch, uneven skin tone, or a bout with acne. A good number of the patients come in for cosmetic reasons, wanting their wrinkles smoothed out or their dark blotches lasered off. The most important part of my job, though, is to prepare surgical trays for the patients with skin cancer and to assist the doctor through the procedure.

2   My initial concern when setting up a surgical tray is that everything is sterile. This means that all the metal instruments, gauze, and applicators (Q-Tips) are put through an Autoclave (steam sterilizer), to ensure sterilization. Once everything is processed, I begin setting up my surgical tray by placing a sterile field on a tray, which has long legs and wheels at the base so it can be rolled. The tray should stand about waist high so the physician can reach the instruments easily. The sterile field is a large white tissue that I carefully take out of a sealed pack, touching it only at the corners to unfold it to its full size. It serves as a base on which to place all the instruments.

3   Next all of the metal instruments are placed on the tray with a long-handled "pick-up." The necessary instruments are a scalpel, a skin hook, large forceps, small forceps, straight scissors, curved scissors, a large needle holder, and a small needle holder. All are placed with handles facing toward me, except the small

needle holder and the straight scissors. These two should be positioned at a corner away from me with the handles facing out. The position of all of the instruments is important so that the doctor can reach them with ease. The ones placed in the corner are for me to use while assisting with suturing. A surgical tray is not complete without a small stack of gauze (large) and about twenty applicators. The entire tray is covered with another sterile field exactly like the one placed initially on the tray.

4 Just prior to surgery, I set up extras. I place on the counter anesthesia—a 3cc syringe of lidocaine with epinephrine—and a disinfectant skin cleanser, along with two pair of surgical gloves, one for the doctor and one for me. I turn on the hyfrecator, which is a cauterizer used to stop bleeding by burning the tissue. I prepare a specimen bottle indicating on its label the patient's name, the date, the doctor's name, and the area of the body from which the specimen is taken. I remove the sterile field on top of the instruments and place the sutures requested by the doctor and a different kind of sterile field, which has a hole in the middle of it, on the tray. This field enables the doctor to place the hole directly over the surgery site, exposing only the area to be worked on and covering the surrounding areas.

5 During surgery, once the doctor removes the section that needs to be tested, I place it in the specimen jar, seal the lid on it, and place it on the counter. I have to be attentive to the surgery at this point to assist in reducing the bleeding. My job is to apply gauze or applicators wherever bleeding occurs and to ready the hyfrecator in case the doctor needs it. When bleeding is minimized, the doctor begins suturing. At this point I have the small needle holder in hand as well as the straight scissors. I use the small needle holder to grab the tip of the needle after the doctor inserts it through the skin, to pull it through for her. This makes her job easier. I use the straight scissors to cut the suture once she is finished with knotting. Sometimes she does some internal suturing for the tissue under the skin, with dissolvable thread, and knots each turn. This is when I cut directly on top of the knot. The surface suturing is usually knotted at the beginning and at the end of the line of sutures and needs cutting down to one-quarter of an inch.

6 After surgery, I use peroxide to clean the patient's surgical site. I apply either a pressure bandage or a plain Band-Aid with antibiotic ointment. The pressure bandage is applied usually when there is a concern of more bleeding post surgery. I explain to the patient how to take care of the surgical area and when to come back to have the sutures removed. This makes my job complete, until it is time for another set-up, when I will repeat the same process of ensuring a sterile environment for the patient.

Discussion and Critical Thinking

1. Underline and label the thesis (in the first paragraph).

2. Annotate the essay for the preparation and the steps of this process analysis. Number the parts of each stage. Underline key words corresponding with your annotations.

3. Why is the preparation stage longer than the steps stage for Birdine?

4. On what principle is Birdine's order of presentation based—time or space?

Workin' at the Car Wash

ROY M. WALLACK

With these secrets from professional detailers, you'll have your car looking good in no time, says Roy M. Wallack, college instructor and freelance writer. His article was first published in the July/August 2002 edition of Westways.

1   In 90 seconds, Mike Pennington changed my life. Well, he changed my car's life, anyway.

2   A minute-and-a-half is all it took Pennington, the director of training at Irvine-based wax- and polish-maker Meguiar's, to gently rub a clay bar in circles over the hood of my long-neglected 1990 Acura Integra. In seconds, the beige bar dripped with a film of brown muck—all of it from a car I'd washed an hour before.

3   When Pennington finished claying the three-foot circle, it felt as smooth as glass—a striking contrast to the scratchy feel of the surface that surrounded it. Then I noticed one more thing: The circle was distinctly lighter than the rest of the hood. It was astounding; he had pulled years of imbedded grime out of my paint in less time than it takes to fill the gas tank. And he'd done it without breaking a sweat.

4   "Car care has come a long way over the last few years," Pennington explained. "Now that we have products like clay bars and spray waxes that make the process so simple and quick, you don't have any excuse for not having a great-looking car. *Comprende?*"

Car Wash 101

5   Yeah, I got the message. But it's some comfort to know there are millions of us who think we understand the simple process of car washing and waxing and yet don't have a clue. So we keep scrubbing our cars with lemon-fresh dishwashing soap, unaware that it'll strip the wax off our paint as fast as it takes the grease off our dinner plates. We still use dirty old rags and break out the old-fashioned cans of rubbing compound we've had lying around the garage for years, oblivious to the

fact that they'll scratch our cars' finish and remove almost as much paint as dirt, respectively.

6   But what do you expect? The average car owner doesn't have the time or expertise to wade through the yards of car-care stuff on display at your typical auto-parts store. So cars get dirtier.

7   Well, no more. A new breed of products is making it easier and faster than ever to care for your car's finish. To get us up to speed, we sought out some of Southern California's best auto detailers and suppliers and enrolled ourselves in what amounted to Car Wash 101.

The Dirty Truth

8   This may sound un-American, but not all car filth is created equal. Sometimes, your car only needs a wash; sometimes, a wash and wax; sometimes, a wash, clay-bar cleaning, polish, and wax. But before you settle on a strategy, remember: It's a war out there.

9   Our automobiles are under constant assault from bird droppings, diesel soot, road grit, pulverized tire rubber, and UV rays. Cars fight back with a line of defense called a "clear coat," a thinner-than-paper (.002-inch) layer of clear acrylic enamel paint. The clear coat has been original equipment on most vehicles manufactured since 1990.

10   Although this clear coat offers advantages over old-style single-stage paint, there's also a downside. "Clear coat is softer than the paint on older cars, so it scratches and develops swirl marks more easily," says Jeff Jeppeson of Classy Cars, a detailer in Huntington Beach. It can also discolor, fade, and develop hairline cracks over time, despite the built-in UV sunscreen. And when airborne contaminants that bombard it daily aren't quickly washed off, they get embedded.

11   The result is, well, my Acura. "Particles build up on clear coat like plaque on your teeth," says Scot Prescott of Detail 301, a Beverly Hills detailer that handles the car fleets of actors Nicholas Cage and Laurence Fishburne. The solution? "You have to wash on a weekly basis," says Prescott, "especially in a place like L.A., which is loaded with airborne contaminants."

Step by Step

12   The most important lesson to be learned in Car Wash 101 is elementary: Wash caked-on dirt off your car every week, and wash the car, regardless, every two weeks. (This has been a very dry year, so be judicious in your water usage.)

13   To make things simpler still, we've broken the process down into six easy steps:

Wash

14   **Frequency:** Weekly or biweekly.

15   **Tools:** Wash bucket, specially designed car-washing soap, lamb's-wool washing mitt or 100 percent cotton terry cloth towel, nonacid spray-on wheel cleaner, and soft-bristled tire and wheel brush.

16   **Technique:** Wash your wheels and tires first, then wash the body and windows from the top down. Wet the entire car before you start to wash, and keep surfaces wet the whole time. To avoid water spots, finish by rinsing the car thoroughly with a stream of water instead of a spray.

Dry

17   **Frequency:** Whenever you wash.

18   **Tools:** Your choice of a microfiber towel, a natural or synthetic chamois, or the squeegee-like Original California Water Blade and tire dressing and specially designed tire-dressing applicators (if desired).

19   **Technique:** Dry painted surfaces first, then windows, going from top to bottom. Always finish by drying inside the doors, hood, and trunk jambs. This is also a good time to apply tire dressing if desired. Next, run your hand over the car. If it feels as smooth as glass, your job is done. If it doesn't, it's got contaminants bonded to the paint, and you'll need to go to Step 3.

Clay

20   **Frequency:** Whenever painted surfaces feel rough. Usually once or twice a year.

21   **Tools:** Clay detailing system. Often sold in a kit ($16–$20) that includes lubricant spray and clay bars.

22   **Technique:** Spray lubricant on a small area and rub the clay over the surface using light pressure. Continue until the surface feels glassy smooth. When you're finished with an area, wipe it clean with a towel. Knead the dirty clay surface into the center of the bar and continue until you've done the whole car, which should take 20 to 30 minutes. Remember that a freshly clayed surface is naked and needs a protective coat of wax immediately afterward.

Shine

23   **Frequency:** As needed. An optional step before waxing to restore a high gloss and remove tiny scratches and swirl marks.

24   **Tools:** Car polish (not to be confused with much harsher polishing compound), sponge applicator pad, 100 percent cotton terry cloth or microfiber towel.

25   **Technique:** Pour a small amount of polish onto a dry terry cloth towel and massage into the surface with a circular motion. Allow to dry, then remove with a dry terry cloth or microfiber towel.

Protect

26   **Frequency:** Three to four times a year if your car is garaged at night, every other month if it's kept outside. Before winter and at the beginning of summer are ideal times.

27   **Tools:** Premium wax, sponge applicator pad or clean 100 percent cotton terry cloth or microfiber towels, detail brush.

28   **Technique:** Apply a small amount of liquid or paste wax onto a dry applicator or towel and massage onto the surface with a circular motion to create a light haze. Allow to dry completely, then remove with a clean towel. Clean wax residue from trim and other tight spaces with a detail brush like the one described in the "Tips" box below.

Interior

29   **Frequency:** Weekly or whenever a crisis arises.

30   **Tools:** Vacuum cleaner, leather or fabric upholstery cleaner, glass cleaner, vinyl dressing.

31   **Technique:** Remove the floor mats and vacuum them and the interior thoroughly, paying special attention to crevices in and around seats. Wipe down all the interior surfaces with a damp cloth or interior dressing. Clean the upholstery and carpet as needed by following the directions on the product's packaging. Finish by cleaning

the windows and mirrors inside and out with a glass cleaner formulated for automotive use.

Tips and Tricks from the Pros

A. Wash and wax your car in a cool, shady area to prevent the rapid drying that leads to water spots.

B. If you drop your wash mitt or towel on the ground, get a new one to avoid scratching paint with the grit it's picked up. Most mitts can be machine washed and dried (skip the liquid fabric softener or dryer sheets).

C. If you like using a bucket of soapy water to wash your wheels and tires, use a separate one for the rest of the car to avoid transferring abrasive grit to painted surfaces.

D. Remember that polishes create gloss and waxes protect. Many car-care products combine these two compounds, allowing you to do both in one step.

E. Use a light coat of wax. Thin coats are easier to apply and remove and are less likely to create excess wax "dust" that can be a hassle to remove.

F. Never use a high-speed buffer because, in the hands of an inexperienced user, the heat it generates can burn right through paint. Instead, buy an orbital model (about $40 at your local hardware store).

G. Make your own detail brush for removing hard-to-get wax residue by cutting the bristles of a two-inch paintbrush in half. Wrap the metal band with electrical tape and soften the bristle tips by running them back and forth over sandpaper before using.

H. Make sure wheels are cool before applying wheel-cleaning solutions; hot rims can be stained by the chemicals they contain.

I. Spray a high-quality interior protectant inside the car's wheel wells to give your car a like-new look.

J. To apply vinyl dressing to the dash without getting it on the windshield, wrap a rag around your hand and apply the dressing only to the bottom side. Otherwise, you'll have to use glass cleaner to fix the mess.

K. When buying and using car-care products, be sure to read and follow all label directions carefully.

L. Paint transfers, like those that come from close encounters with painted curbs, come off easily if you rub them with a soft cloth dampened with paint thinner (mineral spirits). The same goes for tar and adhesive residues from old parking and bumper stickers.

—R.M.W. and Alan Rider

Washin' on the Web

Looking for more information on caring for your car's finish? Trying to find some of the products and tools discussed in this story? Here are a few of our favorite websites:

www.griotsgarage.com
www.meguiars.com
www.mothers.com
www.calcarduster.com

www.eagleone.com
www.properautocare.com
www.topoftheline.com

EXERCISE 5

Discussion and Critical Thinking

1. The standard form for a directive process analysis is preparation followed by steps. How does the article by Wallack deviate from that form?

2. What is the need for the back-and-forth arrangement of preparation and steps?

3. Fill in the blanks with the capital letters from "Tips and Tricks from the Pros" to match tips and tricks with steps.

Step	Tips and Tricks
1	_____
2	_____
3	_____
4	_____
5	_____
6	_____

4. List any suggestions you have for improving this directive process analysis.

Fast-Track French Fries

ERIC SCHLOSSER

In this excerpt from the best-selling Fast Food Nation: The Dark Side of the All-American Meal, *Eric Schlosser explains the sequence by which French fries are the product of a complex, highly mechanized operation. Unlike many of the unsavory fast-food processes Schlosser discusses in his profound exposé, this one doesn't turn your stomach.*

1   Lamb Weston was founded in 1950 by F. Gilbert Lamb, the inventor of a crucial piece of french fry–making technology. The Lamb Water Gun Knife uses a high-pressure hose to shoot potatoes at a speed of 117 feet per second through a grid of sharpened steel blades, thereby creating perfectly sliced french fries. After coming up with the idea, Gil Lamb tested the first Water Gun Knife in a company parking lot, shooting potatoes out of a fire hose. Lamb sold his company to ConAgra in 1988. Lamb Weston now manufactures more than 130 different types of french fries, including: Steak House Fries, CrissCut Fries, Hi-Fries, Mor-Fries, Burger Fries, Taterbabies, Taterboy Curley QQQ Fries, and Rus-Ettes Special Dry Fry Shoestrings.

2   Bud Mandeville, the plant manager, led me up a narrow, wooden staircase inside one of the plant's storage buildings. On the top floor, the staircase led to a catwalk,

and beneath my feet I saw a mound of potatoes that was twenty feet deep and a hundred feet wide and almost as long as two football fields. The building was cool and dark, kept year-round at a steady 46 degrees. In the dim light the potatoes looked like grains of sand on a beach. This was one of seven storage buildings on the property.

3   Outside, tractor-trailers arrived from the fields, carrying potatoes that had just been harvested. The trucks dumped their loads onto spinning rods that brought the larger potatoes into the building and let the small potatoes, dirt, and rocks fall to the ground. The rods led to a rock trap, a tank of water in which the potatoes floated and the rocks sank to the bottom. The plant used water systems to float potatoes gently this way and that way, guiding different sizes out of different holding bays, then flushing them into a three-foot-deep stream that ran beneath the cement floor. The interior of the processing plant was gray, massive, and well-lit, with huge pipes running along the walls, steel catwalks, workers in hardhats, and plenty of loud machinery. If there weren't potatoes bobbing and floating past, you might think the place was an oil refinery.

4   Conveyer belts took the wet, clean potatoes into a machine that blasted them with steam for twelve seconds, boiled the water under their skins, and exploded their skins off. Then the potatoes were pumped into a preheat tank and shot through a Lamb Water Gun Knife. They emerged as shoestring fries. Four video cameras scrutinized them from different angles, looking for flaws. When a french fry with a blemish was detected, an optical sorting machine time-sequenced a single burst of compressed air that knocked the bad fry off the production line and onto a separate conveyer belt, which carried it to a machine with tiny automated knives that precisely removed the blemish. And then the fry was returned to the main production line.

5   Sprays of hot water blanched the fries, gusts of hot air dried them, and 25,000 pounds of boiling oil fried them to a slight crisp. Air cooled by compressed ammonia gas quickly froze them, a computerized sorter divided them into six-pound batches, and a device that spun like an out-of-control lazy Susan used centrifugal force to align the french fries so that they all pointed in the same direction. The fries were sealed in brown bags, then the bags were loaded by robots into cardboard boxes, and the boxes were stacked by robots onto wooden pallets. Forklifts driven by human beings took the pallets to a freezer for storage. Inside that freezer I saw 20 million pounds of french fries, most of them destined for McDonald's, the boxes of fries stacked thirty feet high, the stacks extending for roughly forty yards. And the freezer was half empty. Every day about a dozen railroad cars and about two dozen tractor-trailers pulled up to the freezer, loaded up with french fries, and departed for McDonald's restaurants in Boise, Pocatello, Phoenix, Salt Lake City, Denver, Colorado Springs, and points in between.

6   Near the freezer was a laboratory where women in white coats analyzed french fries day and night, measuring their sugar content, their starch content, their color. During the fall, Lamb Weston added sugar to the fries; in the spring it leached sugar out of them; the goal was to maintain a uniform taste and appearance throughout the year. Every half hour, a new batch of fries was cooked in fryers identical to those used in fast food kitchens. A middle-aged woman in a lab coat handed me a paper plate full of premium extra longs, the type of french fries sold at McDonald's, and a salt shaker, and some ketchup. The fries on the plate looked wildly out of place in this laboratory setting, this surreal food factory with its computer screens, digital readouts, shiny steel platforms, and evacuation plans in case of ammonia gas leaks. The french fries were delicious—crisp and golden brown, made from potatoes that had been in the ground that morning. I finished them and asked for more.

EXERCISE 6   # Discussion and Critical Thinking

1. Is this directive or informative process analysis?

2. Using the steps from this list, complete the following basic outline.

    Stored for shipment   Conveyed by belts to steam boiler

    Sliced into fries   Shipped to restaurants

    Sorted, bagged, and loaded   Corrected if flawed

    Taste-tested

    I. Situation

        A. F. Gilbert Lamb, inventor

        B. The Lamb Water Gun Knife

        C. Development of invention

        D. Mound of potatoes

    II. Sequence

        A. Brought from field

        B. Sorted, sized, cleaned in vats of water

        C. Moved along by flotation

        D. _____

        E. Shot through Lamb Water Gun Knife

        F. _____

        G. Evaluated for flaws

        H. _____

        I. Blanched, dried, and fried

        J. _____

        K. Driven to freezer

        L. Analyzed and adjusted

        M. _____

        N. _____

        O. _____

Topics for Writing Process Analysis

You will find a blank Writing Process Worksheet on page 7, which can be photocopied, filled in, and submitted with each assignment if your instructor directs you to do so.

Reading-Related Topics

"*Pupusas:* Salvadoran Delight"

1. Write about a special food prepared in your family now or in your childhood. The food could be your favorite dish, or it might be a treat prepared for a special holiday. Personalize your process analysis.

"Making Faces"

2. Using this paragraph as a model (omit the hypothetical customer if you like), write about any other grooming or personal service that you either perform for hire or understand very well and can perform. Suggestions: hair, nails, facials, skin art (tattooing or painting), skin alteration (piercing).

"The Skinny of Working for a Dermatologist"

3. Write about a job that required you to play an important supporting role. Explain both how you helped and what the other person did.

"Workin' at the Car Wash"

4. Using this essay as a model, write about another job that could be performed either at home or at the workplace. Suggestions: changing oil in a car, changing a tire, giving a hair permanent, repairing a household utility.

"Fast-Track French Fries"

5. If you have worked in a factory, use this excerpt as a model in writing about how a product is produced.

General Topics

Most of the following topics are directive as they are phrased. However, each can be transformed into a how-it-was-done informative topic by personalizing it and explaining stage by stage how you, someone else, or a group did something. For example, you could write either a directive process analysis about how to deal with an obnoxious person or an informative process analysis about how you or someone else dealt with an obnoxious person. Keep in mind that the two types of process analysis are often blended, especially in personal writing. Many of the following topics will be more interesting to you and your readers if the process is personalized.

Most of the topics 6–14 require some narrowing to be treated in a paragraph or short essay. For example, writing about playing baseball is too broad; writing about how to throw a curve ball may be manageable.

6. How to end a relationship without hurting someone's feelings.

7. How to pass a test for a driver's license.

8. How to get a job at _____

9. How to eat _____

10. How to perform a magic trick

11. How to repair _____

12. How to assemble _____

13. How to learn about another culture

14. How to approach someone you would like to know better

Imagine you will have a houseguest from a country that does not have our household conveniences. You will be away on the day the person arrives and you need to write some instructions on how to operate something (and perhaps a few warnings about the consequences of not following directions).

15. Write an explanation, including the stages of preparation and steps, of how to do something. Include drawings, diagrams, pictures, or other illustrations that are keyed by numbers or letters to your instructions. For potential topics, walk through your house and consider the conveniences you take for granted, such as the dishwasher, the washing machine, the dryer, the toaster, the VCR, the can opener, and so on. Before writing your final draft, have someone follow your directions, doing only what you write.

Cross-Curricular Topics

16. Write about a process related to another class in which you use equipment for a small unit of work. Include drawings, diagrams, or photocopies of images marked with numbers or letters to correspond with your directions. Consider the following processes:

   • viewing a slide of a specific item in a biology lab

   • identifying a rock in a geology class

   • testing soil in an agriculture class

   • preflighting an aircraft

Career-Related Topics

17. Explain how to display, package, sell, or demonstrate a product.

18. Explain how to perform a service or to repair or install a product.

19. Explain the procedure for operating a machine, computer, piece of equipment, or other device at the workplace.

20. Explain how to manufacture, construct, or cook something at the workplace.

Writer's Guidelines: Process Analysis

1. Decide whether your process analysis is mainly directive or informative, and be appropriately consistent in using pronouns and other designations.

   • For directive process analysis, use the second person, addressing the reader as *you*. The *you* may be understood, even if it is not written.

   • For informative process analysis, use the first person, speaking as *I* or *we*, or the third person, speaking about the subject as *he, she, it,* or *they*, or by name.

2. Consider using these basic forms.

Directive	Informative
I. Preparation	I. Background
A.	A.
B.	B.
II. Steps	II. Sequence
A.	A.
B.	B.
C.	C.

3. Listing is a useful prewriting activity for process analysis. Begin with the Roman-numeral headings indicated in number 2.

4. The order of a process analysis will usually be chronological (time based) in some sense. Certain transitional words are commonly used to promote coherence: *first, second, third, then, soon, now, next, finally, at last, therefore,* and *consequently.*

5. Write and revise.

   • Write and then revise your paragraph or essay as many times as necessary for **c**oherence, **l**anguage (usage, tone, and diction), **u**nity, **e**mphasis, **s**upport, and **s**entences (**CLUESS**). Read your work aloud to hear and correct any grammatical errors or awkward-sounding sentences.

   • Edit any problems in fundamentals, such as **c**apitalization, **o**missions, **p**unctuation, and **s**pelling (**COPS**).

Chapter
20

Analysis by Division:
Examining the Parts

Being able to analyze is the key to understanding oneself, mastering subjects, and performing well at work.

Learning Objectives

Working with this chapter, I will learn

~ the principles of writing analysis by division.

~ how to use analysis by division in different contexts.

Writing Analysis by Division

Being able to analyze is the key to learning, performing, and teaching. If you need to explain how something works or exists as a unit, you will write an analysis by division. You will break down a unit (your subject) into its parts and explain how each part functions in relation to the operation or existence of the whole. The most important word here is *unit*. You begin with something that can stand alone or can be regarded separately. Here are some examples of units that can be divided into traits, characteristics, or other parts in different contexts:

Personal
- a relationship
- love
- a role, such as parent, neighbor, friend (traits)
- an activity, such as a hobby

Cross-Curricular
- a musical composition
- a prepared food
- an organism
- a government
- a poem or short story

Career-Related
- a job description
- an evaluation of an individual, product, service, institution, or company
- management style
- management

Procedure

The following procedure will guide you in writing an analysis by division. Move from subject to principle, to division, to relationship:

1. Begin with something that is a unit.

2. State one principle by which the unit can function.

3. Divide the unit into parts according to that principle.

4. Discuss each of the parts in relation to the unit.

You might apply that procedure to writing about a good boss in the following way:

1. Unit	Manager
2. Principle of function	Effective as a leader
3. Parts based on the principle	Fair, intelligent, stable, competent in the field
4. Discussion	Consider each part in relation to the person's effectiveness as a manager.

Organization

In a paragraph or an essay of analysis by division, the main parts are likely to be the main points of your outline or main extensions of your cluster. If they are anything else, reconsider your organization.

A basic outline of analysis by division might look like this:

Thesis: To be effective as a leader, a manager needs specific qualities.
 I. Fairness
 II. Intelligence
 III. Stability
 IV. Competence in the field

Sequence of Parts

The order in which you discuss the parts will vary according to the nature of the unit and the way in which you view it. Here are some possible sequences for organizing the parts of a unit:

- **Time:** The sequence of the parts can be mainly chronological, or time-based (if you are dealing with something that functions on its own, such as a heart, with the parts presented in relation to stages of the function).

- **Space:** If your unit is a visual object, especially if, like a pencil, it does nothing by itself, you may discuss the parts in relation to space. In the example of the pencil, the parts of the pencil begin at the top with the eraser and end at the bottom with the pencil point.

- **Emphasis:** Because the most emphatic location of any piece of writing is the end (the second most emphatic point is the beginning), consider placing the most significant part of the unit at the end.

Practicing Patterns of Analysis by Division

In analysis by division, Roman-numeral headings are almost always parts of the unit you are discussing as your subject. Learning to divide the unit into parts will help you move through your assignment quickly and efficiently.

| EXERCISE 1 | Completing Patterns |

Fill in the blanks in the following outlines to complete each analysis by division. The Roman-numeral items represent major divisions of the unit and consequently would indicate the major parts of a paragraph or an essay.

A. Unit: Federal government

   Principle: Division of power

   Parts based on the principle:

   I. Executive

   II. _____

   III. _____

B. Unit: Newspaper

   Principle: Sections for readers

   Parts based on the principle:

   I. News

   II. Sports

   III. _____

   IV. _____

   V. _____

C. Unit: Doctor

   Principle: Effective as a general practitioner

   Parts based on the principle:

   I. Ability to _____

   II. Knowledge of _____

   III. Knowledge of computers and other equipment

Writing Patterns

Fill in the blanks in the following outlines as if you were organizing material for a paragraph or an essay. Have a specific person, job, service, institution, or product in mind.

A. Unit: Evaluation of a person (one who is on the job or applying for a job)

   Principle: Traits that would make a person praiseworthy (as a worker or an applicant)

   The name of the person (may be fictitious): _____

   I. _____

   II. _____

   III. _____

   IV. _____

   (Add other headings if necessary.)

B. Unit: Product, institution, or service

   Principle: Qualities that would make the unit excellent

   Specific name of the unit: _____

   I. _____

   II. _____

III. _____

IV. _____

(Add other headings if necessary.)

Connecting Reading and Writing: Heroes—Who, Where, and Why

A person once said, "Pity the nation that has no heroes." It is a statement worthy of our consideration, especially since it is often said that we have no heroes today or that a hero is only good for about fifteen minutes, because, with media scrutiny, we're likely to know of any prominent person's flaws soon after the applause has died. That, of course, brings up the question of just how much we should expect from our heroes. Naturally, our heroes should be more than ordinary, but should they be bigger than life? We need a definition, one that fits a special word often used loosely. Are famous athletes and other celebrities "heroes" or even role models? Some pretend to be and disappoint us. Some "big names" don't want to be known as either a hero or a role model. The irascible Charles Barkley said, "Raise your own kids. I'm a basketball player."

Clarance H. Benes and John E. Steinbrink offer a comprehensive view in "Heroes Everywhere." Writing mainly for instructors of social studies, they place the idea of heroism within social, cultural, and historical contexts. In "A Music Legend Fades to Black," Dave Tianen pays tribute to Johnny Cash, a hero from popular culture. Student Susan Miller presents "Susan B. Anthony: Hero in Bloomers," a political leader of noble stature who helped shape our nation's laws.

THE QUIGMANS   by Buddy Hickerson

B. Hickerson, copyright Los Angeles Times Syndicate. All rights reserved.

In the first selection, "More Than Ordinary," student Nancy Samuels was faced with writing on the topic of "a personal, popular, or historical hero." She didn't have to go to the library. Right in her household she found her subject—her mother. She writes of an ordinary person who faced a difficult challenge and succeeded, in a situation in which others gave up too easily. You can follow her writing process by studying her Writing Process Worksheet. To conserve space here, the freewriting and the first draft with revisions and editing have been deleted from her submission.

You will find a full-size blank worksheet on page 7, which can be photocopied, filled in, and submitted with each assignment if your instructor directs you to do so.

Writing Process Worksheet

Title   More Than Ordinary

Name   Nancy Samuels   **Due Date**   Tuesday, May 4, 9:30 a.m.

ASSIGNMENT   In the space below, write whatever you need to know about your assignment, including information about the topic, audience, pattern of writing, length, whether to include a rough draft or revised drafts, and whether your paper must be typed.

Write a paragraph of analysis by division about a personal, popular, or historical hero. Name the hero and stress the traits that make that person a hero. Assume that your readers do not know your subject well. Submit this completed worksheet, one or more rough drafts, and a typed final draft.

STAGE ONE   **Explore**   Freewrite, brainstorm (list), cluster, or take notes as directed by your instructor. Use the back of this page or separate paper if you need more space.

Listing

Unit: Mother
Principle of function: person as hero
Parts based on the principle:
    optimistic
    persevering
    considerate
    courageous
    tolerant
    self-sacrificing

STAGE TWO   **Organize**   Write a topic sentence or thesis; label the subject and the treatment parts.

<u>My mother</u> is the best example of a hero I can think of.
     subject   treatment

Write an outline or an outline alternative.

I. Optimistic
    A. Would not believe bad news
    B. Consulted several doctors
    C. Had a positive goal
II. Persevering
    A. Becomes my brother's therapist
    B. Worked with him for three years
III. Courageous
    A. Does not listen to others
    B. Would not accept failure
IV. Self-sacrificing
    A. Concentrating on helping son
    B. Neglected self

STAGE THREE

Write   On separate paper, write and then revise your paragraph or essay as many times as necessary for **c**oherence, **l**anguage (usage, tone, and diction), **u**nity, **e**mphasis, **s**upport, and **s**entences (**CLUESS**). Read your work aloud to hear and correct any grammatical errors or awkward-sounding sentences.

Edit any problems in fundamentals, such as **c**apitalization, **o**missions, **p**unctuation, and **s**pelling (**COPS**).

More Than Ordinary

Nancy Samuels

Topic sentence   <u>My mother is the best example of a hero I can think of</u>. No one will read about her in a book about heroes, but in her small circle of friends, no one doubts her heroism. Certainly my younger brother doesn't. He is the special beneficiary of her heroism. He was in an accident when he was five years old, and the doctor told us that he would never walk. My mother listened respectfully, but she didn't *Trait*   believe him. She had <u>optimism</u>. She went to another doctor and then another. Finally she found one who prescribed exercises. She worked with my brother for *Trait*   three years. Day after dismal day, she <u>persevered</u>. It wasn't just her working with him that helped my brother. It was her raw courage in the face of failure. My *Trait*   brother worked with her. They both were <u>courageous</u>. We other family members weren't. To us my brother and mother were acting like a couple of people blinded by hope. We thought my mother especially, the leader, was in prolonged denial. But in three years my brother was walking. He won't be an athlete; nevertheless, he gets around. We're proud of him, but we know—and he knows—that without Mother he would never have walked. She sacrificed years of her life for him. Of course, she's not a miracle worker. Most of the time, doctors are right, and some injured people can never walk. But the ones, like my brother, who somewhere have that hidden ability need that special someone like my mother. She's more than ordinary. She's a hero.

EXERCISE 3

Discussion and Critical Thinking

1. What are the main traits of Samuels's heroic mother?

2. Is she a miracle worker?

3. Will her kind of strength always succeed? Explain.

4. Would she have been heroic if she had not succeeded in helping her son?

Susan B. Anthony: Hero in Bloomers

SUSAN MILLER

In reading history, we often discover our heroes. They include those who established the institutions and the basic freedoms that we so often take for granted. In elementary school, student Susan Miller discovered Susan B. Anthony. She remembered so well that for this essay she hardly needed to review the facts about one of the women responsible for women gaining the right to vote.

1   When I first read about Susan B. Anthony, I ran to my mother and asked if I was named after her. The answer was no. I was named Susan because it is a pretty name. So when I think of her, I will not think of the idea of namesake, but I will think of the idea of hero. In fact, she is the best example I know of. Against all odds she was a hero, displaying the qualities any hero needs, in my definition. Thesis   <u>As a hero she was courageous, persistent, and willing to sacrifice self.</u>

2   Those qualities are not easily separated in discussing Anthony. Certainly she was courageous, because she acted as an individual equal to any others in her strong stands against slavery and alcohol. When she was thirty-two years old, she attended a temperance movement meeting and wanted to speak against the sale of alcohol, which she saw as destructive of the family, especially among the poor. Although she was not allowed to speak because she was a woman, she argued individually and was widely criticized and scorned by the men in attendance.

3   Nothing would dissuade her as she persisted in her views. The more she argued about slavery and temperance, the more it became apparent that women were treated unfairly. They did not have equal opportunity in education, social relationships, and politics. She began writing and speaking on all those issues. When she was told that women should stay in their place under their dresses, she began wearing bloomers, loose-fitting trousers that were regarded as scandalous clothing by the male-dominated society.

4   After the Civil War, she rejoiced as black men were given the right to vote. It was a right she had long upheld. But she was disappointed because women, all women, were denied that right. For the remainder of her life, women's suffrage was her passion. In 1872 she dressed as a man and voted, although she was breaking a federal law in doing so. But she believed that the right for women to vote was so fundamental that she put herself at risk.

5   Susan B. Anthony would not be around when women were given the right to

vote in 1919. She had died fourteen years earlier. But her name and reputation remain. Because of heroes like her, women now have opportunities hardly thought of at the beginning of her life.

EXERCISE 4 | **Discussion and Critical Thinking**

1. What were Susan B. Anthony's main traits?

2. Are courage and self-sacrifice almost the same? Explain.

3. If Susan B. Anthony were around today, what causes do you think she would be involved in?

Heroes Everywhere

CLARANCE H. BENES AND JOHN E. STEINBRINK

The word hero *is defined broadly—some would say loosely—but the basic traits of heroism have not lost their significance. In this excerpt from "Be Your Own Heroes," an essay directed mainly at social studies instructors, Clarance H. Benes and John E. Steinbrink discuss the sources of heroic reputation and the various types of heroes across a wide spectrum. This material was first published in the journal* The Clearing House *in 1998.*

1   Virtually all societies have their heroes who are derived from myth (Hercules), legend (Johnny Appleseed), or life (George Washington, Abraham Lincoln, Sam Houston, Rosa Parks). Ancient heroes inevitably performed deeds that required strength, cunning, and boldness. Later, during the medieval period, heroes were characterized by piety, honor, valor, and loyalty. More recently, whether derived from fiction (James Bond, Princess Leia) or from real life (Sojourner Truth, Geronimo, Susan B. Anthony, FDR, Malcolm X, Norman Schwarzkopf), heroes require conflict or an antagonist to demonstrate their heroic qualities.

2   A typical heroic sequence of action exists. The hero may venture forth in a moral quest to save a people (Joan of Arc), to support a moralistic idea (Jesus, Buddha, Mother Teresa), or to support a new idea (Henry Ford, Elizabeth Cady Stanton, Margaret Mead). Thus heroes are commonly founders of something (Jesus, Clara Barton) or people who have created a new standard (John Lennon, Elvis). Heroes alter the world, nearly always changing it for the better (Anne Frank, Nelson Mandela). Heroes are necessarily bold and innovative because, in order to found something new, one must leave behind the old (Jesus, Martin Luther, Christopher Columbus, Martin Luther King Jr.).

3   Heroes are noted for their autonomy and individualism. They create a new standard. Heroes challenge conventional wisdom and commonly transcend peer pressure and conformity. Because they are marching to a different drummer, however, they frequently perceive their remarkable actions as being merely ordinary, as simply a matter of doing their duty.

4   Two types of heroes can be identified. The first type—the superhuman or divine hero—typically is male, preceded by legend (e.g., from the House of David), and of unusual strength (Hercules, Paul Bunyan, Wonder Woman) or cleverness (Robin Hood, Sojourner Truth). David, for example, delivered his people from the Philistines by defeating Goliath. Brigham Young led his followers on a grand odyssey and delivered them to Zion, modern Utah. Harriet Tubman, termed the Moses of her people, led slaves to freedom in the North. Chief Joseph attempted to outrun the federal soldiers and prevent his people from being forced onto reservations. Susan B. Anthony and Elizabeth Cady Stanton were pioneers in the women's suffrage movement, campaigning for female equality. As the leader of the western democracies, Woodrow Wilson made the world safe for democracy by pressing for U.S. involvement in World War I. Rachel Carson introduced the concepts of ecology and environmental protection to Americans in her book *Silent Spring*. Dwight Eisenhower helped orchestrate the coalition of western democracies in their conquest of Germany's Third Reich. In sum, heroes typically perform what appear to be superhuman acts.

5   The second type of hero is the ordinary person hero, a type of hero generated by the needs of the society. The concept of the ordinary person as hero provides virtually everyone with the opportunity to become a hero. For example, teachers, fire fighters, police officers, hard-working parents, outstanding grandparents, and civic volunteers possess many of the characteristics of the second type of hero. The ordinary person hero is distinguished by extraordinary deeds, but he or she seldom becomes famous and rarely is known beyond his or her family, neighborhood, or community.

6   Our media-saturated popular culture transforms hero worship into a secular religion. Ordinary mortals who became legendary heroes include Pocahontas, Charles Lindbergh, the Beatles, John Kennedy, Helen Keller, and Elvis Presley. American political icons who became heroes include the Founding Fathers—George Washington, John Adams, Thomas Jefferson, James Madison, and Benjamin Franklin. Other American political icons include Andrew Jackson, Sam Houston, Theodore Roosevelt, Franklin Roosevelt, Eleanor Roosevelt, Harry Truman, Dwight Eisenhower, Sandra Day O'Connor, and Barbara Jordan. Most significant political heroes are leaders who exercise power without abusing it (Golda Meir, Harry Truman).

7   Heroes represent vision, bold action, and idealism. In our electronic society, however, television, movies, and sports create celebrities and TV personalities who are commonly confused with genuine heroes. John Wayne didn't actually fight in WWII or any war (and neither did Rambo). Yet, John Wayne was declared by the U.S. Congress to be an "All American Hero."

EXERCISE 5

Vocabulary Highlights

Write a short definition of each word as it is used in the essay. (Paragraph numbers are given in parentheses.) Be prepared to use the words in your own sentences.

piety (1)	suffrage (4)
innovative (2)	orchestrate (4)
autonomy (3)	coalition (4)
transcend (3)	secular (6)
odyssey (4)	icons (6)

EXERCISE 6

Discussion and Critical Thinking

1. Complete the following items for analysis by division by using information about ancient heroes in paragraph 1.

   Unit: Individual in ancient times.

   Principle of function: _____

   Parts based on the principle: _____

2. What conditions or situations are necessary to bring out the qualities of a modern hero?

3. According to the definitions given in paragraph 2, why might John Lennon and Elvis be called heroes?

4. What did John Lennon and Elvis create?

5. Do you feel that John Lennon and Elvis can reasonably be called heroes?

6. What are the two types of heroes?

7. What sentence in paragraph 5 indicates the main difference between the super-human hero and the ordinary person hero?

8. Paragraph 6 explains that media personalities are often confused with the parts they play. Then the two examples of that idea are bold action figures. Could media personalities who do not act boldly also be regarded as heroes? If so, name a few.

9. What heroes would you like to add to the many examples given in this excerpt?

A Music Legend Fades to Black

DAVE TIANEN

Journalist and music critic Dave Tianen has written a eulogy about Johnny Cash, the man who always wore black on stage but who had as many shades of uniqueness as the color wheel. Cash was more than another performer with a string of hits. He was, as Tianen indicates, a folk hero for what he was, did, and stood for. This article was first printed in the Journal Sentinel *(Milwaukee).*

Johnny Cash 1932–2003

1   Johnny Cash owned two dogs. One he named Sin, and the other Redemption. That tension between good and evil, darkness and light, echoed through Cash's art and life. He was both outlaw and pilgrim, both rebel and patriot. It was a

lasting duality that endeared him to older traditional country fans and young rockers alike.

2   After years of declining health, Cash, 71, died early Friday in a Nashville hospital from complications of diabetes. It was just four months after the death of his wife, June Carter Cash. His last years were crowded with honors. Although his records were rarely played anymore on mainstream country radio, a series of spare albums cut with rock/rap producer Rick Rubin for American Recordings brought him Grammys and a cult audience among rock fans. His song and video for "Hurt," written by Trent Reznor of Nine Inch Nails, was nominated for several MTV Video Music Awards and is in the running for best single and best video in the November 5 Country Music Association Awards.

3   "Whether anybody knows it or not, they were directly or indirectly influenced by Johnny Cash," country star Kenny Chesney said Friday in an e-mail statement. "Rock 'n' roll, country, gospel—Johnny's music crossed any boundary that was put up in front of him." There was something quintessentially American about Johnny Cash. He had the kind of features that would have looked natural on Mount Rushmore. He had a bond with the luckless, the downtrodden, even the despised, that never felt forced or preachy. There was a strong thread of Americana in his music, and his songbook is dotted with folk tunes such as "Frankie and Johnny," "Long Black Veil" and "Delia's Gone." He celebrated folk heroes such as Casey Jones and John Henry, and over time he became a kind of folk hero himself.

4   He also was a major link between the worlds of rock and country. Emerging in the '50s from the same Sun Records stable in Memphis that produced Elvis Presley, Jerry Lee Lewis, Carl Perkins, Charlie Rich and Roy Orbison, Cash helped to revolutionize the sound of country music with hits such as "I Walk the Line," "Folsom Prison Blues," "Big River" and "Guess Things Happen That Way." Although he had a rockabilly streak that came through on tunes such as "Get Rhythm" and "Hey Porter," Cash remained more anchored in country than his other Sun stablemates. There was a signature chugga-chugga sound to his early hits with the Tennessee Two, but he remained open to new sounds, as well. He was one of the first Nashville figures to record songs by Bob Dylan and Kris Kristofferson. When Dylan turned country on "Nashville Skyline," he opened the 1969 album with a Cash duet on "Girl from the North Country."

5   Eclecticism was a constant in Cash's career. As much as anyone he defined country music in all its varied aspects. His '60s hits included bluegrass songs ("Orange Blossom Special"), TV gunfighter ballads ("The Rebel—Johnny Yuma"), early country blues ("In the Jailhouse Now"), novelty tunes ("Everybody Loves a Nut"), gospel ("Daddy Sang Bass") and folk tunes ("Rock Island Line"). His biggest pop hit of the era was "A Boy Named Sue," a raucous novelty tune recorded before an audience of San Quentin prisoners and written by *Playboy*'s Shel Silverstein. Joan Baez once aptly described Cash as having "a crumbling rock of a voice." Deep and craggy, what it lacked in range it more than made up for in strength and presence. It sounded like the voice of an Old Testament prophet, and it proved adaptable to a remarkable range of material.

6   Cash also was country music's greatest patriarch. His marriage to June Carter Cash linked him with the Carter Family, a seminal force in country music dating back to the 1920s. His daughter Roseanne Cash became a major country star in her own right in the '80s. June's daughter, Carlene Carter, had a string of top-10 hits in the early '90s. Cash's younger brother Tommy has a string of hits, and his sons-in-law have included Marty Stuart and Rodney Crowell.

7   Cash was born February 26, 1932, in Kingsland, Arkansas. It was not an easy childhood. The Cashes were poor cotton farmers struggling to stay solvent in the

depths of the Depression. They were flooded out in 1937, and Cash's older brother Jack was killed in a saw accident when Johnny was a teenager. After a string of odd jobs, Cash joined the Air Force in 1950 and taught himself guitar while stationed in Germany. Following his discharge, he married, moved to Memphis and started selling appliances. He also met a pair of local mechanics—Luther Perkins and Marshall Grant—who played music on the side. He started singing with them unpaid.

8   In 1954, he began recording for Sun, and in 1955 "Cry! Cry! Cry!" by Johnny Cash and the Tennessee Two went to number 14 on the country charts. That was the beginning of a decades-long string that would eventually produce 136 country chart hits. The hits continued when Cash jumped to Columbia in 1958. "Ring of Fire" went top 20 on the pop charts in 1963. Movie roles and a television series followed. Although he was prospering professionally, Cash's health was compromised by an addiction to pills. In 1965, Cash was arrested by narcotics police in El Paso, Texas, and given a 30-day suspended sentence. Album covers of the time show a gaunt figure whose weight had dropped as low as 140 pounds.

9   The bright light in Cash's personal life was his growing relationship with June Carter. The two married in 1968, following Cash's divorce from his first wife. Although chemical addictions continued to sporadically haunt Cash for many years, June remained an anchor for him throughout the rest of their lives together.

10   Cash continued to tour and record successfully for Columbia in the '70s and '80s, although the hits came less consistently. "One Piece at a Time," a novelty about an autoworker who steals a Cadillac part by part over 30 years, hit No. 1 in 1976. Another chart topper followed in 1985 on a supergroup collaboration, the Highwaymen, with Kristofferson, Willie Nelson and Waylon Jennings for "Highwayman." Although he continued to be a successful touring attraction, Cash fell more and more outside country music's youth focus as the '80s waned. Airplay became a struggle. When this reporter interviewed him in 1994, he said, "If I hear the word *demographics* one more time, I'll puke."

11   After a brief stint with Mercury Records, Cash started recording for Rubin and the American label in the early '90s. This was stripped-down, raw, acoustic, guitar-and-voice music that mixed folk and pop tunes with material from young songwriters such as Beck and Glenn Danzig. These songs didn't regain an audience for Cash on mainstream country radio, but they won awards and reaffirmed his outsider hero status within the emerging alternative country movement while confirming his long-standing reputation for stubborn independence. When one of the American albums, "Unchained," won a Grammy in 1998, Cash took out a full-page ad in the trade magazine *Billboard* thanking country radio for its "support." It was a vintage shot of Cash flipping the bird.

12   In 1997, Cash was diagnosed with Shy-Drager Syndrome. That diagnosis was later revised to autonomic neuropathy, but his health problems continued to mount. Public appearances grew rare, and there were frequent hospitalizations for pneumonia, plus advancing diabetes and glaucoma. He had, of course, long since attained a legendary stature few performers ever achieved. Terri Clark, a country songstress two generations removed, captured a sense of it in a statement released Friday. "What really made him stand out, more than the back-beats, the TV shows, the hit records, was how he stood up for the little people, the way he believed in the right things. . . . He was a beacon for both musical and personal integrity, and he set a bar most of us can only gaze at."

EXERCISE 7

Vocabulary Highlights

Write a short definition of each word as it is used in the essay. (Paragraph numbers are given in parentheses.) Be prepared to use the words in your own sentences.

duality (1)   solvent (7)

quintessentially (3)   gaunt (8)

revolutionize (4)   sporadically (9)

eclecticism (5)   demographics (10)

seminal (6)   reaffirmed (11)

EXERCISE 8

Discussion and Critical Thinking

1. What is meant by Cash's "lasting duality that endeared him to older traditional country fans and young rockers alike" (paragraph 1)?

2. Explain the terms "both outlaw and pilgrim, both rebel and patriot."

    Outlaw: _____

    Pilgrim: _____

    Rebel: _____

    Patriot: _____

3. What are the parts of the implied analysis of Cash as a "folk hero" in paragraph 3?

4. In analyzing Johnny Cash as a person who was the founder of something or who "created a new standard" [from paragraph 2 in "Heroes Everywhere], we can apply the following procedure. Use paragraph numbers to indicate where each part is discussed.

    Unit: Johnny Cash

    Principle of function: _____

    Parts based on the principle:

    Range of traits (duality): Paragraph(s) _____

    Range of music and achievements: Paragraph(s) _____

    Appearance: Paragraph(s) _____

    Voice: Paragraph(s) _____

    Reputation: Paragraph(s) _____

Topics for Writing Analysis by Division

You will find a blank Writing Process Worksheet on page 7, which can be photocopied, filled in, and submitted with each assignment if your instructor directs you to do so.

Reading-Related Topics

"More Than Ordinary"

1. Using Samuels's paragraphs as a model, write about a person you know who has struggled mightily and deserves the title ordinary person hero.

"Susan B. Anthony: Hero in Bloomers"

2. Write about some notable person from history (any culture, any field) who could be called heroic. Your writing will define the idea of hero by discussing the achievements and traits of your exemplary person. Include comments on the opposition your hero had to overcome. Use this essay as a basic model, whether you write a paragraph or a short essay.

"Heroes Everywhere"

3. These authors use analysis by division to differentiate types of heroes. Pick one hero specified in this excerpt or come up with your own and explain why your choice deserves to be called a superhuman or an ordinary person hero.

"A Music Legend Fades to Black"

4. Select another legend from music—someone larger than his or her achievements—such as John Lennon, Janis Joplin, Elvis Presley, Bruce Springsteen, Madonna, Jim Morrison, Woody Guthrie, Pete Seeger, Buddy Holly, or Howling Wolf—and write an analysis by division. Consider using some of the same parts pertaining to Johnny Cash.

5. Using this essay as a model, write about a person in some media other than music or in some field other than music—for example, writing, dancing, painting, and so on.

General Topics

Write a paragraph or an essay about one of the following:

6. A machine such as a specific automobile, a computer, a camera

7. A ceremony—wedding, graduation

8. A holiday celebration, a pep rally, a sales convention, a religious revival

9. An offensive team in football (any team in any game)

10. A family, a relationship, a gang, a club, a sorority, a fraternity

11. A CD, a performance, a song, a singer, an actor, a musical group, a musical instrument

12. A movie, a television program, a video game

13. Any well-known person—athlete, politician, criminal, writer

Cross-Curricular Topics

14. For a paragraph or an essay topic pertaining to a current or former class other than English, select a unit that can be divided into parts. Consult your textbook(s) for ideas on that subject. Talk with your instructor(s) in other fields, especially those that relate to your major field of study. Your writing instructor may require you to photocopy a page or more of your source material if your work is largely summary. Following are a few examples from various disciplines:

    • Art History: Points for analyzing a painting or other work of art

    • Music History: Points for analyzing a musical composition or the performance of a musical composition

    • Agriculture: Points for judging livestock

    • History: Characteristics that made a historical figure great

    • Government: Basic organization of the United Nations

    • Biology: Working parts of an organ or organism

    • Physical Education: Parts of a football team in a particular offensive or defensive formation

    • Business: Structure of management for a particular business

    • Law Enforcement: Organization of a specific precinct

Career-Related Topics

15. Explain how the parts of a particular product function as a unit. Consider using a drawing with labeled parts to aid your explanation.

16. Explain how each of several qualities of a specific person—such as his or her intelligence, sincerity, knowledgeability, ability to communicate, manner, attitude, and appearance—makes that individual an effective salesperson, manager, or employee. Looking at copies of workplace evaluation sheets can help you in deciding on the points you will use.

17. Write a self-evaluation of you as a worker or as a student. Keep in mind that most self-evaluations are more generous than evaluations coming from supervisors.

18. Write an evaluation of a product or service that can be analyzed according to its parts. Name the product or service. Use the Internet or library services as source material.

Writer's Guidelines: Analysis by Division

Almost any unit can be analyzed by division—for example, how the parts of the ear function in hearing; how the parts of an idea represent the whole idea; how the parts of a machine function; how the parts of a committee, department, or company function at the workplace. You can also use analysis by division to evaluate programs, products, and persons. Subjects such as these are all approached with the same systematic procedure.

1. This is the procedure.

   - *Step 1.* Begin with something that is a unit.

   - *Step 2.* State the principle by which that unit functions.

   - *Step 3.* Divide the unit into parts according to the principle.

   - *Step 4.* Discuss each of the parts in relation to the unit.

2. This is the way you might apply that procedure to a good boss.

• Unit	Manager
• Principle of function	Effective as a leader
• Parts based on the principle	Fair, intelligent, stable, competent in the field
• Discussion	Consider each part in relation to the person's effectiveness as a manager.

3. This is how a basic outline of analysis by division might look.

   Thesis: To be effective as a leader, a manager needs specific qualities.
     I. Fairness
    II. Intelligence
   III. Stability
   IV. Competence in the field

   This procedure can be modified for assignments in different disciplines. At the workplace you are likely to have forms for evaluations.

4. Write and revise.

   - Write and then revise your paragraph or essay as many times as necessary for coherence, language (usage, tone, and diction), unity, emphasis, support, and sentences (**CLUESS**). Read your work aloud to hear and correct any grammatical errors or awkward-sounding sentences.

   - Edit any problems in fundamentals, such as capitalization, omissions, punctuation, and spelling (**COPS**).

Comparison and Contrast: Showing Similarities and Differences

As a pattern of thinking, comparison and contrast is relevant to all phases of your life. For example, try to think about something without comparing or contrasting it with something else.

FLOW OF WRITING

Learning Objectives

Working with this chapter, I will learn

~ **the principles of writing comparison and contrast.**

~ **how to use comparison and contrast in different contexts.**

Writing Comparison and Contrast

Comparison and contrast is a method of showing similarities and dissimilarities between subjects. **Comparison** is concerned with organizing and developing points of similarity; **contrast** serves the same function for dissimilarity. Sometimes a writing assignment may require that you cover only similarities or only dissimilarities. Occasionally, an instructor may ask you to separate one from the other. Usually, you will combine them in a paragraph or an essay. For convenience, the term *comparison* is often applied to both comparison and contrast, because both use the same techniques and are usually combined into one operation.

Generating Topics and Working with the 4 *P*s

Comparison and contrast is basic to your thinking. In your daily activities, you consider similarities and dissimilarities among persons, things, concepts, political leaders, doctors, friends, instructors, schools, nations, classes, movies, and so on. You naturally turn to comparison and contrast to solve problems and make decisions in your life and in your writing. Because you have had so much experience comparing, finding a topic to write about is likely to be only a matter of choosing from a great number of appealing ideas. Freewriting, brainstorming, and clustering will help you generate topics that are especially workable and appropriate for particular assignments.

Many college writing assignments will specify a topic or ask you to choose one from a list. Regardless of the source of your topic, the procedure for developing your ideas by comparison and contrast is the same. That procedure can be appropriately called the 4 *P*s: purpose, points, patterns, and presentation.

Purpose

Are you trying to show relationships (how things are similar and dissimilar) or to show that one side is better (ranking)? If you want to show that one actor, one movie, one writer, one president, one product, or one idea is better than another, your purpose is to persuade. You will emphasize the superiority of one side over the other in your topic sentence and in your support.

If you want to explain something about a topic by showing each subject in relationship with others, then your purpose is informative. For example, you might be comparing two composers, Beethoven and Mozart. Both were musical geniuses, so you then decide it would be senseless to argue that one is superior to the other. Instead, you choose to reveal interesting information about both by showing them in relation to each other.

Suppose that you are an immigrant from Vietnam and you want to compare the lives of women in Vietnam and women in America. To narrow your topic, you might decide to focus on women who marry and have children. Your intention is to inform: to show how the women in the two cultures are similar and dissimilar, not to show that one is better than the other. Here is a way in which you might proceed.

Points

First, you would develop a list of ideas, or points, that apply somewhat equally to the two sides. Next, you would select two or three related items and circle them. You might soon discover that some of the items on your list could be combined. You might decide to order your points by time (chronological order, as shown here), space, or emphasis (importance).

cultural background
childhood
education ⟶ growing up
marriage
motherhood ⟶ maturity
hopes ⟶ expectations
reality
satisfaction

Patterns

Then you would organize your material. There are two basic comparison and contrast patterns: subject by subject and point by point.

The **subject-by-subject pattern** presents all of one side and then all of the other.

Topic sentence
I. Vietnam
   A. Growing up

   B. Maturity

   C. Expectations

II. America
   A. Growing up

   B. Maturity

   C. Expectations

Concluding Sentence(s)

The **point-by-point pattern** shows the points in relation to the sides (subjects) one at a time. This is the more common pattern.

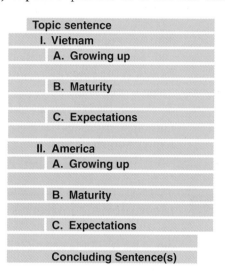

Topic sentence
I. Growing up
   A. Vietnam

   B. America

II. Maturity
   A. Vietnam

   B. America

III. Expectations
   A. Vietnam

   B. America

Concluding Sentence(s)

Presentation

Both patterns of organizing your points can be very effective. The subject-by-subject pattern is strong in that it presents one side completely and then the other, in clear blocks of information. (You can help your reader by occasionally referring to the other side, in phrases such as "Unlike her Vietnamese counterpart," and so on.) The point-by-point pattern groups points closer together and, therefore, establishes connections directly. Each point must be developed; otherwise, this pattern can read like an outline, mechanical and predictable. Some writers believe that the subject-by-subject pattern works best for shorter (paragraph-length) assignments, and the point-by-point pattern works best for longer pieces (essays).

Some assignments may require only comparisons or only contrasts and some a separation of the two, but most assignments require a blending of similarities and dissimilarities in relation to points. Regardless of the pattern you select, you would use your outline (or cluster or list) to begin writing your paper. You would use appropriate explanations, details, and examples for support.

Practicing Patterns of Comparison and Contrast

Shorter compositions such as paragraphs are likely to be arranged subject by subject, and longer compositions such as essays are likely to be arranged point by point, although either pattern can work in either length. In longer works, especially in published writing, the two patterns may be mixed. Being able to organize your material quickly and effectively according to the pattern that is best for your material is important to your success as a writer. Even in a timed assignment, make a simple scratch outline that will guide you in writing a piece that is unified and coherent.

EXERCISE 1   Completing Patterns of Comparison and Contrast

Fill in the blanks to complete the following outlines.

A. Subject-by-subject pattern

Friends: Marla and Justine

    I. Marla   (subject)

        A. Appearance   (point)

        B. _____   (point)

        C. _____   (point)

   II. Justine   (subject)

        A. _____   (point)

        B. Personality   (point)

        C. _____   (point)

B. Point-by-point pattern

Two Bosses: Mr. Santo and Ms. Elliott

    I. Disposition   (point)

       A. Mr. Santo   (subject)

       B. Ms. Elliott   (subject)

    II. Knowledge of _____ (point)

       A. _____ (subject)

       B. Ms. Elliott (subject)

    III. _____ (point)

       A. Mr. Santo (subject)

       B. _____ (subject)

C. Subject-by-subject pattern

Two schools you have attended (or another approved topic)

    I. _____ (subject)

       A. _____ (point)

       B. _____ (point)

       C. _____ (point)

    II. _____ (subject)

       A. _____ (point)

       B. _____ (point)

       C. _____ (point)

D. Point-by-point pattern

Two jobs you have had (or another approved topic)

    I. _____ (point)

       A. _____ (subject)

       B. _____ (subject)

    II. _____ (point)

       A. _____ (subject)

       B. _____ (subject)

    III. _____ (point)

       A. _____ (subject)

       B. _____ (subject)

Connecting Reading and Writing: Cultural Blends and Clashes

Culture here is used in the broad sense to indicate groups of people with recognizable identities. That means generation, ethnic, gender, sexual preference, physical and mental condition, age, and region. As we meet those who are different from us, we may discover up close the considerable range of dissimilarities and at the same time recognize the far greater degree of commonality in human beings. Of course, we can't put an individual into one slot. When we live in a culturally diverse society, we reflect the experiences we have had and the persons we have met; consequently, we come away being a combination of many cultural groups. A person could be an older, female, Asian-American, slightly deaf, Southern, heterosexual individual and thereby take part in six different cultures on the basis of those characteristics alone.

THE QUIGMANS   by Buddy Hickerson

The cultural encounters that we are most aware of concern those we know and those we identify with and, therefore, feel we know. In his essay "The Long and Short of Saying Hello and Good-bye," student Michael Reed discusses some simple accommodations made by families brought together by marriage. In "Superman and Batman," by Judy Urbina, we travel the outer realm of diversity: two imaginary heroes who have become cultural icons. In "A Mixed Tex-Cal Marriage" José Antonio Burciaga discusses what happens when a Texas guy and a California gal get together and sort out differences.

Student Thung Tran takes us on an international journey to explore the different experiences of women in Vietnam and America. Born in Vietnam, Trung Tran emigrated to America as a young girl. After observing her mother make the unsteady transition from Vietnamese woman to American woman, Tran was well qualified to write this comparison and contrast paragraph. Her paragraph "Wives and Mothers in Vietnam and in America" immediately follows with a completed Writing Process Worksheet and her final draft.

Writing Process Worksheet

Title   Wives and Mothers in Vietnam and in America

Name   Thung Tran   **Due Date**   Wednesday, February 16, 10 a.m.

ASSIGNMENT   In the space below, write whatever you need to know about your assignment, including information about the topic, audience, pattern of writing, length, whether to include a rough draft or revised drafts, and whether your paper must be typed.

Write a paragraph of comparison and contrast about two people or two types of people who are culturally different. Use the subject-by-subject pattern. Assume that your readers do not know your subjects well. Turn in this completed worksheet, one or more rough drafts, and a typed final draft.

STAGE ONE   **Explore**   Freewrite, brainstorm (list), cluster, or take notes as directed by your instructor. Use the back of this page or separate paper if you need more space.

Listing

cultural background
childhood
education   ⟶   growing up
marriage
motherhood   ⟶   maturity
hopes   ⟶   expectations
reality
satisfaction

STAGE TWO   **Organize**   Write a topic sentence or thesis; label the subject and the treatment parts.

<u>Vietnamese immigrants discover just how American culture is different</u>
                                    subject
<u>from Vietnamese culture, especially for the women who become wives</u>
                                            treatment
<u>and mothers.</u>

Write an outline or an outline alternative.

I. Vietnam
    A. Growing up
    B. Maturity
    C. Expectations
II. America
    A. Growing up
    B. Maturity
    C. Expectations

Write   On separate paper, write and then revise your paragraph or essay as many times as necessary for **c**oherence, **l**anguage (usage, tone, and diction), **u**nity, **e**mphasis, **s**upport, and **s**entences (**CLUESS**). Read your work aloud to hear and correct any grammatical errors or awkward-sounding sentences.

Edit any problems in fundamentals, such as **c**apitalization, **o**missions, **p**unctuation, and **s**pelling (**COPS**).

Wives and Mothers in Vietnam and in America

Thung Tran

Topic sentence
I.
A.
B.

C.
II.
A.
B.
C.

Concluding sentences

   Fleeing from communism, many Vietnamese left their country to resettle with their families in the United States. <u>Here they discovered just how American culture is different from Vietnamese culture, especially for the women who become wives and mothers</u>. In <u>Vietnam, a young girl</u> is <u>educated in Confucian theories</u>: "Obey your father as a child, and your husband when you get married." Living with her in-laws after marriage, <u>her role</u> is <u>that of child bearer and housekeeper</u>. She has to <u>be</u> a <u>good</u> <u>wife</u>, a <u>good mother</u>, and a <u>good daughter-in-law</u> if she wants to be happy. She is the first to rise and the last to go to bed in a household that includes her husband and his parents. She will seldom make decisions and will always be obedient. <u>She expects</u> her <u>husband to support</u> the <u>family financially</u>, <u>protect her</u>, and <u>help his relatives direct</u> the <u>family</u>. In <u>American</u> society the <u>female</u> has a <u>different pattern</u> of <u>experiences</u>. As <u>a girl</u> she <u>learns to think for herself</u> and <u>develop</u> her <u>talents</u>. <u>After she marries</u>, unlike her Vietnamese counterpart, she <u>is likely to work outside</u> the <u>home</u>. <u>Because she provides a part of</u> the <u>financial support</u>, she <u>expects</u> her <u>husband to share</u> some of the <u>work of raising</u> the <u>children, keeping</u> the <u>house</u>, and <u>maintaining</u> a <u>relationship with</u> the <u>in-laws</u> on <u>both sides, who probably live in</u> a <u>separate house</u>. In <u>America</u>, ideally, the <u>wife</u> and <u>mother</u> will <u>probably</u> have <u>more independence</u> in the <u>home</u> and <u>more responsibilities</u> <u>outside</u> the <u>home</u>. In <u>Vietnam</u> the <u>wife</u> may be left with a <u>secure position</u> but <u>few options</u>.

Discussion and Critical Thinking

1. Has Tran organized her paragraph using a point-by-point or subject-by-subject pattern?

2. List any references to the other side that Tran uses to emphasize her comparison.

3. Does Tran shade the evidence to favor one side?

4. In ideal circumstances what advantages does each woman experience?

The Long and Short of Saying Hello and Good-bye

MICHAEL REED

How people greet each other and say good-bye is a reflection of their culture. Here student Michael Reed analyzes the differences between the behavior of his family and that of his wife's family.

1   After I married Eina, I soon discovered that I had married her family as well and that in the interest of kindness and peace, I should make adjustments. My wife's family is openly emotional, whereas mine tends to be more restrained emotionally. Soon I found myself considering the significance of how each individual is different, each family is different, and each culture is different—even in simple things such as how one says hello and good-bye at family get-togethers.

2   Much of our respective family behavior can be traced to our family size and background. Middle-American from mixed Northern European ancestors, my parents moved to Los Angeles before I was born. My family is very small. It consists of my parents, one sister (married with two daughters), my grandparents (from my mother's side). We live close to each other, but we don't get together very often. My wife's family is very large and is traditionally Italian. Most of her relatives live in Italy or Montreal, Canada. They often have a relative from out of the area staying with one of us in California. My wife has one sister and two brothers, each with a large family, who live a few miles from our house. They love to have family get-togethers to eat, drink wine, and play cards.

3   Regardless of which family is having the party, the same protocol is followed in each, in the sense that we greet and say our farewells. The difference is in how it's done. When my family gets together, it's a small party. When we arrive, I will usually kiss my mother and grandparents. Each of the others gets a "Hello" or "How are you?" The same applies to good-byes. A quick kiss, "See you later," and we're out of there. Nothing that neat and direct occurs at my wife's family get-togethers. First, their parties are larger, and when people start arriving, it's like an orgy of emotional greetings: kissing (one kiss on each cheek), hugging, shaking hands, and more kissing! On some of those occasions, I can have my dinner finished when her family are still kissing, hugging, and saying hello. By this time I'm sometimes ready to go home, but, of course, I don't. When I arrive at one of these parties, I will only kiss my mother- and father-in-law. They have earned and now deserve my respect, which I give them. My brother-in-law, Geno, gets insulted when I don't shake his hand, so I make it a point to give him a special hello and a handshake. All of us get along fine for the duration of the party. Then, from my perspective, it is time for us to simply say good-bye. However, saying good-bye to my wife's family is not simple. This is the time when the kissing and hugging start all over again. While my wife and kids are busy with their more elaborate salutations, I usually just sit down somewhere and wait it out. The time may be as short as ten minutes, but I've timed some at more than an hour.

4   As for me, I like and respect my relatives, and I've made my adjustments. I feel a hello is an excellent greeting and a good-bye is a fine farewell, but people will

naturally do what makes them feel good, which is what they're used to. I think it really doesn't matter if relatives kiss or don't kiss at family get-togethers. What really matters is one's love for family and the things we all do for each other. Regardless of all the superficial differences between my birth and my in-law families, we all have far more in common than not.

EXERCISE 3

Discussion and Critical Thinking

1. Is this essay more comparison or contrast?

2. Is the purpose mainly to inform or to persuade?

3. What are the two main points of contrast Reed uses in his essay?

4. Is the form point by point or subject by subject?

5. Has Michael Reed handled the social situation well?

Superman and Batman

JUDY URBINA

Displaying a keen knowledge of the private lives of Superman and Batman, student Judy Urbina compares these two foremost cultural icons of the comic-book world. We know these crime busters. One leaps over tall buildings, and the other climbs all over the Gotham skyline with his trusty bat hooks. Unfortunately, they never meet face to face, for, despite their many cultural differences, they have much in common. But, Urbina says, we naturally identify more with one than the other. Holy Rhetoric,_____! Which one is it?

1   During the Depression in the 1930s, Superman and Batman were created as the first big comic-book heroes. More than two thousand similar but lesser characters were to follow. Both Superman and Batman have been enormously successful, but one seems to have more personality and is probably closer to most of us emotionally. Which hero wins out in this struggle for our hearts and minds? Taking into account their upbringing, motives, and criminal targets, one can argue that it is Batman who is more credible.

2   Neither came originally from a home environment we are likely to identify with completely. Superman was conceived on the planet Krypton by a highly intelligent couple. His life was threatened because Krypton was going to destruct. Superman's parents bundled him up in a kiddie spacecraft and launched him on a long journey to Earth to save his life. He was raised on a farm by Jonathan and Martha Kent, who adopted him and grew to love him as their own. Batman, on

the other hand, is entirely a product of this planet. Really Bruce Wayne in disguise, Batman was left an orphan by his parents, who were killed in a mugging right in front of him. Fortunately for Bruce Wayne, his parents were rich, and he inherited millions when they died. He was raised by his butler, unlike Superman, who was nurtured by a conventional adoptive mom and dad. Obviously the upbringing of these two heroes had a lot to do with the kind of heroes they grew up to be.

3   Both comic book heroes had different motives for confronting killers and spoilers. Superman instinctively knew he was sent to Earth to fight crime. When his birth parents shipped him off to Earth as an infant, they programmed the spacecraft to educate him on the ways of the Earthlings. Superman's adoptive parents reinforced those lessons by teaching him that he had to hide his powers and use them for the well-being of the human race. On the contrary, Batman soon became a revenge-driven vigilante after his parents were killed in the mugging, so he decided to devote his life to fighting crime, with his butler as a domestic accomplice. To Batman no criminal is a good criminal. Although all of us citizens know we should not take the law into our own hands, nevertheless, we celebrate Superman and Batman as heroes, all the time identifying more with the guy in the fancy bat car.

4   Like all superheroes, each of these two has an arch enemy. Superman's arch enemy is Lex Luther, who has a brilliant criminal mind. Lex Luther is always trying to destroy Superman. He knows everything about Superman, right down to his weakness—the mineral Kryptonite. Batman's main enemy is the Joker. As a teen the Joker killed Batman's parents. Then Batman "accidentally" dropped the Joker into acid and permanently disfigured his face, so they are constantly getting into battles. More people are able to relate to Batman because most of us at least think about vengeance if someone has done us wrong. Superman just wants to fight for "truth, justice, and the American way," all worthwhile values, but they're abstract.

5   Superman does not offer love or self-knowledge as keys to a perfect world. He offers only physical strength. Displaying more cunning and base passion, Batman preys on fears and insecurities of criminals as keys to a perfect world. He wants to keep the bad men and women intimidated and on the run. His presence in Gotham strikes fear in the hearts of the wicked. Neither crime fighter is much concerned about rehabilitation. Mainly they knock heads. But Batman seems to enjoy his work more than Superman because Batman's getting even. The fact that we are in touch with that source of satisfaction says as much about us as it does about Batman.

EXERCISE 4

Discussion and Critical Thinking

1. Does Urbina use a point-by-point or subject-by-subject pattern in this essay?

2. Make a simple point-by-point outline of this essay, using *upbringing, motives,* and *enemies* as Roman-numeral headings.

I. _____

  A. _____

  B. _____

II. _____

  A. _____

  B. _____

III. _____

  A. _____

  B. _____

3. Underline and label the thesis of the essay (in the first paragraph).

4. Underline and label the topic sentences of paragraphs 2, 3, and 4.

5. Why does Superman lose out to Batman, according to the writer, in the battle for credibility?

6. Which character is your favorite? Why?

7. Do these characters resemble your other heroes? Explain.

A Mixed Tex-Cal Marriage

JOSÉ ANTONIO BURCIAGA

A distinguished publisher and writer, José Antonio Burciaga died in 1996, leaving a rich legacy of poems, short stories, and essays. He was a Chicano cultural activist, muralist, humorist, and founding member of the comedy group Culture Clash. His Undocumented Love *won the Before Columbus American Book Award for poetry in 1992. This essay, about him and his wife, is included in his book* Drink Cultura *(1993).*

1   According to Cecilia, my wife, we have a mixed marriage. She's from California, I'm from Texas. Though we have no regrets, this truly proves that love is blind.

2   When Cecilia and I first met, we thought we had a lot in common. As young, professional Chicanos in Washington, D.C., we both supported the United Farm Workers' grape and lettuce boycotts, the Coors boycott, the Gallo Wine boycott,

the Farah Pants boycott, and the Frito Bandito boycott. We still boycott some of those items, for many reasons; health, habit, nostalgia or plain, ordinary guilt if we indulged in any of these.

3   As first-generation Mexican-Americans, we both spoke *Español,* graduated from Catholic schools, and had similar politics.

4   But, as we were soon to discover, the vast desert that separates Texas and California also differentiates the culture and style of Chicanos. Because we met far from Texas and California, we had no idea at first of the severity of our differences.

5   We both liked enchiladas—the same enchiladas, I thought, until the first time Cecilia prepared them. They looked like enchiladas, and they smelled like enchiladas. And then I bit into one.

6   "These are good, *corazón,*" I said. "But these are *entomatadas.* They have more tomato than chili. *Mí Mamá* used to make them all the time."

7   She threw me a piquant stare as I chewed away. "Hmmm, they're great!" I stressed through a mouthful.

8   Californians, like her parents who immigrated from the coastal state of Jalisco, Mexico, use more tomatoes than Texans like my parents, who came from the central states of Durango and Zacatecas and use more chilis.

9   Cecilia grew up with white *menudo,* tripe soup. White menudo? How could anyone eat colorless menudo? And not put hominy in it? Ours was red-hot and loaded with hominy. In Texas, we ate our menudo with bread. In California, it's with tortillas. Texas flour tortillas are thick and tasty, California flour tortillas are so thin you can see through them.

10   She didn't particularly like my Tony Lama boots or my country-western and Tex-Mex musical taste. I wasn't that crazy about Beach Boys music or her progressive, California-style country-western.

11   In California, the beach was relatively close for Cecilia. On our first date she asked how often I went to the beach from El Paso. Apparently, geography has never been a hot subject in California schools. That's understandable considering the sad state of education, especially geography, in this country. But in Texas, at one time the biggest state in the union, sizes and distances are most important.

12   In answer to Cecilia's question, I explained that to get to the closest beach from El Paso, I had to cross New Mexico, Arizona and California to reach San Diego. That's 791 freeway miles. The closest Texas beach is 841 freeway miles to the Gulf of Mexico.

13   Back when we were courting, California Chicanos saw *Texanos* as a little too *Mexicano,* still wet behind the ears, not assimilated enough, and speaking with either thick Spanish accents or "Taxes acksaints."

14   Generally speaking, Texanos saw their *Califas* counterparts as too weird, knowing too little if any Spanish and with speech that was too Anglicized.

15   After our marriage we settled in neutral Alexandria, Virginia, right across the Potomac from the nation's capital. We lived there a couple of years, and when our firstborn came, we decided to settle closer to home. But which home, Califas or Texas? In El Paso we wouldn't be close to the beach, but I thought there was an ocean of opportunity in that desert town. There was some Texas pride and machismo, to be sure. It was a tug-of-war that escalated to the point of seeking advice, and eventually I had to be realistic and agree that California had better opportunities. In EPT, the opportunities in my field were nonexistent.

16   The rest is relative bliss. Married since 1972, I'm totally spoiled and laid-back in Northern Califas, but I still miss many of those things we took for granted in Texas, or Washington, D.C.—the seasonal changes, the snow, the heat, heating

systems, autumn colors, and monsoon rains; the smell of the desert after a rain, the silence and serenity of the desert, the magnified sounds of a fly or cricket, distant horizons uncluttered by trees, and the ability to find the four directions without any problem. I do miss the desert and, even more, the food. El Paso *is* the Mexican-food capital of this country.

17   Today, I like artichokes and appreciate a wide variety of vegetables and fruits. I even like white, colorless menudo and hardly ever drink beer. I drink wine, but it has to be a dry Chardonnay or Fumé Blanc although a Pinot Noir or Cabernet Sauvignon goes great with meals. Although I still yearn for an ice cold Perla or Lone Star beer from Texas once in a while, Califas is my home now—mixed marriage and all.

EXERCISE 5

Discussion and Critical Thinking

1. Which sentence states the thesis most emphatically (see paragraph 1)? Copy it here.

2. In paragraphs 6 through 15, what are the three points used for comparison and contrast?

3. In paragraphs 16 and 17 Burciaga discusses how he has changed. In what ways does that imply comparison and contrast?

4. Because all of us are culturally complex, being the products of many cultures, we frequently blend and clash with others in matters of age, ethnicity, gender, sexual preferences, religion, and so on. As for the broad concept of "mixed marriage," are Cecilia and José fairly typical compared with other marriage partners you know? Do you have some examples of those more extreme and less extreme? You might also discuss this topic in connection with friendships you have or know about.

Topics for Writing Comparison and Contrast

You will find a blank Writing Process Worksheet on page 7, which can be photocopied, filled in, and submitted with each assignment if your instructor directs you to do so.

Reading Related Topics

"Wives and Mothers in Vietnam and in America"

1. Using this paragraph as a model, write about men or women in different societies. Begin with whatever they have in common and then discuss how their experiences are different. You might want instead to consider different aspects of one society: city and suburb, male and female, straight and gay, young and old,

and so on. As you compare and contrast, keep in mind that you are generalizing and that individuals differ within groups—avoid stereotyping.

"The Long and Short of Saying Hello and Good-bye"

2. Compare two families you are familiar with in terms of their temperament, especially their ways of expressing emotion.

"Superman and Batman"

3. Select two other pop-culture icons and compare and contrast them: Rambo and Tarzan, the Terminator and Ghostbusters, two well-known athletes such as Jeter and Sosa or Coleman and James, two other comic-book characters, two characters from sitcom or a cop drama, one character from a television series and a real person (either a well-known person—perhaps a celebrity—or just someone you know, such as a family member or friend).

"A Mixed Tex-Cal Marriage"

4. Using this essay as inspiration, write about a marriage or relationship between two individuals who are significantly different. Consider making a list about their possible differences (such as religion; education; country, city, or suburban background; politics; ethnicity; preferences for food, activities, behavior). In your discussion don't overlook the common characteristics that brought and keep them together, and briefly mention how each person has compromised.

General Topics

Narrow one of the following topics for a paragraph or short essay. For example, "Methods of Disciplining Children" may be too broad, but "Two Parents, Two Styles of Discipline," with names given, might work well.

5. Romantic attachments
6. Methods of disciplining children
7. Courage and recklessness
8. Hope and expectations
9. Relatives
10. Passive student and active student
11. Two dates
12. Married and living together
13. Two neighborhoods
14. Two malls
15. Two businesses you know well: big box stores, restaurants, fast-food places, automobile repair shops, gyms, beauty shops, and so on. Name the places and refer to specific experiences by you or other reliable sources, including rankings and evaluations you can find on the Internet and in the library.
16. Two products. Use library sources such as *Consumer Reports* or the Internet for information. Consider automobiles, motorcycles, appliances, clothing, electronics, furniture, housewares, and so on.

Cross-Curricular Topics

17. In the field of your interest or involvement, compare and contrast two theories, two prominent people, two practices, two products, or two services.

18. In the fields of nutritional science and health, compare and contrast two diets, two exercise programs, or two pieces of exercise equipment.

19. Compare and contrast your field of study (or one aspect of it) as it existed some time ago (specify the years) and as it is now. Refer to new developments and discoveries, such as scientific breakthroughs and technological advances.

Career-Related Topics

20. Compare and contrast two products or services, with the purpose of showing that one is better.

21. Compare and contrast two management styles or two working styles.

22. Compare and contrast the operations of a public school and a business.

23. Compare and contrast the operations of an athletic team and a business.

Writer's Guidelines: Comparison and Contrast

1. Work with the 4 *P*s:

- *Purpose:* Decide whether you want to inform (show relationships) or to persuade (show that one side is better).

- *Points:* Decide which ideas you will apply to each side. Consider beginning by making a list to select from. Order can be based on time, space, or emphasis.

- *Patterns:* Decide whether to use subject-by-subject or point-by-point organization.

- *Presentation:* Decide to what extent you should develop your ideas. Use references to the other side to make connections and use examples and details to support your views.

2. Your basic subject-by-subject outline will probably look like this:

I. Subject 1

    A. Point 1

    B. Point 2

    C. Point 3

II. Subject 2

    A. Point 1

    B. Point 2

    C. Point 3

3. Your basic point-by-point outline will probably look like this:

   I. Point 1

      A. Subject 1

      B. Subject 2

   II. Point 2

      A. Subject 1

      B. Subject 2

   III. Point 3

      A. Subject 1

      B. Subject 2

4. Write and revise.

- Write and then revise your paragraph or essay as many times as necessary for coherence, language (usage, tone, and diction), unity, emphasis, support, and sentences (**CLUESS**). Read your work aloud to hear and correct any grammatical errors or awkward-sounding sentences.

- Edit any problems in fundamentals, such as capitalization, omissions, punctuation, and spelling (**COPS**).

Argument: Writing to Persuade

*Often one side is demanding freedom,
and the other is insisting on regulation for
public good.*

To Regulate or Not?

FLOW OF WRITING

Learning Objectives

Working with this chapter, I will learn to

~ structure an argument.

~ use different kinds of supporting
   evidence.

~ avoid logical fallacies.

~ write patterns of argument that
   persuade.

Writing Argument

Persuasion and Argument Defined

Persuasion is a broad term. When we persuade, we try to influence people to think in a certain way or to do something. **Argument** is persuasion on a topic about which reasonable people disagree. Argument involves controversy. Whereas exercising appropriately is probably not controversial because reasonable people do not dispute the idea, an issue such as gun control is. In this chapter we will be concerned mainly with the kind of persuasion that involves argument.

Components of Argument

Statements of argument are informal or formal in design. An opinion column in a newspaper is likely to have little set structure, whereas an argument in college writing is likely to be tightly organized. Nevertheless, the opinion column and the college paper have much in common. Both provide a proposition, which is the main point of the argument, and both provide support, which is the evidence or the reasons that back up the proposition.

For a well-structured paragraph or essay, an organizational plan is desirable. Consider these elements when you write, and ask yourself the following questions as you develop your ideas.

Background: What is the historical or social context for this controversial issue?

Proposition (the topic sentence of a paragraph of argument and the thesis of an essay): What do I want my audience to believe or to do?

Qualification of proposition: Can I limit my proposition so that those who disagree cannot easily challenge me with exceptions? If, for example, I am in favor of using animals for scientific experimentation, am I concerned only with medical experiments or with any use, including that pertaining to the cosmetic industry?

Refutation (taking the opposing view into account, mainly to point out its fundamental weakness): What is the view on the other side, and why is it flawed in reasoning or evidence?

Support: In addition to sound reasoning, can I use appropriate facts, examples, statistics, and opinions of authorities?

The basic form for a paragraph or an essay of argument includes the proposition (the topic sentence) and support. The support sentences are, in effect, *because* statements; that is, the proposition is valid *because* of the support. Your organization should look something like this.

Proposition (topic sentence): It is time to pass a national law restricting smoking in public places.

 I. Discomfort of the nonsmoker (support 1)

 II. Health of the nonsmoker (support 2)

 III. Cost to the nation (support 3)

Kinds of Support

In addition to sound reasoning generally, you can use these kinds of support: facts, examples, statistics, and authorities.

First, you can offer facts. Martin Luther King Jr. was killed in Memphis, Tennessee, on April 4, 1968. Because an event that has happened is true and can be verified, this statement about King is a fact. But that James Earl Ray acted alone in killing King is to some questionable. That King was the greatest of all civil rights leaders is also opinion because it cannot be verified.

Some facts are readily accepted because they are general knowledge—you and your reader know them to be true because they can be or have been verified. Other "facts" are based on personal observation and are reported in various publications but may be false or questionable. You should always be concerned about the reliability of the source for both the information you use and the information used by those with other viewpoints. Still other "facts" are genuinely debatable because of their complexity or the incompleteness of the knowledge available.

Second, you can cite examples. If you use examples, you must present a sufficient number, and the examples must be relevant.

Third, you can present statistics. Statistics are facts and data of a numerical kind that are classified and tabulated to present significant information about a given subject.

Avoid presenting a long list of figures; select statistics carefully and relate them to things familiar to your reader. The millions of dollars spent on a war in a single week, for example, become more comprehensible when expressed in terms of what the money would purchase in education, highways, or urban renewal.

To test the validity of statistics, either yours or your opponent's, ask: Who gathered them? Under what conditions? For what purpose? How are they used?

Fourth, you can cite evidence from, and opinions of, authorities. Most readers accept facts from recognized, reliable sources—governmental publications, standard reference works, and books and periodicals published by established firms. In addition, they will accept evidence and opinions from individuals who, because of their knowledge and experience, are recognized as experts.

In using authoritative sources as support, keep these points in mind:

- Select authorities who are generally recognized as experts in their field.

- Use authorities who qualify in the field pertinent to your argument.

- Select authorities whose views are not biased.

- Try to use several authorities.

- Identify an authority's credentials clearly in your paragraph or essay.

EXERCISE 1

Fact or Opinion?

Identify the italicized statements as fact (F) or opinion (O). (See Answer Key for answers.)

Elvis deserves to be called the King of Rock and Roll. Born in 1935 in Tupelo, Mis-
                                    1   **2**
sissippi, he went on to become *the greatest entertainer of the mid-twentieth century.*
                                                            3
Eighteen of his songs were No. 1. His movie musicals are still seen and loved by tele-
            4
vision viewers. Who can watch *Viva Las Vegas* and not admire his versatility? His

fans are still enthusiastic. *More than 500,000 people go to Graceland each year* to
                              5
visit his grave and see his former home, and *every month over fifty letters arrive*
                                                                              6
there, all addressed to Elvis Presley. *That kind of attention is appropriate for the King.*
                                                                          7

1. _____   5. _____

2. _____   6. _____

3. _____   7. _____

4. _____

EXERCISE 2

Fact or Opinion?

Identify each sentence as one based on fact (F) or opinion (O).

_____ 1. Blue jeans were first worn by miners in the 1849 Gold Rush.

_____ 2. They were made of canvas that originally had been ordered to use in constructing tents.

_____ 3. They became the best pants the miners ever wore.

_____ 4. Later, jeans were sold to American farmers.

_____ 5. By the 1960s, blue jeans caught on with several prominent fashion designers.

_____ 6. Europeans adopted blue jeans as the natural clothes style for rock-and-roll music.

_____ 7. Blue jeans are still scarce in Eastern Europe.

_____ 8. They were once smuggled in and sold there on the black market.

_____ 9. Some people apparently regarded blue jeans as a symbol of rebellion.

_____ 10. The love of blue jeans will never end.

Logical Fallacies

Certain flawed patterns in thought, commonly called **logical fallacies,** are of primary concern in critical thinking.

These are among the most common logical fallacies:

1. *Post hoc, ergo propter hoc* (After this, therefore because of this): When one event precedes another in time, the first is assumed to cause the other.

   > "I knew I'd have a day like this when I saw that black cat run across the driveway this morning."

   > "See what I told you. We elected him president, and now we have high inflation."

2. *False analogy:* False analogies ignore differences and stress similarities, often in an attempt to prove something.

   > "A person has to get a driver's license because unqualified drivers could have bad effects on society. Therefore, couples should also have to get a license to bear children because unqualified parents can produce delinquent children."

   > "The leader of that country is a mad dog dictator, and you know what you do with a mad dog. You get a club and kill it."

3. *Hasty generalization:* This is a conclusion based on too few reliable instances.

   > "Everyone I've met this morning is going to vote for the incumbent. The incumbent is going to win."

   > "How many people did you meet?"

   > "Three."

4. *False dilemma:* This fallacy presents the reader with only two alternatives from which to choose. The solution may lie elsewhere.

   > "Now, only two things can be done with the school district. You either shut it down now or let it go bankrupt."

   > "The way I see it, you either bomb them back into the Stone Age or let them keep on pushing us around."

5. *Argumentum ad hominem* (Arguing against the person): This is the practice of abusing and discrediting your opponent instead of keeping to the main issues of the argument.

   > "Who cares what he has to say? After all, he's a wild-eyed liberal who has been divorced twice."

   > "Let's put aside the legislative issue for one moment and talk about the person who proposed it. For one thing he's a southerner. For another he's Catholic. Enough said."

EXERCISE 3   ## Critical Thinking

Each of the following sentences is based on a logical fallacy. Identify the logical fallacies with these labels: post hoc (PH), false analogy (FA), hasty generalization (HG), false dilemma (FD), or ad hominem (AH). (See Answer Key for answers.)

_____ 1. It's no wonder she had a terrible honeymoon. She didn't wear something blue during the wedding ceremony.

_____ 2. My kids' loud music is driving me crazy. There are only two possible solutions: either the boom boxes go or the kids go.

_____ 3. After reading two Harlequin romances, I can say that the French are the most romantic people in the world.

_____ 4. I'm not surprised. You elect a liberal mayor, and now taxes have gone up.

_____ 5. Larry Brown says that practice makes perfect. So I plan to get married lots of times before I settle down.

_____ 6. I can't recommend the fiction of F. Scott Fitzgerald. What could an admitted alcoholic have to say that would be of value?

_____ 7. I'm not surprised. I knew I'd win the Pillsbury bake-off when I found that lucky penny this morning.

_____ 8. Today I met a group of ten Russian tourists. Now I can see why people say the Russians are friendly.

_____ 9. Joe DiMaggio has always liked his coffee, and now he's in the Hall of Fame. Obviously the secret to becoming a great baseball player is in your coffee maker.

_____ 10. How can you take heavy metal music seriously? The musicians who play that stuff are druggies with long hair and tattoos.

EXERCISE 4   ## Critical Thinking

Each of the following sentences is based on a logical fallacy. Identify the logical fallacies with these labels: post hoc (PH), false analogy (FA), hasty generalization (HG), false dilemma (FD), or ad hominem (AH).

_____ 1. I trained my dog not to wet on the carpet by rubbing his nose in the "mess" he created; therefore, I will potty train my children by rubbing their noses in the "messes" they make.

_____ 2. The continued use of nuclear energy will lead to either nuclear war or catastrophic nuclear accidents.

_____ 3. Everyone in the front office is dipping Lippy Snuff. I figure it's the hottest item on the market.

_____ 4. Our dog eats only once a day, and look how healthy he is. I don't know why you kids keep yellin' for three meals a day.

_____ 5. No wonder she's been going around crying all day. Yesterday the government slapped a tax on Lippy Snuff.

_____ 6. I refuse to listen to his musical interpretation of the Yalta Conference because he's a card-carrying member of the ACLU.

_____ 7. Either we cave in to the terrorist demands, or we strike back with nuclear weapons.

_____ 8. After watching the high school kids on the bus today, I would say that the whole education system could use a required course in manners.

_____ 9. It's no wonder my Winnebago exploded today. Yesterday I bought a tank of cheap gasoline.

_____ 10. I wouldn't trust him as far as I can throw a heifer. He rides a Harley and drinks Rebel Yell.

Practicing Patterns of Argument

The formal pattern of argument is not always followed in a set sequence, but the main components—the proposition and support—are always included. As your own argument evolves, you should also consider whether to qualify your proposition and whether to include a refutation.

EXERCISE 5

Completing Patterns of Argument

Fill in the blanks with supporting statements for each proposition. Each outline uses the following pattern:

Proposition

    I. Support 1

    II. Support 2

    III. Support 3

A. Proposition: College athletes should be paid.

    I. _____

    II. They work long hours in practice and competition.

III. They have less time than many other students for study.

B. Proposition: Zoos are beneficial institutions.

I. _____

II. They preserve endangered species by captive breeding.

III. They study animal diseases and find cures.

EXERCISE 6

Completing Patterns of Argument

Complete the following outline. Use your own topic or write on the topic "There should be no curfew for teenagers" or "There should be a curfew for teenagers."

Proposition: _____

I. _____ (Support 1)

II. _____ (Support 2)

III. _____ (Support 3)

EXERCISE 7

Completing Patterns of Argument

Complete the following outline. Use your own topic or write on the topic "Known gang members should be prohibited from using public parks" or "Known gang members should not be prohibited from using public parks."

Proposition: _____

I. _____ (Support 1)

II. _____ (Support 2)

III. _____ (Support 3)

Connecting Reading and Writing: To Regulate or Not

Automobile speed, drinking, skateboarding, taxes, benefits, bicycling, concerts, the price of milk, imports, immigration, HMOs, housing density, interest rates, voting, seat belts, helmets for cyclists, insecticides, wetlands, airport noise—what do those words make you think of? Probably laws and restrictions—and people arguing. Often one side is demanding freedom, and the other is insisting on regulation for public good. Ideally, the opposing sides will express their views calmly and logically, moderating the heat of their passion with the coolness of reason.

That is the tone we seek in argumentation. Two essays may surprise you with their propositions: "A Modest Proposal: Guys Shouldn't Drive Till 25" and "Let Granny Drive If She Can." Another essay carries the issue as a title: "Is It Time for Cameras in the Classroom?"

Student Eric Miller has written both a paragraph and an essay version of "A New Wind Blowing," demonstrating how a well-constructed paragraph can be expanded into an essay. Miller argues that in certain circumstances restrictions should be imposed on smokers. He isn't asking people to stop smoking, he's just asking them only to stop smoking in public places. Reading his Writing Process Worksheet, we can trace his exploration of the topic and the organization of his short and long papers. His rough drafts are not included here.

You will find a full-size blank worksheet on page 7, which can be photocopied, filled in, and submitted with each assignment if your instructor directs you to do so.

THE QUIGMANS   **by Buddy Hickerson**

"I'm gonna let you off with a warning this time, but from here on in, try and keep your conversation at a pretentions level."

B. Hickerson, copyright Los Angeles Times Syndicate. All rights reserved.

Writing Process Worksheet

Title   A New Wind Blowing

Name   Eric Miller   **Due Date** Monday, September 5, 10 a.m.

ASSIGNMENT   In the space below, write whatever you need to know about your assignment, including information about the topic, audience, pattern of writing, length, whether to include a rough draft or revised drafts, and whether your paper must be typed.

Write a paragraph of argumentation on an approved topic. Length: about 250 to 300 words. Audience: general, some who disagree with your view. Research your topic. Include different kinds of evidence. Submit this completed worksheet, one or more rough drafts, and a typed final draft.

STAGE ONE   **Explore**   Freewrite, brainstorm (list), cluster, or take notes as directed by your instructor. Use the back of this page or separate paper if you need more space.

Clustering

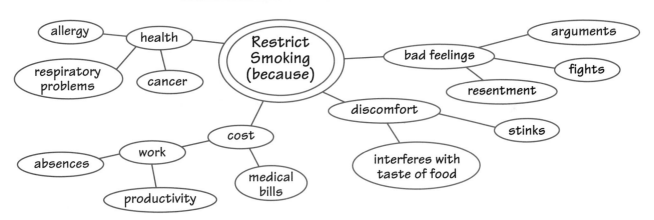

STAGE TWO   **Organize**   Write a topic sentence or thesis; label the subject and the treatment parts.

Smoking in public places should be restricted by a national law.
          subject   treatment

Write an outline or an outline alternative.

I. Smokers unhappy if restricted
  A. Belief of violation of their rights
  B. But could benefit
II. Main reason to restrict smoking: health
  A. Illness and death from secondhand smoke
    1. Many people with respiratory illness
    2. Califano estimates 5,000 deaths a year
  B. Cancer from secondhand smoke
    1. Secondary smoke listed as a carcinogen
    2. Nonsmokers with smokers, 80 percent more likely to get cancer

III. Second reason: discomfort
   A. Disagreeable odor
   B. Must be seen in relation to whole problem
IV. Third reason: cost
   A. Medical bills
   B. Lost productivity

STAGE THREE

Write   On separate paper, write and then revise your paragraph or essay as many times as necessary for **c**oherence, **l**anguage (usage, tone, and diction), **u**nity, **e**mphasis, **s**upport, and **s**entences (**CLUESS**). Read your work aloud to hear and correct any grammatical errors or awkward-sounding sentences.

Edit any problems in fundamentals, such as **c**apitalization, **o**missions, **p**unctuation, and **s**pelling (**COPS**).

A New Wind Blowing
(paragraph)
Eric Miller

One of the most common complaints heard in restaurants and work places pertains to smoking. In all crowded public places, when a smoker lights up, people get upset for reasons they believe are valid. Along with them, I say <u>it is time to pass a national law restricting smoking in public places</u>. <u>Reasonable exceptions can be worked out</u>. Three reasons make this proposition right. <u>One is discomfort</u>. Most people don't like to breathe secondhand smoke. It smells bad. <u>That reason is coupled with the health reason</u>. Studies indicate (as reported by Joseph Califano, former Secretary of Health, Education, and Welfare) <u>that more than 5,000 Americans die each year from secondhand smoke and that people living with smokers are 80 percent more likely to get lung cancer than those who do not live with smokers</u>. In 1993 <u>the Environmental Protection Agency formally classified secondhand smoke as a potent carcinogen</u>—in a class with asbestos. <u>Connected with this health problem is the matter of cost</u>. The last five surgeons general have agreed that secondhand smoke is a significant health problem, with a huge cost to society in medical bills and lost job productivity. Although many smokers concur with the proposal for restriction, <u>others feel that they would lose their rights. They shouldn't</u>. They can continue to smoke, but only if they do not jeopardize the health of others in public places. <u>Discomfort, bad health, and bills for taxpayers are too much for society to pay to live without restriction</u>.

Proposition (topic sentence)
Qualification
Support 1

Support 2
Authoritative statement with statistics

Authoritative statement

Support 3

Refutation

Concluding sentence

EXERCISE 8

Discussion and Critical Thinking

1. Why does Miller qualify his proposition?

2. What are the different kinds of support offered by Miller?

3. Assume the position of those who take the other view. How would you argue against Miller?

A New Wind Blowing
(essay)
Eric Miller

Fact

Confusion prevails on the issue of smoking in public places. Both smokers and nonsmokers are confused and would like the problem solved. On one side are many who, because of preference or addiction, desire to smoke. On the other side are primarily those who do not smoke and do not want to breathe the smoke of those who do. Laws vary from community to community; businesspersons wonder what is morally right and what price they may eventually have to pay in relation to this issue. For all the right reasons, the solution has become quite clear.

Thesis/proposition

It is time to pass a national law restricting smoking in public places.

Refutation

Smokers may be disturbed by this proposition. They may feel that their rights would be violated both at work and elsewhere. They shouldn't, because a national law restricting them can benefit them also. This law would eliminate the hostility felt by a large percentage of the nonsmokers and, therefore, improve relationships between smokers and nonsmokers. Moreover, no one will be fired, and no one will be deprived of the privilege of visiting public places; the only restriction is on smoking. The smokers can continue to puff away—as long as they do not imperil the health of others.

Support

Authoritative statement

The main reason that smoking should be restricted is the issue of health, the health of those who breathe secondhand smoke. Joseph Califano, former Secretary of Health, Education, and Welfare, reports that more than 5,000 Americans die each year because of secondhand smoke, and that nonsmokers who live with smokers are 80 percent more likely to get lung cancer than those who are married to nonsmokers. Moreover, some people are allergic to tobacco smoke, and some have respiratory illnesses that are made worse by the tobacco smoke. In 1993, the Environmental Protection Agency classified tobacco smoke as a carcinogen and placed it in a group with asbestos. The study by the EPA discovered that all people tested—and many were nonsmokers—had nicotine in their blood.

Statistics

Statistics

Examples

Fact

Support

A second reason is the discomfort factor. Tobacco smoke has a disagreeable odor to most nonsmokers. In a restaurant, the pleasing aroma of food is altered, if not destroyed, by tobacco smoke, and because the senses of smell and taste are so closely related, tobacco smoke interferes with the pleasure of eating. The smell also clings to the clothes and hair of nonsmokers. There are, of course, other unpleasant clinging odors created by human beings, and were it not for the fact that secondhand smoke is a health issue, the discomfort factor might not be enough to warrant the proposed restriction.

Support

Authoritative statement

Fact

Another factor is the cost involved. The last five surgeons general have agreed that secondhand smoke is a significant problem with huge costs to the entire nation. Nonsmokers and all taxpayers pay large sums to take care of problems caused by secondhand smoke. People who are made ill by secondhand tobacco smoke miss work, losing time and money, and their employers lose productivity. Some may argue that creating nonsmoking areas, installing signs, and enforcing the rules would cost money, but the bill for these adjustments is nowhere close to what we are paying in the absence of a national law.

Concluding sentence

Powerful lobbies for tobacco companies are on the other side. But on the side of restriction are logic, honesty, and an abundance of scientific information. On the side of restriction is also a large group of smokers who are unable or unwilling to quit smoking and see the rightness of such a proposal. A new wind is blowing across the nation—and it is smoke free, at least in public places.

A Modest Proposal: Guys Shouldn't Drive Till 25

JOYCE GALLAGHER

Freelance writer Joyce Gallagher says we should look at the national problem of motor vehicle accidents and take a "drastic" step. To Gallagher, statistics tell the story, and the solution is as inevitable to her as it may be unthinkable to you.

1   In the year 2001, 57,480 people were killed in motor vehicle accidents. That figure is within a few hundred of being the same number as those killed in the Vietnam War. We took drastic measures back in the early 1970s and ended that war in a way shocking to some: we left. The time has come for another drastic scheme. We need to recognize the main causes of this highway carnage and take action. According to the U.S. Department of Transportation, 25.1 percent of the roadway fatalities involve an age group constituting only 14.5 percent of the driving public. That group is the age range from 15 to 25. Within that group, one half are males. They are three times more likely to be involved in roadway fatalities, meaning that the about 7 percent males are responsible for more than 16 percent of roadway fatalities. This proposal may be a hard sell for politicians, but it is time for us to step forward boldly and raise the legal driving age for males nationally to 25.

2   Some may protest that it is unfair to punish the good young male drivers for the sins of their irresponsible peers. But we're already discriminating by group. Surely we all agree that drivers of a certain age should not be allowed to drive. That age varies from state to state, but it is around 15 or 16. We have concluded that those younger than 15 are too immature. We don't say those under 15 should be treated individually, not even on the basis of gender. Instead, we exclude the offending group. With my proposal, we would simply move the legal age of male drivers to 25, lumping those of similar age and sex together for the good of society.

3   For you who would like to point out that some oldsters are also menaces on the roadways, I would say that those over 88 are equal only to those between 15 and 25 for being involved in fatal crashes. Moreover, the crashes by super-seniors are likely to be caused by physical and mental impairments, which can be detected by periodic tests and remedied by pulled licenses, whereas the young, often irresponsible and impatient, are more likely to be guided by thrill-seeking impulses, tantrums, and other byproducts of testosterone, all of which are hopelessly glandular.

4   Although one salient reason—that this group of young males is responsible for the deaths of so many fellow citizens—is enough support for the proposed law, there are many side benefits for society.

- While the male 15–25 age group is waiting to drive motor vehicles, they would have time to improve their cultural lives and to lay groundwork for better driving skills and improved mental and physical health.

- Many youngsters would customarily ride with statistically superior female or elder drivers and could learn from the relatively good examples they witness.

- Being no more dependent on driving almost everywhere, the male youngsters would walk more or ride bikes or skateboards, providing them wholesome exercise so often neglected in our paunchy, weight-challenged society.

- As a group they would also use more public transportation, relieving traffic congestion on our roadways and reducing congestion in the air we breathe.

- Support for public transportation projects would soar, and cars might cease to be near the center of our lives.

- Car payment money now impoverishing so many young males might go toward savings, education, home improvement, self-improvement, and family activities.

- Gratitude from young male drivers for the rides provided by female spouses and other loved ones could promote affectionate and appreciative relationships and diminish road rage.

5   The only exceptions to this new national law would be for the military and for public security and emergency agencies. Within the armed services, male personnel under 25 would be allowed to drive on foreign soil or on military property at any time. Male drivers working for police, fire, rescue, and ambulance services would drive only when on duty and their permits would be terminated for any serious traffic infraction. No doubt, some male youngsters, obsessed with driving motor vehicles, would join our public service sectors, making our national security and infrastructural services stronger so we could all sleep more peacefully.

6   Probably some males would protest this law and would try to circumvent it with devious strategies. Such resistance could be easily combated. For example, those who attempt to cross-dress or dye their hair gray for the purpose of obtaining a drivers' license could be charged with a felony.

7   Several people who have read my modest proposal have suggested that young men are victims of their own bodies and could plead a "testosterone dementia defense." Therefore, they should be allowed to take injections of estrogen to neutralize the male hormones raging like tiny bulls within their systems. However, even these critics would surely concede that there could be a feminizing reaction to estrogen, one both psychological and physiological. Because of those possible side effects, wives of young men might find estrogen therapy unacceptable. A youthful bride might willingly bear the burden of transporting her husband to work and back, whereas she would almost certainly recoil at the thought of his wearing her bra.

8   Some might argue that improved drivers' education programs in our school system, better public transportation, the production of vehicles that are no more powerful and threatening than they need be, a reduced speed limit, counseling and restrictions for repeat offenders, and a stricter enforcement of existing laws represent a wiser approach to our national problem. However, because those ideas have failed to resonate, and young males have continued to put the pedal to the metal in a flood of blood, it is time for a simple statement that will fit on your bumper sticker:

> # Guys Shouldn't Drive Till 25

EXERCISE 9

Vocabulary Highlights

Write a short definition of each word as it is used in the essay. (Paragraph numbers are given in parentheses.) Be prepared to use the words in your own sentences.

carnage (1)   salient (4)

constituting (1)   terminated (5)

impairments (3)   sectors (5)

testosterone (3)   circumvent (6)

glandular (3)   estrogen (7)

EXERCISE 10

Discussion and Critical Thinking

1. What is the proposition?

2. How is the proposition introduced in the first paragraph?

3. How is the proposition qualified?

4. Which paragraph covers the main rebuttal (addressing the main anticipated point(s) of the opposition)?

5. What is Gallagher's main support?

6. In what way are the bulleted items related to support?

7. Would this law create some problems not discussed by the author?

8. Which of the bulleted items would you disagree with and why?

9. Do you think the author is entirely serious about this argument? What author comments might suggest that she is not?

10. Does it make any difference that the author is female?

Let Granny Drive If She Can

SUZANNE FIELDS

A syndicated columnist for the Washington Times, *Suzanne Fields writes opinion articles twice a week on topics that often polarize her readers. Here she addresses the idea of restricting drivers' privileges because of age.*

1   My mother at 85 was alert, with good vision and sharp reflexes for her age, but one day she smashed into three parked cars on a supermarket parking lot. We never found out exactly how it happened—she was not sure, either—but the investigators figured Mom hit the accelerator instead of the brake. When the car didn't slow down, she panicked and pushed down harder on the wrong pedal. This may be what happened to the 86-year-old man who plowed through that California farmers' market.

2   Mom was lucky, even though she spent two weeks in the hospital with two broken ribs. But we reluctantly concluded that it was time to take Mom's car keys. This was the hardest thing I have ever had to do. She pleaded, cajoled and demanded to keep her car. I was "mean" and "unfeeling," and her gentle voice grew strident. Tears trickled down her cheeks. I think she never felt old until that moment, when I took away the independence provided by the car. I felt like the wicked witch of the west, and the other points of the compass as well.

3   In the days that followed, we suggested that she take taxis to visit friends and to shop, but she wouldn't do it: "That's not my style." A driver was out of the question because she had no set places she had to go. She was not a lady for "Driving Miss Daisy." Fortunately, she lived in the city and quickly slipped into the routine of taking the bus, which she hadn't done since high school. She got to know the bus drivers and waved at them as they drove past her on her frequent strolls through the neighborhood. She began to enjoy her new life. But most old people have no convenient public transportation or shops within walking distance.

4   Hard as it was on both of us, we made the right decision in Mom's case. But is tragedy like that in Santa Monica a reason to take away the car keys of the elderly? I think not. Unless we learn how to play God, foreseeing accidents, that's the wrong lesson to learn.

5   Age doesn't necessarily prove anything. Slower reflexes or not, senior citizens are much better drivers than, for example, teenagers. They usually drive more slowly. They get honked at a lot, but their slower speed reduces the risk of death and destruction that accompanies speeding tons of metal. The worst risk-takers on the highway are young men between the ages of 18 to 25, but no one suggests taking away their keys or raising the driving age to 26.

6   The fatality rate in 2001 for motorists between 16 and 20, according to the National Highway Traffic Safety Administration, was more than double that for drivers over 70. The AARP estimates that drivers 55 and older compose a quarter of the driving population, but have only 18 percent of the accidents. The older the driver, the fewer miles he puts on his car. As the baby boomers age, the numbers of older drivers will increase. Large majorities of them live in the suburbs or in the countryside without public transportation. Rural and suburban communities must arrange for alternative kinds of transportation for those who are failing in their driving ability; demand can drive public and entrepreneurial innovation.

7   Preventive remedies for the aging driver abound. Their licenses could be renewed at shorter intervals, with tougher physical tests. At the first signs of diminished alertness, a designated adult in the family should monitor the elderly driver closely

for the good of everyone else. They shouldn't drink and drive, but who should? Doctors who prescribe medications for the elderly must make them aware of their influence on driving.

8   The older citizen who tries to avoid danger is likely to take personal responsibility with considerably more seriousness than a younger person who courts danger through partying and risk. I like the example of Lord Renton, the 94-year-old "Father of the House of Lords" in London, who volunteered the other day to take his first driving test. He first drove a car in England before 1935, the year a driver's license was first required. He enjoyed a grandfather clause, you might say.

9   Deciding he owed it to himself and his fellow drivers to submit to a test, he submitted himself to the indignity of taking the test on a small and unfamiliar Ford sedan, not his usual cup of tea. He succeeded brilliantly. We could expect no less from seniors on this side of the Atlantic. So, let's let Granny drive for as long as she can. Road age is a lot less dangerous than road rage.

EXERCISE 11

Discussion and Critical Thinking

1. What two paragraphs state the author's proposition and summarize her support?

2. What two other patterns of writing (narration, exemplification, comparison and contrast, process analysis, analysis by division) does Fields use significantly to advance her argument?

3. List the several forms of evidence Fields uses.

4. She mentions that young men between the ages of 18 and 25 are the worst drivers, but no one suggests taking their licenses away because of age. Why does that view prevail?

5. What is your reaction to Fields's argument?

6. Fields personalizes her argument by discussing her mother's situation. What effect does that approach have on her overall presentation?

Is It Time for Cameras in the Classroom?

CLAUDE LEWIS

Would you mind if a camera were covering you as you read this sentence? One argument goes, "Why should you mind if you are not doing anything wrong?" The other side of the issue would call the surveillance an invasion of privacy. In this essay, Claude Lewis, retired columnist for the Philadelphia Inquirer, *makes his case for cameras in the classroom.*

1   Something new is happening in public schools across America. Round-the-clock cameras are coming into the classroom, and their introduction is stirring a wide range of emotions. Reactions range from quiet acceptance by many parents to the

shrillest outrage by those who insist the practice is a clear attack on the Fourth Amendment prohibition against unreasonable searches.

2   Cameras are appearing not only in classrooms, but also in school hallways, cafeterias, gymnasiums, auditoriums, parking lots, and practically everywhere else on school grounds. School districts throughout America and England are beginning to experiment with cameras hovering silently above students and teachers. But in Biloxi, Mississippi, of all places, school districts are out in front of the pack.

3   I abhor the idea of what some have labeled "spying" on schoolchildren. And I shudder when I think of the draconian measures other societies use to monitor childhood—and adult—behavior. But since many of us have transferred our parental responsibility to our schools, the burden of teachers and school officials has increased dramatically. The evidence is ample that we live in extraordinary times, times that call for sterner measures to help keep our schools and other public institutions safe. But really, cameras in the classroom should not lead to paranoia. Nearly any public space where Americans gather is already under the camera eye. Americans are often quietly photographed at work, on the road, at public events, in shopping malls, banks, in court, and nearly everywhere else. Who are the photographers? Any of a number of private and government agencies. So why not in school?

4   A Philadelphia school district spokesman, Cameron Kline, tells me that Philadelphia uses security cameras on the grounds of some schools but not in the classroom except, perhaps, for special projects or programs. "We don't presently use cameras for monitoring students or teachers in our schools," Kline said. But if it's found that monitoring classes with cameras could benefit students, teachers and the administration, "we might consider their use," Kline said.

5   Up to now, Biloxi is the only school district in the nation that has installed Web cameras in nearly all its classrooms. When the new school term began on Monday, more than 500 cameras peeked down from ceilings all over campus. According to a district spokesman, "students, parents and teachers don't mind them at all." Many privacy advocates do. They worry that cameras in schools could be misused and may even interfere with the learning process. But some argue that cameras can fill in where personnel is lacking: With the large school complexes of today, it is nearly impossible for teachers and security guards to cover every blind spot on campus.

6   Some are reluctant to concede that their acceptance of cameras was shaped by the Columbine High killings in 1999. But ever since then, school officials have engaged in a national conversation concerning ways to monitor their populations more closely. That conversation began immediately after thirteen were slaughtered by students Eric Harris and Dylan Klebold, who were armed with a semiautomatic rifle, two sawed-off shotguns, a semiautomatic handgun, and dozens of homemade bombs. No one should argue that cameras would have prevented Columbine—but they may have helped somewhat. Had cameras been on campus back then, the students at Columbine who survived the killings would have had to plant fewer crosses to mark their funereal grief. As it happened, they planted four pink ones for the females, nine blue ones for the males—and two black ones, a distance away, for the young killers.

7   So now, in our unending search for answers, some of us reluctantly move toward cameras. It is a move that stems, at least in part, from that awful day in April 1999, a day that continues to haunt us, a day our nation lost a little more of its innocence.

EXERCISE 12   Discussion and Critical Thinking

1. According to Lewis, what is the current background to the issue of cameras in classroom; that is, how does he frame the argument?

2. How does Lewis handle the refutation in paragraph 3?

3. What is the main point of reasoning on which Lewis's argument is based?

4. How does Lewis use the example in paragraph 6?

5. Is there an argument against the conclusion that camera use could have diminished the tragedy at Columbine? Explain.

6. In addition to safety, what are other possible practical uses of cameras in the classroom?

7. Overall, do you agree or disagree with Lewis's proposition? Why or why not?

Topics for Writing Argument

You will find a blank Writing Process Worksheet on page 7, which can be photo-copied, filled in, and submitted with each assignment if your instructor directs you to do so.

Reading-Related Topics

"A New Wind Blowing"

1. Using either the paragraph or the essay as a model, write from the other side of the issue.

"A Modest Proposal: Guys Shouldn't Drive Till 25"

2. Write an argument in which you either agree or disagree with Gallagher's views. Make it an independent statement or a critique of specifically what she said. Consider using examples from your own experience.

"Let Granny Drive If She Can"

3. Write an argument in which you disagree with Fields's views. Make it independent or a critique of Fields's article.

4. Write an argument in which you agree with Fields's views. Your argument should be either personalized with your own examples or presented as a more formal argument without personal examples.

"Is It Time for Cameras in the Classroom?"

5. Write an argument in which you agree with Lewis but for additional reasons such as for better control of bullying, cheating, bad teaching, and theft.

6. Write an argument in which you disagree with Lewis because you believe cameras in the classroom violate laws of privacy (Fourth Amendment). Discuss possible or likely abuses by those who operate the system.

General Topics

The following are broad subject areas. You will have to limit your focus for a paragraph or an essay of argument. Modify the subject to correspond with your experiences and interests. Some of these subjects will benefit from research in the library or on the Internet. Some will overlap with subject material from classes you have taken and with studies you have made.

7. School drug tests.

8. School metal detectors

9. Sex education

10. Defining sexual harassment

11. Changing the juvenile justice system

12. Endangered species legislation

13. Advertising tobacco

14. Combatting homelessness

15. State-run lotteries

16. Jury reform

17. Legalizing prostitution

18. Censoring rap or rock music

19. Cost of illegal immigration

20. Installation of local traffic signs

21. Foot patrols by local police

22. Change in (your) college registration procedure

23. Local public transportation

24. Surveillance by video (on campus, in neighborhoods, or in shopping areas)

25. Zone changes for stores selling liquor

26. Curfew for teenagers

27. Laws keeping known gang members out of parks

Cross-Curricular Topics

From a class you are taking or have taken or from your major area of study, select an issue on which thoughtful people may disagree and write an essay of persuasion or argument. It could be an interpretation of an ambiguous piece of literature for an English class; a position on global warming, public land management, or the Endangered Species Act for a class in ecology; an argument about the effectiveness of a government program in a political science class; a view on a certain kind of diet in a food-science class; a preference for a particular worldview in a class on philosophy; or an assertion on the proper role of chiropractors as health care practitioners in a health-science class.

Career-Related Topics

Write a proposal to solve a problem in your family, neighborhood, school, or workplace. The problem is likely to be the purchase or modification of something, the introduction or modification of a procedure, or the introduction of a service. For this assignment, use basically the same form regardless of the location or circumstances of the problem. For this assignment, you can use a basic pattern, background, solution (as a proposition), support (how it can be done, when it can be done, what it will cost, if anything). The problem that you are proposing to alleviate or eliminate can be based on your experiences or it can be purely fictional. If you are suggesting the purchase of an item or items to solve a problem, the Internet can provide you with prices and specifications. That data could be integrated into your proposal or photocopied and attached, with references.

Following are a few specific topic suggestions:

28. Home

    Contracting with a gardener or a housekeeper
    Dividing the chores
    Respecting the privacy and space of others

29. Neighborhood

    Limiting noise
    Dealing with dogs—vicious, wandering, barking
    Parking recreational vehicles out front

30. College

    Parking
    Enrollment and registration
    Classroom procedure
    Safety

31. Workplace

    Time-saving equipment
    Doing your job (or part of it) at home rather than at the workplace
    Fringe benefits
    Evaluation procedures
    Staggering lunch hours and work breaks
    Communication between workers on different shifts

Writer's Guidelines: Argument

1. Ask yourself the following questions; then consider which parts of the persuasive statement or argument you should include in your essay.

   - *Background:* What is the historical or social context for this controversial issue?

   - *Proposition* (the topic sentence of the paragraph or the thesis of the essay): What do I want my audience to believe or to do?

   - *Qualification of proposition:* Can I limit my assertion so that those who disagree cannot easily challenge me with exceptions?

   - *Refutation* (taking the opposing view into account, mainly to point out its fundamental weakness): What is the view on the other side, and why is it flawed in reasoning or evidence?

   - *Support:* In addition to sound reasoning, can I use appropriate facts, examples, statistics, and opinions of authorities?

2. The basic pattern of a paragraph or an essay of persuasion or argument is likely to be in this form:

   Assertion (the topic sentence of the paragraph or the thesis of the essay)
   I. Support 1
   II. Support 2
   III. Support 3

3. Write and revise.

   - Write and then revise your paragraph or essay as many times as necessary for **c**oherence, **l**anguage (usage, tone, and diction), **u**nity, **e**mphasis, **s**upport, and **s**entences (**CLUESS**). Read your work aloud to hear and correct any grammatical errors or awkward-sounding sentences.

   - Edit any problems in fundamentals, such as **c**apitalization, **o**missions, **p**unctuation, and **s**pelling (**COPS**).

Chapter

23

Celebrations

When we study the celebration of another culture, we feel a special warmth, and we immediately relate it to something we do in our own family.

Learning Objectives

Working with this chapter, I will learn

~ **how patterns can be combined.**

More Similar Than Different

If you want to know what a culture values, study its celebrations. What holidays does it have? What songs does it sing? What dances does it do? What foods does it consume, especially in the name of celebration?

Except for those of Native Americans, all of these customs were brought to America by immigrants, brought as surely as baggage, picture albums, and language. The practices may become Americanized over the years, but that does not mean they lose their meaning. Even back in the home lands, different regions practiced their own variations, and towns and families have always individualized customs to some extent.

Travel across America and you will encounter various festivals—the German Octoberfest in Milwaukee and other cities, the Kolache Festival begun by the Czechs who settled in Oklahoma a hundred years ago, the Hispanic-American Cinco de Mayo in East Los Angeles, the numerous Native American corn festivals across the Southwest, the elaborate family reunions of African-Americans (especially in the South), and hundreds more.

Many of these ceremonies are simple and appeal to the basic human instinct to enjoy life. When we study the celebrations of another culture, we feel a special warmth, and we immediately relate it to something that we do in our own family. We may learn that a Thanksgiving Day in the fall exists in many cultures, and that spring festivals abound also, and even the small behaviors give us pause and delight.

Last summer I traveled to Russia where I had an opportunity to visit people who lived in villages and on collective farms. They were friendly, but because I knew practically no Russian and they knew little English, we had some difficulty in communicating, usually resorting to gestures, grunts, and body language. Remarkably, this exercise in charades worked pretty well. One incident stands out.

B. Hickerson, copyright Los Angeles Times Syndicate. All rights reserved.

I was on a country road near Smolensk, somewhere between Moscow and Poland, when I came upon a woman and two small girls. The children were prettily dressed, and I gestured for permission to take their picture. The mother agreed, and I posed the children with the village well in the background. The little girls stood there, looking very serious. In order to break through their reserve and shyness, I picked a common flower from the roadside and handed it to one. She looked down, smiled, and began plucking the petals, saying merrily, *"Lubit, ne lubit. Lubit, ne lubit. Lubit, ne lubit."* I picked another flower and also began plucking the petals, saying, "She loves me, she loves me not. She loves me, she loves me not." The girls giggled, and I laughed. For a moment the *amerikanets* and the *russkiye* were one. The simplest of cultural connections had been established.

The five reading selections in this chapter connect cultures in much the same fashion. They are more similar than different. They commingle ritual and spontaneous behavior. In the presence of celebration, the feelings of joy, warmth, and pride are common denominators.

As noted in previous chapters, the patterns of writing seldom appear alone, though one often provides a particular structure to convey the writer's main intent. Because the authors of these selections are telling you about their experiences, they use various combinations of forms, especially narration, description, and process analysis. Your responsive writing will no doubt use your own combination of those forms; however, one, such as process analysis or comparison and contrast, may very well stand out.

Festival of the Dead

TERESITA CASTELLANOS

On November 2, Mexicans celebrate the Festival of the Dead. It is a time of joy when the living go to cemeteries to pay homage to the dead. Children eat candies shaped like skulls, adults clean tombstones, and they all remember and pray. Student Teresita Castellanos, an immigrant from Mexico, knows this day well from her childhood experiences.

The Day of the Dead, which falls on November 2 each year, is a great national holiday in Mexico. Introduced into Mexico by the Spaniards after the Conquest, it is one of the most peculiar and important Mexican religious celebrations. Several days before the occasion, markets and bakeries are filled with special breads baked in human forms, sweets shaped into skulls, and toy coffins, skeletons, and masks made of papier-mâché. Flower shops overflow with marigolds, the flower that in Aztec times was sacred to the dead. On that day Mexicans carry gifts of food and flowers to the graves of those who have died. But they do not feel sad, for they believe that the dead return to earth in spirit on this special day. People clean tombstones, set out offerings of treats, salt, and sugar, and welcome the dead as honored guests. Then people celebrate by eating the food and by wearing masks that look like grinning skulls. The children pretend to frighten each other with jack-in-the-boxes that look like skeletons jumping out of their coffins. This celebration helps people not to be afraid of the dead and of death itself.

EXERCISE 1

Discussion and Critical Thinking

1. Why is the Festival of the Dead not an occasion of sadness?

2. What are the basic steps in the celebration?

EXERCISE 2

Reading-Related Writing

1. Write about your experience with the Festival of the Dead or another holiday that also has a long history.

2. If the Festival of the Dead is not part of your culture, write about your initial reaction to it and your reaction to it after you learned of its history and meaning.

3. Because of the close proximity of Halloween and the Festival of the Dead, the two may be celebrated by the same people at almost the same time. Some Hispanics may feel that the wildness of Halloween tends to corrupt the seriousness of their holiday. Interview a few Hispanics (incorporating your own view if you are Hispanic), and write a report on the issue. Include comments on any blending that occurs.

Soul Food at a Black American Family Reunion

SHEILA FERGUSON

Sheila Ferguson is the author of Soul Food: Classic Cuisine from the Deep South. *Let her tell you about soul food in the proper setting, the black American family reunion.*

1 Soul food . . . is a legacy clearly steeped in tradition; a way of life that has been handed down from generation to generation, from one black family to another, by word of mouth and sleight of hand. It is rich in both history and variety of flavor.

2 To cook soul food you must use all of your senses. You cook by instinct, but you also use smell, taste, touch, sight, and, particularly, sound. You learn to hear by the crackling sound when it's time to turn over the fried chicken, to smell when a pan of biscuits is just about to finish baking, and to feel when a pastry's just right to the touch. You taste, rather than measure, the seasonings you treasure; and you use your eyes, not a clock, to judge when that cherry pie has bubbled sweet and nice. These skills are hard to teach quickly. They must be felt, loving, and come straight from the heart.

3 Ah, but when you taste good soul food then it'll take ahold of your soul and hang your unsuspecting innards out to dry. It's that shur-'nuf everlovin' down-home stick-to-your-ribs kinda food that keeps you glued to your seat long after the meal is over and done with, enabling you to sit back, relax, and savor the gentle purrings of a well satisfied stomach, feeling that all's right with the world. . . .

4   It was down South . . . that I went to my first family reunion. Now, I know I should be telling you that the highlight of this affair was the prayers that one member was chosen to deliver. But if I were to tell the gospel truth, and I think I'm a-gonna, it was definitely the dishes that everybody turned out. Oh, dear, I'm making myself sound like some kinda pagan, but all that food, spread out majestically, on a long banquet-sized picnic table, sure was one sight for a small girl to behold. The table at the farm on Blanton Street in Charlotte kinda sloped with the terrain, but that didn't stop us from keeping the food well-balanced and from swatting the flies away from the pecan pies, stacked a mile high, I might add. With one long and narrow slice you had a hunk of pie big enough to last you for quite a spell.

5   I should explain, though, that a black American family reunion stands for a great deal more than just the sharing of a really fine meal. It is a testimonial both to the past and to what the future holds in store for the entire family. We gather to share all that is most precious to us, especially with those family members we don't get to see that often. We eat, we drink, and we pray, but also we encourage each other and lift our heads in praise of what our offspring have accomplished. We share in each other's joys and good fortunes and offer solace when the chips are down. We comfort each other and this enables us to retain a special kind of closeness, even when we're hundreds of miles apart.

6   Every time our family gets together we try to pay some humble tribute to the accomplishments of our race in one way or another. My family, for example, after discovering the existence of my great-great-grandfather Dennison Harrell, now meets annually for a grand family reunion expressly in his honor. We come together from all over the States—and in my case from across the Atlantic each time—tracing new family members we have never met before, as we continue to pay homage to the man who founded our family in America. Everyone who attends gives in the best of spirit and puts all of their personality into the dishes they concoct. At the same time, we are remembering all of our forebears and all that they gave, often against apparently insurmountable odds.

7   This is precisely why we feel we must get down to some real serious cookin' at the time of a family reunion. It represents sharing the very best with those we love the very most and that love is best conveyed in the pride we take in preparing our food. By now, it has become a family tradition. And believe you me, can we burn when we cook. Everyone is asked to bring a dish, usually their specialty, and each cook has to maintain an exceedingly high standard of cooking, baking, and innovation. One dish just walks all over and surpasses another, and we always delight in sharing and comparing recipes. Once Aunt Peacie brought along her "Jesse Jackson Sweet Potato Pie." Well, it was gone before you had a chance to take a good look. Man, that pie was "the T"—the talk of the day. But another thing is for dang sure: if your cooking isn't quite up to scratch, you sure as shootin' won't be asked to bring a dish next time round! You'll be nicely passed over with, "Oh, honey, that's OK, why don't you just sit this one out."

8   Even if it's not a big family reunion, it is still considered an extreme insult if you don't put yourself out and cook a fine and exquisite meal. I wouldn't dream of presenting my family and friends with a meal consisting of frozen fried chicken, frozen collard greens, store-bought cartons of buttermilk sausage biscuits and gravy made out of some sorry old box of granules. Oh, they'd eat it all right. But they would just feel so put down and outright insulted that they would commence telling me off, royally, right on the spot. Then, they would continue to talk about me for fifteen more years! My folks pull no punches when it comes to telling you off and they don't necessarily wait until they're politely out of earshot either. I can just hear them signifying now: "Well, she sure didn't sweat long over that sad plate of

stuff." "Do you call that food? Sure was pathetic." "I don't care how busy the girl is, she could certainly take a little time to think about her family once in a while, humph!" That is the spirit through which soul food traditions continually evolve—*pressure!*

EXERCISE 3   ## Discussion and Critical Thinking

1. How does one use all five senses to prepare soul food?

2. According to Ferguson, why is soul food, soul food?

3. What does a black American family reunion stand for?

4. What have Ferguson and her family done on a personal level?

5. What are the standards of cooking?

EXERCISE 4   ## Reading-Related Writing

1. Write about the tradition of reunions or the celebration of a certain holiday in your family. Explain how people work together and what they take pride in.

2. Write about a particular reunion you have gone to.

3. Write about the equivalent of soul food in another culture. Use Ferguson's description as a framework for your discussion.

4. Write about the significance of particular foods at a specific cultural holiday.

Thanksgiving

LINDA HOGAN

Prominent Native American writer and member of the Chickasaw Nation, Linda Hogan writes reverently of a time of thanksgiving for her and her people. But for the Native Americans she writes of, the celebration is not one meal, one ceremony, one day. For them Thanksgiving is a series of dances that are held throughout the growing season. These ceremonies bind her people to the land in a deeply spiritual and cultural fashion. She conveys how Native Americans love the land, the products of the land, and their brothers and sisters, who are all part of nature.

1   In Pueblo country, throughout the yearly growing season, the corn dances take place. The dancing begins at the time of planting and ends with the time of harvest.

2   It is a serious dance, a long and hard barefoot dance on burning hot southwestern earth. It is a dance of community, not only between people, but a larger sense of community that includes earth, the new young plants, and the fiery sun. It's a dance of human generosity, as the dancers lend their energy to the kernels sowed in newly turned soil. There is drumming and singing. There is feasting on loaves of bread baked outdoors in clay ovens, on watermelons the color of the mountains, on meats, and varieties of chile sauces. But mostly there is prayer in the dance, and thankfulness.

3   A few years ago I was asked, as part of a ceremony, to grind light-giving blue corn with a grinding stone and metate. I didn't know then that corn was as dependent on people as people have been, throughout history, on corn. But 90-year-old writer Meridel Le Sueur has written that ancient women gatherers were free travelers who loved the tiny grass of early corn, hand-pollinated it, and "created the great cob of nutrition which cannot free itself from the cob without the hand of human."

4   During that ceremony, I also drank bitter tea, telling the herb in the cup, *thank you,* telling the sun, *thank you,* and thanking the land. Gratitude and a human connectedness with food is part of many ceremonies of life that are centered on hunting, picking, planting, and healing.

5   In my own tribal history, too, corn has meant life. The people eat cornbread and ear corn, parched corn, cornmeal mush. My grandmother, like many other Chickasaw women, made hominy with lye and ashes in a large black kettle on the wood stove. Still, in a single kernel of that swollen white corn, people swallow the light of sun and the rich mineral earth, eat of the rains in the milky sweetness of yellow corn, eat the rich loamy smell of turned earth, of planter's moons, of seeds planted in the sacred land.

6   The reciprocity among land, food, and people also exists farther north where ricers' boats move among the wild rice plants in the swampy, humid land as the boat is pushed with a pole through lily pads and plants and the distant call of a loon. In the diffuse, soft light of the sun, the people are covered with rice dust and dried pollen and insects. They, too, sing their thankful song to the rice, and the songs, like those of others, come to life within the food.

7   Here a woman works with a digging stick. There a child chases crows away from the crops. Old men break ground and turn the soil. Women plant by the moon. There are the berry-pickers, and the grateful people who bring in the twisting, shining fish from the river. The herb gatherers know to pick plants at certain times of the year and month, and they speak with the plants as they work, thanking them. And there is the native woman I met in Hawaii; it fell to her to be the

traditional hunter of wild pigs, to take only what was needed, to feed others, to be thankful. Sometimes in the hurry sickness of our time, we forget to return the gift of what we've taken from the rich land that feeds us. Sometimes we do not remember that millions of years of life have grown from this verdant, muddy, yielding terrain where we live in the land of our ancestors. We forget the long years of hunger, the starving times of history we have survived, and the years of living on lard and flour. We forget the meaning of food, which is both beginning and end of a divine alchemy, an infinite movement of sun into fruit, of windborne seeds falling to earth, seeds being carried in the fur of animals and the stomachs of birds, of rain water, of life rising up again. In our food all things come together in an elemental dance of magic and mystery; brother water, sister light, mother land, and the sacred fire all rise up in stalks and stems, opening a blossom and becoming red fruit of grass eaten by the deer, or the ripening yellow ears of corn planted and harvested by our short-lived hands.

8   Now it is autumn, and in the cool, plastered corners of houses are the seed pots. The pots are smooth, rounded clay that has been painted with lines thin as a strand of corn silk and they hold the seeds of pumpkin, beans, and squash in a loving embrace before they go back to land. Even last summer's sun is held there, dormant and ready to turn over and surge to life in incredible germinations of renewal.

9   Near here grew the green spring pastures with onions growing at the borders. Now, in autumn, they are the golden stubble of harvested hay, the road is damp and silty with fallen red leaves that are turning back into soil, waiting for spring's rich rains and sun. On the next hill are the five wild turkeys I saw last month as they walked through the tall, dry grasses, and beyond them are the caves of mineral salt that generations of people have used. This is the vulnerable land shared among us. Not far from here the ancient plants are listening and moving again toward the ripening.

EXERCISE 5

Vocabulary Highlights

Write a short definition of each word as it is used in the essay. (Paragraph numbers are given in parentheses.) Be prepared to use the words in your own sentences.

metate (3)   alchemy (7)

reciprocity (6)   dormant (8)

verdant (7)

EXERCISE 6

Discussion and Critical Thinking

1. Hogan writes about more than the process of the dances that take place during the corn growing and harvesting season. She writes about the intricate relationship between human beings and all aspects of nature and even the spiritual world. She sees a reciprocal relationship, an interdependency. What are some of those interdependencies? How do they represent process?

2. To what do the dances relate?

3. How have corn and people been interdependent?

4. In the Southwest, how do different family members participate in corn production? What process is described here?

5. In her next-to-last sentence, Hogan says, "This is the vulnerable land shared among us." Although she is concerned about the life-sustaining forces of larger nature, what understated idea does she bring up here?

EXERCISE 7 | **Reading-Related Writing**

1. If you are familiar with Native American culture, write a process analysis about a particular ceremony that is consistent in thought with Hogan's essay.

2. Write a process analysis about gratitude and a feeling of interdependence from any perspective other than Native American.

3. Write about the interdependency Hogan considers.

4. Write about the American Thanksgiving in terms of its original idea and current practice.

5. Discuss the relevance of Hogan's statement "This is the vulnerable land shared among us" to current environmental problems.

6. Discuss how the Native American Thanksgiving as presented by Hogan is different from the American Thanksgiving.

Grandmother's Sunday Dinner

PATRICIA HAMPL

In this excerpt from her book A Romantic Education *(1981), Patricia Hampl writes on one of her favorite topics, her Czech-American heritage. Born in 1946, she grew up in St. Paul, Minnesota, and graduated from the University of Minnesota. After studying writing at the Iowa Writer's Workshop, she returned to the University of Minnesota, where she still teaches and continues with her writing.*

1   Food was the potent center of my grandmother's life. Maybe the immense amount of time it took to prepare meals during most of her life accounted for her passion. Or it may have been her years of work in various kitchens on the hill and later, in the house of Justice Butler: after all, she was a professional. Much later, when she was dead and I went to Prague, I came to feel the motto I knew her by best—*Come eat*—was not, after all, a personal statement, but a racial one, the *cri de coeur* of Middle Europe.

2   Often, on Sundays, the entire family gathered for dinner at her house. Dinner was 1 P.M. My grandmother would have preferred the meal to be at the old time of noon, but her children had moved their own Sunday dinner hour to the more fashionable (it was felt) 4 o'clock, so she compromised. Sunday breakfast was something my mother liked to do in a big way, so we arrived at my grandmother's hardly out of the reverie of waffles and orange rolls, before we were propped like rag dolls in front of a pork roast and sauerkraut, dumplings, hot buttered carrots, rye bread and rollikey, pickles and olives, apple pie and ice cream. And coffee.

3   Coffee was a food in that house, not a drink. I always begged for some because the magical man on the Hills Brothers can with his turban and long robe scattered with stars and his gold slippers with pointed toes, looked deeply happy as he drank from his bowl. The bowl itself reminded me of soup, Campbell's chicken noodle soup, my favorite food. The distinct adultness of coffee and the robed man with his deep-drinking pleasure made it clear why the grownups lingered so long at the table. The uncles smoked cigars then, and the aunts said, "Oh, those cigars."

4   My grandmother, when she served dinner, was a virtuoso hanging on the edge of her own ecstatic performance. She seemed dissatisfied, almost querulous until she had corralled everybody into their chairs around the table, which she tried to do the minute they got into the house. No cocktails, no hors d'oeuvres (pronounced, by some of the family, "horse's ovaries"), just business. She was a little power crazed: she had us and, by God, we were going to eat. She went about it like a goose breeder forcing pellets down the gullets of those dumb birds.

5   She flew between her chair and the kitchen, always finding more this, extra that. She'd given you the *wrong* chicken breast the first time around; now she'd found the *right* one: eat it too, eat it fast, because after the chicken comes the rhubarb pie. Rhubarb pie with a thick slice of cheddar cheese that it was imperative every single person eat.

6   We had to eat fast because something was always out there in the kitchen panting and charging the gate, champing at the bit, some mound of rice or a Jell-O fruit salad or vegetable casserole or pie was out there, waiting to be let loose into the dining room.

7   She had the usual trite routines: the wheedlings, the silent pout ("What! You don't like my brussels sprouts? I thought you liked *my* brussels sprouts," versus your wife's/sister's/mother's. "I made that pie just for you," etc., etc.). But it was the way she tossed around the old clichés and the overused routines, mixing them up and dealing them out shamelessly, without irony, that made her a pro. She tended to peck at her own dinner. Her plate, piled with food, was a kind of stage prop, a mere bending to convention. She liked to eat, she was even a greedy little stuffer, but not on these occasions. She was a woman possessed by an idea, given over wholly to some phantasmagoria of food, a mirage of stuffing, a world where the endless chicken and the infinite lemon pie were united at last at the shore of the oceanic soup plate that her children and her children's children alone could drain . . . if only they would try.

8   She was there to bolster morale, to lead the troops, to give the sharp command should we falter on the way. The futility of saying no was supreme, and no one ever tried it. How could a son-in-law, already weakened near the point of imbecility by the once, twice, thrice charge to the barricades of pork and mashed potato, be expected to gather his feeble wit long enough to ignore the final call of his old commander when she sounded the alarm: "Pie, Fred?"

9   Just when it seemed as if the food-crazed world she had created was going to burst, that she had whipped and frothed us like a sack of boiled potatoes under her masher, just then she pulled it all together in one easeful stroke like the pro she was.

10   She stood in the kitchen doorway, her little round Napoleonic self sheathed in a cotton flowered pinafore apron, the table draped in its white lace cloth but spotted now with gravy and beet juice, the troops mumbling indistinctly as they waited at their posts for they knew not what. We looked up at her stupidly, weakly. She said nonchalantly, "Anyone want another piece of pie?" No, no more pie, somebody said. The rest of the rabble grunted along with him. She stood there with the coffeepot and laughed and said, "Good! Because there *isn't* any more pie."

11   No more pie. We'd eaten it all, we'd put away everything in that kitchen. We were exhausted and she, gambler hostess that she was (but it was her house she was playing), knew she could offer what didn't exist, knew us, knew what she'd wrought. There was a sense of her having won, won something. There were no divisions among us now, no adults, no children. Power left the second and third generations and returned to the source, the grandmother who reduced us to mutters by her art.

12   That wasn't the end of it. At 5 P.M. there was "lunch"—sandwiches and beer; the sandwiches were made from the left-overs (mysteriously renewable resources, those roasts). And at about 8 P.M. we were at the table again for coffee cake and coffee, the little man in his turban and his coffee ecstasy and his pointed shoes set on the kitchen table as my grandmother scooped out the coffee and dumped it into a big enamel pot with a crushed eggshell. By then everyone was alive and laughing again, the torpor gone. My grandfather had been inviting the men, one by one, into the kitchen during the afternoon where he silently (the austere version of memory— but he must have talked, must have said *something*) handed them joggers of whiskey, and watched them put the shot down in one swallow. Then he handed them a beer, which they took out in the living room. I gathered that the *little* drink in the tiny glass shaped like a beer mug was some sort of antidote for the *big* drink of beer. He sat on the chair in the kitchen with a bottle of beer on the floor next to him and played his concertina, allowing society to form itself around him—while he lived he was the center—but not seeking it, not going into the living room. And not talking. He held to his music and the kindly, medicinal administration of whiskey.

13   By evening, it seemed we could eat endlessly, as if we'd had some successful inoculation at dinner and could handle anything. I stayed in the kitchen after they all reformed in the dining room at the table for coffee cake. I could hear them, but the little man in his starry yellow robe was on the table in the kitchen and I put my head down on the oil cloth very near the curled and delighted tips of his pointed shoes, and I slept. Whatever laughter there was, there was. But something sweet and starry was in the kitchen and I lay down beside it, my stomach full, warm, so safe I'll live the rest of my life off the fat of that vast family security.

EXERCISE 8

Vocabulary Highlights

Write a short definition of each word as it is used in the essay. (Paragraph numbers are given in parentheses.) Be prepared to use the words in your own sentences.

potent (1)   imperative (5)

compromised (2)   mirage (7)

reverie (2)   phantasmagoria (7)

virtuoso (4)   nonchalantly (10)

ecstatic (4)   torpor (12)

querulous (4)   antidote (12)

EXERCISE 9 | ## Discussion and Critical Thinking

1. In this mixture of patterns, one is description. Use two words to state the dominant impression.

2. As a narrative pattern, what unit of time provides the framework for this account?

3. What phrases does Hampl use to portray her grandmother as a military figure?

4. What two techniques does Hampl's grandmother use to get people to eat more?

5. What does the figure of the little "magical man" on the Hills Brothers coffee can seem to represent?

6. What is the role of food in this account? Just what does it do for the family and individuals?

EXERCISE 10 | ## Reading-Related Writing

1. Write about family get-togethers you have experienced. Provide a unit of time for the framework and develop it as a simple narrative. Include description and, if it fits, some dialogue. Try to recall some inanimate object (think of the image on the Hills Brothers coffee can) that related to what occurred.

2. Compare and contrast Hampl's experience with her grandmother's Sunday dinner with your own.

3. Write a character study of the grandmother, in which you discuss her main traits—those that make her such a memorable person to Hampl.

4. Write a paragraph or an essay in which you expand on Hampl's last sentence, which includes the words "I'll live the rest of my life off the fat of that vast family security."

The Loudest Voice

GRACE PALEY

Sometimes an immigrant group may find itself in the middle of a cultural experience that is fundamentally alien to their thinking. In this short story, Grace Paley writes of first-generation Jewish people participating in a play celebrating the birth of Jesus Christ. Ever eager to avoid offending the citizens of their host country, most of the parents and children cooperate, with ironic results.

1   There is a certain place where dumb-waiters boom, doors slam, dishes crash; every window is a mother's mouth biding the street shut up, go skate somewhere else, come home. My voice is the loudest.

2   There, my own mother is still as full of breathing as me and the grocer stands up to speak to her. "Mrs. Abramowitz," he says, "people should not be afraid of their children."

3   "Ah, Mr. Bialik," my mother replies, "if you say to her or her father 'Ssh,' they say, 'In the grave it will be quiet.'"

4   "From Coney Island to the cemetery," says my papa. "It's the same subway; it's the same fare."

5   I am right next to the pickle barrel. My pinky is making tiny whirlpools in the brine. I stop a moment to announce: "Campbell's Tomato Soup. Campbell's Vegetable Beef Soup. Campbell's S-c-otch Broth . . ."

6   "Be quiet," the grocer says, "the labels are coming off."

7   "Please, Shirley, be a little quiet," my mother begs me.

8   In that place the whole street groans: Be quiet! Be quiet! but steals from the happy chorus of my inside self not a tittle or a jot.

9   There, too, but just around the corner, is a red brick building that has been old for many years. Every morning the children stand before it in double lines which must be straight. They are not insulted. They are waiting anyway.

10 I am usually among them. I am, in fact, the first, since I begin with "A."

11 One cold morning the monitor tapped me on the shoulder. "Go to Room 409, Shirley Abramowitz," he said. I did as I was told. I went in a hurry up a down staircase to Room 409, which contained sixth-graders. I had to wait at the desk without wiggling until Mr. Hilton, their teacher, had time to speak.

12 After five minutes he said, "Shirley?"

13 "What?" I whispered.

14 He said, "My! My! Shirley Abramowitz! They told me you had a particularly loud, clear voice and read with lots of expression. Could that be true?"

15 "Oh yes," I whispered.

16 "In that case, don't be silly; I might very well be your teacher someday. Speak up, speak up."

17 "Yes," I shouted.

18 "More like it," he said. "Now, Shirley, can you put a ribbon in your hair or a bobby pin? It's too messy."

19 "Yes!" I bawled.

20 "Now, now, calm down." He turned to the class. "Children, not a sound. Open at page 39. Read till 52. When you finish, start again." He looked me over once more. "Now, Shirley, you know, I suppose, that Christmas is coming. We are preparing a beautiful play. Most of the parts have been given out. But I still need a child with a strong voice, lots of stamina. Do you know what stamina is? You do?

Smart kid. You know, I heard you read 'The Lord is my shepherd' in Assembly yesterday. I was very impressed. Wonderful delivery. Mrs. Jordan, your teacher, speaks highly of you. Now listen to me, Shirley Abramowitz, if you want to take the part and be in the play, repeat after me, 'I swear to work harder than I ever did before.'"

21   I looked to heaven and said at once, "Oh, I swear." I kissed my pinky and looked at God.

22   "That is an actor's life, my dear," he explained. "Like a soldier's, never tardy or disobedient to his general, the director. Everything," he said, "absolutely everything will depend on you."

23   That afternoon, all over the building, children scraped and scrubbed the turkeys and the sheaves of corn off the schoolroom windows. Goodbye Thanksgiving. The next morning a monitor brought red paper and green paper from the office. We made new shapes and hung them on the walls and glued them to the doors.

24   The teachers became happier and happier. Their heads were ringing like the bells of childhood. My best friend Evie was prone to evil, but she did not get a single demerit for whispering. We learned "Holy Night" without an error. "How wonderful!" said Miss Glacé, the student teacher. "To think that some of you don't even speak the language!" We learned "Deck the Halls" and "Hark! The Herald Angels." . . . They weren't ashamed and we weren't embarrassed.

25   Oh, but when my mother heard about it all, she said to my father: "Misha, you don't know what's going on there. Cramer is the head of the Tickets Committee."

26   "Who?" asked my father. "Cramer? Oh yes, an active woman."

27   "Active? Active has to have a reason. Listen," she said sadly, "I'm surprised to see my neighbors making tra-la-la for Christmas."

28   My father couldn't think of what to say to that. Then he decided: "You're in America! Clara, you wanted to come here. In Palestine the Arabs would be eating you alive. Europe you had pogroms. Argentina is full of Indians. Here you got Christmas. . . . Some joke, ha?"

29   "Very funny, Misha. What is becoming of you? If we came to a new country a long time ago to run away from tyrants, and instead we fall into a creeping pogrom, that our children learn a lot of lies, so what's the joke? Ach, Misha, your idealism is going away."

30   "So is your sense of humor."

31   "That I never had, but idealism you had a lot of."

32   "I'm the same Misha Abramovitch, I didn't change an iota. Ask anyone."

33   "Only ask me," says my mama, may she rest in peace. "I got the answer."

34   Meanwhile, the neighbors had to think of what to say too.

35   Marty's father said: "You know, he has a very important part, my boy."

36   "Mine also," said Mr. Sauerfeld.

37   "Not my boy!" said Mrs. Klieg. "I said to him no. The answer is no. When I say no! I mean no!"

38   The rabbi's wife said: "It's disgusting!" But no one listened to her. Under the narrow sky of God's great wisdom she wore a strawberry-blond wig.

39   Every day was noisy and full of experience. I was Right-hand Man. Mr. Hilton said: "How could I get along without you, Shirley?"

40   He said: "Your mother and father ought to get down on their knees every night and thank God for giving them a child like you."

41   He also said: "You're absolutely a pleasure to work with, my dear, dear child."

42   Sometimes he said: "For God's sakes, what did I do with the script? Shirley! Shirley! Find it."

43   Then I answered quietly: "Here it is, Mr. Hilton."

44   Once in a while, when he was very tired, he would cry out: "Shirley, I'm just

tired of screaming at those kids. Will you tell Ira Pushkov not to come in till Lester points to that star the second time?"

45   Then I roared: "Ira Pushkov, what's the matter with you? Dope! Mr. Hilton told you five times already, don't come in till Lester points to that star the second time."

46   "Ach, Clara," my father asked, "what does she do there till six o'clock she can't even put the plates on the table?"

47   "Christmas," said my mother coldly.

48   "Ho! Ho!" my father said. "Christmas. What's the harm? After all, history teaches everyone. We learn from reading this is a holiday from pagan times also, candles, lights, even Chanukah. So we learn it's not altogether Christian. So if they think it's a private holiday, they're only ignorant, not patriotic. What belongs to history, belongs to all men. You want to go back to the Middle Ages? Is it better to shave your head with a secondhand razor? Does it hurt Shirley to learn to speak up? It does not. So maybe someday she won't live between the kitchen and the shop. She's not a fool."

49   I thank you, Papa, for your kindness. It is true about me to this day. I am foolish but I am not a fool.

50   That night my father kissed me and said with great interest in my career, "Shirley, tomorrow's your big day. Congrats."

51   "Save it," my mother said. Then she shut all the windows in order to prevent tonsillitis.

52   In the morning it snowed. On the street corner a tree had been decorated for us by a kind city administration. In order to miss its chilly shadow our neighbors walked three blocks east to buy a loaf of bread. The butcher pulled down black window shades to keep the colored lights from shining on his chickens. Oh, not me. On the way to school, with both my hands I tossed it a kiss of tolerance. Poor thing, it was a stranger in Egypt.

53   I walked straight into the auditorium past the staring children. "Go ahead, Shirley!" said the monitors. Four boys, big for their age, had already started work as propmen and stagehands.

54   Mr. Hilton was very nervous. He was not even happy. Whatever he started to say ended in a sideward look of sadness. He sat slumped in the middle of the first row and asked me to help Miss Glacé. I did this, although she thought my voice too resonant and said, "Show-off!"

55   Parents began to arrive long before we were ready. They wanted to make a good impression. From among the yards of drapes I peeked out at the audience. I saw my embarrassed mother.

56   Ira, Lester, and Meyer were pasted to their beards by Miss Glacé. She almost forgot to thread the star on its wire, but I reminded her. I coughed a few times to clear my throat. Miss Glacé looked around and saw that everyone was in costume and on line waiting to play his part. She whispered, "All right. . . ." Then:

57   Jackie Sauerfeld, the prettiest boy in first grade, parted the curtains with his skinny elbow and in a high voice sang out:

> *"Parents dear*
> *We are here*
> *To make a Christmas play in time.*
> *It we give*
> *In narrative*
> *And illustrate with pantomime."*

58   He disappeared.

59   My voice burst immediately from the wings to the great shock of Ira, Lester, and Meyer, who were waiting for it but were surprised all the same.

60   "I remember, I remember, the house where I was born. . . ."

61   Miss Glacé yanked the curtain open and there it was, the house—an old hayloft, where Celia Kornbluh lay in the straw with Cindy Lou, her favorite doll. Ira, Lester, and Meyer moved slowly from the wings toward her, sometimes pointing to a moving star and sometimes ahead to Cindy Lou.

62   It was a long story and a sad story. I carefully pronounced all the words about my lonesome childhood, while little Eddie Braunstein wandered upstage and down with his shepherd's stick, looking for sheep. I brought up lonesomeness again, and not being understood at all except by some women everybody hated. Eddie was too small for that and Marty Groff took his place, wearing his father's prayer shawl. I announced twelve friends, and half the boys in the fourth grade gathered round Marty, who stood on an orange crate while my voice harangued. Sorrowful and loud, I declaimed about love and God and Man, but because of the terrible deceit of Abie Stock we came suddenly to a famous moment. Marty, whose remembering tongue I was, waited at the foot of the cross. He stared desperately at the audience. I groaned, "My God, my God, why hast thou forsaken me?" The soldiers who were sheiks grabbed poor Marty to pin him up to die, but he wrenched free, turned again to the audience, and spread his arms aloft to show despair and the end. I murmured at the top of my voice, "The rest is silence, but as everyone in this room, in this city—in this world—now knows, I shall have life eternal."

63   That night Mrs. Kornbluh visited our kitchen for a glass of tea.

64   "How's the virgin?" asked my father with a look of concern.

65   "For a man with a daughter, you got a fresh mouth, Abramovitch."

66   "Here," said my father kindly, "have some lemon, it'll sweeten your disposition."

67   They debated a little in Yiddish, then fell in a puddle of Russian and Polish. What I understood next was my father, who said, "Still and all, it was certainly a beautiful affair, you have to admit, introducing us to the beliefs of a different culture."

68   "Well, yes," said Mrs. Kornbluh. "The only thing . . . you know Charlie Turner—that cute boy in Celia's class—a couple others? They got very small parts or no part at all. In very bad taste, it seemed to me. After all, it's their religion."

69   "Ach," explained my mother, "what could Mr. Hilton do? They got very small voices; after all, why should they holler? The English language they know from the beginning by heart. They're blond like angels. You think it's so important they should get in the play? Christmas . . . the whole piece of goods . . . they own it."

70   I listened and listened until I couldn't listen any more. Too sleepy, I climbed out of bed and kneeled. I made a little church of my hands and said, "Here, O Israel. . . ." Then I called out in Yiddish, "Please, good night, good night. Ssh." My father said, "Ssh yourself," and slammed the kitchen door.

71   I was happy. I fell asleep at once. I had prayed for everybody: my talking family, cousins far away, passersby, and all the lonesome Christians. I expected to be heard. My voice was certainly the loudest.

EXERCISE 11 — Vocabulary Highlights

Write a short definition of each word as it is used in the essay. (Paragraph numbers are given in parentheses.) Be prepared to use the words in your own sentences.

a tittle or a jot (8)   resonant (54)

stamina (20)   harangued (62)

pogroms (28)   declaimed (62)

EXERCISE 12 — Discussion and Critical Thinking

1. What is the conflict in this story?

2. What is the significance of the setting (where the story takes place)?

3. Who is the main character?

4. Why are Shirley Abramowitz's beliefs unshaken by this experience?

5. This story has a humorous tone. What makes it funny? Might the same basic story be told in a different tone for a very different effect?

6. What does having Shirley tell the story contribute to its effect?

7. Why does Shirley speak softly at times?

8. What is her father's view? Her mother's view?

EXERCISE 13 — Reading-Related Writing

1. Write about a time when you were expected to do something (religious, cultural) that made you feel uncomfortable. Using informative process, explain how the incident took place.

2. Compare and contrast Shirley's mother and father.

3. Write about events in this story as examples of cultural confrontation. Include comments on sensitivity and insensitivity, tolerance and intolerance.

Topics for Writing About Celebrations

You will find a blank Writing Process Worksheet on page 7, which can be photocopied, filled in, and submitted with each assignment if your instructor directs you to do so.

Reading-Related Topics

"Festival of the Dead"

1. Write a paragraph or an essay about a festival or ceremony that is important to a cultural group but is much misunderstood by the American public.

"Soul Food at a Black American Family Reunion"

2. Use this essay as an example to write about a family reunion you attended. Explain how the reunion was important in keeping the family connected and in maintaining family history. Give details about individuals, food, ceremony, and traditions.

"Thanksgiving"

3. Write a paragraph or an essay about a cultural event such as this one by Hogan, in which people feel reverence for what they have and what they are.

"Grandmother's Sunday Dinner"

4. Write a paragraph or an essay in which you discuss how the Sunday dinner is actually a ceremony because it has become a ritual. Be sure to discuss each part of the ritual.

"The Loudest Voice"

5. If you have ever participated in a festival or ceremony that was outside your belief system, relate that experience in a paragraph or an essay. Include comments on your feelings and your behavior. Usually we go along with the larger group, not wanting to stand out or offend those who are well meaning, but what we keep to ourselves probably reveals much about our values.

Collaborative Learning

6. Make a list of all the cultures in your class and establish committees to organize a multicultural holiday—a Thanksgiving, a New Year, or one that you invent. Select ethnic foods for the meal—salads, soups, appetizers, main courses, desserts, and drinks (before, during, and after the meal). Then make a list of ethnic activities, especially dances, music, and games. Next invent, adapt, or borrow ceremonies or rituals. Finally, combine these elements in a report, using collaborative techniques as directed by your teacher. If time and other circumstances permit, celebrate the holiday, complete with food, song, and activities, and invite other classes or friends.

7. Divide the class into four groups, with each selecting a reading from this chapter showing process, especially a ceremony, that reveals much about a particular culture. Then, in a cooperative procedure established by your instructor,

write a report on that reading, probing for what it reveals about such ideas as family, nature, religion, and philosophy. A single group may choose more than one reading.

Writer's Guidelines

1. Writing in this chapter is likely to include more than one pattern of writing, although one, such as narration or process analysis, may provide the main framework for your paragraph or essay.

2. Write and revise.

   • Write and then revise your paragraph or essay as many times as necessary for coherence, language (usage, tone, and diction), unity, emphasis, support, and sentences (**CLUESS**). Read your work aloud to hear and correct any grammatical errors or awkward-sounding sentences.

   • Edit any problems in fundamentals, such as capitalization, omissions, punctuation, and spelling (**COPS**).

Appendixes

Appendix A: Parts of Speech

To classify a word as a part of speech, we observe two simple principles:

- The word must be in the context of communication, usually in a sentence.

- We must be able to identify the word with others that have similar characteristics—the eight parts of speech: nouns, pronouns, adjectives, verbs, adverbs, prepositions, conjunctions, or interjections.

The first principle is important because some words can be any of several parts of speech. The word *round*, for example, can function as five:

1. I watched the potter *round* the block of clay. [verb]

2. I saw her go *round* the corner. [preposition]

3. She has a *round* head. [adjective]

4. The astronauts watched the world go *round*. [adverb]

5. The champ knocked him out in one *round*. [noun]

Nouns

- **Nouns** are naming words. Nouns may name persons, animals, plants, places, things, substances, qualities, or ideas—for example, *Bart, armadillo, Mayberry, tree, rock, cloud, love, ghost, music, virtue.*

- Nouns are often pointed out by noun indicators. These noun indicators—*the, a, an*—signal that a noun is ahead, although there may be words between the indicator and the noun itself.

the slime	*a* werewolf	*an* aardvark
the green slime	*a* hungry werewolf	*an* angry aardvark

Pronouns

A **pronoun** is a word that is used in place of a noun.

- Some pronouns may represent specific persons or things:

I	she	they	you
me	her	them	yourself
myself	herself	themselves	yourselves
it	he	we	who
itself	him	us	whom
that	himself	ourselves	

- Indefinite pronouns refer to nouns (persons, places, things) in a general way:

each   everyone   nobody   somebody

- Other pronouns point out particular things:

Singular	Plural
this, that	*these, those*
This is my treasure.	*These* are my jewels.
That is your junk	*Those* are your trinkets.

- Still other pronouns introduce questions.

  Which is the best CD player?

  What are the main ingredients of a Twinkie?

Verbs

Verbs show action or express being in relation to the subject of a sentence. They customarily occur in set positions in sentences.

- **Action verbs** are usually easy to identify.

  The aardvark *ate* the crisp, tasty ants. [action verb]

  The aardvark *washed* them down with a snoutful of water. [action verb]

- The **being verbs** are few in number and are also easy to identify. The most common *being* verbs are *is, was, were, are,* and *am.*

  Gilligan *is* on an island in the South Pacific. [being verb]

  I *am* his enthusiastic fan. [being verb]

- The form of a verb expresses its tense, that is, the time of the action or being. The time may be in the present or past.

  Roseanne *sings* "The Star-Spangled Banner." [present]

  Roseanne *sang* "The Star-Spangled Banner." [past]

- One or more **helping verbs** may be used with the main verb to form other tenses. The combination is called a *verb phrase.*

  She *had sung* the songs many times in the shower. [Helping verb and main verb indicate a time in the past.]

  She *will be singing* the song no more in San Diego. [Helping verbs and main verbs indicate a time in the future.]

- Some helping verbs can be used alone as main verbs; *has, have, had, is, was, were, are, am.* Certain other helping verbs function only as helpers: *will, shall, should, could.*

The most common position for the verb is directly after the subject or after the subject and its modifiers.

  At high noon only two men [subject] *were* on Main Street.

  The man with a faster draw [subject and modifiers] *walked* away alone.

Adjectives

Adjectives modify nouns and pronouns. Most adjectives answer the questions *What kind? Which one?* and *How many?*

- Adjectives answering the *What kind?* question are descriptive. They tell the quality, kind, or condition of the nouns or pronouns they modify.

red convertible	*dirty* fork
noisy muffler	*wild* roses
The rain is *gentle*.	Bob was *tired*.

- Adjectives answering the *Which one?* question narrow or restrict the meaning of a noun. Some of these are pronouns that become adjectives by function.

my money	*our* ideas	the *other* house
this reason	*these* apples	

- Adjectives answering the *How many?* question are, of course, numbering words.

some people	*each* pet	*few* goals
three dollars	*one* glove	

- The words *a, an,* and *the* are adjectives called *articles.* As "noun indicators," they point out persons, places, and things.

Adverbs

Adverbs modify verbs, adjectives, and other adverbs. Adverbs answer the questions *How? Where? When?* and *To what degree?*

Modifying Verbs: They <u>did</u> their work <u>quickly</u>.
　　　　　　　　　　　　　v　　　　　　　　adv

He <u>replied</u> <u>angrily</u>.
　v　　　adv

Modifying Adjectives: They were <u>somewhat</u> <u>happy</u>.
　　　　　　　　　　　　　　　　adv　　　adj

- Adverbs that answer the *How?* question are concerned with manner or way.

  She ate the snails *hungrily.*

  He snored *noisily.*

- Adverbs that answer the *Where?* question show location.

  They drove *downtown.*

  He stayed *behind.*

  She climbed *upstairs.*

- Adverbs that answer the *When?* question indicate time.

  The ship sailed *yesterday.*

  I expect an answer *soon.*

- Adverbs that answer the *To what degree?* question express extent.

  She is *entirely* correct.

  He was *somewhat* annoyed.

Most words ending in *-ly* are adverbs.

>He completed the task <u>skillfully</u>. [adverb]

>She answered him <u>courteously</u>. [adverb]

However, there are a few exceptions.

>The house provided a <u>lovely</u> view of the valley. [adjective]

>Your goblin mask is <u>ugly</u>. [adjective]

Prepositions

A **preposition** is a word or group of words that function as a connective. The preposition connects its object(s) to some other word(s) in the sentence. A preposition and its object(s)—usually a noun or pronoun—with modifiers make up a **prepositional phrase**.

>Bart worked <u>against</u> great <u>odds</u>.
>
>   prep   object
>
>   prepositional phrase

>Everyone <u>in</u> his <u>household</u> cheered his effort.
>
> prep   object
>
> prepositional phrase

Some of the most common prepositions are the following:

about	before	but	into	past
above	behind	by	like	to
across	below	despite	near	toward
after	beneath	down	of	under
against	beside	for	off	until
among	between	from	on	upon
around	beyond	in	over	with

Some prepositions are composed of more than one word and are made up from other parts of speech:

according to	as far as	because of	in spite of
ahead of	as well as	in back of	instead of
along with	aside from	in front of	together with

Caution: Do not confuse adverbs with prepositions.

>I went *across* slowly. [without an object—adverb]

>I went *across* the field. [with an object—preposition]

>We walked *behind* silently. [without an object—adverb]

>We walked *behind* the mall. [with an object—preposition]

Conjunctions

A **conjunction** connects and shows a relationship between words, phrases, or clauses. A phrase is two or more words acting as a part of speech. A clause is a group of words with a subject and a verb. An independent clause can stand by itself: *She plays bass guitar.* A dependent clause cannot stand by itself: *when she plays bass guitar.*

There are two kinds of conjunctions: coordinating and subordinating.

Coordinating conjunctions connect words, phrases, and clauses of equal rank: noun with noun, adjective with adjective, verb with verb, phrase with phrase, main clause with main clause, and subordinate clause with subordinate clause. The seven common coordinating conjunctions are *for, and, nor, but, or, yet,* and *so.* (They form the acronym FANBOYS.)

> **Two Nouns:**   Bring a <u>pencil</u> <u>and</u> some <u>paper</u>.
>   noun   conj   noun

> **Two Phrases:**   Did she go <u>to the store</u> <u>or</u> <u>to the game</u>?
>   prep phrase conj prep phrase

Paired conjunctions such as *either/or, neither/nor,* or *both/and* are usually classed as coordinating conjunctions.

> <u>Neither</u> the coach <u>nor</u> the manager was at fault.
>   conj   conj

Subordinating conjunctions connect dependent clauses with main clauses. The most common subordinating conjunctions include the following:

after	because	provided	whenever
although	before	since	where
as	but that	so that	whereas
as if	if	till	wherever
as long as	in order that	until	
as soon as	notwithstanding	when	

Sometimes the dependent clause comes *before* the main clause, where it is set off by a comma.

> <u>Although</u> <u>she</u> <u>was</u> in pain, she stayed in the game.
>   conj   sub   v
>   dependent clause

Sometimes the dependent clause comes *after* the main clause, where it usually is *not* set off by a comma.

> She stayed in the game <u>because</u> <u>she</u> <u>was needed</u>.
>   conj   sub   v
>   dependent clause

Caution: Certain words can function as either conjunctions or prepositions. It is necessary to look ahead to see if the word introduces a clause with a subject and verb—conjunction function—or takes an object—preposition function. Some of the words with two functions are these: *after, for, since, until.*

> *After* the concert was over, we went home. [clause follows—conjunction]

> *After* the concert, we went home. [object follows—preposition]

Interjections

An **interjection** conveys strong emotion or surprise. When an interjection appears alone, it is usually punctuated with an exclamation mark.

Wow!   Curses!   Cowabunga!   Yabba dabba doo!

When it appears as part of a sentence, an interjection is usually followed by a comma.

Oh, I did not consider that problem.

The interjection may sound exciting, but it is seldom appropriate for college writing.

EXERCISE 1

Identifying Parts of Speech

Identify the part of speech of each italicized word or group of words by placing the appropriate abbreviations in the blanks. (See Answer Key for answers.)

n	*noun*	*pro*	*pronoun*
v	*verb*	*adj*	*adjective*
adv	*adverb*	*conj*	*conjunction*
prep	*preposition*		

_____ _____ 1. The *turtle* can be defined as a reptile *with* a shell.

_____ _____ 2. It is a *toothless* creature that *can smell* and see well.

_____ _____ 3. Some live *mostly* in the water, whereas others live mostly *in* places as dry as the desert.

_____ _____ 4. Both sea *and land* turtles will burrow and hibernate.

_____ _____ 5. Turtles are well known *for their* longevity.

_____ _____ 6. *Some live* to be more than a hundred years old.

_____ _____ 7. *Many* people purchase turtles for *pets*.

_____ _____ 8. Young turtles *eat chopped* raw meat, greens, fish, and worms.

_____ _____ 9. *They* need both sunlight *and* shade.

_____ _____ 10. *Some* people paint their *pet* turtles, a practice that can damage the turtles' shells.

_____ _____ 11. *Most* turtles are not *suitable* for pets.

_____ _____ 12. The snapping turtle *is* one such *species*.

_____ _____ 13. *It* can be *vicious* when cornered.

_____ _____ 14. The *common* snapper weighs up to sixty pounds and can snap off a set of fingers *with* one bite.

_____ _____ 15. Folklore holds that *when* a snapping turtle bites someone, it will not let go *until* it hears thunder.

_____ _____ 16. Stories *circulate* about a farmer who cut off the head of a snapping turtle that was biting someone, *yet* even without its body, the snapper would not let go.

_____ _____ 17. The box turtle is a *gentle creature* and makes a good pet.

_____ _____ 18. It has a *hooked* beak, red eyes, and a splotchy *yellow* and brown shell.

_____ _____ 19. It eats worms, snails, berries, *and* other *fruit.*

_____ _____ 20. In the summer in the Midwest, one *can find* many box turtles crawling about, their solemn beaks red from a *meal* of blackberries.

EXERCISE 2

Identifying Parts of Speech

Identify the part of speech of each italicized word or group of words by placing the appropriate abbreviations in the blanks.

n	*noun*	*pro*	*pronoun*
v	*verb*	*adj*	*adjective*
adv	*adverb*	*conj*	*conjunction*
prep	*preposition*		

_____ _____ 1. *Before* gunpowder was invented, soldiers *often* wore armor.

_____ _____ 2. The armor *protected* the soldiers against *sharp* blows.

_____ _____ 3. Early armor was designed *from* layers of animal *hide.*

_____ _____ 4. The *first* designs were in the form *of* shields.

_____ _____ 5. Other designs *covered* the *entire* body.

_____ _____ 6. Whole battles were *sometimes* won or *lost* because of armor.

_____ _____ 7. *Armor* craftsmen had *important* positions in society.

_____ _____ 8. Chain mail *armor* was made *of* small connected rings.

_____ _____ 9. *Japanese* armor of the 1500s was made *of* thousands of fishlike scales.

_____ _____ 10. Most European armor was made of *large* metal plates shaped to the *body.*

_____ _____ 11. *Some* of it was designed with precious metals and decorated with *artistic* patterns.

_____ _____ 12. The metal was *heavy, and* soldiers needed special assistance in mounting their horses.

_____ _____ 13. Because the metal was *so* strong, knights *often* tried to unseat their opponents instead of trying to pierce the armor.

_____ _____ 14. One famous soldier fell off his horse *and* into a stream *fifteen* inches deep.

_____ _____ 15. His armor *filled* with water *and* he drowned.

_____ _____ 16. *During* the crusades, European soldiers wore their *metal* armor into the deserts.

_____ _____ 17. The *armor* often became so hot the soldiers fell off their horses *in* exhaustion.

_____ _____ 18. With the development of the longbow *and* gunpowder, traditional armor *lost* its popularity.

_____ _____ 19. Lightweight *armor* has been used in *modern* warfare.

_____ _____ 20. The helmet is one *carryover* from earlier *designs*.

EXERCISE 3   ## Identifying Parts of Speech

Identify the part of speech of each italicized word or group of words by placing the appropriate abbreviations in the blanks.

n	noun	pro	pronoun
v	verb	adj	adjective
adv	adverb	conj	conjunction
prep	preposition		

_____ _____ 1. *For* about forty years, the Three Stooges were a popular *comedy* team.

_____ _____ 2. They were *often* accused of making films *in* bad taste, but no one accused them of being good actors.

_____ _____ 3. For decades they *made seven* or more pictures a year.

_____ _____ 4. Actually six *different* actors *played* the parts.

_____ _____ 5. The *most* famous threesome *was* Moe, Curley, and Larry.

_____ _____ 6. The Stooges specialized *in physical* comedy.

_____ _____ 7. They *took* special *delight* in hitting each other in the head and poking each other's eyes.

_____ _____ 8. Moe was the on-screen *leader* of this *zany* group.

_____ _____ 9. He assumed leadership in each film *because he* was more intelligent than the others, which isn't saying much.

_____ _____ 10. Curley was not bright, but he made up for his *dumbness* by having the *hardest* head in the world, at least in the world of Stooge movies.

_____ _____ 11. Larry *often got caught* between the flailing arms and kicking feet of Moe and Curley.

_____ _____ 12. The movies made *by* the Stooges *usually* came in two reels and were shown along with feature-length films.

_____ _____ 13. The Stooge movies *were given* such *titles* as *Half-Wits, Three Hams on Rye, Slap Happy Sleuths,* and *Matri Phony.*

_____ _____ 14. They made fun of *dignity* and physically abused each other with all kinds *of* lethal instruments, but they never got hurt.

_____ _____ 15. They received *little respect* from the filmmaking community.

_____ _____ 16. Only Moe saved *his* money *and* became wealthy.

_____ _____ 17. Apparently Curley *at* times lived his *movie* role off stage.

_____ _____ 18. After a *brief* marriage, Curley's wife *left* him, saying he punched, poked, pinched, and pushed her and left cigar butts in the sink.

_____ _____ 19. Moe tried to gain *respectability* as a character actor, but the audiences could never accept *him* in serious roles.

_____ _____ 20. A whole new television *audience has made* the Three Stooges the stars they never were in their lifetimes.

Appendix B: Taking Tests

Good test-taking begins with good study techniques. These techniques involve, among other things, how to read, think, and write effectively. Those skills have been covered in this book. Here we will discuss only a few principles that apply directly and immediately to the test situation.

At the beginning of the semester, you should discover how you will be tested in each course. Match your note-taking and underlining of texts to the kind or kinds of tests you will take. Objective tests will usually require somewhat more attention to details than will subjective or essay tests.

For both types of tests—and you will probably have a combination—you should carefully apportion your time, deciding how much to spend on each section or essay and allowing a few minutes for a quick review of answers. For both, you should also read the directions carefully, marking key words (if you are permitted to do so) as a reminder to you for concentration.

Objective Tests

Here are some tips on taking objective tests.

- Find out whether you will be graded on the basis of the number of correct answers or on the basis of right-minus-wrong answers. This is the difference: If you are graded on the basis of the number of correct answers, there is no penalty for guessing; therefore, if you want the highest possible score, you should leave no blanks. But if you are graded on the basis of right-minus-wrong (meaning one or a fraction of one is subtracted from your correct answers for every miss), then answer only if the odds of being right are in your favor. For example, if you know an answer is one of two possibilities, you have a 50 percent chance of getting it right; consequently, guess if the penalty is less than one because you could gain one by getting it right and lose less than one by getting it wrong. Ask your teacher to explain if there is a right-minus-wrong factor.

- If you are going to guess and you want to get some answers correct, you should pick one column and fill in the bubbles. By doing that, you will almost certainly get some correct.

- Studies show that in a typical four-part multiple-choice test section, more answers are B and C than A and D.

- Statements with absolutes such as *always* and *never* are likely to be false, whereas statements with qualifications such as *usually* and *probably* are likely to be true.

- If you don't know an answer, instead of fixating on it and getting frustrated, mark it with what seems right, put a dot alongside your answer, and go back later for a second look if time permits.

- When (and if) you go back to check your work, do not make changes unless you discover that you obviously marked one incorrectly. Studies have shown that first hunches are usually more accurate.

Subjective, or Essay, Tests

Here are some tips on taking subjective tests.

- Consider the text, the approach taken by the instructor in lectures, and the overall approach in the course outline and try to anticipate essay questions. Then, in your preparation, jot down and memorize simple outlines that will jog your memory during the test if you have anticipated correctly.

- Remember to keep track of time. A time-consuming A+ essay that does not allow you to finish the second half of the exam will result in a failing grade.

- Study the essay questions carefully. Underline key words. Each essay question will have two parts: the subject part and the treatment part. It may also have a limiting part. If you are required, for example, to compare and contrast President Clinton and President George W. Bush on their environmental programs, you should be able to analyze the topic immediately in this fashion:

> The *subject* is President Carter and President Bush.
>
> The *limitation* is their environmental programs.
>
> The *treatment* is comparison and contrast.

Hence, you might mark it in this fashion:

> <u>Compare and contrast</u> the <u>environmental programs</u> of
>   treatment   limitation
>
> <u>President Carter and President Bush.</u>
>   subject

The treatment part (here "compare and contrast") may very well be one of the forms of discourse such as definition, description, or analysis, or it may be something like "evaluate" or "discuss," in which a certain form or forms would be used. Regardless of what the treatment word is, the first step is to determine the natural points of division and to prepare a simple outline or outline alternative for organization.

- In writing the essay, be sure to include specific information as support for your generalizations.

Appendix C: Writing a Job-Application Letter and a Résumé

Two forms of practical writing that you may need even before you finish your college work are the job-application letter and the résumé. They will often go together as requirements by an employer. In some instances, the employer will suggest the form and content of the letter and résumé; in others, you will receive no directions and should adjust your letter and résumé to match the requirements and expectations as you perceive them. The models on pages 463 and 464 are typical of what job applicants commonly submit. The *Sentences, Paragraphs, and Essays* student website contains more extensive instruction on writing résumés.

Job-Application Letter

The following basic guidelines will serve you well:

- Use standard letter-size paper and type size and style.

- Do not apologize and do not brag.

- Do not go into tedious detail, but do relate your education, work experience, and career goals relevant to the available job.

- Begin your letter with a statement indicating why you are writing the letter and how you heard about the job opening.

- End the letter by stating how you can be contacted for an interview.

Résumé

Employers are especially concerned about your most recent work experiences and education, so include them first, as indicated in the example on page 464. The heading "College Activities" can be replaced with "Interests and Activities." Your main concern is presenting relevant information in a highly readable form. Always end with a list of references.

203 Village Center Avenue
Glendora, CA 91740
July 11, 2003

Mr. Roy Ritter
Computers Unlimited
1849 N. Granada Avenue
Walnut, CA 91789

Dear Mr. Ritter:

I am responding to your advertisement in the Los Angeles *Times* for the position of salesperson for used computers. Please consider me as a candidate.

In one more semester I will have completed my Associate in Arts degree at Mt. San Antonio College with a major in business management and a minor in computer technology.

My experience relates directly to the job you offer. As a result of my part-time work for two years as lab technician at my college, I have come to know the operations of several different computers. I have also learned to explain the operations to people who have very little knowledge of computers. In my business classes, I have studied the practical approaches to advertising and sales while also learning theory. Each semester for the past two years, I have worked in the college bookstore, where I helped customers who were buying various products, including computers.

This job would coincide perfectly with my work at school, my work experience, and even my goal of being a salesperson with a large company.

Enclosed is my résumé with several references to people who know me well. Please contact them if you want information or if you would like a written evaluation. I am available for an interview at your request.

Sincerely yours,

Benjamin Johanson
Benjamin Johanson

Benjamin Johanson
203 Village Center Avenue
Glendora, CA 91740
(626) 987-5555

WORK EXPERIENCE
Lab Assistant in the Mt. San Antonio College Computer Lab   2001–03
Sales and Stock Technician in the Mt. San Antonio College Bookstore   2001–03

EDUCATION
Full-time student at Mt. San Antonio College   2001–03
High school diploma from Glendora High School   2001

COLLEGE ACTIVITIES
Hackers' Club (2001–02)
Chess Club (2001–02)
Forensics Club (2001–03)—twice a regional debate champion

REFERENCES
Stewart Hamlen
Chairperson, Business Department
Mt. San Antonio College
Walnut, CA 91789
(909) 594-5611, ext. 4707

Bart Grassmont
Human Resources Director, Bookstore
Mt. San Antonio College
Walnut, CA 91789
(909) 594-5611, ext. 4706

Howard McGraw
Coach, Forensics Team
Mt. San Antonio College
Walnut, CA 91789
(909) 594-5611, ext. 4575

Appendix D: Brief Guide for ESL Students

If you came to this country knowing little English, you probably acquired vocabulary first. Then you began using that vocabulary within the basic patterns of your own language. If your native language had no articles, you probably used no articles; if your language had no verb tenses, you probably used no verb tenses, and so on. Using the grammar of your own language with your new vocabulary may initially have enabled you to make longer and more complex statements in English, but eventually you learned that your native grammar and your adopted grammar were different. You may even have learned that no two grammars are the same, and that English has a bewildering set of rules and an even longer set of exceptions to those rules. Part 2 of this book presents grammar (the way we put words together) and rhetoric (the way we use language effectively) that can be applied to your writing. The following are some definitions, rules, and references that are of special help to writers who are learning English as a second language (ESL).

Using Articles in Relation to Nouns

Articles

Articles are either indefinite (*an, a*) or definite (*the*). Because they point out nouns, they are often called *noun determiners*.

Nouns

Nouns can be either singular (*book*) or plural (*books*) and are either count nouns (things that can be counted, such as "book") or noncount nouns (things that cannot be counted, such as "homework"). If you are not certain whether a noun is a count noun or a noncount noun, try placing the word *much* before the word. You can say "much homework," so *homework* is a noncount noun.

Rules

- **Use an indefinite article (*a* or *an*) before singular count nouns and not before noncount nouns.** The indefinite article means "one," so you would not use it before plural count nouns.

Correct:	I saw a book. [count noun]
Correct:	I ate an apple. [count noun]
Incorrect:	I fell in a love. [noncount noun]
Correct:	I fell in love. [noncount noun]
Incorrect:	I was in a good health. [noncount noun]
Correct:	I was in good health. [noncount noun]

- **Use the definite article (*the*) before both singular and plural count nouns that have specific reference.**

Correct:	I read the book. [a specific one]
Correct:	I read the books. [specific ones]
Correct:	I like to read a good book. [nonspecific, therefore the indefinite article]

Correct: A student who works hard will pass. [any student, therefore nonspecific]

Correct: The student on my left is falling asleep. [a specific student]

- **Use the definite article with noncount nouns only when they are specifically identified.**

  Correct: Honesty [as an idea] is a rare commodity.

  Correct: The honesty of my friend has inspired me. [specifically identified]

  Incorrect: I was in trouble and needed the assistance. [not specifically identified]

  Correct: The assistance offered by the paramedics was appreciated. [specifically identified]

- **Place the definite article before proper nouns (names) of**

  oceans, rivers, and deserts (for example, *the* Pacific Ocean and *the* Red River).

  countries, if the first part of the name indicates a division (*the* United States of America).

  regions (*the* South).

  plural islands (*the* Hawaiian Islands).

  museums and libraries (*the* Los Angeles County Museum).

  colleges and universities when the word *college* or *university* comes before the name (*the* University of Oklahoma).

These are the main rules. For a more detailed account of rules for articles, see a comprehensive ESL book in your library.

Sentence Patterns

Chapter 3 of this book defines and illustrates the patterns of English sentences. Some languages include sentence patterns not used in standard English. The following principles are well worth remembering:

- **The conventional English sentence is based on one or more clauses, each of which must have a subject (sometimes the implied "you") and a verb.**

  Incorrect: Saw the book. [subject needed even if it is obvious]

  Correct: I saw the book.

- **English does not repeat a subject, even for emphasis.**

  Incorrect: The book that I read it was interesting.

  Correct: The book that I read was interesting.

Verb Endings

- **English indicates time through verbs.** Learn the different forms of verb tenses and the combinations of main verbs and helping verbs.

Incorrect:	He watching the game. [A verblike word ending in *-ing* cannot be a verb all by itself.]
Correct:	He is watching the game. [Note that a helping verb such as *is, has, has been, will,* or *will be* always occurs before a main verb ending in *-ing*.]

- **Take special care in maintaining consistency in tense.**

Incorrect:	I went to the mall. I watch a movie there. [verb tenses inconsistent]
Correct:	I went to the mall. I watched a movie there.

All twelve verb tenses are covered with explanations, examples, and exercises in Chapter 6.

Idioms

Some of your initial problems with writing English are likely to arise from trying to adjust to a different and difficult grammar. If the English language used an entirely systematic grammar, your learning would be easier, but English has patterns that are both complex and irregular. Among them are idioms, word groups that often defy grammatical rules and mean something other than what they appear to mean.

The expression "He kicked the bucket" does not mean that someone struck a cylindrical container with his foot; instead, it means that someone has died. That example is one kind of idiom. Because the expression suggests a certain irreverence, it would not be the choice of most people who want to make a statement about death; but if it is used, it must be used with its own precise wording, not "He struck the long cylindrical container with his foot," or "He did some bucket-kicking." Like other languages, the English language has thousands of these idioms. Expressions such as "the more the merrier" and "on the outs" are ungrammatical. They are also very informal expressions and therefore seldom used in college writing, although they are an indispensable part of a flexible, effective, all-purpose vocabulary. Because of their twisted meanings and illogic, idioms are likely to be among the last parts of language that a new speaker learns well. A speaker must know the culture thoroughly to understand when, where, and how to use slang and other idiomatic expressions.

If you listen carefully and read extensively, you will learn English idioms. Your library will have dictionaries that explain them.

More Suggestions for ESL Writers

1. Read your writing aloud and try to detect inconsistencies and awkward phrasing.

2. Have others read your writing aloud for the same purposes.

3. If you have severe problems with grammatical awkwardness, try composing shorter, more direct sentences until you become more proficient in phrasing.

4. On your Self-Evaluation Chart, list the problems you have (such as articles, verb endings, clause patterns), review revelant sections of Part 1 of this book, and concentrate on your own problem areas as you draft, revise, and edit.

Correcting a First Draft

Make corrections in the use of articles, verbs, and phrasing. (See Answer Key for answers.)

George Washington at Trenton

One of most famous battles during the War of Independence occur at Trenton, New Jersey, on Christmas Eve of the 1776. The colonists outmatched in supplies and finances and were outnumbered in troop strength. Most observers in other countries think rebellion would be put down soon. British overconfident and believe there would be no more battles until spring. But George Washington decide to fight one more time. That Christmas, while large army of Britishers having party and thinking about the holiday season, Americans set out for surprise raid. They loaded onto boats used for carrying ore and rowed across Delaware River. George Washington stood tall in lead boat. According to legend, drummer boy floated across river on his drum, pulled by rope tied to boat. Because British did not feel threatened by the ragtag colonist forces, they unprepared to do battle. The colonists stormed living quarters and the general assembly hall and achieved victory. It was good for the colonists' morale, something they needed, for they would endure long, hard winter before fighting again.

Copyright © Houghton Mifflin Company. All rights reserved.

Answer Key

Chapter 1

Exercise 1

The Leadership of Martin Luther King Jr.

1   On December 1, 1955, in Montgomery, Alabama, a <u>black woman</u> named <u>Rosa Parks</u> was <u>arrested</u> for <u>refusing to give up</u> her <u>bus seat</u> to a <u>white man</u>. In <u>protest</u>, <u>Montgomery blacks</u> organized a <u>year-long bus boycott</u>. The boycott <u>forced white city leaders</u> to <u>recognize</u> the <u>blacks' determination and economic power</u>.

2   <u>One of</u> the <u>organizers</u> of the bus boycott was a Baptist minister, the Reverend <u>Martin Luther King Jr</u>. King <u>soon</u> became a <u>national leader</u> in the growing <u>civil rights movement</u>. With stirring speeches and personal courage, he <u>urged blacks</u> to <u>demand their rights</u>. At the same time, he was completely <u>committed to nonviolence</u>. Like Gandhi, . . . he believed that justice could triumph through moral force.

3   In April 1963, <u>King began</u> a <u>drive</u> to <u>end segregation</u> in <u>Birmingham, Alabama. He</u> and his <u>followers boycotted segregated businesses</u> and <u>held peaceful marches</u> and <u>demonstrations</u>. Against them, the Birmingham <u>police used electric cattle prods, attack dogs, clubs</u>, and <u>fire hoses</u> to break up marches.

4   <u>Television cameras</u> brought those <u>scenes into</u> the <u>living rooms of millions of Americans</u>, who were <u>shocked</u> by what they saw. On <u>May 10</u>, Birmingham's <u>city leaders gave in</u>. A <u>committee</u> of <u>blacks and whites oversaw</u> the gradual <u>desegregation of the city</u> and <u>tried</u> to <u>open more jobs</u> for <u>blacks</u>. The <u>victory</u> was later <u>marred</u> by grief, however, when a <u>bomb exploded</u> at a Birmingham <u>church, killing four black children</u>.

Steven L. Jantzen, *World History: Perspectives on the Past.*

Chapter 2

Exercise 1

1. Mahatma Gandhi
2. he
3. You (understood)
4. good
5. fasts, writings, speeches
6. He
7. Gandhi
8. British
9. leaders, agitators
10. Gandhi

Exercise 3

1. live, travel
2. varies
3. is
4. spend
5. make
6. will beat
7. are, live
8. hoots, shakes
9. hear, go
10. are

Exercise 5

Verbs are underlined.

1. You (understood) <u>Read</u>, <u>learn</u>
2. cities <u>were</u>
3. Government, religion <u>were</u>
4. <u>was</u> difference
5. They <u>built</u>, <u>sacrificed</u>
6. ceremonies <u>related</u>
7. society <u>had</u>
8. family <u>included</u>
9. boys <u>went</u>; girls <u>went</u>, <u>learned</u>
10. Aztecs <u>wore</u>; they <u>lived</u>; they <u>ate</u>
11. Scholars <u>developed</u>
12. calendars <u>are</u>
13. language <u>was</u>
14. language <u>was</u>, <u>represented</u>
15. religion, government <u>required</u>
16. soldiers <u>could capture</u>, <u>enlarge</u>
17. Hernando Cortez <u>landed</u>
18. He <u>was joined</u>
19. Aztecs <u>rebelled</u>
20. Spaniards <u>killed</u>; they <u>defeated</u>

Review 1

Verbs are underlined.

1. You (understood) <u>Read</u>
2. What <u>causes</u>
3. <u>can</u> they <u>do</u>
4. Earthquakes <u>shake</u>
5. <u>is</u> answer
6. earth <u>is covered</u>
7. they <u>are</u>
8. plates <u>bump</u>, <u>pass</u>
9. rocks <u>are squeezed</u>, <u>stretched</u>
10. They <u>pull</u>, <u>pile</u>, <u>cause</u>
11. breaks <u>are called</u>
12. formation <u>is</u>
13. wave <u>travels</u>
14. vibrations <u>are</u>
15. force <u>is</u>
16. scientists <u>have tried</u>
17. <u>has been</u> success
18. Earthquakes <u>are identified</u>
19. states <u>experience</u>
20. quake <u>is occurring</u>

Chapter 3

Exercise 6

___S___ 1. The most popular ⟨sport⟩ in the world <u>is</u> soccer.

___CC___ 2. ⟨People⟩ in ancient China and Japan <u>had</u> a form of soccer, and even ⟨Rome⟩ <u>had</u> a game ⟨that⟩ <u>resembled</u> soccer.

___CX___ 3. The ⟨game⟩ as ⟨it⟩ <u>is played</u> today <u>got</u> its start in England.

___S___ 4. In the Middle Ages, whole ⟨towns⟩ <u>played</u> soccer on Shrove Tuesday.

___CC___ 5. ⟨Goals⟩ <u>were built</u> at opposite ends of town, and ⟨hundreds⟩ of people ⟨who⟩ <u>lived</u> in those towns <u>would play</u> on each side.

_____S_____ 6. Such (games) resembled full-scale brawls.

_____S_____ 7. The first (side) to score a goal won and was declared village champion.

_____CP_____ 8. Then both (sides) tended to the wounded, and (they) didn't play again for a whole year.

_____S_____ 9. The (rules) of the game were written in the late 1800s at British boarding schools.

_____CP_____ 10. Now nearly every European (country) has a national soccer team, and the (teams) participate in international tournaments.

Exercise 8

_____S_____ 1. The (American Society of Civil Engineers) (ASCE) compiled a list of the seven wonders of the modern world.

_____CC_____ 2. These engineering (experts) based their decisions upon several factors; for example, (they) evaluated the pioneering quality of structures' design or construction, the structures' contributions to humanity, and the engineering challenges (that) were overcome to build the structures.

_____CX_____ 3. One (structure) on the list is the 31-mile Channel Tunnel, or Chunnel, (which) connects England and France through a system of tunnels under the English Channel.

_____CP_____ 4. Another (marvel) is the Panama Canal; (it) took 42,000 workers ten years to dig a canal across Panama to connect the Atlantic and Pacific oceans.

_____CX_____ 5. Although (it) was completed back in 1937, San Francisco's (Golden Gate Bridge) remains the world's tallest suspension bridge.

_____CP_____ 6. The bridge's (construction) involved many difficulties, for (workers) faced strong tides, frequent storms and fog, and the problem of blasting rock under deep water for earthquake-resistant foundations.

_____S_____ 7. (Two) of the structures on the ASCE's list of wonders are buildings.

_____ **CP** 8. (One) of them <u>is</u> New York's Empire State Building, and the (other) <u>is</u> the CN Tower in Toronto, Canada.

_____ **CC** 9. Even though (it) <u>is</u> no longer the tallest building in the world, the well-engineered (Empire State Building) <u>held</u> that record for forty years, and its (construction) <u>revolutionized</u> the skyscraper construction industry.

_____ **CP** 10. The (Itaipu Dam) at the Brazil/Paraguay border and the (dams, flood-gates,) and storm surge (barriers) of the Netherlands' North Sea Protection Works <u>illustrate</u> humanity's ability to master the forces of nature, so (they) <u>are</u> the sixth and seventh items on the list.

Review 1

_____ **S** 1. For more than forty years, (dolphins) <u>have served</u> in the U.S. Navy.

_____ **CX** 2. (Dolphins) <u>use</u> *echolocation,* (which) <u>involves</u> transmitting sound waves at objects and then <u>reading</u> the "echoes" from those objects.

_____ **S** 3. (They) <u>can distinguish</u> a BB pellet from a kernel of corn from fifty feet away.

_____ **CP** 4. (They) <u>can</u> also tell the difference between natural and man-made objects, so the (navy) <u>has trained</u> dolphins to detect explosive anti-ship mines.

_____ **CX** 5. After unmanned undersea (vehicles) <u>use</u> sonar to identify suspicious objects, a (dolphin) and his (team) of humans <u>go</u> into watery combat zones to evalute those objects.

_____ **CC** 6. When a (dolphin) positively <u>identifies</u> a mine, the (location) <u>is marked,</u> and (divers) <u>arrive</u> later to remove the mine.

_____ **S** 7. During the 2003 war with Iraq, (dolphins) <u>helped</u> disarm 100 mines and underwater booby traps planted in the water near the port city of Umm Qasr.

_____ **CX** 8. The (dolphins) <u>are</u> not in jeopardy because (they) <u>are trained</u> to stay a safe distance from the mines.

_____CP_____ 9. (Dolphins) also <u>protected</u> warships during the Vietnam War; in 1970,

for example, the (presence) of five navy dolphins <u>prevented</u> enemy

divers from destroying an army pier.

_____CC_____ 10. Many (people) do not <u>realize</u> that (dolphins) <u>have used</u> their extrordi-

nary abilites to protect American lives during wartime, so the (navy)

<u>considers</u> them to be very valuable assets.

Chapter 4

Exercise 1

1. James Francis "Jim" Thorpe, a Sac and Fox Indian, was born in 1888 near

   Prague, Oklahoma, **, but** At the age of sixteen, he left home to enroll in the Carlisle

   Indian School in Pennsylvania.

2. He had had little experience playing football, **, yet** He led his small college to victo-

   ries against championship teams.

3. He had scarcely heard of other sports, **, but** He golfed in the 70s, bowled above

   200, and played varsity basketball and lacrosse.

4. In the 1912 Olympic Games for amateur athletes at Stockholm, Jim Thorpe

   entered the two most rigorous events, the decathlon and the pentathlon, **, and** He

   won both.

5. King Gustav V of Sweden told him, "You, Sir, are the greatest athlete in the

   world," **; and** Jim Thorpe said, "Thanks, King."

6. Later it was said he had once been paid fifteen dollars a week to play baseball,

   making him a professional athlete, **, so** The Olympic medals were taken from him.

7. Soon a major league baseball scout did offer Thorpe a respectable contract, **, and** He

   played in the National League for six seasons.

8. Not content to play only one sport, he also earned a good salary for that time

   in professional football, **, yet** After competing for fifteen years, he said he had never

   played for the money.

9. Many regard Jim Thorpe as the greatest athlete of the twentieth century/He `, for`
excelled in numerous sports at the highest levels of athletic competition.

10. Off the playing fields, he was known by his friends as a modest, quiet man/On `, but`
the fields, he was a person of joyful combat.

Exercise 3

1. The legendary island of Atlantis has fascinated people for centuries/It probably `; however,`
never existed.

2. According to the Greek writer Plato, the people of Atlantis were very ambitious and warlike/They planned to conquer all of the Mediterranean. `; in fact,`

3. Initially, they were successful in subduing areas to the west/They became wealthy. `; therefore,`

4. Then the people of Atlantis became proud/They became corrupt and wicked. `; moreover,`

5. They were confident and attacked Athens/Athens and its allies defeated the `; however,`
invaders.

6. The story of Atlantis is probably just a tale/Many people have believed it. `; however,`

7. Some writers have tried to link the legend with such real places as America
and the Canary Islands/No link has been found. `; nevertheless,`

8. The Minoan civilization on Crete was destroyed by tidal waves/A similar fate `;`
may have befallen Atlantis.

9. Some people speculate about a volcanic explosion on Atlantis/A volcanic `; in fact,`
eruption did destroy part of the island Thera in the Eastern Mediterranean in
1500 B.C.E.

10. Some writers have conjectured that American Indians migrated to the New
World by way of Atlantis/Archaeologists dispute that idea. `; however,`

Exercise 5

1. The freeway congestion was under study. ~~The problem~~ that occurred every Friday
at noon/

2. The vacationers had a good time/The bears destroyed a few tents and ate `, even though`
people's food.

, although
3. The teenagers loved their senior prom,/The band played badly.

because
4. Farmers gathered for miles around,/Jeff had grown a fifty-pound cucumber.

If
5. Back-seat drivers make unwanted suggestions in the nag-proof model,/They

can be ejected from the vehicle.

who
6. The marriage counselor gave bad advice,/~~He~~ charged only half price.

that
7. The robots would not do their work. ~~They~~ needed fresh batteries,/

Because
8. The hurricane was expected to hit during the night,/The residents checked

their flashlights.

When
9. The ice sculptor displayed his work in the dining hall,/The customers

applauded.

After
10. Someone stole the artwork of ice,/No evidence was found.

Exercise 7

Although
1. A grumpy bear had stalked the grounds,/Summer camp had been a great expe-

, and
rience for the campers,/They vowed to return.

After   **, and**
2. The stuffed cabbage ran out,/The party ended,/The guests went home.

Because   **, and**
3. It was a costume party,/All the guests dressed as movie legends,/Ten were Elvis

impersonators.

When   **, and**
4. A new Elvis theme park opened in our town,/I attended,/I think I saw the King.

Because   **, and**
5. My father encouraged me to take up a hobby,/I began collecting stamps,/Now

my hobby has become a business.

, and   **, although**
6. They were in a wilderness camp,/They were not allowed to bring pets,/They

were allowed to bring toys.

Because   **, but**
7. He had no leather shoes to wear,/Young Stu could not go to the prom,/He hoped

there would be a prom next year.

, and   **, though**
8. People were hungry,/They ate massive quantities of hot dogs at the game,/They

knew the dogs were made of mystery meat.

While   **, and**
9. The ambulance drivers were taking a break,/A man had a choking fit,/The

drivers came to his rescue.

Even though
10. ∧The film was filled with scenes of violence,/It included a charming love story,/ *, and* The public liked it.

Exercise 9

1. Ernest Hemingway won the Nobel Prize for literature in 1954. ~~He was mainly~~ an American writer of fiction,/

3. After high school he became a reporter,/ ~~He worked~~ for the Kansas City *Star.*

5. In 1920 he returned to journalism with the Toronto *Star*, *and* ~~He~~ met his future first wife, Hadley Richardson.

7. ~~Hemingway~~ work~~ed~~ *ing* conscientiously on his writing,/He soon became a leader of the so-called Lost Generation.

9. During World War II Hemingway armed his fishing boat and hunted for German submarines,/ *in* ~~He patrolled~~ the waters of the Caribbean.

Review 1

1. The Mercury Comet was judged the winner. ~~It had~~ imitation zebra-skin seat *, with* covers,/ ~~It had~~ *and* an eight-ball shift knob,/

2. Koko had a great plan to make some money,/ *, but* ∮he had financial problems,/ *and* could not develop her plan.

3. The mixture could not be discussed openly,/ *because* ¢ompetitors were curious,/ *, and* ¢orporate spies were everywhere.

4. Babette's bowling ball is special. It is red and green,/ *, and* /t is decorated with her phone number in metal-flake.

5. *Although* ∧The young bagpiper liked Scottish food,/ *and* He enjoyed doing Scottish dances,/ Wearing a kilt in winter left him cold.

6. Ruby missed the alligator farm. She fondly remembered the hissing and snapping of the beasts as they scrambled for raw meat,/ *, but* Her neighbors were indifferent to the loss.

7. *Although* ∧Many people are pleased to purchase items with food preservatives,/ Øthers are *because* fearful,/They think these chemicals may also preserve consumers.

                                           because
8. Leewan loves her new in-line roller skates/They look and perform much like
                      , but
   ice skates/They are not as safe as her conventional roller skates.
              ^

9. Fish sold at Discount Fish Market were not of the highest quality; some of
                                                                         ^
                                                  and
   them had been dead for days without refrigeration/~~They~~ were suitable only
                                                     ^
   for bait.

                                         , so
10. Cliff wanted to impress his date/~~He~~ splashed on six ounces of He-Man
                                     ^
              and
   cologne/~~He~~ put on his motorcycle leathers and a flying scarf.
           ^

Chapter 5

Exercise 1

1. <u>When Leroy Robert Paige was seven years old</u>/~~He~~ was carrying luggage at a
                                                     ;
   railroad station in Mobile, Alabama.

2. He was a clever young fellow/<u>Who invented a contraption for carrying four</u>
   <u>satchels (small suitcases) at one time.</u>

3. <u>After he did that</u>/~~He~~ was always known as Satchel Paige.
                         ;

4. His fame rests on his being arguably the best baseball pitcher/<u>Who ever played</u>
   <u>the game.</u>

5. <u>Because of the so-called Jim Crow laws</u>/~~He~~, as an African American, was not
                                                ;
   allowed to play in the major leagues/<u>Until 1948 after the Major League color</u>
   <u>barrier was broken.</u>

6. By that time he was already forty-two/<u>Although he was in excellent condition.</u>
                                         ;

7. He had pitched/<u>Wherever he could, mainly touring around the country.</u>

8. <u>When he faced Major Leaguers in exhibition games</u>/~~He~~ almost always won.
                                                          ;

9. <u>Because people liked to see him pitch</u>/~~He~~ pitched almost every day/<u>While he</u>
                                              ;
   <u>was on tour.</u>

10. One year he won 104 games. During his career he pitched 55 no-hitters and
    won more than 2,000 games.

11. He pitched his last game in the majors at the age of fifty-nine.

12. In 1971 he was the first African-American player/ Who was voted into the Baseball Hall of Fame in a special category for those/ Who played in the old Negro Leagues.

Exercise 3

1. As a subject of historical record/ Dancing seems to be a natural human act.

2. Even prehistoric cave paintings depict dancing figures/ Scrawled outlines of people in motion.

3. Dancing takes many forms, but mainly it is a matter of moving rhythmically/ In time to music.

4. Most children jump up and down when they are excited. They sway back and forth when they are contented.

5. Having studied the behavior of many ethnic groups/ Anthropologists confirm that dancing reveals much/ About a group's culture.

6. People dance for various reasons/ Such as to entertain others, to relax, to inspire others, and to celebrate life.

7. One stylized form of dancing is the ballet/ A story told with graceful, rhythmic movement and music.

8. Folk dances relate stories/ Of the dancers' culture.

9. Young people can get to know each other at social dances/ While enjoying themselves.

10. Each generation of social dancers seems to have its own style/ Sometimes a modified revival, such as swing.

Exercise 5

1. Harry polished his vehicle, a Ford Ranger truck with fine Corinthian leather seats.

2. He drove to pick up Jane for their date.

3. Jane wanted to go to the opening-day baseball game at Dodger Stadium.

4. She hoped for a new memory, a never-to-be-forgotten experience.

5. Jane dreamed of being seen on big-screen Diamond Vision in the stadium.

6. They arrived with the first sound of the bat on ball.

7. Harry bought peanuts and Crackerjacks for Jane.

8. Jane had brought a baseball glove so that she might catch a well-hit ball.

9. She brought her portable television set so that she could hear and see her heroes up close.

10. Seeing the rain clouds, they feared that the game might be canceled.

Exercise 7

(1) Two ice hotels $\overset{are}{\underset{\wedge}{}}$ the ultimate place for "chilling out." (2) One of these hotels $\overset{is}{\underset{\wedge}{}}$ in Quebec, Canada. (3) The other ~~being~~ $\overset{is}{}$ in Sweden. (4) These structures $\overset{are}{\underset{\wedge}{}}$ built of 4,500 tons of snow and 250 tons of ice, like giant igloos. (5) The hotels' rooms even ~~in-cluding~~ $\overset{include}{\underset{\wedge}{}}$ furniture made of ice. (6) Room temperatures do not rise above 27 degrees Fahrenheit. (7) But outside temperatures $\overset{are}{\underset{\wedge}{}}$ well below freezing. (8) The hotels' ice walls actually ~~trapping~~ $\overset{trap}{}$ and ~~holding~~ $\overset{hold}{\underset{\wedge}{}}$ some of the heat inside. (9) Guests still sleep in thick sleeping bags piled with animal skins for warmth. (10) In the hotels' bars, even the glasses are made of ice. (11) Drinks $\overset{are}{\underset{\wedge}{}}$ served "in the rocks" instead of "on the rocks."

(12) Construction $\overset{occurs}{\underset{\wedge}{}}$ in December of every year. (13) In January, the hotels open for business. (14) $\overset{The\ hotels}{\underset{\wedge}{}}$ ~~Stay~~ open until late March. (15) Then $\overset{they}{\underset{\wedge}{}}$ begin to melt. (16) These ~~are~~ two hotels ~~having~~ $\overset{have}{\underset{\wedge}{}}$ to be totally rebuilt every year.

Exercise 9

1. Delete "which"
2. People go to
3. Delete "who"
4. Tourists regard the
5. St. Augustine has the
6. teams go to
7. Tourists can
8. displays are available at
9. Delete "who"
10. Delete "which"

Exercise 12

1. CS; optimism, but a
2. RO; winter, and they
3. OK
4. RO; winter, yet they
5. CS; branches, and some
6. RO; managing, for they
7. CS; food, so they
8. CS; winter, and the
9. RO; depressed, but they
10. RO; help, and seven

Exercise 14

1. CS; Although Chris
2. CS; Because she
3. RO; While she . . . teens, she
4. RO; 1974, when she
5. CS; When she

6. RO; Although Evonne . . . first, Martina
7. RO; notable because she
8. CS; Because Chris
9. RO; "ice princess" because she
10. OK

Exercise 16

1. CS; 1980s; however, she
2. RO; dance; moreover, she
3. CS; school; therefore, with
4. OK
5. OK

6. CS; singer; moreover, she
7. RO; *Susan;* she
8. CS; media; consequently, she
9. CS; prospered; however, she
10. RO; herself; similarly, other

Exercise 18

1. CS; coat. They
2. RO; parades. The
3. OK
4. RO; distance. Enemies
5. OK

6. RO; uniform. The
7. CS; hand. The
8. CS; India. They
9. OK
10. RO; color. They

Review 1

    Dinosaurs were giant lizardlike animals, ~~they~~ **They** lived more than a hundred million years ago. Some had legs like lizards and turtles, **and** some had legs more like birds. The ones with legs like birds, ~~c~~ould walk easily with raised bodies. They varied in size, **and** many were huge. The largest, the diplodocus, **was** about ninety feet long, equal to the distance between the bases in baseball. ~~Weighing~~ **It weighed** more than ten elephants. The smallest weighed no more than two pounds and was no bigger than a chicken. Some dinosaurs ate meat, **and** almost certainly some dinosaurs ate other dinosaurs. ~~U~~**They used** their strong claws and fierce teeth to tear at their victims. Dinosaurs were different, ~~i~~n design as well as size. They had horns, spikes, bills, armorlike plates, clublike tails, bony crests, and teeth in many sizes and shapes ~~their~~ **Their** heads were proportionately tiny or absurdly large, **and** ~~t~~heir mouths varied, ~~d~~epending on their eating habits.

Chapter 6

Exercise 1

1. created
2. built
3. went, asked
4. returned, threw
5. dug, constructed

6. began
7. jilted
8. hoped, became
9. worked, knows
10. saw, change

Exercise 3

1. lost
2. laid
3. did, won
4. became, ran
5. eaten, served

6. ruined, put
7. cost, raise
8. sit, liked
9. rose, headed
10. knew, lusted

Exercise 6

1. said
2. is
3. had
4. could have, would have
5. had

6. have decided
7. determined
8. are considering
9. may be
10. will worry

Exercise 8

1. is
2. are
3. is
4. is
5. is

6. is
7. are
8. is
9. are
10. are

Exercise 10

Lizzie Borden was famous for being arrested and tried for the gruesome ax murder of her father and stepmother. On August 4, 1892, when Andrew Borden was taking a nap in his home, someone ~~hits~~ hit him in the head eleven times with a hatchet. His wife, Abby Borden, had already been killed in an upstairs bedroom with the same weapon. The police ~~investigate~~ investigated and ~~conclude~~ concluded that Andrew's thirty-two-year-old daughter Lizzie ~~is~~ [was] the murderess. Lizzie ~~is~~ [was] arrested but pleaded not guilty to the

crimes. Her sensational trial was followed by people all over the country. The pros-

ecution ~~presents~~ [presented] an overwhelming amount of circumstantial evidence. Many people

thought that she ~~is~~ [was] guilty. Nonetheless, Lizzie's jury acquitted her. The case remains

unsolved to this day.

Exercise 12

1. A

2. P

3. P; Pirates seized cargo and plundered coastal towns.

4. P; Also, pirates kidnapped people and held them for ransom.

5. A

6. P; Writers such as Rafael Sabatini and Lord Byron created the swashbuckling pirate of our imagination.

7. P; Books like *Captain Blood* and poems like "The Corsair" gave readers the romantic portrait of a sword-wielding, treasure-hunting ruffian in gold earrings.

8. P; As a result, people have often perceived pirates as ruthless but adventurous heroes.

9. P; Actually, though, these desperate criminals lived a drunken, violent, and short life.

10. P; The development of national navies in the nineteenth century caused the decline of piracy.

Exercise 14

1. Like most people, Bob fears public speaking.

2. Most people fear public speaking more than death!

3. Bob worries about looking foolish.

4. Bob needs to learn more about public speaking.

5. So Bob now attends Santa Ana College.

6. He has enrolled in a speech class.

7. Bob learns how to prepare a speech.

8. Bob now can control his anxiety.

9. To relax, Bob takes deep breaths.

10. Bob gives speeches confidently.

Exercise 16

1. were

2. were

3. were

4. were

5. be

Review 1

From	*To*
1. is	was
2. is	was
begins	began
3. runs	ran
4. works	worked
5. gives	gave

Review 2

1. was

2. were

3. was

4. was

5. were

Review 4

1. Whitney is rebuilding her desktop.

2. Anika can lead our group.

3. Matthew scored the last touchdown.

4. Maria works at the department store.

5. Jonathan attracts favorable attention.

Chapter 7

Exercise 1

1. me, her

2. He, I

3. she

4. them, us

5. us, me

6. We

7. us

8. who

9. whomever

10. me

Exercise 3

1. Whom		6. Who	
2. whom		7. whom	
3. who		8. whom	
4. whom		9. Whom	
5. who		10. who	

Exercise 5

1. me		6. who	
2. me		7. whom	
3. who		8. me	
4. I		9. who	
5. who		10. who, who	

Exercise 8

	From	*To*
1.	you	they
	you	they
2.	you	they
	your car	their cars
3.	you	they
4.	you	I
5.	you	he
6.	you	she
7.	you	they
8.	you	we
	you	we
9.	you	they
10.	you	they

Exercise 10

1. its		6. their	
2. he or she		7. his or her	
3. his or her		8. their	
4. it		9. their	
5. he, his		10. its, its, its	

Exercise 12

1. they, their
2. he or she, his or her
3. its
4. their
5. their
6. his or her
7. her
8. their
9. his
10. his or her

Exercise 14

1. (a) V
   (b) OK
2. (a) OK
   (b) V
3. (a) V
   (b) OK
4. (a) V
   (b) OK
5. (a) V
   (b) OK
6. (a) V
   (b) OK
7. (a) V
   (b) OK
8. (a) V
   (b) OK
9. (a) V
   (b) OK
10. (a) V
    (b) OK

Review 1

1. me
2. who
3. me
4. me
5. We

Review 2

	From	To
1.	you	one
2.	you	they
3.	one	she
4.	you	I
5.	your	his or her

Review 3

	From	To
1.	C	
2.	her	their
3.	their	his or her
4.	his	their
5.	her	their

Review 4

	From	To
1.	their	his or her
2.	their	his or her
	they are	he or she is
3.	he or she doesn't	they don't
4.	their	his
5.	his or her	their

Review 5

1. He joined the Marine Corps and that choice straightened him out.

2. Joe said to Rick, "I want to cut my hair."

3. According to an old saying, you can fool some of the people some of the time, but you can't fool all of the people all of the time.

4. Doctors say that senior citizens should get a flu shot every year.

5. Betty Sue told Rhonda Ann, "Your sauerkraut is the best in town."

Chapter 8

Exercise 3

1. most	6. best
2. really	7. real
3. hardly	8. hardly
4. badly, really	9. bad
5. well	10. most

Exercise 4

	From	*To*
1.	real	really
2.	worser	worse
3.	most biggest	biggest
4.	no	any
5.	never	ever
6.	real	really
7.	good	well
8.	very unique	unique
9.	well	good
10.	no	any

Exercise 5

1. really, good	6. really
2. any	7. strangest
3. not	8. well
4. oddest	9. best, fastest
5. most	10. more

Exercise 7

1. D; Driving through the Brazilian rainforest, we spotted leafcutter ants going about their work.

2. M; This tribe of ants is one of the few creatures that grow food on this planet.

3. M; Leafcutter ants cleverly learned to farm over 50 million years ago.

4. D; Climbing trees, the ants cut down the leaves and bite them into the shape of half-moons.

5. M; Then, each ant hoists a leaf, weighing ten times more than it does, and carries it back down the tree toward the nest.

6. M; Marching home with their leaves, the ants resemble a parade of fluttering green flags.

7. M; Carried into the subterranean tunnels of the nest, the cargo is deposited by the leafcutters.

8. M; Taking over, tiny gardener ants clean, clip, and spread the leaves with secreations from their bodies.

9. M; The ants place fungus on the hunks of leaves, lines up in neat rows.

10. M; Cultivated for food, the ants' fungus garden is fertilized by the leaves.

Review 1

In 1951, Sir Hugh Beaver, who was the managing director of the Guinness Brewery, became embroiled in an argument about which bird was the ~~faster~~ _fastest_ game bird in Europe. He wondered if a book that supplied the answers to such burning questions would sell ~~good.~~ _well._ So he worked with a fact-finding agency to compile what became _The Guinness Book of World Records_, first published in 1955. The book proved to be ~~popularer~~ _more popular_ than all other books ~~climbing~~ _Climbing_ to the top of the British bestseller lists. Over the years, more than 94 million copies of the book's editions have been sold in 100 different countries and 37 different languages, making it the top-selling copyrighted book of all time. Today, of course, Guinness World Records is still a household name. The organization continues to be the ~~better~~ _best-_ known collector and verifier of records set around the globe.

Chapter 9

Exercise 1

1. vicious, relentless, (and) inexplicable
2. family moves (and) it finds
3. to make (and) to ignore
4. invited (but) neglected
5. has inherited (and) has caused

6. physician separates (and) they hate
7. twin is (and) other is
8. embittered (and) vindictive
9. unreasoning, angry, (and) brutal
10. crashes (and) devours

Exercise 3

1. X; change *eating* to *eat*
2. X; change *escaping* to *escapes*
3. X; delete "he finds"
4. X; delete "having"
5. P

6. X; change *dish,* to *dish and*
7. X; change *upsetting* to *upset*
8. X; delete "who had"
9. P
10. X; change *becoming* to *become*

Exercise 5

1. color, amazement
2. action-packed
3. how to save them
4. to live
5. joys, sorrows

6. truth, justice, freedom
7. survives, triumphs
8. love, care
9. fly, float
10. loves, sends

Exercise 6

1. hulking, unrelenting
2. to destroy
3. life, woman
4. survive
5. humans are the slaves

6. begins
7. attack
8. to destroy
9. ugly, harmless
10. arrogant, obnoxious

Exercise 7

1. (not only) robbed . . . (but also) gave
2. (Both) Humphrey Bogart (and) Katharine Hepburn
3. (either) himself (or) Mr. Hyde
4. (neither) . . . jobs (nor) compassion
5. (either) die . . . (or) go
6. (either) develop . . . (or) go
7. (not only) gets . . . (but also) goes

8. (both) who framed . . . (and) who is playing

9. (not only) heartaches (but also) . . . joy

10. (either) his dignity (or) his life

Review 1

Ken Kesey wrote *One Flew Over the Cuckoo's Nest* as a novel. It was later made into a stage play and a film. The title was taken from a children's folk rhyme: "One flew east, one flew west, / One flew over the cuckoo's nest."

The narrator in the novel is Chief Bromden, the central character is Randle McMur-

the villain is

phy, and Nurse Ratched ~~is the villain~~. Bromden sees and ~~can~~ hear but does not speak.

s

He is a camera with a conscience. McMurphy is both an outcast and ~~serves as~~ a

individuality.

leader, and he speaks out for freedom and ~~as an individual~~. Nurse Ratched is the

voice of repression. She is the main representative of what Bromdon calls the "Com-

s

bine." She organizes, directs, controls, and, if necessary to her purposes, ~~will~~ destroy.

Chapter 10

Exercise 1

1. ?	6. .
2. .	7. !
3. .	8. ?
4. .	9. .
5. !	10. .

Exercise 3

1. Teach, . . . Blackbeard,

2. ships, . . . hostage,

3. coins, gold, silver,

4. Blackbeard, . . . menacing,

5. fierce,

6. battles,

7. swords, pistols,

8. South Carolina,

9. skull-and-crossbones,

10. flag,

11. Charleston, South Carolina,

12. ransom,

13. short,

14. 1718,

15. Ocracoke Island,

16. cheap, . . . goods,

17. ended, however, . . . November,

18. Virginia, . . . crimes,

19. battle, . . . times,

20. pirates,

Exercise 5

1. monster, . . . desperate,
2. house,
3. simple,
4. however,
5. monster, . . . dejected,
6. innocent, . . . brother,
7. horror,
8. demands,
9. him,
10. away, . . . parts,
11. anticipation,
12. project,
13. say, . . . unexpected,
14. away,
15. married, . . . fully, . . . enraged,
16. wedding, . . . horrified,
17. monster,
18. desolate, . . . North,
19. visit,
20. friend, love, . . . soul, and, therefore,

Exercise 7

1. Italian Alps,
2. summoned;
3. corpse;
4. corpse,
5. Neolithic human;
6. stone tools; consequently,
7. died;
8. wounds; for example, . . . cut,
9. battle;
10. injuries,
11. difficult,
12. interesting,
13. principles;
14. fire;
15. clothing;
16. cloth;
17. ax,
18. Italy;
19. Neolithic age,
20. him,

Exercise 9

1. Professor Jones said, "Now we will read from <u>The Complete Works of Edgar Allan Poe</u>."

2. The enthusiastic students shouted, "We like Poe! We like Poe!"

3. The professor lectured for fifty-seven minutes before he finally said, "In conclusion, I say that Poe was an unappreciated writer during his lifetime."

4. The next speaker said, "I believe that Poe said, 'A short story should be short enough so that a person can read it in one sitting.'"

5. Then, while students squirmed, he read "The Fall of the House of Usher" in
   sixty-eight minutes.

6. "Now we will do some reading in unison," said Professor Jones.

7. Each student opened a copy of <u>The Complete Works of Edgar Allan Poe</u>.

8. "Turn to page 72," said Professor Jones.

9. "What parts do we read?" asked a student.

10. "You read the words, or maybe I should say 'word,' of the raven," said the professor.

Exercise 11

1. Many of literature's great works—poems, stories, and novels—began as dreams.

2. Robert Louis Stevenson (1850–1894)—the author of *Treasure Island*— often dreamed complete stories that he would later write.

3. He had the following to say of his tale about Jekyll and Hyde: "I dreamed the scene . . . in which Hyde, pursued for some crime, took the powder and underwent the change in the presence of his pursuers."

4. Mary Shelley (1797–1851)—she was married to Romantic poet Percy Bysshe Shelley—said that a nightmare gave her the idea for her novel *Frankenstein*.

5. English Romantic poet Samuel Taylor Coleridge, who is famous for the poem "The Rime of the Ancient Mariner," is another literary artist inspired by a dream.

6. One of his best-known poems is titled "Kubla Khan: Or, a Vision in a Dream."

7. This poem begins with these famous lines: "In Xanadu did Kubla Khan/A stately pleasure-dome decree."

8. Coleridge said that he fell asleep after reading in a history book: "Here the Khan Kubla [another spelling of the name is Kublai Khan] commanded a palace to be built and a stately garden thereunto. And thus ten miles of fertile ground were enclosed within a wall."

9. Poet, philosopher, and literary critic—Coleridge had a fertile imagination and a huge intellect.

10. Unfortunately, though, he was interupted as he composed his verse about Xanadu, and his vision completely evaporated, forcing him to subtitle the poem "A Fragment."

Exercise 13

1. "I've heard that you intend to move to El Paso, Texas," my brother-in-law said.

2. "My date of departure on United Airlines is July 11," I answered.

3. "Then you've only thirty-three days remaining in California," he said.

4. My mother gave me some Samsonite luggage, and Dad gave me a Ronson razor.

5. Jennifer does not know I am leaving for the University of Texas.

6. Jennifer, my mother's dog, is one-quarter poodle and three-quarters cocker spaniel.

7. That dog's immediate concern is almost always food rather than sentimentality.

8. I wouldn't have received my scholarship without the straight A's from my elective classes.

9. I am quite indebted to Professor Jackson, a first-rate teacher of English and several courses in speech.

10. I wasn't surprised when Grandma gave me a box of stationery and a note asking me to write Mother each Friday.

Review 1

1. Everyone defines the term *success* differently; how do you define it?

2. According to American author and editor Christopher Morley, the only success is being able to spend your life the way you want to spend it.

3. Margaret Thatcher, former leader of Great Britain, said that success is being good at what you're doing but also having a sense of purpose.

4. Author Vernon Howard had this to say on the subject: "You have succeeded in life when all you really want is only what you really need."

5. Albert Einstein, however, believed that if A equals success in life, then A = x + y + z.

6. X is work, y is play, and z is keeping your mouth shut.

7. One of the most well-known quotes about success comes from philosopher Ralph Waldo Emerson, who wrote that to have succeeded is "to leave the world a bit better" and "to know that even one life has breathed easier because you have lived."

Chapter 11

Exercise 1

1. hear
2. than
3. their
4. through
5. piece
6. all right
7. passed
8. too
9. advice
10. a lot
11. already
12. chose
13. receive
14. quite
15. could have
16. lose
17. it's
18. accept
19. know
20. paid

Review 1

1. famous
2. location
3. noticeable
4. dropped
5. likely
6. hopeless
7. management
8. hottest
9. robbed
10. stopped
11. safely
12. argument
13. judgment
14. courageous
15. swimming
16. committed
17. occurrence
18. omitted
19. beginning
20. preferred

Chapter 14

Exercise 1

Young voters are not voting ~~the way~~ [as often as] they should. The latest figures show that only 20 percent are going to the ~~poles~~ [polls]. The next-older generation ~~is,~~ the so-called baby boomers, ~~they~~ are going to the ~~poles~~ [polls] at about twice that rate. Because I'm part of the young group, I'm concerned, but the answers to why we usually don't bother to vote are ~~as~~ obvious ~~as the nose on your face. For one thing the~~ [One factor is that many] younger people don't think voting changes anything. The political parties are all about the same, and the candidates look and talk alike, even though they seem angry with each other. ~~For~~ [A]nother [factor is that many] ~~a lot of~~ young voters don't have parents ~~that~~ [who] voted or even talked about politics when they were growing up, [so] they don't either. Still another ~~thing~~ [point] is that the issues ~~going around~~ don't ~~move~~ [inspire] [current] young people that much. The politicians talk about the national debt and social security and health care ~~and~~ [but] we're concerned about jobs and the high cost of education. If ~~they could get people we~~ [political parties would offer candidates we] could believe in and ~~they~~ [those candidates] would talk about issue[s] that matter to us, then maybe ~~they'd see more of us at the polls.~~ [we'd vote.]

Chapter 22

Exercise 1

1. O
2. F
3. O
4. F

5. F
6. F
7. O

Exercise 3

1. PH
2. FD
3. HG
4. PH/AH
5. FA

6. AH
7. PH
8. HG
9. PH
10. AH

Appendix A

Exercise 1

1. n, prep
2. adj, v
3. adv, prep
4. conj, adj
5. prep, adj
6. pro, v
7. adj, n
8. v, adj
9. pro, conj
10. adj, adj

11. adj, adj
12. v, n
13. pro, adj
14. adj, prep
15. conj, conj
16. v, conj
17. adj, n
18. adj, adj
19. conj, n
20. v, n

Appendix D

Exercise 4

George Washington at Trenton

One of [the] most famous battles during the War of Independence ~~occur~~ [occurred] at Trenton, New Jersey, on Christmas Eve of ~~the~~ 1776. The colonists [were] outmatched in supplies and finances and ~~were~~ outnumbered in troop strength. Most observers in other countries ~~think~~ [thought the] rebellion would be put down soon. [The] British [were] overconfident and ~~believe~~ [believed] there would be no more battles until spring. But George Washington ~~decide~~ [decided] to fight one more time. That Christmas, while [a] large army of Britishers [were] having [a] party and thinking about the holiday season, [the] Americans set out for [a] surprise raid. They loaded onto boats used for carrying ore and rowed across [the] Delaware River. George Washington stood tall in [the] lead boat. According to legend, [the] drummer boy floated across [the] river on his drum, pulled by [a] rope tied to [a] boat. Because [the] British did not feel threatened by the ragtag colonist forces, they [were] unprepared to do battle. The colonists stormed [the] living quarters and the general assembly hall and achieved victory. It was good for the colonists' morale, something they needed, for they would endure [a] long, hard winter before fighting again.

Text Credits

Clarance H. Benes and John E. Steinbrink, "Heroes Everywhere," from "Be Your Own Hero: Activities for Middle-Level Social Studies Classes" by The Clearing House, Vol. 71, No. 6, pp. 367–371, July/August 1998. Reprinted with permission of the Helen Dwight Reid Educational Foundation. Published by Heldref Publications, 1319 Eighteenth Street, NW, Washington, DC 20036-1802. Copyright © 1998.

Rick Bragg, "100 Miles per Hour, Upside Down and Sideways," from *All Over but the Shoutin'* by Rick Bragg. Copyright © 1997 by Rick Bragg. Used by permission of Pantheon Books, a division of Random House, Inc.

José Antonio Burciaga, "A Mixed Tex-Cal Marriage," from *Drink Cultura* by José Antonio Burciaga, Joshua Odell Editions, Santa Barbara, 1993. Reprinted with permission of Cecilia P. Burciaga.

Bob Cullen, "Testimony from the Iceman." Originally appeared in *Smithsonian,* February 2003. Reprinted by permission of the author.

Sheila Ferguson, "Soul Food at a Black American Family Reunion," from *Soul Food* by Sheila Ferguson. Copyright © 1989 by Sheila Ferguson. Used by permission of Grove/Atlantic, Inc.

Suzanne Fields, "Let Granny Drive If She Can," from *The Washington Times,* Op-Ed, July 24, 2003. Reprinted by permission of the author.

Patricia Hampl, "Grandmother's Sunday Dinner," from *A Romantic Education* by Patricia Hampl. Copyright © 1981 by Patricia Hampl. Used by permission of W. W. Norton & Company, Inc.

Linda Hogan, "Thanksgiving," from *Elle,* 1990. Reprinted by permission of the author.

Robert F. Howe, "Covert Force." Originally appeared in *Smithsonian,* October 2002. Reprinted by permission of the author.

Jennifer Kirkpatrick, "Blackbeard: Pirate Terror at Sea," from *National Geographic World,* November 1996 issue. Reprinted by permission of the National Geographic Society.

Claude Lewis, "Is It Time for Cameras in the Classroom?," from Knight Ridder/Tribune News Service, August 15, 2003. Copyright © 2003. Reprinted by permission of Knight Ridder.

Leo N. Miletich, "Sleepless in El Paso," from *Newsweek,* July 17, 1995. Copyright 1995 Newsweek, Inc. All rights reserved. Reprinted by permission.

Mary Beth Norton, "Women and Witchcraft," from *Major Problems in American Women's History,* 3rd edition. Copyright © 2003 by Houghton Mifflin Company. Reprinted with permission.

Grace Paley, "The Loudest Voice," from *The Little Disturbances of Man* by Grace Paley. Copyright © 1956, 1957, 1958, 1959 by Grace Paley. Used by permission of Penguin, a division of Penguin Group (USA) Inc.

Roy Rivenburg, "The Mean Season," from *Los Angeles Times,* July 14, 1995. Copyright © 1995 by the Los Angeles Times. Reprinted by permission.

Eric Schlosser, "Fast-Track French Fries," from *Fast Food Nation* by Eric Schlosser. Copyright © 2001 by Eric Schlosser. Excerpted and reprinted by permission of Houghton Mifflin Company. All rights reserved.

Gary Soto, "The Jacket," from *A Summer Life.* Copyright © 1990 by University Press of New England. Reprinted by permission.

Dave Tianen, "A Music Legend Fades to Black," from *Milwaukee Journal Sentinel,* September 13, 2003. © 2003 Journal Sentinel, Inc., reproduced with permission.

Roy M. Wallack, "Workin' at the Car Wash," from *Westways,* July/August 2002. Reprinted by permission of the author.

Yi-Fu Tuan, "American Space, Chinese Place." Copyright © 1974 by *Harper's Magazine.* All rights reserved. Reproduced from the July issue by special permission.

Author and Title Index

Subject Index

reading-related writing, 2
  defined, 12, 17
  guidelines for, 27
  outlining, 17–18
  reaction statement, 21
  summaries, 19–20
  two-part response, 21–22
real, really, 178, 187
receive, recieve, 252
"recipe language," 355
recursive, writing process as, 2,
  283, 286
references, parentheses for, 229
refutation, in argument, 411, 431
regular verbs, 117–118, 140
relative clauses
  in complex sentences, 52, 71–72,
    82
  defined, 47–48
  as fragments, 89
  punctuation for, 71–72, 82
  restrictive and nonrestrictive, 89
relative pronouns, 47–48, 71–72,
  82
repetition
  avoiding unnecessary, 284
  for emphasis, 284
  for unity, 284
representative examples, 337, 352
research papers, point of view for,
  156
restatement
  punctuation for, 228
  of thesis, 294
résumé writing, 463, 464
revision process, 283–285, 290–
  291
  CLUESS acronym for, 284
  coherence in, 284
  emphasis in, 284
  evaluating support in, 284–285
  language in, 284
  for sentences, 285
  unity in, 284
rise, raise, 123
rough draft. *See* first draft
run-on sentences, 101–110
  commas and coordinating con-
    junctions for, 102, 112
  defined, 101–102, 111–112
  identifying, 110–111
  semicolons for, 106, 112
  separate sentences for, 108, 112
  subordinating conjunctions for,
    104, 112

second person perspective
  applications for, 156, 354
  common problems with, 157
  and pronoun case, 148–149
Self-Evaluation Chart, 5–6, 246
self-improvement strategies, 4–6
semicolons
  after parentheses, 229
  for comma splices and run-ons,
    106, 112
  common usage for, 219, 238

for compound-complex sentences,
  74
in compound sentences, 50, 58,
  67, 81, 89
with conjunctive adverbs, 67, 219
with quotation marks, 225
sensory impressions, in description,
  321–322
sentence fillers, 35, 130
sentence outline, 276
sentences
  balance in, 193–194
  basics for ESL students, 466
  beginnings for, 80
  clauses in, 47–48, 57–58
  combining (*see* sentences, com-
    bining)
  comma splices, 101–110
  complex, 49, 51–52, 58, 69–72
  compound, 49, 58, 64–69
  compound-complex, 49, 52, 58,
    74
  fragments, 88–101 (*see also* frag-
    ments)
  illogical omissions in, 78
  length of, 80
  order in, 80
  parallel structure in, 193–194
  procedure for analysis of, 53
  in revision process, 285, 291
  run-on, 101–110
  self-evaluation of, 5, 6
  simple, 49, 58
  techniques for spotting problem,
    110–111
  types of, 47, 49–52, 58, 79
  using variety, 79–80
  weak, 136, 141
  and wordy phrases, 254
sentences, combining
  coordination, 64–69, 81
  coordination and subordination,
    74, 82
  other methods for, 76, 82–83
  subordination, 69–72, 81–82
sequence words, 284, 294
series
  comma use in, 211, 237
  with coordinating conjunctions,
    211
  parentheses for numbers in, 229
  semicolon use in, 219
sex bias, avoiding, 161, 167
signal words, for parallel structure,
  194, 200, 203
simple sentences, 47, 49, 58, 64, 79
simple subject, 33, 41
simple verb tenses, 126, 127
sit, set, 123
situation
  in description, 323, 335
  in narratives, 304
slang
  avoiding, 175, 284
  and ESL students, 467
  quotation marks for, 224, 238
sources, in argument, 412

space order
  for analysis by division, 378
  for comparison and contrast, 395
  for description, 322–323
  for exemplification, 338
specific examples, 337, 352
specific words, 322, 335
spell checkers, 6, 247, 256, 285
spelling
  commonly confused and mis-
    spelled words, 250–252
  in editing process, 285
  frequently misspelled words, 250
  general rules for, 247–249, 255–
    256
  importance of correct, 246
  self-evaluation of, 5, 6
  steps to efficient, 246–247
  using spell checkers, 247
standard usage, 117, 140, 148,
  284
stationary, stationery, 252
statistics, in argument, 412
strong verbs, 138, 141
struggle, in narratives, 304
style checkers, 6
subject (of paragraph)
  defined, 262, 271, 281
  in developmental paragraph,
    262–264
  in topic sentence, 273
subject (of sentence), 33–36
  agreement with verb, 130–133,
    140
  alternative, 131, 159
  complete, 33
  compound, 34, 131, 159
  defined, 33, 41
  illogical omissions of, 78
  implied, 34, 97
  location of, 39, 41
  missing, as fragment, 88, 97
  nouns as, 33
  and prepositional phrases, 34
  pronouns as, 33–34, 148–149
  simple, 33, 41
  trouble spots with, 34–35
subject-by-subject pattern, 395,
  396, 408
subjective-case pronouns, 148–149,
  166
subjective description, 321, 334,
  335
subjective tests, 461–462
subjunctive mood, 139–140, 141
subordinating conjunctions
  for comma splices and run-ons,
    104, 112
  in complex sentences, 70–71
  defined, 70, 456
  fragments with, 88–89, 111
  list of common, 71, 104, 456
  punctuation with, 71
subordination, for combining sentences, 69–72, 74, 81–82
suffixes, spelling rules for adding,
  248–249, 256